BYZANTIUM AND THE SLAVS

DIMITRI OBOLENSKY

BYZANTIUM AND THE SLAVS

ST VLADIMIR'S SEMINARY PRESS
CRESTWOOD, NEW YORK 10707
1994

Library of Congress Cataloging-in-Publication Data

Obolensky, Dimitri, 1918-
    Byzantium and the Slavs / Dimitri Obolensky.
        p.   cm.
    Includes bibliographical references and index.
    ISBN 0-88141-008-X
    1. Russia—Relations—Byzantine Empire.
    2. Byzantine Empire—Relations—Russia.   3.   Russia—
    Civilization—Byzantine influences.   4.   Russia—History—
    To 1533/   5.   Byzantine Empire—History—527-1081.
    6.   Byzantine Empire—History—1081-1453.   7.   Cyril,
    Saint, Apostle of the Slavs, ca. 827-869.   8.   Methodius,
    Saint, Apostle of the Slavs, ca. 825-884 or 5.   I.   Title
    DK67.5.B95026   1994   94-25507
    303.48'21749180495—dc20   CIP

BYZANTIUM AND THE SLAVS

published by

ST VLADIMIR'S SEMINARY PRESS

ISBN 0-88141-008-X

PRINTED IN THE UNITED STATES OF AMERICA

Contents

INTRODUCTION

The chapters of this book are reprinted from two volumes of my Collected Studies published by Variorum Reprints: the first ten from *Byzantium and the Slavs* (1971), the last two from *The Byzantine Inheritance of Eastern Europe* (1982). The first of these volumes has long been out of print.

These twelve studies may be divided thematically into three groups. The first is concerned with the general aspects of Slavo-Byzantine relations; the second with specific features of the acculturating process, and with the reciprocal nature of these relations; while the third group of studies is concerned with the contacts between Byzantium and medieval Rus'.

I

Our picture of Slavo-Byzantine relations will gain focus and clarity when seen in the wider context of Byzantium's relations with its northern neighbors (*Chapter Two*). Only the early phase of these relations — from the death of Justinian I (565) to the conquest of Bulgaria by Basil II (1018) — is examined here. In the history of eastern and south-eastern Europe these four-and-a-half centuries proved both formative and dramatic. The invasion of Byzantium's Balkan provinces by the Slavs, which began on a massive scale in Justinian's reign and threatened in the seventh century the Empire's very existence, was followed, after A.D. 800, by the revival of its military and political fortunes and by the Byzantine reconquest, in the early years of the eleventh century, of virtually the entire Balkan peninsula. Though it proved temporary, this reconquest marked the highest point achieved by Byzantine imperialism in Europe during Middle Ages. By the same date and by peaceful means the Slavo-Varangian state of Rus' had been induced to accept the religion and many of the cultural values of Byzantium.

This expansion owed much to the success of Byzantine diplomacy. Based on Roman foundations and seeking its warrant in the Christian tradition, this diplomacy has a triple aim: to defend the Empire's security in the hour of danger; to forestall attacks by its neighbors by building beyond the frontiers a chain of dependent states and communities, half-subjects and half-allies of Byzantium, which, like the *foederati* of ancient Rome, were supposed to guard its borders in exchange for imperial protection and the right of self-government; and thirdly to bring to these pagan 'barbarians' the message and the benefits of Christianity. Mainly defensive in character, Byzantine diplomacy repeatedly saved the Empire from destruction, gaining for Christendom and for Europe extensive territories in the Balkans and to the north of the Black Sea. The principles and methods of diplomacy (*Chapter One*) deserve further study.

Byzantine diplomacy usually operated across frontiers, military, political, or cultural. The study of these frontier zones is an integral part of the historical geography of the Byzantine Empire. Ambassadors and missionaries used land routes, travelling up river valleys, over plains and across mountain passes, to the South Slav neighbors of the Empire south and north of the Danube; while the envoys to the more distant Russians sailed across the Black Sea, landing in one of the Byzantine dependencies in southern Crimea, especially in Cherson. In the history of Slavo-Byzantine relations the frontier appears either as a barrier or as a bridge. These frontiers were often shifting and impermanent, moving outward from the political centres of the Empire and following a movement of colonization which in some respects resembled that of the North American frontier. The frontier was thus an essential factor in a process that social anthropologists and some historians call acculturation. It occurs when societies with different cultures come into direct and prolonged contact with each other, a contact resulting from ethnic migration and leading to cultural diffusion (*Chapter Twelve*).

II

A form of cultural diffusion which is given special prominence in medieval sources are Byzantine missions. These often fulfilled a dual purpose: to establish or confirm the emperor's sovereingty over neighboring pagan tribes and nations; and to bring to these same pagans the knowledge of the Christian Gospels. Hence the Byzantine missionary usually acted as the representative abroad both of his emperor and his church.

This was true of most celebrated of all Byzantine missions to the Slavs, led by Constantine (Cyril) and Methodius. It was born in the second half of the ninth century out of the Byzantine need to evangelize the Slavs beyond the empire's frontier in their native language, a need which in 862 became urgent and specific. Envoys from the ruler of Moravia, a Slav principality in central Europe, arrived in Constantinople asking for a Slav-speaking Christian missionary. Moravia had already been partly converted by German priests under Frankish control, but its ruler, fearful for its country's independence, probably wished to counter their influence by that of a Slav-speaking clergy owing allegiance to Byzantium. The two brothers from Thessalonica, whom the emperor chose to head this religious and political mission, translated from Greek and Slavic, with the help of the newly invented Slav alphabet, the Byzantine liturgical offices, the Christian scriptures and other religious and secular works. Thus was created, by Constantine and Methodius and their closest disciples, a new literary language, known today as Old Church Slavonic. In the early Middle Ages it became, after Greek and Latin, the third international language of Europe and the common literary idiom of the Bulgarians, the Serbs, the Ukrainians, the Russians and the Rumainians, who through their conversion to Christianity gained entry into the Byzantine cultural commonwealth. The nature of Cyrillo-Methodian tradition — Slavic in form, and at first largely Greek in content — made it an effective channel for the diffusion of Byzantine culture in Eastern Europe (*Chapters Seven and Nine*).

During most of the Middle Ages Constantinople and Thessalonica were the mainsprings of this diffusion. Constantinople, the birthplace of the Cyrillo-Methodian mission, remained until Methodius' death in 885 its principal point of reference. Thessalonica, the second city of the empire, was only slightly less involved in this mission's subsequent history. Not only was it the two missionaries' native city, and the object, during their long sojourn abroad, of their nostalgia and longing for home. It was also the centre of the cult of Thessalonica's heavenly protector, the "great martyr" St Demetrius, the patron of the Cyrillo-Methodian mission (*Chapter Eleven*).

In more than one Slav country the cult of St Demetrius of Thessalonica, and the enthusiastic acceptance of the Cyrillo-Methodian tradition, combined to instill both in the educated and unlettered classes a veneration of Byzantium and its religion: not least in Russia, where a number of early medieval writings breathe a heady air of a cultural springtime, coming from an awareness that the Slavs, by receiving the Christian scriptures and the liturgy in their own language, have acquired a distinct historical identity (*Chapter Eight*).

The history of the Cyrillo-Methodian mission is an example — one of the most successful — of the cultural influence exerted by Byzantium upon its Slav proselytes. But acculturation is by definition a two-way process; so in studying it we would expect to find evidence of a reverse movement, from the periphery towards the center, or — in historical terms — of an influence exerted on Byzantium by the Slavs.

Perhaps the most notable example of such a reverse influence is offered by the relations between Bulgaria and Byzantium in the tenth and eleventh centuries. In the first half of the tenth century there arose on Bulgarian soil a movement known as Bogomilism. Its founder appears to have been a Bulgarian Slav priest, by the name of Bogomil. The sect to which he gave his name was historically an offshoot of the Dualist movement which, through its Paulician and Manichaean antecedents, goes back at least as far as Gnosticim. From its original home, probably in Slavic Macedonia, the Bogomil movement spread to many areas of the Byzantine Empire, enjoyed a brief though spectacular vogue in Constantinople, survived in Bulgaria until the late Middle Ages, spread westward to Serbia and Bosnia and, in the late twelfth century, exerted a powerful influence upon the Cathar (or Albigensian) movement in Southern France. It is an example —the most strikingly successful in the whole of the Middle Ages — of a spontaneous and popular movement of resistance to the patterns of Byzantine culture, fighting Orthodox Christianity on its own ground and with its own weapons (*Chapter Ten*).

III

In the third group of studies the focus shifts to medieval Russia. The country's relations with Byzantium and its heritage are discussed from several angles. In the field of ecclesiastical politics the Russians appear to have wrested from the Empire in the late Middle Ages significant concessions, the nature of which can probably teach us a much about the aims of this diplomacy as about the Russians' attitude to Byzantium and to its claims of hegemony (*Chapter Four*). This attitude, complex, ambiguous and at time shifting, is explored in relation to the same late medieval period, and reasons are sought for the presence in this attitude of a curious blend of attraction and repulsion (*Chapter Five*). In modern times as well, Byzantium has figured in the historical and philosophical speculations of the Russians, affecting in various and often contradictory ways their ideas of national self-determination. Finally, in the 1870s the rise in Russia of a genuine tradition of Byzantine scholarship diminished, without altogether eradicating, the inveterate proclivity to value judgements passed on Byzantium (*Chapter Six*). In one of these pieces an attempt is made to discuss the nature of Russia's Byzantine Heritage in more general terms, by viewing it in a European context. This essay, published in 1950, and some others as well, seem in retrospect to contain in embryo some of the ideas I later developed more fully in my book *The Byzantine Commonwealth* (1971).

The author whose shorter writings are reprinted in this way may well find it difficult to avoid the occasional overlap or repetition. The reader patient enough to peruse these chapters consecutively will find no difficulty in identifying these recurrent passages. I have thought it best not to remove them, leaving the text more or less as it was in its original form.

Another problem arises from the time-span measured by these pieces: together they cover a period of some thirty years. Had my views on a number of problems not changed at all during that length of time, this might well have been cause for alarm. I am well aware that, writing today, I would at the very least have altered the tenor of some of the arguments and phrased certain passages differently. Yet here again I have resisted the temptatiion to rewrite extensively, believing that most readers would prefer to have these studies as they originally were. Mostly I have confined myself to citing in the notes recent editions of primary sources, and adding references to what seemed to me the more important new secondary material.

It remains to thank the original publishers of these pieces for permission to reprint them in this volume, Variorum Reprints and Dr John Smedley for similar permission, and SVS Press for its help and forbearance. I am particularly indebted to Dr Paul Meyendorff, my copy-editor, for the care, vigilance and learning he brought to preparing the text for publication.

D. O.

Oxford
1 April 1993

CHAPTER I

THE PRINCIPLES AND METHODS
OF BYZANTINE DIPLOMACY*

It is scarcely surprising that the diplomacy of the Byzantine Empire still awaits its historian. A full-length and comprehensive survey of this subject — involving of necessity a study of the Empire's relations with almost every nation of Europe, with the whole of western and part of central Asia, and with northern and eastern Africa as well — would be indeed a formidable undertaking. Attempts have been made to survey the whole field of Byzantine diplomacy, but only briefly and sketchily: the most successful, perhaps, are those of Charles Diehl and Louis Bréhier. For the rest, the student must gleam his information from the standard text-books of Byzantine history, from the existing studies of the Empire's relations with specific foreign powers, and especially from monographs devoted to particular reigns — for instance from Diehl's book on Justinian I, from Runciman's monograph on Romanus Lecapenus, from Rambaud's study of Constantine VII, and from D. J. Geanakoplos' recent work on the western policy of Michael VIII.[1]

These studies, brief or partial, of Byzantine foreign policy have done much to pave the way for some future scholar possessed with the necessary knowledge and industry to attempt a comprehensive study of the Empire's diplomacy. Such a scholar would find, moreover, that much of the source material relating to this subject has already been listed and analyzed with admirable clarity: Professor Dölger's *Regesten* and Professor Moravcsik's *Byzantinoturcica*, for example, have amply supplemented and extended K. Dieterich's older, but still useful, compedium of Byzantine ethnology. It seems to me, however,

---

*Actes du XIIᵉ Congrès International d'Études Byzantines, I (Belgrade, 1963), 45-61.

that more preparatory work must be done before we can have any detailed and comprehensive account of Byzantine diplomacy as a whole — of its principles and methods, its ideals and techniques, its failures and achievements; and that in the meantime more limited studies of the Empire's foreign policy in specific areas may well provide the most fruitful starting point.

The aim of this paper is to attempt such a limited study in relation primarily to one such area. From the spectacle of Byzantine diplomacy at work, grappling with concrete problems, in this area during the course of centuries, a general picture will, it is hoped, emerge which will be used in the second half of the paper as a basis for an overall assessment of some of the principles and methods of Byzantine diplomacy.

The area to which I shall, in the main, confine myself in the first part of this paper lay beyond the northern borders of the Empire. This, broadly speaking, was the region limited in the west by the plain of Hungary and in the east by the Caspian Sea. It stretches over the Carpathian Mountains, the south Russian steppe and the lowlands to the north of the Caucasus. It is bounded in the north by a semicircle extending over the lower courses of the great Russian rivers — the Dniester, the Dnieper and the Don — and whose tips come to rest on the middle Danube in the west and on the lower Volga in the east. It coincides exactly with the area of which a geo-political description is given in the forty-second chapter of the *De Administrando Imperio*; and the scrupulous care with which this region is described therein is in itself sufficient evidence of the importance it possessed in the eyes of the Byzantine statesmen of the tenth century.

In stressing the crucial importance to Byzantium of the lands that lay beyond the Empire's northern borders Constantine Porphyrogenitus was giving expression to a concern that underlies the whole history of Byzantine diplomacy. For it was from this area that issued that never-ending procession of tribes and nations which, in war and in peace, were irresistibly drawn into the orbit of Byzantium, whose attacks and invasions fill the military records of the Empire, and whose fears, ambitions and lust taxed so severely the ingenuity of the statesmen in Constantinople. For a considerable part of its history the Empire was fighting to defend its frontiers — and often its very life —against the thrust of the northern invader, of Hun and Bulgar, of Avar and Slav, of Russian and Pecheneg. The role played by Byzantium in standing for a millennium and more as the guardian of Europe's eastern frontier against oriental expansion and northern attacks is now, indeed, widely recognized; but it is perhaps not always appreciated how much the preservation of civilization in Eastern Europe was due to the skill and resourcefulness of Byzantine diplomacy. And it was partly in response to the northern challenge that was forged, in the course of centuries, by steadfast faith and lucid thinking, by careful study and observation, by trial and error, that Imperial diplomacy which surely remains one of Byzantium's lasting contributions to the history of Europe. The fact that Byzantium in its dealings with the barbarians generally preferred diplomacy to war is not surprising: for the East Romans, faced with the ever-present necessity of having to battle on two fronts — in the east against Persians, Arabs and Turks, in the north against the steppe barbarians and the Balkan Slavs — knew from personal experience how expensive in money and manpower is war.

In considering the ways in which the statesmen of Byzantium endeavoured to meet the challenge presented to the security of the state by its northern neighbors, it may be convenient to consider in turn the principal sectors in which these neighbors impinged on the strategic and diplomatic position of the Empire. There were, it seems to me, three such sectors, which served as the pivots of Byzantine diplomacy on the northern frontier: the Caucasus, the Crimea and the Danube.

The importance of the Caucasian sector to the Empire's security was a matter of elementary geo-politics: for at the two extremities of this great isthmus separating the Black Sea from the Caspian the Graeco-Roman civilization of the Mediterranean met and frequently clashed with the westward expansion of Asiatic powers: in the north with the nomads of Eurasia, pressing toward the Black Sea and the Danube; in the south with the great powers of the Middle East, pushing toward Asia Minor and the Bosphorus. Both these westward movements spelled constant danger to Byzantium, and the efforts of Imperial diplomacy in this sector were directed as much at achieving a favorable balance of power in the lowlands north of the Caucasus, as to creating a bulwark against possible attacks of Persians, Arabs and Turks through Asia Minor towards Constantinople itself. The close relationship that always existed, in the strategy of the Empire's generals, in the mind of its diplomatists and in actual fact, between Byzantium's eastern and northern fronts is nowhere more apparent than in the Caucasus sector. And the basic aim of Byzantine policy in this sector was always the same: to build a chain of allied, or vassal, states from the lower Volga and the Sea of Azov to Lake Van in Armenia. Their peoples could render the Empire services consonant with their geographical position and military resources: in the sixth century, for instance, on the eastern coast of the Black Sea the Zichi and the Abasgi could enable the Byzantine fleet to operate in Caucasian waters and could hold the left flank of the Empire's north-eastern front; further south the Lazi and the Tzani guarded the approaches to the northern coast of Asia Minor; the Georgians in the central Caucasus and the Alans further north stood guard over the Caspian Gates and could prevent the steppe nomads from Asia from striking south across this mountain pass at Byzantine Asia Minor. All these Caucasian peoples were successfully wooed by the diplomacy of Justinian; the first four were converted to Christianity in the sixth century by Byzantine missionaries, and the new ecclesiastical organization set up in their lands proved a powerful means of keeping them within the political orbit of East Rome. And the roads and fortresses which the Byzantines built in these countries were the material counterpart of the flattering but less tangible links which their rulers were induced to cement with the Imperial court of Constantinople. These outposts of Byzantine influence in the Caucasus could also be of considerable economic value to the Empire: thus the relations established by Byzantium with the Turks of Central Asia between 568 and 576, which enabled the Empire to import silk while circumventing the Persian control of the silk routes from China to the Black Sea, depended at least in part on the trade route that skirted the northern shores of the Caspian, crossed the central Caucasus range, reached the Black Sea coast of Abasgia, and continued by sea via Phasis to Trebizond.[1a]

The central Caucasus region retained its strategic value for the Empire until the second half of the eleventh century. The Alans, already described by Procopius as "friends of the Romans from of old,"[2] had become in the tenth century the linchpin of Byzantine diplomacy in the Caucasian sector. They were converted to Christianity by Byzantine missionaries in the first half of that century. The Alans were held in high esteem in Byzantium, and Constantine Porphyrogenitus stresses their usefulness in checking possible Khazar encroachments in the Crimea.[3] Their ruler, who held the Byzantine title of ἐξουσιαστής, was one of the three Imperial satellites of that period to be honored as the Emperor's "spiritual son."[4] The importance of Armenia — that bone of contention between Byzantium and the Arabs — was fully recognized by the Imperial diplomatists of the Macedonian period. Their policy of bestowing high-sounding titles on Armenian princes to ensure their political docility led to the annexation of part of the country by Basil II, and of the remaining part in 1064. But soon the battle of Mantzikert sealed the doom of Byzantine hegemony in Transcaucasia.

At the northern extremity of the Empire's Caucasian front lay a region of peculiar strategic importance: the lowlands between the lower Volga and the Sea of Azov offered easy transit to nomadic invaders from Asia heading towards the Black Sea and the Danube, or southward to the Caucasus and beyond. The peoples who dwelt in this area, if they were friendly to the Empire and sufficiently powerful, could be counted on to guard the eastern extremity of the European "steppe corridor" and, generally, to help preserve the balance of power along the whole length of the Empire's northern front. The Byzantine statesmen were quick to realize the urgent need of securing a strong ally in this sector: and on two occasions they succeeded in this task. In the first half of the seventh century a powerful barbarian kingdom arose in the triangle between the sea of Azov, the lower Volga and the northern Caucasus; known to the Byzantines as "Old Great Bulgaria," its rise to power was undoubtedly due to East Roman support. Its ruler Kovrat had been brought up and baptized at the court of Constantinople, and the spell cast upon him by his memories of the Imperial city served the Empire in good stead: Kovrat, a close friend of the Emperor Heraclius, his vassal, ally and godson, himself a patrician of the Roman Empire, offers a striking example of a satellite ruler, faithfully guarding the interest of Byzantium in the north. This successful experiment was soon repeated by the Empire: for when in the middle of the seventh century, "Old Great Bulgaria" was displaced and conquered by the Khazars, the Byzantines transferred their support to the newcomers. And during the next two centuries the Khazar Empire, the most civilized and ordered of states created by the Turkic peoples in the early Middle Ages, remained Byzantium's most constant and valued ally in the north. It is possible that in the eighth century the Khazar alliance did much to save Byzantium from the Arab menace, for if the Khazars had not halted the northward thrust of Islam on the Caucasus, the Arabs might well have invaded the steppes of South Russia, appeared on the lower Danube, and outflanked the whole Byzantine system of defence. Though the interest of the two powers occasionally clashed — notably in the Crimea — relations between

Constantinople and the Khazar capital of Itil' on the lower Volga were generally friendly and close; as the Book of Ceremonies shows, in the diplomatic protocol of Byzantium the Khazar khagan ranked among non Christian foreign rulers second only to the khalife of Baghdad. Once again — in the second half of the thirteenth century — did the lands to the north of the Caucasus play their part in that balance of power which the Byzantine statesmen always sought to establish in the Pontic steppes: for, in accordance with the age-long traditions of Byzantine diplomacy in this sector, the alliance concluded by Michael VIII with the Tatars of the Golden Horde was partly aimed at exerting pressure upon a hostile neighbor of the Empire — the Bulgarians.

In the central segment of the great semi-circle that marked the effective limits of Byzantium's sphere of interest in the north, half-way between its tips that rested on the middle Danube and the lower Volga, lay the second sector of the Empire's northern front. Until the early thirteenth century the Byzantine possessions in the Crimea, above all the city of Cherson, acted as the northern outpost of Byzantine diplomacy in the steppe: their importance was partly economic, for the Crimea provided Byzantium with the raw materials of the hinterland — fish from the rivers of South Russia, salt from the Azov region, furs and honey from the forests further north, and sold to the barbarians the manufactured articles of Byzantine industry. Politically, Cherson and its neighboring region, subject or vassal of the Empire, was an invaluable observation post, a watch-tower planted on the very fringe of that barbarian world of south Russia which Byzantine diplomacy was ever anxious to influence and control. It was from the Crimea that Justinian's government could follow the moves of the Hunnic tribes, encamped on both sides of the sea of Azov, and, by a timely bribe or by stirring up internal strife among them, ward off their attacks on the Balkans. Thus, from Byzantine Crimea, could the Emperors pursue towards the northern barbarians, the traditional Roman policy of "divide and rule," or at least, when this proved impracticable, in the words of Rostovtzeff, "weaken and watch." And, true again to the time-honored methods of Roman diplomacy, Byzantium had secured in that region, to counterbalance the Huns, a useful satellite, part vassal and part ally — the Crimean Goths. The security of the Empire's Balkan provinces depended as much upon the watchfulness of its agents in the Crimea as upon the influence it wielded in the north Caucasian sector; it is no wonder that Byzantium hung on to its Crimean outpost with grim determination, struggling to preserve it from Khazar domination, attempting, not always successfully, to canalize into lawful channels the traditions of Greek municipal autonomy, which were always strong in Cherson. And in the late ninth century the wisdom of this policy of hanging on to the Crimea became forcibly apparent. The appearance of new barbarians on the northern horizon forced the Empire hastily to build up a new balance of power in the steppes. The first of these new intruders were the Pechenegs. This barbarous Turkic people was then threatening the whole western section of the Empire's northern front, from the sea of Azov to the Danube. Byzantine diplomacy met this challenge by a policy of readjustment. For the past two centuries it had relied, for preserving order in the steppes, mainly on the Khazars, but their power was fast declining; so, in the early tenth century, Byzantium turned to the Pechenegs. One has but to re-read the opening chapters of *De Administrando Imperio* to be persuaded of the crucial importance of the Pecheneg alliance to the Empire during that century. They show quite clearly that for Constantine VII alliance with the Pechenegs is the corner-stone of Byzantine diplomacy in the north; for — as Constantine is at pains to explain to his son — if this alliance is kept, Byzantine Crimea is safe, trade with Russia can flourish, and the Empire's northern enemies, Bulgars and Magyars and Russians, who tremble with fear before the Pechenegs, will not dare to attack. "I conceive, then," the Emperor writes, "that it is always greatly to the advantage of the emperor of the Romans to be minded to keep the peace with the nation of the Pechenegs and to conclude conventions and treaties of friendship with them and to send every year to them from our side a diplomatic agent with presents befitting and suitable to that nation."[5] It is understandable and significant that the responsibility for negotiating with the Pechenegs lay on the Governor of Cherson.

The other factor which enhanced the importance of Byzantine Crimea in this period was the southward movement of the Swedish Vikings down the Russian rivers, and the foundation of the Varangian Russian principalities along the Dnieper waterway. The attacks they launched from Kiev in the century following their massive raid on Constantinople in 860 could be forestalled, if not prevented, by the intelligence bureau of the στρατηγός of Cherson. "Behold," the Chersonites informed the Emperor in 944, "the Russians are coming in countless ships, and the ships have covered the sea."[6] In vain the Russians sought to mop up this dangerous observation post. Cherson, it is true, fell to the armies of Vladimir of Russia in 989-90: but, by a providential irony of fate, the city, so long a focus of missionary work among the pagans of the north, took her captor captive: for Vladimir's *coup de main* resulted in his marriage to the Emperor's sister and in the conversion of Russia to Christianity, and Cherson was returned to the Emperor by the Russian ruler in exchange for his bride. Thus did the missionaries and diplomatists of East Rome gain for Christianity and for Byzantine civilization a territory which in size exceeded the Empire itself.

The third sector of the Empire's northern front was on the lower and middle Danube, the ancient "limes Romanus": and the Danube, in the true sense of the word, was much more of a "front" than the Crimea or the northern Caucasus. This too was a matter of geopolitics: for the lower Danube lies near the terminus of the "steppe corridor," that immemorial highway for nomadic invaders from Asia: and for many of them, who had succeeded in avoiding the entanglements and traps laid for them by the Byzantine diplomats in the Caucasian and Crimean sectors, the Danube proved no insuperable obstacle, and the road into the Balkans lay open. There is a significant contrast in the strategic position of Constantinople, which explains much in the medieval history of south-eastern Europe: admirably protected from attack by sea, the city lies open to a chance invasion by land, across the lowlands of Thrace; and we find that contrast stressed as early as the second century BC by Polybius; his remarks on the tragic exposure of the ancient Greek city of Byzantium to attacks from the north-west are worth quoting, for they seem to be almost a prophecy of the East Roman Empire's relations with its northern neighbors. "As Thrace" — Polybius writes — "surrounds the territory of the Byzantines on all sides, reaching from sea to sea, they are involved in an endless and troublesome war against the Thracians, for it is not feasible, by making preparations on a grand scale and winning one decisive victory over them, to get rid once for all of their hostilities; the barbarous nations and dynasts are too numerous. If they overcome one, three more worse than the first arise and advance against their country. Nor can they gain any advantage by submitting to pay tribute and making definite contracts; for if they make any concession to one prince, such a concession raises up against them five times as many foes. For these reasons they are involved in a never-ending and troublesome war. For what is more dangerous than a bad neighbor, and what is more dreadful than a war with barbarians? And besides the other evils that attend on war, they have to undergo (to speak poetically) a sort of Tantalean punishment, for when they. . .have been rewarded by the production of an abundant and surpassingly fine crop, then come the barbarians, and having reaped part of the fruits to carry off with them, destroy what they cannot take away. The Byzantines can only murmur indignantly, and endure."[7] If for Polybius' invading Thracians we substitute the northern foes of the Eastern Empire — Huns, Slavs, Avars, Bulgars, Magyars, Pechenegs, Russians and Cumans — and if to the patient endurance of the ancient Byzantines we add the capacity for military resistance so marvellously displayed by their East Roman successors in the city of Constantine, we shall have an admirable summary of the Empire's position on the Danubian front.

It was in this Danubian sector — and in its southern extension into the Balkans — that Byzantine diplomacy met its most powerful and sustained challenge. Byzantine policy in this sector was dominated by the Empire's relations with the Slavs. The story is as chequered and painful as Polybius' remarks would lead one to expect. Its main episodes are prominently recorded in the contemporary sources: Justinian's attempts — only partly successful — to hold the Danube by an intricate web of defensive diplomacy; the efforts of his successors — notably Justian II and Maurice — to replace Justinian's balance of power by a policy of strength against the Avar pressure on the Danube; Heraclius' alliance with the Serbs and the Croats against the Avars and his great victory against the northern barbarians in 626, offset by the continued and irresistible spread of the Slavs over the Empire's Balkan provinces; the collapse of Byzantium's Danubian frontier between 679 and 681, the invasion of the Bulgars and the foundation of the First Bulgarian Empire, which was several times to bring Byzantium to the brink of destruction; Byzantium's diplomatic counter-offensive north and south of the Danube in the second half of the ninth century; the desperate struggle with Symeon of Bulgaria who by his imperialist designs presented the diplomatists of Byzantium with a challenge the like of which they had never encountered; the uneasy equilibrium that followed, until the victorious armies of John Tzimisces, tearing asunder what remained of the First Bulgarian Empire, carried Byzantium's northern frontier back to the Danube; the rise of the Second Bulgarian Empire in the late twelfth century; the struggle of the dying Empire against the imperial designs of Ste-

phen Dušan of Serbia, which in so many ways recalls Byzantium's
contest with Symeon of Bulgaria four centuries earlier: such were, in
the Danubian and Balkan sectors, the main phases of the Empire's
diplomatic and military resistance against its northern neighbors.

* * *

From this picture of Byzantine diplomacy at work in the three
sectors of the Empire's northern front — the Caucasus, the Crimea
and the Danube — there emerges, it would seem, a certain constant
and recognizable pattern. To defend the borders of the Empire by
nipping in the bud the attacks of the barbarians, the ἔθνη of the
steppes; to extend as far as possible the boundaries of the Empire's
political and cultural hegemony by creating beyond the frontiers a
chain of satellite states, whose loyalty to Byzantium was cemented by
their acceptance of the religion and the political supremacy of the
Emperor in Constantinople: these were surely the unchanging aims of
East Roman diplomacy in the north. And I believe that there is no
better way of testing the essential continuity of this diplomacy than to
compare the foreign policy of Justinian, as described by Procopius,
with that of the Macedonian Emperors, as epitomized in the writings
of Constantine Porphyrogenitus; it is difficult to resist the impression
that Constantine, for all his greater sophistication and, perhaps, a
clearer grasp of essentials, is a pupil of Justinian. For it was above all
Justinian who developed and bequeathed to his successors that conception of diplomacy as an intricate science and a fine art, in which
military pressure, political intelligence, economic cajolery and religious
propaganda were fused into an almost irresistible weapon of defensive
imperialism. And finally, to test this continuity on a still deeper level,
we may pass from the realm of technique to that of first principles
and ask ourselves the question: what did the East Romans understand
by foreign policy?

It has often been stated that the Byzantine Empire, in its essential
features, was a synthesis of the three traditions of Rome, Hellenism
and Christianity. The Roman conception of law and government, the
Greek language, literature and philosophy, the Christian faith with its
Jewish foundations — these, it may fairly be claimed, were the basic
ingredients that went into the making of Byzantine civilization. And it
seems to me possible to detect the influence of these same three traditions in the principles of Byzantine foreign policy. For these principles

were not just the product of *ad hoc* decisions: they were rooted in the view held by the East Romans of the nature and purpose of their Empire. The Byzantines believed that their Empire was, in principle, coextensive with the civilized universe, the *Oikoumene*, of which their Emperor was the sole legitimate sovereign. This, of course, is a characteristically Roman idea, for the Romans had already suffered from the egocentric illusion that their Empire embraced the civilized world. It was only natural that the *Rhomaioi* of Constantine's city inherited this uncompromising belief in the one Universal Empire. Thus Agathias, writing in the reign of Justinian, could state that the Emperor's dominions "embrace the whole world;"[8] and four centuries later Constantine Porphyrogenitus, the standard authority on Byzantine political theory, compared the Emperor's power, in its rhythm and order, to the harmonious movement given to the Universe by its Creator.[9] And this doctrine of the one Universal Empire, ruled by the Emperor who was the supreme legislator and the living law, was intransigently held by the Byzantines till the last days of the Empire. More particularly, the *Oikoumene* was held to extend over all countries whose inhabitants professed Orthodox Christianity and were bound, in a sense not easily definable in terms of constitutional law, by a common allegiance to the Emperor of Byzantium, the supreme head of the whole Christian world and God's representative on earth. By the middle of the tenth century, as we see from *The Book of Ceremonies,* the Byzantine diplomatic protocol had evolved with some precision this notion of an Oecumenical society, an ordered hierarchy of subordinate states, satellites revolving in obedient harmony round the throne of the universal Autocrat in Constantinople. In this vast Commonwealth each nation was theoretically assigned its particular place, according to the excellence of its culture, the degree of political independence enjoyed by its ruler, the military resources he commanded, and the services he and his subjects could render to the Empire. This Byzantine *Oikoumene*, which Professor Ostrogorsky and Professor Dölger have described so vividly, and which was evoked with great eloquence by the Russian scholar Lamansky in 1875,[10] included the Orthodox Slav countries — Serbia, Bulgaria and Russia; and, with scarcely an exception, the medieval rulers of these countries never questioned this vision of the one universal Christian Empire, destined to foreshadow on earth the Heavenly Kingdom, until the last days and the coming of Antichrist. When in the early tenth century Symeon of Bulgaria led his armies against Constantinople and defiantly assumed the title of Emperor, he knew full well that to establish a Bulgarian βασιλεία of his own was out of the question: his aim was not to rival or to supplant Byzantium, but to set himself up as a Roman Emperor in Constantinople. And the Byzantine Patriarch Nicholas Mysticus, who exerted all his diplomatic skill in an attempt to persuade Symeon to abandon this venture, saw this very clearly. Symeon's claim to world domination he castigated as *Tyrannis*, an unlawful revolt against the sovereign Emperor.[11] And it is remarkable that the Patriarch, who was prepared to go to almost any length to appease the Bulgarian ruler, refused to concede the one essential point; against Symeon's imperialistic claims he solemnly reiterated the fundamental tenet of Byzantine political philosophy: the Empire, he wrote to Symeon, "stands above all earthly authority and alone on this earth was established by the King of all."[12] It is remarkable that even Byzantium's bitterest enemies in Eastern Europe implicitly accepted this notion of the *Oikoumene*, centered in Constantinople. This is just as evident in the policy of Stephen Dušan and in the title he assumed of βασιλεὺς καὶ αὐτοκράτωρ Σερβίας καὶ Ῥωμανίας, as it is in Symeon's designs. And the rulers of medieval Russia who, no less than those of Serbia and Bulgaria, jealously guarded their political sovereignty and independence, likewise recognized that the Emperor in Constantinople possessed supremacy and a measure of jurisdiction over all Christian nations, including their own. It is true that in the closing years of the fourteenth century the Patriarch of Constantinople strongly rebuked the Grand Duke of Moscow for causing the Emperor's name to be omitted from the diptychs of the Russian Church, and reminded him of his obligations towards the oecumenical Emperor: "My son," he wrote to Basil I of Moscow, "you are wrong in saying 'we have a Church, but not an Emperor.' It is not possible for Christians to have a Church and not to have an Empire." And the Patriarch makes it quite clear that the sovereignty of the Byzantine Emperor extends over Russia: "The Emperor. . .is appointed *basileus* and *autokrator* of the Romans — to wit, of all Christians."[13] But this revolt of the Russian sovereign against the basic principle of the *Oikoumene* was, it seems, quite exceptional; and his son and successor Basil II, in the very last years of the Empire's history, wrote to the Emperor Constantine XI in these terms: "You have received your great imperial sceptre. . .in order to establish all Orthodox Christianity in your realm and to render great assistance to our dominions of Russia and to all our religion."[14]

But the universality of the Empire was in fact, of course, a very relative thing: for beyond the confines of the Empire, beyond even those Christian countries which could still be regarded as part of the Byzantine *Oikoumene*, there dwelt in outer darkness the pagan ἔθνη, lesser breeds without the law. The Byzantines called them barbarians; now βάρβαρος, of course, is a Greek word, and for the ancient Greeks the barbarians were people outside the Hellenic world whose way of living, thinking and behaving was un-Greek. And the Byzantines borrowed this concept of "barbarians" from the ancient Greeks, but with the new cultural emphasis it had acquired in the Hellenistic age. In the remarkable mixture of races that made up the Byzantine Empire there was no place for any ethnic distinction between the Rhomaios and the barbarian. The Byzantines, it is true, would still call the non-Greek languages "barbarian;"[15] but the true distinctive mark of the Rhomaios was his membership of the Orthodox Church and his allegiance to the Emperor, the vicegerent of God. The barbarian, in principle, was now the pagan, outside the Emperor's direct jurisdiction. Once you accepted Orthodox Christianity you generally ceased, whatever your race and the language you spoke, to be a barbarian. Writing of Kovrat, ruler of Old Great Bulgaria in the seventh century, the contemporary chronicler John of Nikiu states: "After he had been baptized with life-giving baptism he overcame all the barbarians and heathens through virtue of holy baptism."[16] The culture of this Bulgar Christian ruler may have been somewhat crude: but it is clear that, in Byzantine eyes, he was no longer a barbarian. Similarly, in the late twelfth century the Christian Russians (τὸ χριστιανικώτατον οἱ 'Ρὼς γένος), allies of Byzantium, are contrasted with the "barbarian" and pagan Cumans.[17]

The Roman idea of the One Universal Empire and the Greek, or rather Hellenistic, concept of "barbarians" were infused by the Byzantines with a metaphysical interpretation, borrowed from the tradition of Judaism and Christianity. The Byzantines believed that the political organization of this world is part of God's universal plan and is intimately bound up with the history of man's salvation. As the universal organism of the Roman Empire had providentially paved the way for the victorious advance of the Christian faith, so were the Rhomaioi, dedicated to the service of Christ by the Emperor Constantine, to reap where the First Rome had sown, and to bring the Gospel to all the peoples of the earth. So the *Pax Romana* was equated with the *Pax Christiana,* and the interests of the Empire coincided with the advancement of the Christian faith. It is easy to say that the Byzantine missionary was the agent of East Roman imperialism. But it is perhaps not always realized how seriously most Emperors took their duty of converting the barbarians. To test the effectiveness of Byzantine foreign policy in any given period, the work of the Christian missions is nearly always a sure criterion. And there can be little doubt that the greatest period in the history of Byzantine missions begins in the middle of the ninth century when the Empire's foreign policy, long on the defensive, and recently crippled by the Iconoclast crisis, regained the initiative in all three sectors of the northern front. This expansion of Byzantine culture in the north led to the emergence, by the beginning of the eleventh century, of a new community of European nations, with a nascent Christian culture and a common allegiance to the Church and Emperor of East Rome. The leading role in this peaceful conquest was played by the Byzantine missionary. In the history of Byzantine missions there is surely no greater period than the sixties of the ninth century; in this single decade, the Khazar khagan, who favored the Jewish faith, was induced to follow a policy of toleration towards the Christians of his realm; Constantine and Methodius were sent to Moravia, there to implant among the Slavs of Central Europe a vernacular Christianity under Byzantine auspices; Bulgaria was converted to the Christian faith; and the Patriarch Photius, the instigator of all these missions, was able to announce that the Russians themselves had accepted baptism and acknowledged the Emperor's supremacy.

Such then, it may be suggested, were the principles which determined the foreign policy of the Byzantine Empire: a universalism derived from ancient Rome; a distinction between the Rhomaios and the barbarian, that combined the Hellenistic idea of a common culture with the Christian notion of a common Church; and the Judaeo-Christian conception of the Chosen People, the pre-ordained carrier of the true faith to all corners of the earth.

It is obvious that these principles, and especially the first, were often at variance with observable reality. And yet, for all their attachment to theory, the Byzantine politicians were no pedantic doctrinaires. How then did they square the theory with the facts?

The main problem was, of course, to reconcile the Emperor's universal sovereignty with the existence of barbarians outside his effective control. The Byzantines, with their characteristically Greek tendency to rationalize phenomena, had to explain and justify these limitations of the Emperor's power: the barbarian ἔθνη, they argued, may today be outside the Empire's hegemony, or in revolt against the authority of the *autokrator*; but ideally and potentially they were still his subjects; if their lands remained outside the *Oikoumene*, this was the result of God's permissive will, of the divine *oikonomia*, and some day they would bow down before their legitimate sovereign. To induce them to do so was the unvarying aim of Byzantine diplomacy: and in several periods of the Empire's history, when the authority and prestige of Byzantium were on the ascendant, it must have seemed to the statesmen of East Rome that this universal mission was on the way to being fulfilled: such epochs of great diplomatic achievement were the reigns of Justinian and Heraclius, the period that extends from the accession of Michael III in 842 to the death of Basil II in 1025, and the age of the Comnenian emperors.

The methods employed by the Byzantine diplomatists to induce the barbarians to enter the *Oikoumene*, or at least to associate themselves with it, varied greatly according to circumstances. The simplest — and one frequently used until the financial crisis of the late eleventh century — was money. In the belief that every man has his price, the Byzantine governments from Justinian to Basil II paid out considerable sums to ensure the loyalty of the Empire's satellite peoples. In many cases this money was undoubtedly tribute, extorted by the barbarians at the point of the sword. But the Byzantines themselves, characteristically enough, regarded these contributions, especially when they were periodic, as payments by the beneficent Emperor for services the recipients had rendered, or would render, to the Empire. Thus tribute itself became a means of associating the barbarians with the *Oikoumene*. The exact nature of this association cannot easily be defined in constitutional terms. But it would, I believe, be interesting to consider the meaning of several technical terms used by Byzantine writers to describe the peoples thus associated with the Empire. Six of these seem particularly significant: ἔνσπονδοι, ὑπόσπονδοι, σύμμαχοι, κατήκοοι, ὑπήκοοι and πρόξενοι.

The term ἔνσπονδος ("ally;" cf. σπονδαί = "a solemn treaty") is in a sixth-century source significantly related to the word μισθοφόρος ("mercenary;" οἱ μισθοφόροι = mercenaries).[18] The term ἔνσπονδοι was also applied in the sixth century to the Crimean Goths,[19] to the Lombards,[20] and to the Saracens on the south-eastern borders of the Empire;[21] and in the early thirteenth century the Bulgarian ruler Kaloyan was termed one of the ἔνσπονδοι of the Byzantine Emperor.[22]

Ὑπόσπονδοι ("under a treaty") is clearly synonymous with ἔνσπονδοι. The term is applied in the fifth century to the Thracian Goths,[23] in the sixth century to the Tzani.[24] In a *chrysobullon* issued shortly after the conquest of the Empire of Samuel in 1018, Basil II stated that the country was now his ὑπόσπονδον.[25] In the twelfth century the same word is applied to the Russian prince of Galicia[26] and to the King of Hungary.[27]

Σύμμαχοι ("allies") denoted the Heruli in the sixth century,[28] the Russians in the eleventh,[29] and the Hungarians in the twelfth;[30] in the same century Manuel Comnenus is said to have offered a συμμαχία to the prince of Kiev,[31] and in the early years of the thirteenth century Kaloyan of Bulgaria is described as a σύμμαχος of Alexius III.[32]

The term κατήκοοι ("obedient;" cf. κατακούω — "to be subject") was somewhat less common; it is applied to the Tzani in the sixth century,[33] and to the Serbs in the twelfth.[34] The two other terms, ὑπήκοοι ("subjects") and πρόξενοι ("public friends"), are used by the Patriarch Photius in his encyclical letter of 867 to define the relationship of the newly-converted Russians to the Empire.[35] The choice of the last two terms, both of which go back to classical antiquity, is, I believe, significant: ὑπήκοοι was a word applied to the subject allies of Athens, while one of the meanings of πρόξενος was a citizen who had been nominated by a foreign state to be its friend.

It seems to me that these six technical terms have, in their given contexts, much the same significance. The first three were earlier applied to the "foederati" and "socii populi Romani," autonomous subjects of the Roman Empire who, by virtue of a treaty (foedus) concluded with Rome, guarded her frontier in exchange for a regular subsidy, imperial protection and the right of self-government. The "foederati" are explicitly identified with the ὑπόσπονδοι in a fifth-century source;[36] and it seems that in the sixth century the "foederati" came to be called σύμμαχοι.[37] It would perhaps be unwise, in view of the linguistic traditionalism of the Byzantines, to attach too much significance to the recurrence of these technical terms. Yet such was the continuity of Romano-Byzantine institutions that it seems by no means impossible that the Byzantines still thought of their satellites in terms of Roman administration; and that the position within the *Oikoumene* of these satellites, theoretically subject to the Emperor, independent in practice, may to some extent be understood in the light of the Roman conception of "foederatio," which expresses the status of the Empire's subject-allies. In this manner Byzantium could safeguard its universal claims, without being obliged to press them too far; while the "barbarians," gaining a new prestige from their legal association with the Empire, could preserve their political autonomy.

The association of the "barbarians" with the Empire was further expressed by the bestowal upon their rulers of titles taken from the hierarchy of the Byzantine court. The purpose of such titles was three-fold: to flatter the vanity of the Imperial satellites; to bind them to the Empire by a relationship of dependence; and to signify the particular rank occupied by the ruler and his people within the *Oikoumene*. The significance of this *Herrschertitulatur* has often been discussed by Byzantinists; it need only be pointed out here that the highest of all titles in the hierarchy dependent on the supreme authority of the βασι-λεὺς καὶ αὐτοκράτωρ τῶν Ῥωμαίων — that of simple βασιλεύς — was granted several times by Byzantium to foreign rulers: to Charlemagne in 812; to Peter of Bulgaria in 927; probably, as Professor Ostrogorsky has demonstrated, to Symeon of Bulgaria in 913; and possibly, as I have argued elsewhere,[38] to Vladimir of Rus' around 989.

These concessions of Imperial diplomacy, sometimes accompanied by bestowals of Byzantine brides and Byzantine insignia (including crowns), were reinforced by the work of East Roman missionaries. For the most powerful instrument of Byzantine universalism was the Orthodox Christian faith which united the barbarian proselytes to the Rhomaioi by membership of the same Church and by direct allegiance to the Emperor, head of the Christian *oikoumene*. When the King of the Caucasian Lazi sought the protection of Justin I, he is said to have addressed the Emperor in these terms: "We wish thee to make us Christians like thyself, and we shall then be subjects of the Roman Empire."[39] The dependence of the new Christian satellites on Byzantium was often expressed in spiritual terms, the barbarian proselyte becoming the Emperor's "spiritual son." And this dependence was further strengthened by the work of the Byzantine missionary clergy, who by their own teaching and through the collection of Byzantine canon law which they brought to the new converts abroad, spread the notion of the universal sovereignty of the *basileus*.

Byzantine ecclesiastical diplomacy, in certain periods at least, showed, no less then its secular counterpart, a genius for combining a program of Imperial hegemony with a policy of concessions to the national aspirations of Byzantium's satellites. A curious instance of this policy of concessions is provided by the evidence of an agreement, concluded between the authorities of Byzantium and Russia, according to which the primates of the Russian Church were to be appointed alternately from among Byzantine and Russian candidates.[40] But the most effective of all instruments used by Byzantine missionaries in Eastern Europe was the Slavonic liturgy and translations of the Scriptures with which Cyril and Methodius provided the Moravian Slavs in the second half of the ninth century. This vernacular tradition enabled the Empire's Slavonic converts in Eastern Europe — the Bulgarians, the Russians and the Serbs — to build up their Christian life under Byzantine auspices without fear of losing their cultural autonomy; and though this policy of linguistic liberalism was to suffer a temporary eclipse in the late eleventh and twelfth centuries, the legacy of Cyril and Methodius, perhaps the greatest of Byzantine missionaries, enabled the Slavs to assimilate something of that cosmopolitan universalism which, in their finest and most successful hour, the Church and Empire of East Rome preached to the newly converted nations of Europe.

This work of Byzantine envoys abroad was supported, and indeed made possible, by the diplomatists at home. No effort was spared to impress the barbarian rulers, or their ambassadors who travelled to Constantinople, with the power and majesty of the Roman peace. The officials of the Ministry of Foreign Affairs — the Master of Ceremonies, the Master of the Offices and, later, the Logothete of the Course, knew how to combine an elaborate mise-en-scène with the requirements of military security. If the foreign ambassadors came from a powerful nation, strict security measures were enforced. Constantine Porphyrogenitus, who knew so well what he describes as the "ravening greed and brazenly submitted claims of the tribes of the North," and the fondness of their rulers for Byzantine princesses, urged that they be not allowed to see too many riches of Constantinople or to contemplate the beauty of Greek women.[41] Rather were they to be pointedly shown the smartness of the troops and the height of the city walls.[42] But in Constantinople itself, the envoys would generally be treated to a splendid reception. Historians are fond of citing Liutprand's famous description of an Imperial audience in the palace — the immense throne which by some hidden mechanism could suddenly levitate to the ceiling, with the Emperor upon it; the gilded tree with singing birds of bronze; the mechanical lions which roared and beat the ground with their tails.[43] But one may be permitted to wonder how far, to impress the barbarians, the Byzantines really needed all this paraphernalia, which must have struck even the less sophisticated envoys from abroad as a little childish. For their greatest asset was their City, protected by God, with all its glory. Its palaces and churches could provide far more effective means of propaganda. The Byzantine poet Paul the Silentiary describes a scene he saw in the atrium of St. Sophia: a group of Africans were being shown round —and so impressed they were with the beauty and majesty of Rome, symbolized by Justinian's Church, that they submitted of their own free will to the Church and the Emperor of Byzantium.[44] And four centuries later there comes from a Slav source the exact counterpart to this suggestive scene: when the envoys of the Russian prince Vladimir, sent abroad to test the different religions of the earth, returned home, they are said to have made this report to their pagan sovereign: "We came to the Greeks [i.e. into St. Sophia] and we knew not whether we were in heaven or on earth; for on earth there is no such beauty or splendour. . .we know only that in that place God dwells among men, and their service is more beautiful than that of other nations: for we cannot forget that beauty."[45]

* * *

To attempt an overall estimate of the achievements and failures of Byzantine diplomacy on the basis of the fragmentary picture sketched in this paper would, no doubt, be hazardous. But a few tentative suggestions may be advanced in conclusion. In the first place, it would be wrong to idealize this diplomacy. Not all the northern barbarians appreciated that ingenious and elaborate mythology by which the Byzantines justified the claims of their Emperor to exercise universal jurisdiction. When Bayan, khagan of the Avars, demanded of Justin II the surrender of Sirmium, he cynically mocked the Emperor's rights of adoption: if the Emperor was his father, he asserted, let him grant him what was due to a son.[46] Moreover, the art of instigating one barbarian tribe against another, in which Byzantine diplomatists excelled, and the treachery with which the Empire sometimes acted towards its erstwhile allies, were not always calculated to enhance its prestige among the victims of this diplomatic game of chess. When Valentinus, envoy from Justin II to the Turks of Central Asia, presented his credentials to the khagan, he was met by an explosion of rage; putting his hands to his mouth, the Turkish sovereign exclaimed: "are you not those Romans, who have ten tongues, and one deceit?. . .As my ten fingers are now in my mouth, so you use many tongues: with one you deceive me, with another the Avars, my slaves. You flatter and deceive all peoples with the artfulness of your words and the treachery of your thoughts, indifferent to those who fall headlong into misfortune, from which you yourselves derive benefit." "It is strange and unnatural," he added in stinging rebuke, "for a Turk to lie."[47] On occasion the traditionalism of Byzantine foreign policy could lapse into archaistic romanticism. Ernst Stein has pointed out that Justinians' failure to protect adequately the Danube frontier can be partly explained by his obsession with classical reminiscences: his wars with Persia, with the memories of Marathon and Salamis, and his reconquest of Roman lands offered more appeal than a border warfare on the Danube against miserable barbarians:[48] and for this failure, Justinian's successors paid dearly.

As we look closer into the history of Byzantine diplomacy we may detect in its methods a curious duality: a mixture of conservatism and elasticity, of overbearing pride and extreme open-heartedness, of aggressive imperialism and political generosity. This duality is particularly apparent in the attitude of Byzantium to the Slav language: in the ninth and tenth centuries the Empire actively encouraged its Slavonic proselytes to build up their own cultural life on vernacular foundations; in the following centuries a policy of hellenization and cultural oppression was at times initiated. It is perhaps difficult to decide which was the normal, and which the aberrant, tendency; possibly both were always in existence. But it is worth reminding ourselves that a policy of cultural liberalism and self-interested generosity was the hall-mark of the Emperors of the Macedonian house; and of these Basil I and Basil II were perhaps the greatest.

There can be no doubt that, on an overall view, Byzantine diplomacy was remarkably successful. By saving the Empire many times from invasion and destruction, by attracting so many of the pagan ἔθνη into the orbit of Graeco-Roman civilization, by gaining for Christendom and for Europe so many lands of the Balkans and to the north of the Black Sea, this diplomacy was a factor of major importance in European history. As such, it is a subject not unworthy of further study. Nor has its influence on our cultural inheritance been negligible: for the nations of Eastern Europe received much of their education in foreign policy from the statesmen of Byzantium; the East European sovereigns of the Middle Ages learnt much from their masters; while some at least of the traditions of Byzantine diplomacy were passed on to the West through the intermediary of Venice. And in the world today, a foreign policy that could combine in so outstanding a degree an uncompromising belief in the truth of its own values with an ability to negotiate with its opponents, may have its relevance as well.

FOOTNOTES ON CHAPTER I

[1]See now, however, *Byzantine Diplomacy*, ed. J. Shepard and S. Franklin (London, Variorum Reprints, 1992).

[1A]Menander, fr. 21-22.

[2]*Bellum Persicum*, II, c. 29, ed. Teubner, pp. 291-2.

[3]*DAI*, c. 10, 11.

[4]*De Cerimoniis*, ed. Bonn., p. 688.

[5]*DAI*, c.1. English translation by R.J.H. Jenkins.

[6]*Povest' Vremennykh Let*, s. a. 944.

[7]Polybius, IV, 45. Cited in an English translation by J. B. Bury (*A History of the Later Roman Empire*, II (London, 1889), pp. 11-12.

[8]Cited in P. N. Ure, *Justinian and His Age* (Penguin Books, 1951), p. 248.

[9]*De Cerimoniis*, ed. Bonn, p. 5.

[10]*Slavyansky Sbornik*, I (St. Petersburg, 1875), pp. 464-9.

[11]Ed. R.J.H. Jenkins and L.G. Westerink (Washington, D.C., 1973), pp. 27-38.

[12]*Ibid.*, p. 48.

[13]Miklosich und Müller, *Acta Patriarchatus Constantinopolitani*, II, 190-2. English transl. by Ernest Barker, *Social and political thought in Byzantium* (Oxford, 1957), pp.194-6.

[14]*Russkaya Istoricheskaya Biblioteka*, VI, 577.

[15]Cf. the use of the Homeric term βαρβαρόφωνος by Paul the Silentiary, *Descriptio S. Sophiae*, ed. Bonn, 1. 985.

[16]*The Chronicle of John, Bishop of Nikiu*, transl. R. H. Charles (London, 1916), p. 197.

[17]Nicetas Choniates, ed. Bonn, 691.

The distinction between "barbarian"and "Christian" was, however, not an absolute one; Christian satellites of the Empire are sometimes styled "barbarians" in Byzantine sources, mainly, it seems, when they forgot their duty of obedience to the Emperor: thus the Russians who attacked the Empire in 1043 are described by Psellos as τὸ βάρβαρον...τοῦτο φῦλον: *Chronographie*, ed. E. Renauld (Paris, 1928), II, 8.

[18]The ruler of the Utigurs was Justinian's ἔνσπονδον. . . καὶ μισθοφόρον: Agathias, *Hist.*, V, 24 (Bonn 332); (Berlin, 1967), p. 195.

[19]Procopius, *De aedificiis*, III, 7, ed. Teubner, p. 101.

[20]Procopius, *Bellum gothicum*, III, 33, ed. Teubner, p. 444.

[21]*Ibid.*, IV, 11; *Bellum persicum*, I, 17, ed. Teubner, p. 90.

[22]Nicetas Choniates: Sathas, *Bibl. gr. medü aevi*, I, 95. This relationship is held by Nicetas to constitute a form of δουλεία.

[23]Malchus (Bonn 237).

[24]Agathias, *Hist.* (Berlin, 1967), p. 164. Procopius states that the Tzani were αὐτόνομοι (*Bell. pers.*, I, 15).

[25]*Byz. Zeitschrift*, II (1893) 44; *Seminarium Kondakovianum*, IV (1931), 50.

[26]Cinnamus, *Hist.* (Bonn 115).

[27]*Ibid.* (Bonn 120).

[28]Procopius, *Bell. goth.* II, 14, ed. Teubner, p. 208.

[29]John Skylitzes, *Synopsis Historiarum*, ed. I. Thurn (Berlin, 1973), pp. 336-355.

[30]Cinnamus, 299.

[31]Cinnamus, 235.

[32]Nicetas Choniates: Sathas, *Bibl. gr. medii aevi*, I, 95.

[33]Agathias V, 1 (Bonn 278); (Berlin, 1967), p. 164. 32 *ibid.*

[34]Cinnamus, 236, 299.

[35]Photius, *Epistolae*, P.G. CII, 736-7.

[36]Malchus (Bonn 237): τῶν ὑποσπόνδων Γότθων, οὓς δὴ καὶ φοιδεράτους οἱ Ῥωμαῖοι καλοῦσιν. Cf.: "Griechisch entspricht dem *foederatus* ἔνσπονδος": Th. Mommsen, *Römisches Staatsrecht*, III (Leipzig, 1887), p. 654.

[37]L. Bréhier, *Les Institutions de l'Empire Byzantin* (Paris, 1949), p. 337.

[38]*Messager de l'Exarchat du Patriarche Russe en Europe Occidentale*, no. 29 (Paris, 1959), pp. 28-33.

[39]John of Nikiu, cited by A. Vasiliev, *Justin the First* (Cambridge, Mass., 1950), p. 260.

[40]This agreement has escaped the notice of historians owing to the accidental omission of a crucial passage from the Bonn edition of Nicephorus Gregoras' *History*. See D. Obolensky, "Byzantium,

Kiev and Moscow," *Dumbarton Oaks Papers*, XI (1957), pp. 23-78, and below pp. 109-65.
[41]See A. Rambaud, *L'Empire Grec au dixième siècle* (Paris, 1870), p. 304.
[42]*Ibid.*
[43]*Antapodosis*, cap. V.
[44]*Descriptio Magnae Ecclesiae seu Sanctae Sophiae*, ed. Bonn, lines 983-990.
[45]*Povest' Vremennykh Let*, s. a. 987.
[46]Rambaud, *op. cit.*, p. 302.
[47]Menander, *Excerpta de legationibus*, I, pp. 205-6.
[48]*Histoire du Bas Empire*, II, 310.

CHAPTER II

THE EMPIRE AND ITS NORTHERN NEIGHBORS*
565-1018

The Empire's relations with the countries of the north during the four and a half centuries between the death of Justinian I and the conquest of the First Bulgarian Empire by Basil II are marked by three main characteristics. In the military annals of Byzantium this was an heroic age, during which, with few intermissions, the Empire fought to defend its frontiers — and sometimes its very life — against the ever-recurring thrust of the northern invader, of Avar and Slav, of Bulgar and Magyar, of Russian and Pecheneg.[1] Secondly, in these centuries was forged, in reply to the northern challenge, by steadfast faith and lucid thinking, by careful study and observation, by trial and error, that essential weapon of East Roman policy — the imperial diplomacy which remains one of Byzantium's lasting contributions to the history of Europe. Finally, it was this period that the Byzantine statesmen became fully aware of the importance of the north in the Empire's system of security; and a study of the relevant sources — accounts of military missions, ambassadors' reports, handbooks of military strategy, confidential guides to foreign policy, academic histories and monastic chronicles — reveals their growing preoccupation with the area that lay immediately beyond the northern border of the Empire. This, broadly speaking, was the area limited in the west by the Hungarian plain and in the east by the Caspian Sea; it stretched over the Carpathian Mountains, the South Russian steppe, and the lowlands to the north of the Caucasus, and was bounded in the north by a semi-circle extending over the lower course of the great Russian rivers — the Dniester, the Dnieper and the Don — and whose tips

*Cambridge Medieval History, IV, part 1 (Cambridge, 1966); 473-518. Reprinted with the permission ©Cambridge University Press.

came to rest on the middle Danube in the west and on the lower
Volga in the east. It was from the periphery of this semi-circle that
issued the never-ending flow of tribes and nations which, in war and
in peace, were irresistibly drawn into the orbit of Byzantium, whose
attacks and invasions fill the military records of the Empire, and
whose fears, ambitions and lust for conquest taxed so severely the
ingenuity of the statesmen of Constantinople. And within this semi-
circle, the encounter of Byzantium with its northern neighbors was
particularly felt in three sectors which served as the pivots of the
Empire's policy in the north: the Danube, the Crimea and the Caucasus.

The importance of these three sectors had become fully apparent
during the reign of Justinian; it was this Emperor above all who developed and bequeathed to his successors a conception of diplomacy as
an intricate science and a fine art, in which military pressure, political
intelligence, economic cajolery and religious propaganda were fused
into a powerful weapon of defensive imperialism. A brief survey of the
Empire's position along its northern frontier in the closing years of his
reign is thus a fitting introduction to the policy of his successors.

The significance of the Caucasian sector for the Empire's security
was a matter of political geography: for at the extremities of this great
isthmus separating the Black Sea from the Caspian the Graeco-
Roman civilization of the Mediterranean met and clashed with the
westward expansion of Asian cultures: in the north, with the nomads
of Eurasia, moving to the Black Sea and the Danube; in the south
with the occupiers of the Iranian plateau, pushing towards Asia
Minor and the Bosphorus. Both these westward movements spelled
constant danger to Byzantium; and the effort of the imperial diplomacy in this sector was directed as much towards achieving a favorable balance of power in the lowlands north of the Caucasus, as to
creating a bulwark against possible attacks of Persians and Arabs
through Asia Minor towards Constantinople itself. The basic aim of
Byzantine policy in this sector was always the same: to build up a
chain of allied, or vassal, states from the lower Volga and the Sea of
Azov to Lake Van in Armenia. Their peoples could render the
Empire services consonant with their geographical position and military resources: on the eastern coast of the Black Sea, the Zikhi and
the Abasgians could help the Byzantine fleet to operate in Caucasian
waters and thus hold the left sector of the Empire's north-eastern
front: further south, along the coast, the Lazi and the Tzani guarded
the approaches to the northern coast of Asia Minor; the Georgians in

The northern neighbours of the Byzantine Empire.

the central Caucasus and the Alans further north on the Terek stood guard over the Pass of Darial and could prevent the Eurasian nomads from striking south at Byzantine Asia Minor. All these Caucasian tribes were successfully wooed by the diplomacy of Justinian; the first four were converted to Christianity in the sixth century by Byzantine missionaries, and the new ecclesiastical organization set up in their lands was to prove, on the whole, an effective means of keeping them under the political influence of East Rome. And the roads and fortresses which the Byzantines built in these countries were the material counterpart of the flattering though less tangible links which their rulers were induced to form with the imperial court of Constantinople. The tribes which inhabited the steppe land between the lower Volga and the Sea of Azov, at the northern extremity of this sector, could, if they were friendly and sufficiently powerful, be counted upon to guard the eastern end of the European "steppe corridor" and generally to help preserve the balance of power along the whole length of the Empire's northern front. Here too, by his alliance with the Sabiri on the western shores of the Caspian and with the Utigurs on the eastern coast of the Sea of Azov, Justinian pointed the way to his successors.

In the central segment of the semi-circle that marked in the sixth century the effective limit of Byzantium's sphere of interest in the north, half-way between its tips which rested on the middle Danube and on the lower Volga, lay the second pivot of the Empire's northern front. During the whole period covered by this chapter Byzantine possessions and dependencies in the Crimea — above all the city of Cherson (the ancient Χερσόνησος) — acted as the northern outpost of the Empire's diplomacy in the steppe; their importance was partly economic, for the Crimea provided Byzantium with the raw materials of the hinterland — fish from the rivers of South Russia, salt from the Azov region, furs and honey from the forests further north — and sold to the barbarians the manufactured articles of Byzantine industry. Politically, Cherson and its neighboring region, subject or vassal of the Empire during the greater part of the period under review, was an invaluable observation post, a watch-tower planted on the very fringe of that barbarian world of South Russia which Byzantine diplomacy was ever anxious to influence and control. It was from the Crimea that Justinian's government could follow the moves of the Utigurs and the Kutrigurs, encamped on both sides of the Sea of Azov, and, by a timely bribe or by stirring up internal strife among them, divert their attacks from the Balkans. It was from Byzantine Crimea that his successors were able to pursue towards the northern barbarians the traditional Roman policy of "divide and rule," or at least, when this proved impracticable, "weaken and watch." And, true again to the time-honored methods of Roman diplomacy, Byzantium had secured in the mountains of southern Crimea, as a counterbalance to its enemies in the steppe, a useful satellite, half-vassal and half-ally, the Crimean Goths. The security of the Empire's Balkan provinces, as later events were so frequently to confirm, depended as much upon the watchfulness of its agents in the Crimea as upon the influence it wielded in the north Caucasian area.

The third sector of the Empire's northern front was on the lower and middle Danube; and this section of the *limes Romanus* was, in the military sense, much more of a "front" than the Crimea or the northern Caucasus. This too was a matter of geography: for the lower Danube lay near the terminus of the "steppe corridor," that immemorial highway taken by nomadic invaders from Asia; and for many of them, who had succeeded in avoiding entanglements and traps laid for them by the Byzantine diplomats in the Caucasian and Crimean sectors, the Danube proved no insuperable obstacle, and the road into the Balkans lay open. The contrast in the strategic position of Constantinople, admirably protected from attack by sea, but open to a chance invasion by land across the plains of Thrace — already observed by Polybius[2] — provides a constant and tragic background to the medieval history of the Balkans. Justinian had seen his Danubian frontier constantly threatened and frequently overrun by Kutrigurs and Slavs. The Slavs, whose incursions into the Balkans had started in the reign of his predecessor Justin I and increased in strength throughout the sixth century, had expanded from their European homes north of the Carpathians and were then divided into two main groups: the Sclaveni, north of the middle and lower Danube, and the Antes (or Antae), further east, between the Carpathians and the Donets.[3] The havoc wrought by the Slavs in the Balkans, described by Procopius,[4] was a harbinger of worse things to come. Justinian's fortifications and skillful diplomacy could not compensate for the lack of soldiers. It has been suggested that the Emperor's failure to protect adequately the Danube frontier can be partly explained by his obsession with classical reminiscences: his wars with Persia, which evoked memories of Marathon and Salamis, and his reconquest of Roman lands, offered more appeal than border warfare on the Danube against barbarians.[5] Whether this is so or not, his successors were certainly left to deal with the problem of the Balkans.

Justinian's death in 565 ushered in a new period in the history of the Empire's Danubian frontier: for the next sixty years Byzantine policy in this sector was conditioned by the Avar threat. The Avars, whose hordes included, it would seem, Mongol and Turkic tribes, had arrived in the north Caucasian region at the close of Justinian's reign, in headlong flight from their erstwhile subjects, the Central Asian Turks.[6] Through the intermediary of the Alans they sought the Empire's protection, and in 558 concluded a *foedus* with East Rome, promising to submit to the Emperor and to fight his enemies. Justinian could not but welcome this chance of easing the pressure on the northern front, believing, as Menander saw it, that "whether the Avars are victorious, or whether they are defeated, in either case the Romans will profit."[7] The Avars played their part as imperial *foederati* only too thoroughly: by 561 they were on the lower Danube, having subjected in their westward advance the Sabiri, the Utigurs, the Kutrigurs and the Antes of Bessarabia. Their relations with the Empire now entered a new and more critical phase. Their requests to be allowed to cross the Danube and to settle in the Dobrudja were studiously ignored by Justinian: thus was created the first of the many bones of contention between Byzantium and the Avars.

Justin II inherited this increasingly tense situation. A few days after his accession he received an Avar embassy in the palace. The Emperor, determined to abandon Justinian's humiliating policy of buying off the northern barbarians,[8] haughtily rejected their request for tribute.[9] The Avars, meanwhile, had become entangled in the affairs of Central Europe: as allies of the Lombards they defeated the Gepids, seized their lands in Dacia and Eastern Pannonia (567) and, on the departure of the Lombards to Italy in the following year, occupied the whole of the Hungarian plain. The establishment of the Avars as the dominant power in Central Europe, lords of an empire that stretched from Bohemia to the lower Danube and from the Alps to the steppes of South Russia and was centered in the Theiss (Tisza) valley, drastically altered the balance of power along Byzantium's northern frontier. It was not long before the supreme ruler of the Avars, the Khan Bayan, a ruthless conqueror and an able diplomatist, showed where his true ambitions lay. The city of Sirmium on the lower Sava, the key to the Byzantine fortifications in northern Illyricum, had, in the confusion of the Lombard-Gepid war, eluded his grasp. And now, with a clear perception of its strategic importance, combining force with diplomacy, Bayan concentrated on this objective. But Sirmium stood firm, and in 574 a treaty was concluded between Byzantium and the Avars, Justin II undertaking to pay a yearly tribute of 80,000 *nomismata*.[10]

At this stage Byzantium's relations with the Avars were suddenly entangled with the Empire's diplomatic activity on the North Caucasian front. In 568 there arrived in Constantinople an embassy from the Central Asian Turks (the T'ou Kiue of the Chinese), whose Empire stretched from Mongolia to Turkestan and was now expanding westwards towards the Northern Caucasus; the envoys brought Justin II peace proposals from Silzibul,[11] khan of the western branch of the T'ou Kiue. The Turks, and their vassals, the Sogdians, controlled the eastern sector of the silk route from China to Europe; the western sector, leading to Byzantium, crossed Persian territory. The Turks were as interested in the silk trade as the Byzantines: the former, aspiring to the role of commercial intermediaries between China and Byzantium, sought an outlet to the south-west; the East Roman government now saw in the Turks a means of circumventing Persian control of the silk routes from China to the Black Sea, which so often in the past threatened to make the Empire economically dependent on its traditional enemy. To the realization of this joint plan the Sassanid Empire was the main obstacle; and it seems that the agreement concluded in Byzantium between Justin II and the Turks provided — next to a clause relating to the silk trade — for a military alliance against Persia. "It was thus," Menander observes, "that the Turkish nation became friends of the Romaioi."[12] A Byzantine embassy, headed by Zemarchus, journeyed to Silzibul's capital in the Ektag mountain in the Tekes valley, in the eastern Tiem Shan.[13] During the next few years relations between Byzantium and the Turks were friendly and close, to judge at least from the numerous embassies that travelled between Constantinople and Central Asia. But in 576 the situation altered dramatically. When the Byzantine envoys, headed by Valentinus, presented their credentials to the Khan Tourxath,[14] Silzibul's son and successor, they were met with an explosion of rage. Placing his fingers to his mouth, the Turkish sovereign exclaimed: "Are you not these Romans, who have ten tongues, and one deceit?... As my ten fingers are now in my mouth, so you have many tongues, using one to deceive me, another to deceive the Varchonites [i.e. the Avars], my slaves. You flatter and deceive all peoples with the artfulness of your words and the treachery of your thoughts, indifferent to those who fall headlong into misfortune, from which you yourselves derive benefit." "It is strange and unnatural," he added in stinging rebuke, "for a Turk to lie." Bitterly reproached with the alliance which their Emperor had concluded with the hated enemies of the Turks, the Avars, "slaves that had fled from their masters," the Byzantine envoys barely escaped with their lives; the alliance between the Empire and the Turks, which had lasted for eight years, was abruptly terminated;[15] and in the same year (576) a Turkish army, moving westwards from the Caspian Sea, captured the Byzantine city of Bosporus in the Crimea and threatened the Empire's whole defensive system in the peninsula.

The collapse of the Turko-Byzantine alliance was probably due as much to the new turn the Empire's diplomacy was taking on its northeastern front as to its activity on the Danube. Menander's frank reporting affords us a suggestive glimpse of the moral indignation which the methods of this diplomacy so often provoked among its victims in the Eurasian steppe. The Turks, it may be surmised, had come to realize that the Byzantine statesmen were losing interest in so distant an ally; and the agreement which the Empire, two years previously, had concluded with the Avars they chose to regard as a hostile act.

Tiberius (578-82), whose realism led him to prefer negotiation to the intransigent imperialism of his predecessor, tried to use the Avars to check the Slavs whose raids across the Danube were causing grave concern in Constantinople.[16] But Bayan proved a treacherous ally: the Danubian frontier was continually sagging throughout Tiberius' reign, and between 578 and 586 Avar raids, alternating and frequently combining with invasions of Slavs, spread havoc in Thrace, Illyricum and Greece.[17] John of Ephesus describes a formidable invasion of the Balkans by the Slavs in 581; they reached the "Long Wall" outside Constantinople and, having "learnt to fight better than the Romans," were still at the time of writing (584) in possession of the conquered lands.[18] Many of them remained on imperial territory, and the first important Slav settlements in Thrace, Macedonia and Northern Greece undoubtedly date from this time. The position was no less perilous in northern Illyricum, where the Avar threat to Sirmium was growing. To Bayan's demand to surrender the city Tiberius replied that he would sooner give one of his daughters to the khan than abandon the fortress of his own free will. But Bayan, who knew that Tiberius was fully occupied with the Persian war, was not to be bluffed; and after a siege of two years Sirmium, inadequately defended and provisioned, was surrendered on the Emperor's orders to the Avars (582).[19]

With the key to the northern Balkans now in Avar hands, the Empire for the next ten years was forced on to the defensive. In vain did the Emperor Maurice attempt to buy off the Avars by agreeing to increase their annual subsidy (584);[20] Thrace, Macedonia, Greece, and it seems the Peloponnese itself, were raided and partly overrun during the next few years by the Avars and their subjects, the Slavs.[21] But Maurice's genius succeeded to some extent in restoring the Empire's position on the Danube during the decade from 592 to 602. In 591 the successful completion of the Persian war enabled him to bring his seasoned troops back to Europe. Priscus, his greatest commander, was entrusted with the double task of maintaining the Danube as a frontier line against the Avars and stopping the incursions of the Slavs. The latter were still able to launch, under the auspices of the khan, a massive attack against Thessalonica in 586 or 597.[22] But on the whole Priscus was remarkably successful, crossing the Danube to subdue the Slavs and recapturing Singidunum from the Avars. In 600 a treaty between Byzantium and the Avars fixed the Empire's frontier on the Danube, Maurice undertaking to increase the tribute.[23] But in 601 Priscus was across the Danube and, carrying the war into the enemy's territory, inflicted a crushing defeat on Bayan's forces on the Theiss. Not since the days of Justinian had the arms of Byzantium won such a triumph in Europe.[24]

But Maurice's successes on the Danube were soon undone. In 602 the Emperor's order that the troops were to winter beyond the Danube provoked a mutiny. The rebellious army marched on Constantinople, seized the city and proclaimed their leader Phocas Emperor. Phocas' disastrous reign (602-10) marks a turning point in the history of the Empire's northern frontier. The *limes* on the lower Danube and on the Sava, held — albeit imperfectly and precariously — by Justinian's three successors, now collapsed, and the barbarians surged over the Balkans. The three-pronged attacks of the Avaro-Slav hordes towards the Adriatic, the Aegean and the Bosphorus in the reigns of Phocas and Heraclius led to a permanent occupation by the Slavs of Illyria, Dalmatia, Macedonia and Thrace. Salona was sacked (c.614), Thessalonica was attacked several times, and then in 617 the Avars reached the suburbs of Constantinople itself.[25] It was then, in all probability, that the Slavs, spreading south irresistibly, settled in large numbers in Greece and the Peloponnese, forming independent

communities (*Sclaviniae*) over which the Byzantine authorities were
for nearly two centuries incapable of exercising effective control. In
623 they ravaged Crete. Without much exaggeration, Isidore of Seville
could write that at the beginning of Heraclius' reign "the Slavs took
away Greece from the Romans."[26] The supreme crisis came in 626
when a vast Avar horde, supported by Slavs, other northern barbarians and — ineffectually — by a Persian army encamped on the Asian
side of the Bosphorus, hurled itself for ten days at the defences of
Constantinople. The courage of the garrison, inspired by the Patriarch
Sergius, and the naval victory gained by the Byzantines over the Slavs,
saved the city. The khan abandoned the siege, and the Avars, badly
defeated, withdrew to Pannonia.[27] Never again did they seriously
threaten the Empire.

Though incapable of stemming the flow of Slavs into his Balkan
provinces, Heraclius could at least, to prevent further Avar invasions,
attempt to stabilize the northern frontier by diplomatic means. This
policy was attended with a measure of success. About 623, the Slavs
of Bohemia, Moravia and Slovakia were liberated from the yoke of
the Avars by Samo, who founded a short-lived realm stretching from
the upper Elbe to the middle Danube. Whether or not Samo's revolt
was instigated by Heraclius' diplomacy, there is no doubt that the rise
of his kingdom, by weakening the power of the Avars on the eve of
their assault on Constantinople, served the interests of Byzantium. Of
more lasting significance were the measures taken by Heraclius, probably soon after 626, to relieve the Avar pressure on the middle
Danube and in Illyricum. Constantine Porphyrogenitus tells us that
the Emperor called in the Croats against the Avars. The Croats, who
came from "White Croatia" north of the Carpathians, defeated the
Avars, expelled them from Illyricum, and, together with the Serbs
from "White Serbia," were then settled by Heraclius as subjects of the
Empire in their present homes in the Balkans. The Serbs and the
Croats were subsequently converted to Christianity by missionaries
sent from Rome on Heraclius' orders;[28] and these new subjects of
Byzantium must have provided some measure of stability in the chaos
which the Avaro-Slav invasions had brought into the Balkans.

The desire to keep the Avars in check was also, it seems, a prime
factor in Heraclius' diplomacy on the Empire's north-eastern, Caucasian, front. The collapse of the alliance with the T'ou Kiue and the
Turkic threat to the Crimea in the eighth and ninth decades of the
sixth century had, moreover, made it necessary for Byzantium to

acquire a strong and reliable ally in this sector. In 619, Heraclius received in Constantinople the visit of a "Hunnic" ruler, had him baptized at his own request, together with his retinue, and before sending him home granted him the title of *patricius*.[29] His subjects were undoubtedly the Onogurs, a people of West Siberian origin, belonging to the Bulgaric (West Turkic) linguistic group, who had lived since the fifth century between the Sea of Azov and the Northern Caucasus.[30] About 635 Kovrat, ruler of the Onogurs, rose against the Avars and drove them out of his country; whereupon he concluded an alliance with the Emperor and was made a patrician in his turn.[31] Kovrat, John of Nikiu tells us, had been baptized as a child and brought up at the court of Constantinople where he became a life-long friend of Heraclius.[32] Kovrat's loyalty served the Empire in good stead. His kingdom, known to the Byzantines as "Old Great Bulgaria" (ἡ παλαιὰ Βουλγαρία ἡ μεγάλη), which stretched from the Caucasus to the Don, and perhaps as far as the Dnieper, successfully withstanding the Avars in the west and the Turks in the east, acted until Kovrat's death in 642 as the guardian of the Empire's interests in the North Caucasian sector.[33]

Shortly after Kovrat's death "Old Great Bulgaria" broke up under the blows of the Khazars who in the middle of the seventh century struck westward from the lower Volga to the Sea of Azov. In the scattering of tribes that followed, two branches of the Onogur people salvaged enough of their national heritage to play a significant part in the destinies of Eastern Europe. The one, it seems, migrated northward and, settling by the junction of the middle Volga and the Kama, built up a powerful trading state, the kingdom of the Volga Bulgars, which became in the tenth century a northern outpost of Islam.[34] The other group, led by Kovrat's son Asparuch (Isperich),[35] left their homes in the North Caucasus region, moved westwards across the Pontic steppes and appeared on the Danube delta. But southern Bessarabia proved only a temporary resting place: doubtless anxious, like the Avars a century earlier, to exchange the hazards of the steppe for the security of cis-Danubian Dobrudja, Asparuch's Bulgars began in the eighth decade of the seventh century to push further south. It was the traditional policy of Byzantium to welcome potential allies on the north bank of the Danube, but to oppose their crossing of the river by every means; so in 680 Constantine IV rushed his armies to the Danube. But the victorious Bulgars swept through Moesia and the Dobrudja, occupying the imperial lands between the Danube and the

Balkan Mountains. Byzantium bowed to the *fait accompli*: in 681
Constantine IV concluded peace with the Bulgars and undertook to
pay them an annual tribute, thus accepting perforce the existence of
an independent barbarian state on imperial territory.[36] The collapse of
the Empire's Danubian frontier, which the Slav invasions had already
brought about in the first half of the century, was now at last
acknowledged by the Byzantine government. Asparuch had carved
himself a kingdom that stretched from the Dniester to the Haemus
range, a limpet that was to cling to the Empire's flank for more than
three hundred years and was to become in the ninth and tenth centuries one of the great powers of Europe. From his new capital of
Pliska, at the southern extremity of the Dobrudja plain, the Sublime
Khan and his military aristocracy of Onogur Bulgar boyars ruled over
a population of Slav immigrants who, in the course of time, assimilated their conquerors;[37] from this gradual fusion of Bulgars and Slavs
the First Bulgarian Empire was born.

It was not long before this new Balkan state began to loom large
in the policy and destinies of Byzantium. In the burst of diplomatic
activity which took place along the Empire's northern front at the
turn of the century, its three main sectors — the north Caucasian,
the Crimean and the Balkan — linked within an intricate web of
power politics, jointly affected the fate of Constantinople itself. In 695,
Justinian II was dethroned and exiled to Cherson. A few years later,
hoping to regain his throne and fearing the loyalty professed by the
Chersonites to Tiberius III, he fled to Khazaria. The khan received
Justinian with honor and married him to his sister, the Khazar princess being baptized as Theodora, a name which, with its patent allusion to her more celebrated namesake, doubtless symbolized the
khan's ambitions for the restoration of his brother-in-law to the
throne of the Romans. Soon, however, an embassy from Constantinople demanding Justinian's extradition made him change his mind.
Warned by his wife of his imminent arrest, Justinian fled from Khazaria to the mouth of the Danube. The final scene of the drama was
enacted in the Balkans. The exiled Emperor appealed for help to Tervel, Asparuch's successor; and in the autumn of 705 Tervel's army of
Bulgars and Slavs appeared before the walls of Constantinople. The
city fortifications proved impregnable, but Justinian slipped in unob-
served, and in the panic that ensued regained his throne. The timely,
though hardly disinterested, services of the Bulgar Khan were not forgotten: seated by the Emperor's side, Tervel was invested by him with

the dignity of Caesar.[38] The event was a notable one, for next to the imperial dignity the rank of Caesar was the highest in the hierarchy of Byzantium. No barbarian ruler had ever risen so high, and the Bulgarians were not soon to forget that their Khan had received, as an associate of the imperial majesty, the homage of the people of East Rome.[39] But in Byzantine eyes the ceremony of 705 had a different significance: Tervel's title carried no power with it, and could indeed be regarded as a sign of his recognition of the Emperor's supreme and universal authority.[40]

Justinian's adventures on the northern shores of the Black Sea illustrate the struggle that took place in the late seventh and early eighth centuries between Byzantium and the Khazars for the control of southern Crimea and of the straits of Kerch. The Turkic threat to the Crimea which led to the fall of Bosporus in 576 was removed by the dissensions that weakened the Empire of the T'ou Kiue and by the rise of the Old Great Bulgaria; by the end of the sixth century Byzantine authority had been restored in Bosporus. But the Empire's whole position in the peninsula was once again challenged by the westward expansion of the Khazars, who were in possession of the city by the end of the seventh century. The intrigues of Justinian II, and, even more, the three largely unsuccessful expeditions which, upon his restoration, he sent to the Crimea to punish the Greek cities for their former conspiracy against him, threw the Byzantine possessions in the peninsula into the hands of the Khazars: by about 705 Cherson as well was controlled by the khan, and the revolution of 711 which led to the assassination of Justinian was organized in the Crimea with Khazar support.

The Khazar pressure on the Crimea relaxed about this time, and Cherson seems to have remained under Byzantine sovereignty after 711. Circumstances were drawing Byzantium and the Khazars closer together. The Byzantines had long since realized their usefullness in the Empire's strategy on the north Caucasian front. Heraclius, on the eve of his great offensive against the Persian Empire in 627, had concluded a military agreement with them. And in the first half of the eighth century the common threat of Islam cemented that alliance between Byzantium and the Khazars which was an essential factor in the Empire's diplomacy for the next two hundred years. During this period the Khazar Khanate, that most civilized and ordered of states created by the Turkic people in the early middle ages, centered on the territory between the lower Volga, the northern Caucasus and the Sea

of Azov, remained Byzantium's most constant and valued ally in the
north-east. It is probable that in the eighth century the Khazar alliance
did much to save Byzantium from the Arab menace, for had the
Khazars not halted in the Caucasus the northward thrust of Islam, the
Arabs might well have invaded the Pontic steppe and, appearing on
the lower Danube, have outflanked the Empire's whole defensive system in the north. At the same time the Khazars played a not unimportant role in the foreign trade of Byzantium; for by supplying Constantinople with gold from the Urals and with raw silk from China,
they helped the Empire to readjust its economy after the loss of Syria
and Egypt to the Arabs.[41] In spite of occasional clashes in the Crimea,
relations between Constantinople and the Khazar capital of Itil in the
Volga delta were friendly and close. In 733, Leo III married his son,
the future Emperor Constantine V, to the khan's daughter; christened
Irene, the Khazar princess introduced her national dress, the *tzitza-
kion*, into the court of Constantinople.[42]

The Byzantine statesmen would have been false to the time-
honored traditions of East Roman diplomacy if they had not
attemped to sanctify and consolidate this political alliance by converting the Khazars to Christianity. It is, however, remarkable that their
missionary efforts in Khazaria seem to have derived some impetus
from the iconoclast movement. For on the one hand, Constantine V's
(741-75) persecutions of the iconophiles caused a mass exodus of
Orthodox monks from Constantinople and the central provinces to
the outlying regions of the Empire, notably to the Crimea, a fact
which strengthened the influence of Byzantine culture in Cherson,
Bosporus and Gothia and enhanced the role of the peninsula as a
missionary outpost. On the other hand, the East Roman authorities,
while persecuting the defenders of the images nearer home, appear to
have used them in the Crimea to propagate Christianity among the
peoples of the North.[43] Christianity certainly spread to Khazaria in the
eighth century,[44] partly from the Crimea,[45] and the Byzantine authorities must have actively encouraged this development. And it is not
unreasonable to suppose that the list of eight bishoprics subject to the
Patriarchate of Constantinople, forming the "Eparchy of Gothia"
administered by the Metropolitan of Doros (the chief city of the Crimean Goths), and covering a territory that extended from the Crimea
to the lower Volga and the Caucasus — a list contained in C. de
Boor's *Notitia Episcopatuum* — embodies a project, conceived by the
Byzantine authorities in the middle of the eighth century, to set up a

missionary Church over the length and breadth of the Khazar Empire.[46] There is no evidence, however, that this vast ecclesiastical network was ever put into operation. In the second half of the eighth century the progress of Christianity in Khazaria was curtailed by the rival propaganda of Judaism and Islam. The former especially was gaining ground; medieval Hebrew sources, whose reliability is still a matter of dispute, date the first success of Judaism in Khazaria about 730-40 when some of its tenets are said to have been adopted by the Khan Bulan.[47] While recognizing the controversial nature of this problem, the present writer believes that the conversion of the ruling circles of Khazaria to Judaism took place in gradual stages and that their final acceptance of the Mosaic law was delayed until the ninth century.[48] The failure to convert the Khazars to Christianity did not, on the whole, affect the friendly relations between Byzantium and its northern ally. Meanwhile the attention of Byzantine statesmen was shifting increasingly to the Balkan sector.

In the century between 650 and 750 the situation in the Balkans had, from the standpoint of the Empire, much deteriorated. Almost the whole peninsula was occupied by the Slavs, the Greek population being temporarily either submerged or pushed back to the coastal regions along the Black Sea and the Aegean. Thus most of Greece, and practically the entire Peloponnese, were for nearly two centuries outside Byzantine control, while to the north lay an endless expanse of Slav territory, stretching continuously from the Adriatic, the Aegean and the Black Sea to the Baltic.[49] And this vast barbarian world, pressing down on Byzantium from all sides, had been reinforced by the creation on the borders of Thrace of the Bulgar kingdom which was showing, under Tervel and his successors, an assertiveness that augured ill for the future.

Yet in this dark period of Balkan history that extends from the death of Maurice (602) to Irene's accession to power (780) Byzantine influence did not vanish from the peninsula. In the cities of eastern Greece and on the rugged east coast of the Peloponnese the Greek population held on, and was indeed reinforced by emigration from the interior, and this, together with the cultural inferiority of the Slavs at that time and their inability to form strong political groups in this region, made possible the work of rehellenization and reconquest.[50] This work began in the second half of the seventh century, with the campaigns of Constans II (in 658) and Justinian II (in 688-9) against the Slavs of Macedonia; the creation of the imperial themes of Thrace

(between 680 and 687) and of Hellas (between 687 and 695)[51] marks
the result of the first serious counter-offensive against the Slavs since
the reign of Maurice. But its effects were limited, and it was not until
the late eighth century that the tide in the southern part of the Balkans
began to turn against the Slavs. In 783, Irene's chief minister Stauracius marched through Greece and the Peloponnese, subduing Slav
tribes; the establishment of the Peloponnesian theme at the end of the
century was possibly a result of this expedition.[52] The real turning
point in the history of the Peloponnese, however, was under Nicephorus I (802-11) whose forces suppressed a large-scale revolt of the Slavs
round Patras (805) and settled Christian communities in various parts
of the peninsula. The process of absorption and hellenization of the
Slavs in Greece and in the Peloponnese was now well under way. By
the middle of the ninth century Byzantine authority was restored
throughout most of these lands, and what was left undone by the
imperial *strategoi* and tax collectors was later completed by the East
Roman missionaries.

Before this reconquest of Greece and the Peloponnese had begun,
the Empire made a desperate, and almost successful, effort to regain
Moesia from the Bulgars and restore its northern frontier to the
Danube. For some twenty years (756-75) Constantine V strove to
conquer Bulgaria. He cleverly exploited the country's social weakness
by fanning the constant antagonism between the boyar aristocracy
and the Slavs, and in a series of nine campaigns, mostly successful,
which usually combined — in the time-honored fashion — land
attacks through Thrace with naval expeditions to the Danube, he
routed the Bulgarian armies again and again. But even his victory over
the Khan Telets at Anchialus in 763 — the greatest of his reign — did
not subdue the country. Constantine's death on his last campaign (775)
left the Empire stronger in the Balkans than it had been since the
reign of Maurice; but Bulgaria, though crippled and exhausted, was
still on the map, its ruling classes bitterly hostile to Byzantium.

The vitality of the Bulgarian state and its powers of recovery were
demonstrated when Krum, the mightiest of its early rulers, became
Sublime Khan in the opening years of the ninth century. The destruction of the Avar Empire by Charlemagne had enabled the Bulgarians
to annex eastern Pannonia, and Krum became the sovereign of a
realm that stretched from northern Thrace to the northern Carpathians and from the lower Sava to the Dniester and adjoined the Frankish Empire on the Theiss. He was long remembered with terror by

the Byzantines. The aggressive policy of Nicephorus I towards Bulgaria set Krum on a campaign of devastation: in 809 he captured Sardica (the modern Sofia) and in July 811 gained his most celebrated triumph: the Byzantine army was trapped by the Bulgarians in a defile of the Balkan Mountains and slaughtered almost to a man. Nicephorus himself perished in the fray, and from his skull Krum made a goblet, lined with silver, out of which he drank with his boyars. This was a terrible blow to the Empire's prestige: not since the death of Valens on the field of Adrianople in 378 had a Emperor fallen in battle. The triumphant khan swept into Thrace, captured Develtus and Mesembria (812) and in July 813, having routed another Byzantine army, arrived at the walls of Constantinople. But "the new Sennacherib"[53] was impressed by the fortifications of the city and opened negotiations. In the meeting that followed with the Emperor Leo V on the shore of the Golden Horn, Krum barely escaped a Byzantine plot to murder him; breathing vengeance he laid waste the environs of the city and stormed Adrianople, transporting its inhabitants, numbering, it was said, ten thousand, to his own dominions north of the Danube. But the following spring, as he was preparing a huge assault on Constantinople, Krum burst a blood vessel and died (April 814).

The Empire had had a narrow escape. But the balance of power in the Balkans had radically altered. Bulgaria, a country which fifty years before had seemed on the verge of extinction, was now one of the great military powers of Europe. Byzantium's northern line of defence was seriously undermined, since the border fortresses in Thrace — Sardica, Develtus, Mesembria and Adrianople — had been either destroyed or crippled by Krum. But fortunately for the Empire, Krum's aggressive policy was abandoned by his successors. In 815-16, the Khan Omortag concluded a thirty year's peace with Byzantium: the frontier between the two realms was to run along the Great Fence of Thrace from Develtus to Macrolivada, and thence northward to the Balkan Mountains, thus coinciding with the boundary established exactly a century before by the treaty between Tervel and Theodosius III. Save for a few frontier clashes, the Empire and Bulgaria were to remain at peace with one another until the end of the century. The new policy could not fail to strengthen Byzantine influence in Bulgaria, and together with men and ideas from Constantinople, and partly through the thousands of Greek prisoners whom Krum had settled in his realm, Christianity was beginning to spread in this country. The authorities, and especially the boyars who regarded Christianity as an insidious form of Byzantine imperialism, were understandably alarmed. So Omortag, largely it seems for political motives, persecuted his Christian subjects. But the progress of the new ideas which, under the cloak of the thirty years' peace, were spreading from Byzantium to Bulgaria could not be arrested for very long by these reactionary measures.

Meanwhile, with peace restored in the Balkans, the East Roman government was free to devote its attention to the other sectors of the Empire's northern front. The emergence of Bulgaria as a major power, and the uncertain situation in the Pontic steppes, more than ever required a favorable balance of power in the Crimea and northern Caucasus; yet all was not well in these areas: Byzantine Crimea, and especially Cherson, was restive under imperial control, and if the Empire was not to lose its invaluable outpost in the north, the local traditions of Greek municipal autonomy had to be diverted into lawful channels. Khazaria, moreover, on whose friendship the Byzantine statesmen had so long depended, now threatened, owing to the progress of Judaism in the land, to elude their grasp. During the reign of Theophilus, however, the Empire's position in these sectors suddenly improved. About the year 833 the Khazar khan sent an embassy to the Emperor, asking for engineers to build a fortress on the lower Don; whereupon the *spatharocandidatus* Petronas Camaterus, escorted by a squadron of the imperial navy, went on Theophilus' orders to Khazaria by way of Cherson. After building the fortress of Sarkel for the Khazars, he returned to report to the Emperor on the situation in the Crimea. On Petronas' advice, Theophilus raised Cherson and its surroundings into an imperial theme, directly subordinated to the central government, and appointed Petronas its *strategos,* with authority over the local magistrates.[54] It seems clear that the building of Sarkel and the establishment of the theme of Cherson were due to the same cause — the pressure of unidentified barbarians on the lower Don.[55] The Cherson-Sarkel axis, which may well have included a chain of fortifications up the Don,[56] thus served both as an inner line of defence for the Khazar Khanate, whose sphere of influence extended by then to the Dnieper and the Oka, and as a pivot of Byzantium's strategic position in the steppes between the lower Volga and the Danube. Common problems of military security had once again confirmed the traditional alliance between the Empire and the Khazars.

The role played by the Khazar alliance in the Empire's diplomacy became even more apparent in the reign of Michael III. Probably at the end of 860, a Byzantine embassy left Constantinople for Khazaria, headed by a young priest from Thessalonica, named Constantine, who was accompanied by his elder brother, the monk Methodius. Their route lay through Cherson, where Constantine spent the winter and prepared for his mission by learning Hebrew. At the Khan's residence, which seems to have been then at Samandar, on the lower Terek, he engaged in theological disputations with Jewish rabbis who held a dominant position at the Khazar court. But Constantine's ninth-century biographer, while depicting the khan and his subjects as monotheists and people of the Book, clearly implies, in the present writer's opinion, that their final conversion to Judaism had not yet taken place.[57] This inference could be reconciled with the earlier dates at which Hebrew and Islamic sources set the conversion of the Khazars to Judaism[58] by supposing that some of the khans had adopted Jewish monotheism between 730 and 860, without, however, submitting to all the requirements of the Mosaic law.[59] It seems significant that the earliest reference to the Khazars practising circumcision and observing "all the traditions of Judaism" dates from about 864-6,[60] and it is thus difficult to escape the conclusion that the ruling circles of Khazaria formally accepted the Mosaic law soon after Constantine's mission.[61]

But if Constantine's embassy was no great success on the religious plane — some two hundred conversions and an ambiguous declaration from the khan of his sympathy for Christianity were the measure of his missionary achievement at Samandar — politically he seems to have secured his object. The alliance between Byzantium and Khazaria was reaffirmed, the khan wrote to Michael III, professing his readiness to serve the Empire whenever he was needed.[62] The exact nature of the "services" which the Empire required from the Khazars in 860-1 is not known, but it is safe to assume that Constantine's mission was connected with a new danger that threatened Byzantium from the north, and must be viewed in the light of the Empire's policy in that region during the seventh decade of the ninth century. The remarkable achievements of this policy, which were to leave a permanent mark on the history of Europe, were perhaps due to three main factors: to the vigor and initiative which, after the barbarian invasions of the post-Justinian period and the iconoclast crisis, Byzantine diplomacy was now able to display beyond the Empire's northern frontier; to an unprecedented expansion of the Church's missionary work, now linked closer than ever to the aims of East Roman diplomacy, which

made the seventh decade of this century one of the greatest in the
history of Byzantine missions; and to the fact that in this period the
religious and cultural influence of the Empire was able to strike out
beyond the traditional perimeter of Byzantium's northern front and,
thrusting deep into eastern and central Europe, to gain the allegiance
of a substantial part of the vast Slav world.

The story of this achievement begins on 18 June 860, when a fleet
of two hundred Viking ships, coming from the Black Sea, sailed into
the Bosphorus and turned against Constantinople. The city's position
was serious indeed: the Byzantine fleet was probably in the Mediterranean, fighting the Arabs, the army and the Emperor were campaign-
ing in Asia Minor. The suburbs and the coastline were defenseless
against the savage depredations of the barbarians. Inside the invested
city the Patriarch Photius urged the people to faith and repentance.
The strong fortifications once again saved Constantinople; and probably before the Emperor hastily brought his army back, the invaders
raised the siege and withdrew to their homes in the north.[63] The violent emergence of these Vikings—known to the Byzantines as 'Ρῶς,[64]
to the Slavs as Rus' and to the Arabs as Rūs[65] — on the horizon of
East Rome was the outcome of a century-long process of expansion
which led the Scandinavians, mostly Swedes from Upland, Söderman-
land and East Gotland, to sail up the Baltic rivers over the great
watershed of the East European plain. In the second half of the eighth
century, drawn by the extensive trade that flourished, through the
intermediary of the Volga Bulgars and the Khazars, between the fur
and slave dealers of the northern forests and the luxury markets of
Baghdad, they began to go down the Volga to Itil, and over the Caspian to the lands of the Caliphate. Somewhat later, in search of fresh
markets and easier plunder, the Vikings explored the shorter routes to
the warm and rich countries of the South: probably by the early ninth
century, sailing down the Don[66] and the Dniester, they reached the
Black Sea. Towards the middle of the ninth century began the third
and most significant stage in the southward expansion of the Swedes:
by moving up the rivers of the eastern Baltic—the Neva, the western
Dvina, and the Niemen—and by dragging their ships over portages
that lay beyond, the Varangians (as the Russian Swedes came to be
known in eastern Europe) discovered the Dnieper which flowed into
the Black Sea; and the whole of this elaborate network of rivers, lakes,
portages and seas which led from Scandinavia to the Bosphorus, the
"route from the Varangians to the Greeks" of the Russian Chronicle,

became in the second half of the century the true Swedish *Austrvegr*, the classic highway for the great Eastern adventure.[67] Along this waterway, on territory inhabited by Finns and eastern Slavs, the Varangians founded their trading colonies and carved out their military kingdoms. By the middle of the century an important "Russian" settlement, ruled by the Viking Ryurik, existed in Novgorod. Some time between 850 and 860 two Varangians from Novgorod, Askold and Dir, went down the Dnieper and captured the city of Kiev from the Khazars.[68] This was an event of considerable importance: for when the Vikings replaced the Khazars as overlords of the middle Dnieper valley, the strong oriental influences to which the eastern Slavs in this region had for centuries been subjected suffered a sharp setback; while the lure of Byzantium, the fabulous Mikligardr, that deflected the Varangian ships from the Volga and the Caspian to the Dnieper and the Black Sea, was a premonition and a cause of that irresistible attraction which the city of Constantinople was to exert on the minds of the Russians for many centuries to come. It was Askold and Dir who led the Russian campaign on Constantinople in 860, and it can scarcely be doubted that the expedition was launched from Kiev.[69]

The Byzantines' response to the Russian attack, whose failure they ascribed to the protection of the Mother of God, was swift and characteristic. It is highly probable that the main political object of Constantine's mission to Khazaria in 860-1 was to concert with the khan on a joint policy against the Russians, the common enemy of Constantinople and Itil. This diplomatic encirclement of Kiev was followed up by an attempt to convert the Russians to Christianity. Soon after 860 ambassadors from the Rhos were baptized in Constantinople,[70] and in 867 the Patriarch Photius was able to announce that the Russians, who formerly surpassed all peoples in cruelty, had now accepted Christianity and were living under the spiritual authority of a Byzantine bishop as "subjects and friends" of the Empire.[71] Finally, in the reign of Basil I, possibly about 874, the Russians concluded a treaty with Byzantium and an archbishop was sent to them by the Patriarch Ignatius.[72] The scantiness of the sources does not allow us to follow the fate of this first Byzantine ecclesiastical organization on Russian soil; it is natural to suppose that its centre was at Kiev and that it was engulfed in the pagan reaction that swept over South Russia later in the century. Yet the bridgehead which Byzantine Christianity had secured beyond the Pontic steppe was never completely destroyed.

It is an impressive sign of the vision and resourcefulness which the Empire's foreign policy had acquired by the seventh decade of the ninth century that, while the missionaries of Photius and Ignatius were laboring to convert the Slavs and their Viking overlords on the middle Dnieper, the cultural and political influence of Byzantium was able to strike out equally far to another region of the North. In 862, there arrived in Constantinople an embassy from Rastislav, prince of the Moravian Slavs. Its purpose was twofold: the Moravians, whose realm stretched from Bohemia to the Theiss and from the Carpathians to the middle Danube, desired to form an alliance with Byzantium to counteract the coalition recently made against them by Louis the German and the Bulgarian Khan Boris. Rastislav also requested Michael III to send him a missionary capable of teaching Christianity to his people in their own Slavonic tongue. Hitherto the Christian preachers in Moravia had been German missionaries and servants of the Frankish Emperor; a Slav-speaking clergy dependent on Constantinople, Rastislav believed, would help him preserve his independence and ensure a more rapid progress of Christianity in his land. The Moravian proposals were favorably received in Byzantium: the Franko-Bulgarian pact, which threatened to bring Carolingian influence to the very doors of Constantinople, could not but alarm so experienced a diplomatist as the Emperor's chief minister, Bardas; while the Patriarch Photius must have foreseen that Byzantine influence in Moravia would provide a means of exerting pressure on the Bulgarians and of bringing them too into the Christian fold. The Moravo-Byzantine alliance was concluded, and early in 863 an East Roman embassy left for central Europe, headed by Constantine, accompanied once again by his brother Methodius.

The two brothers were natives of Greek Thessalonica and well acquainted with the Slavonic language of the hinterland. Constantine was also an unusually gifted philologist: before embarking on his new mission he invented an alphabet for use of the Moravian Slavs. This first unequivocally attested Slavonic script, identified by most modern authorities as Glagolitic, was adapted to a dialect of southern Macedonia. By gradually translating into this dialect the Scriptures and liturgy of the Christian Church, Constantine and Methodius created a new literary language, known as Old Church Slavonic, which became in the course of time the sacred idiom of a large section of the Slavs and the third international language of Europe. The two brothers began their work in Moravia by translating the liturgical offices into

Slavonic: it seems that at first they used only the Byzantine rite, but in the course of time also adopted and translated the Roman mass.[73] Their activities, which included the training of the clergy of Rastislav's new Slav Church, were viewed with open hostility by the Frankish clergy in Moravia who regarded them not only as dangerous innovators in matters of faith — for the Roman Church, in whose jurisdiction Moravia lay, did not favor the use of vernacular liturgies — but also, no doubt, as agents of Byzantine imperialism. In the winter of 867-8, Constantine and Methodius travelled to Rome at the invitation of Pope Nicholas I, and were received by his successor Hadrian II. They could scarcely have chosen a more propitious moment to plead their cause before the Holy See: for the work of these Byzantine missionaries in Moravia had suddenly become a crucial factor in the ecclesiastical politics of Europe, owing to the remarkable change that had befallen the relations between the Empire and Bulgaria.

The peace that prevailed between Byzantium and Bulgaria during Omortag's reign was endangered after his death (831) by the assertiveness of the Bulgarians who occupied Sardica and Philippopolis and annexed central Macedonia,[74] and by the pro-Frankish policy followed by the Khan Boris (852-89) at the beginning of his reign. In 864, fearing that Boris would carry out his promise to accept Christianity from the German court, the Emperor moved his army to the frontier and sent his fleet along the Black Sea coast. The khan was forced to capitulate: he undertook to renounce the Frankish alliance, to receive Christianity from Constantinople and — at least in the Byzantine reading of the facts — to submit himself and his people to the Emperor's authority.[75] In the same year Boris was baptized,[76] being christened Michael in honor of his imperial godfather. A revolt of the boyars against his decision to enforce baptism on all his subjects was ruthlessly surpressed, and the triumph of Byzantine Christianity in Bulgaria seemed assured. The Patriarch Photius wrote a long and carefully worded letter to Boris, explaining the doctrines of the Church and the duties of a Christian ruler.[77] The khan, however, was not altogether satisfied by this learned disquisition: how was he to reconcile his recognition of Byzantine supremacy with his desire to remain master in his own country? A separate ecclesiastical hierarchy, under a Bulgarian Patriarch, or at least under a bishop owing allegiance to Constantinople, seemed to provide a solution to his dilemma; but on this matter Photius was ominously silent. And so, disappointed with the Greeks, Boris turned to his former ally, Louis

the German, and in 866 requested him to send a bishop and priests to
Bulgaria; at the same time he sent an embassy to Rome asking the
Pope for a Patriarch. Determined to make full use of this opportunity
to subject the Bulgarian Church to the Holy See, Nicholas I at once
sent two bishops to Bulgaria and composed a reply to a list of 106
questions which Boris had sent him.[78] This shrewd and sagacious
document shows that Boris was concerned at the social effects of the
clash between the new Christian and the old Bulgarian traditions in
his realm, that his understanding of Christianity was still rudimentary,
but that he was prepared to exploit the rivalry between the Eastern
and Western Churches to gain as much independence and prestige as
possible for his own Church. Boris' request for a Patriarch was, however, adroitly side-stepped by the Pope: for the time being, the khan
was told, he would have to content himself with an archbishop. But
since Byzantium had grudged him even a bishop, Boris considered
that he had got the better deal out of Rome and swore to remain for
ever the faithful servant of St Peter.

Such was the situation when Constantine and Methodius arrived
in Rome. The Papacy, after its triumph over the Byzantine Church in
Bulgaria, now seemed in a good position to regain the whole of Illyricum from the Patriarch of Constantinople and to impose its spiritual
authority over the Slav world. The Slavonic liturgy was no doubt a
break with traditional Roman practice; yet as a means of evangelizing
the Slavs it commended itself, particularly as it was enthusiastically
supported by two Slav rulers in central Europe, Rastislav of Moravia
and Kocel of Pannonia. And so the new Pope Hadrian II gave his
unqualified approval to the work of Constantine and Methodius and
publicly authorized the use of the Slavonic liturgy. After Constantine's
death in Rome in February 869 (he died as a monk under the name
Cyril), Methodius was sent back by the Pope to central Europe to set
up a new Slav Church in Pannonia and Moravia. A few months later,
however, he was back in Rome. Again his visit to the Pope coincided
with an event of European importance which was causing a great stir
in Rome; and again the cause of this stir was the unaccountable
behavior of Boris of Bulgaria.

In the course of the past three years, Boris had realized that the
Pope had no intention of allowing him to manage his own ecclesiastical affairs. Meanwhile, the full resources of Byzantine diplomacy were
being marshalled in an attempt to detach Bulgaria from Rome.[79] In
February 870, the last session of the anti-Photian Council in Con-

stantinople was attended by a Bulgarian embassy which asked the assembled Fathers, on behalf of their ruler, whether his Church should be subject to Rome or Constantinople. A special conference of the eastern Patriarchs' representatives, summoned under the Emperor's chairmanship to deal with this doubtless not unprepared intervention, and from which the protesting papal legates were excluded, decided that Bulgaria should return to the jurisdiction of the See of Constantinople. Boris naturally accepted this decision, the Roman clergy were expelled from his country, and an archbishop consecrated by the Patriarch Ignatius was sent to Bulgaria.[80]

The news of Boris' defection, or at least a warning that it was impending, probably arrived in Rome while Methodius was still there; it seemed hardly calculated to inspire the Pope with confidence in the good faith of the Slavs. But once again Hadrian II proved himself a statesman: he appointed Methodius Archbishop of Pannonia and Legate of the Holy See to the Slavonic nations, extending his diocese to the Bulgarian frontier and thus hoping, with the help of the Slavonic liturgy, to link the Slavs of central Europe still closer to Rome. But Methodius' work in his new archdiocese was crippled by the continued opposition of the Frankish clergy who considered that his Slavonic policy impinged on their own rights. For two and a half years they kept the archbishop a prisoner in Germany; and under their influence the Papacy, after the death of John VIII, lost interest in the Slavonic liturgy. About 882, at the invitation of the Emperor Basil I, Methodius journeyed to Constantinople, where he was received with honor and affection. Two of his disciples, armed with the sacred books in Slavonic, remained in Byzantium as an instrument of further missionary work among the Slavs and Methodius' last gift to his fatherland.

In 885 Methodius, powerless against the intrigues of the Frankish party, the hostility of the new Moravian ruler Svatopluk and the indifference of Rome, died in Moravia, his work among the Slavs of central Europe on the brink of ruin. His principal disciples, including his successor Gorazd, were sentenced to perpetual exile. Yet the Slavonic liturgy and the Slavo-Byzantine culture which St Cyril and St Methodius had implanted north of the Danube and on both sides of the northern Carpathians did not vanish from these lands for another two centuries. In Bohemia, and possibly in southern Poland, their influence can be traced well into the eleventh century,[81] a sure sign of the appeal which Byzantine Christianity, in its vernacular Slavonic form, retained in what had been in the ninth century a distant outpost of the East Roman missions.

It may be assumed that Methodius' work in Moravia and Pannonia enjoyed at least the moral support of his sovereign Basil I. The value of the Slavonic liturgy as a means of evangelizing the Slavs and attracting them into the political orbit of Byzantium was certainly appreciated by this Emperor,[82] whose policy towards the Balkan Slavs was marked by high statesmanship and crowned with remarkable success. Thus the Serbian tribes in the valleys of the Tara, the Lim and the Ibar, together with the piratical Narentani on the Adriatic coast, were forced to acknowledge the Emperor's sovereignty and to accept Christianity, but were left some political autonomy. In 878, through its agent, the Croatian prince Zdeslav, the Empire strengthened its hold over Dalmatia. And though in the following year the Croats accepted the ecclesiastical sovereignty of the Roman See, the political and cultural influence of East Rome, ably furthered by Basil I and clothed in the attractive garb of the Cyrillo-Methodian vernacular tradition, remained paramount in the Balkans.

It was in Bulgaria, however, that the legacy of Cyril and Methodius yielded its greatest dividends and was saved for Europe and the Slavs. The Byzantines were careful in 870 to avoid repeating the mistake that had thrown Boris into the arms of the Papacy, especially since Pope John VIII was making desperate attempts to regain his allegiance. The Archbishop of Bulgaria, though a suffragan of the See of Constantinople, was granted a measure of autonomy.[83] Yet, as Boris must have realized, it was only by acquiring a native clergy and the Slavonic liturgy and letters that his people could safely continue to assimilate Byzantine civilization without prejudice to their cultural and political independence. And so, when the disciples of Methodius, on their expulsion from Moravia, travelled down the Danube valley and arrived in Bulgaria, they were enthusiastically received by Boris. Clement, one of their leaders, was sent to Macedonia about 886, where he labored among Boris' Slav subjects for thirty years, converting the pagans, establishing the Slavonic liturgy of the Byzantine rite, building churches and training large numbers of Slav-speaking priests. On Clement's appointment as bishop in 893, his companion Naum, who had founded a school of Slavonic letters at Preslav in north-eastern Bulgaria, joined him in Macedonia. Thanks to St Clement and St Naum, Macedonia became a renowned centre of Slavo-Byzantine culture, and its chief city of Ohrid became the metropolis of Slavonic

Christianity. At Ohrid and Preslav, during the next few decades, much Byzantine literature was translated into Slavonic: liturgical hymns, Greek patristic works, Byzantine chronicles and encyclopaedias, stories of Troy and of Alexander the Great, were made accessible to the Slavs in the Cyrillic script.[84] The literary wealth that accumulated during this "first golden age" of Bulgarian literature, which included some original creations, was to nourish throughout the middle ages the religious and intellectual life of the Russians, the Serbs and the Rumanians.[85]

This cultural work was further stimulated when Boris' third son Symeon succeeded to the throne (893) after his father had emerged from the monastery to which he had retired four years earlier, to depose his elder son Vladimir, whose pagan excesses had endangered the state. Symeon seemed peculiarly well fitted to continue his father's work: like Boris, he combined a devotion to Byzantine culture with an enthusiasm for Slavonic letters; much of his youth had been spent in Constantinople, where, so Liutprand was informed, he became proficient in the "rhetoric of Demosthenes and the syllogisms of Aristotle," earning the nickname of *hemiargos*, the half-Greek;[86] and on his return to Bulgaria he actively sponsored the literary movement. His new capital of Preslav he intended to make a second Constantinople; the splendor of its churches and palaces, we are assured by a contemporary Bulgarian writer, defied description; and in the royal palace sat Symeon "in a garment woven with gold, a golden chain round his neck, girt with a purple girdle covered with pearls, and wearing a golden sword."[87]

The imperial diplomatists, in observing the progress of Byzantium's northern proselyte, could congratulate themselves on the dividends which the Slav policy, devised by Photius and Basil I and carried out by Cyril and Methodius and their disciples, was yielding in Bulgaria. But in 894 these achievements were compromised by the carelessness of the Emperor Leo VI. An intrigue at the imperial court enabled two Byzantine merchants to secure the monopoly of the Bulgarian trade and to transfer the market to Thessalonica, where they imposed heavy taxes on Bulgarian goods.[88] Symeon thought this an outrage. He promptly invaded Thrace, defeated a Byzantine army and advanced towards Constantinople. The peace which, save for a few minor encounters, had reigned in the Balkans for the past eighty years was at an end. Leo VI, whose best troops were in Asia, resorted to the traditional method of imperial diplomacy: he sent an embassy to Bulgaria's northern neighbors, the Magyars, who then inhabited the steppes between the lower Dnieper and the lower Danube, to persuade them to attack Symeon in the rear. This Finno-Ugrian people, considerably mixed with and influenced by Turkic elements, had in all probability formed part of Kovrat's Onoguric realm; they had remained east of the Maeotis as subjects of the Khazars and in the course of the ninth century had moved westward across the Don and the Dnieper. Ferried across the Danube by the Byzantine fleet, the Magyars raided north-eastern Bulgaria, inflicting several defeats on Symeon's armies (895). But Symeon was capable of outplaying the East Romans at their own game: he opened negotiations with the Empire, arrested the Byzantine ambassador Leo Choerosphactes and, entangling him in a semi-ironic correspondence in which both parties quibbled about word and punctuations,[89] called in the Magyars' eastern neighbors, the Pechenegs. This Turkic people had recently been driven westward from their homes between the Emba and the Volga by the Uzes and had reached the Dnieper. Doubtless bribed by Symeon, they now combined with the Bulgarians to plunder the lands of the Magyars. Finding on their return from Bulgaria their homes occupied by the fearsome Pechenegs, the Magyars had no option but to migrate further west: so they crossed the Carpathians and in 895 entered the Pannonian plain. By 906 they had destroyed the Moravian realm and founded the medieval kingdom of Hungary. Symeon, meanwhile, invaded Thrace and routed the Byzantines at Bulgarophygon (896). Peace was then concluded and the Empire undertook to pay Bulgaria a yearly subsidy.

The events of these three years had seriously undermined the Empire's position in the Balkans. A hostile and ambitious Symeon now stood at the gates of Thrace, and the Slavs of Serbia and of the coastal region of Dyrrachium were falling under his influence. Further north, between the Danube and the Don, the Pechenegs had emerged as a disturbing factor in the steppes. In one respect only did these new barbarian invasions offer some prospect of relief: hitherto Byzantium had been hemmed in by a solid mass of Slavs, stretching from Thrace and Macedonia to the Baltic sea; the coming of the Magyars to Pannonia, the result of Symeon's diplomacy, had driven a wedge into the centre of the Slav world, for ever precluding the formation of a united Slav empire and decisively halting any further expansion of Bulgaria into central Europe.

Menacing clouds were gathering in Leo VI's reign in another sector of the north. The Christian missions planted in Russia by Photius and Ignatius had fallen upon evil days. About 882 the Varangian Oleg, sailing south from Novgorod, captured Kiev from Askold and Dir.[90] The whole of the waterway from the gulf of Finland to a point on the lower Dnieper some hundred miles north of the rapids[91] was now united for the first time under a single Viking ruler, round Kiev, the capital of the new Russian state. The notorious controversy between the "Normanist" and the "anti-Normanist" schools of historians as to whether the ninth-century Russian state was a Scandinavian creation or the product of earlier Slavonic or oriental traditions is now gradually abating;[92] in the present writer's opinion, it can no longer be doubted that the Slavs in the Dnieper basin had been taking an active part in the political and commercial life of the Iranian and Turkic overlords of the steppe for centuries before the Viking era; and that the pre-existing Slav land-owning aristocracy and merchant class remained the mainstay of the country's territorial stability and economic growth under its Scandinavian overlords. But it is equally clear that it was the Vikings who united the scattered tribes of Eastern Slavs into a single state based on the Baltic-Black Sea waterway, to which they gave their "Russian" name.[93] In this sense Oleg was certainly the founder of the Kievan realm. A wave of paganism swept over the Dnieper region during his reign and the predatory lust of the Vikings revived. In 907, with an amphibious host of Varangians and Slavs, Oleg appeared before Constantinople; after laying waste the suburbs of the city, he retired, and in 911 a treaty was signed between the Russians and the Empire.[94] The preferential treatment it accorded the Russian merchants in Constantinople[95] seems to have ensured Byzantium against new attacks from Kiev for the next thirty years. The commercial relations established in 911 mark a further stage in the gradual assimilation of the Vikings into the East European world. But so long as the Varangian rulers of Kiev were pagan, and regarded their capital largely as a stepping-stone on the road to more alluring horizons, the Russians remained a potential threat to both Cherson and Byzantium.

Leo VI's diplomacy at least succeeded in keeping the peace with Bulgaria after 896. But the Emperor's death in 912 precipitated a war with Symeon which lasted for eleven years, brought the Empire's power in the Balkans to the brink of ruin, and presented the Byzantine statesmen with a challenge the like of which they had never yet experienced. Symeon, meanwhile, was waiting for a chance to further his ambitions at the expense of a weakened Empire. The Byzantines seemed to be playing into his hands: his envoys, sent to renew the treaty of 896, had been brutally insulted by the Emperor Alexander. And after Alexander's death in June 913, the Empire, nominally ruled by a delicate child, Constantine Porphyrogenitus, and precariously governed by a regency council under the Patriarch Nicholas Mysticus, was rent by a severe internal crisis. Symeon at the head of a large army invaded Thrace and appeared in August before Constantinople. Like Krum exactly a century before, he was daunted by the fortifications and resolved to negotiate.

The nature and result of these negotiations, concluded at a meeting between Symeon and the Patriarch Nicholas,[96] are obscure and controversial. It is practically certain, however, that Symeon was then promised that one of his daughters would marry the Emperor Constantine, and it is possible that he obtained from the Byzantine government on the same occasion the title of "Emperor of the Bulgarians" (βασιλεὺς Βουλγάρων).[97] It is probable in any case that Symeon's great ambition, which was to haunt him for the rest of his life, took shape as early as 913. The promised position of *Basileopator*, as the Emperor's father-in-law, offered power in Constantinople and seemed to point the way to the very throne of the Empire. The title of "Emperor of the Bulgarians"— if it was ever granted — was at best a makeshift: for Symeon was too well grounded in the Byzantine doctrine of sovereignty to imagine for a moment that there could ever be two Empires in the Balkans; by its nature the Empire was universal and its only centre was Constantinople. It was not a national Bulgarian βασιλεία that Symeon desired, but the *imperium* of the Romans, the throne of the *οἰκουμένη*. And the Patriarch Nicholas, who for twelve years exerted all his diplomatic skill in an attempt to induce him to abandon this venture,[98] saw this very clearly: Symeon's bid for world domination he castigated as *tyrannis*, a rebellious usurpation of the imperial authority.[99] The Patriarch, who was prepared to go to almost any length to appease the Bulgarian ruler, significantly refused to concede this one vital point; against Symeon's claims to hegemony he solemnly reiterated the essential tenet of Byzantine political philosophy: the Empire, he wrote to Symeon, "stands above all earthly authority and alone on this earth was established by the King of all."[100]

But Symeon's hopes proved vain. Hardly was he back in Preslav before the Empress Zoe seized control of the government in Constantinople; the Patriarch's influence declined and the plan of a marriage alliance was conveniently forgotten. Baulked in his immediate ambition, Symeon invaded Thrace and Macedonia. In vain did Nicholas urge him to desist from aggression: Symeon's retort was to demand that the Byzantines recognise him as their Emperor.[101] Zoe's government, determined to crush him, sent an army into Bulgaria. On 20 August 917, by the Achelous river near Anchialus, it was utterly routed by Symeon; the Bulgarians swept into Thrace, and at Catasyrtae, not far from Constantinople, gained another victory. Symeon, whose dominions now extended from the Black Sea to the Adriatic and from Sirmium to the neighborhood of Thessalonica, was master of the Balkans.

In the dark days between 917 and 919, when the fate of the Empire hung in the balance, Byzantium was saved once again by its diplomacy and by its capacity for producing great leaders. Zoe gained a precious respite by entangling Symeon with Serbia; and while the regency government was sinking into disaffection and intrigue, the Admiral Romanus Lecapenus began his steady climb to power. In May 919, through the marriage of his daughter to Constantine VII, he became *Basileopator*; on 17 December 920 he was crowned co-Emperor. Symeon had lost the race for power: the son of an Armenian peasant had gained the throne by the very means the Bulgarian sovereign had planned to use. In vain did Nicholas try to appease his impotent fury by sending him conciliatory letters: Symeon now demanded the deposition of Romanus in favor of himself;[102] every year now he invaded the Empire, reaching the approaches of Constantinople in 921, 922 and 924, and retaking Adrianople in 923. But Romanus had a policy for dealing with the Bulgarians: he allowed Symeon to exhaust himself in fruitless attacks on the capital, while Byzantine diplomacy stirred up trouble against him in Serbia, negotiated for a grand anti-Bulgarian coalition of northern peoples — Magyars, Pechenegs, Russians and Alans — and successfully countered his attempt to secure the use of the Egyptian Fatimid navy against Byzantium.

In the autumn of 924 Symeon's army appeared for the last time before Constantinople. Realizing no doubt that he could not hope to storm the city without a fleet, he opened negotiations. At Cosmidium, on a pier built out into the Golden Horn, Symeon and the Emperor Romanus met and conversed. Contemporary chroniclers, whose imagination was fired by this interview between the two most powerful monarchs of Europe, give a dramatic picture of the Bulgarian ruler, at first mocking and flippant, gradually cowed by the majesty of imperial

Rome and humbled by the Emperor's moral authority.[103] Be that as it may, the meeting with Romanus sounded the death-knell of Symeon's ambitions: Constantinople, he must have realized by then, would never be his. Back in his own country, however, his insolence revived: he spurned the last pathetic appeals of the Patriarch Nicholas;[104] defiantly entitled himself "Emperor of the Bulgarians and of the Romans," to the indignation of Romanus who protested to Symeon in 925, not so much against his title of $\beta\alpha\sigma\iota\lambda\epsilon\upsilon\varsigma$, as against his "tyrannical" claim to the throne of the Romaioi;[105] and, perhaps about 926, raised the Archbishop of Bulgaria to the rank of Patriarch.[106] But these constitutionally vacuous gestures could not conceal the fact that Symeon's bid for world hegemony had broken against the impregnable walls of Constantinople, the patient defensive policy of Romanus and the skill of Byzantine diplomacy. His armies were still able to subdue and devastate Serbia, where the Empire had been active against him; but in 926 a Bulgarian army which invaded Croatia was completely routed by the Emperor's ally, the Croatian king Tomislav. On 27 May 927 Symeon died.

The death of the Bulgarian tsar altered the whole balance of power in the Balkans. Exhausted and ruined by his wars, Bulgaria ceased for the next sixty years to play an active part in the politics of eastern Europe. In the autumn of 927 a peace treaty was signed between Byzantium and the Bulgarian government:[107] Peter, Symeon's son and successor, was married to Maria Lecapena, Romanus' granddaughter, and was acknowledged by the Byzantine authorities as Emperor of Bulgaria ($\beta\alpha\sigma\iota\lambda\epsilon\upsilon\varsigma$ $Bov\lambda\gamma\alpha\rho i\alpha\varsigma$); the autocephalous Bulgarian Patriarchate was also recognized. But these flattering concessions were but a cloak that barely concealed the extent of the Empire's diplomatic victory over Symeon's mild and saintly son. The Byzantine tsaritsa of Bulgaria ensured the dominance of Constantinople over the court of Preslav; while her husband, for all his imperial rank, sank to the level of a docile satellite of Byzantium, honored and chastened at once by the title of "spiritual son" of the Emperors of East Rome.[108]

The decline of Bulgarian power affected the Empire's northern policy in another sense: an effective buffer which had long prevented the trans-Danubian nations of the steppe from raiding Thrace was removed in 927, and the defense of the Empire's northern frontier now depended more and more on the skill of its diplomatists. Freed from the Bulgarian peril, and forced to meet a changing and complex situation between the middle Danube and the northern Caucasus, during the rest of Romanus' reign (i.e. 927 to 944) and the personal reign of Constantine VII (945-59) Byzantine diplomacy embarked upon one of its most successful periods.

In each of the three sectors of the Empire's northern front solid results were achieved. In the Balkans, next to an increasingly byzantinized Bulgaria, the Empire restored its sovereignty over the Serbs (c.927); kept a somewhat nominal control over the coastal cities of Dalmatia, which since the seventies of the ninth century formed an imperial theme under the *strategos* resident at Zara;[109] and retained some political authority in Croatia. The only serious danger to its Balkan provinces in this period came from the Magyars who ravaged Thrace in 934 and 943. The imperial diplomatists were equal to the occasion: in or about the year 948 the Magyar chieftain Bulcsu came to Constantinople, was baptized in the city and, before returning home, was made a *patricius* by the Emperor. Soon afterwards another Hungarian leader named Gyula followed his example; and on his homeward journey Gyula was accompanied by the monk Hierotheus, whom the Patriarch had consecrated as "Bishop of Hungary" (Turkia) (ἐπίσκοπος Τουρκίας) and who appears to have labored successfully in his missionary diocese.[110] This new expansion of Byzantine Christianity to Pannonia, less than a century after the work of St Methodius in that land, did not prevent the Magyars from resuming their attacks on Thrace between 958 and 968; but at least it ensured a respite from their raids during the previous decade.

At no time was the Crimean sector of more vital importance to the Empire than in the reigns of Romanus I and Constantine VII. Never was Byzantium's traditional policy of hanging on to Cherson more clearly vindicated. From here alone could the East Roman statesmen effectively adjust their northern policy to the changes that had taken place in the steppes since the end of the ninth century. For the past two hundred years they had relied for preserving order in that region mainly on the Khazars, but Khazar power was declining; so in the first half of the tenth century Byzantium turned to the Pechenegs, who were then encamped along the Black Sea coast between the Danube and the Don. By the middle of the century alliance with the Pechenegs had become the corner-stone of the Empire's diplomacy in the north. Of this new and urgent preoccupation the opening chapters of the *De administrando imperio* have preserved a striking memorial: for, as Constantine is at pains to explain to his son, if this alliance is kept Byzantium Crimea is safe, trade with Rus' can flourish, and the

Empire's northern neighbors, Bulgarians and Magyars and Russians, who tremble with fear before the Pechenegs, will not dare to attack Byzantium. "I conceive, then," the Emperor writes, "that it is always greatly to the advantage of the Emperor of the Romans to be minded to keep the peace with the nation of the Pechenegs and to conclude conventions and treaties of friendship with them and to send every year to them from our side a diplomatic agent with presents befitting and suitable to that nation."[111] The responsibility for negotiating with the Pechenegs inevitably lay with the *strategos* of Cherson.

Another factor which enhanced the importance of Byzantine Crimea in this period was the continued growth of Kievan Rus'. In 941 Igor, Oleg's successor, led a great sea-borne expedition against Byzantium. Repulsed from the northern entrance of the Bosphorus, the Russians landed on the coast of Bithynia and plundered the country from Heraclea to Nicomedia; but, as they were withdrawing, their ships were attacked by the imperial navy under the *protovestiarius* Theophanes: the Greek fire wrought terrible destruction, and the Russian armada was all but annihilated. In 944, at the head of a large army of Varangians and Slavs, Igor set off once more against Byzantium. An embassy from Romanus succeeded, however, in buying off the Russians and their Pecheneg allies on the Danube. Then, as in 941, the Byzantines were forewarned of the approaching danger by the intelligence bureau of the *strategos* of Cherson: the Emperor was informed by the Chersonites that "the Rus' are advancing with innumerable ships, and have covered the sea with their vessels."[112] The desire to safeguard the security of Cherson is evident in the treaty concluded between Russia and the Empire in 944.[113] A comparison between the *pacta* of 911 and 944 suggests that the balance of power was shifting in favor of Byzantium: the trading privileges of the Russians were now considerably curtailed,[114] and, most significantly, a notable proportion of the envoys sent to Constantinople by Igor to ratify the treaty belonged to a Christian community in Kiev. Gradually, through trade and diplomacy, the Christian and imperial propaganda was breaking down the pagan isolation of the Viking rulers of Rus'. Some time between 946 and 960, Igor's widow, Olga, regent of the realm, went on a mission of peace to Constantinople; there she was baptized into the Byzantine Church, adopting the name, symbolic by its past associations, of the reigning Empress Helena, wife of Constantine VII.[115] And though Olga was unwilling or unable to impose her religion on her subjects at large, and made an abortive attempt in

959 to obtain a German bishop from Otto I,[116] her relations with the Empire paved the way for the triumph of Byzantine Christianity in Rus' in the reign of her grandson.

The diplomacy of Romanus I and Constantine VII was no less successful in the North Caucasian area. Relations with the Khazars had become cooler since the khan's conversion to Judaism and the arrival of the Pechenegs in the Pontic steppes. It is true that in the Empire's diplomatic protocol the khan still ranked, among non-Christian rulers, second only to the Caliph of Baghdad.[117] But Byzantium no longer really trusted the Khazars. And just as their task of policing the steppes in the interests of the Empire had recently devolved upon the Pechenegs, so the role they had formerly been assigned by the Byzantine diplomatists of guarding the Northern Caucasus was now transferred to the Alans, whose lands marched with the Khanate in the south. Since the sixth century the Alans had been the most loyal of the Empire's satellites in this area, for all their strong attachment to paganism; it was not until the early years of the tenth century that the ruler of Alania accepted Christianity and an archbishop from the Patriarch Nicholas Mysticus. Despite a subsequent and brief relapse into paganism, the Alans were held in high esteem in Byzantium, and Constantine Porphyrogenitus stressed their usefulness in checking possible Khazar encroachments on the Crimea.[118] Their ruler, who held the Byzantine title of ἐξουσιαστής, was one of the three imperial satellites to glory in the title of the Emperor's "spiritual son."[119] Of comparable importance was the ἐξουσιαστής of Abasgia, who guarded Byzantium's interests in the strategically vital area between Alania, Armenia and the Black Sea coast.[120]

Thus within the semi-circle which, in the tenth as in the sixth century, marked the effective limits of the Empire's influence in the north, in the vast area that extended from the Hungarian Alföld, over the steppes and rivers of South Russia to the lower Volga and the North Caucasian lowlands, the diplomacy of Romanus and Constantine had built up by the middle of the century a chain of vassal and allied states, satellites supposedly revolving in obedient harmony round the throne of the universal Autocrat in Constantinople, barbarians rendered quiescent by the power or the liberalities of the Emperor, or proselytes attracted by the prestige and spiritual appeal of Byzantium's Christian culture. It was the work of these two emperors that paved the way for the forces of expansion which in the next fifty years were to carry the armies of East Rome to the Danube and the influence of its civilization to the confines of the Baltic Sea.

From the death of Romanus II (963) to the year 1018 the Empire's northern policy was dominated by its relations with Bulgaria and Rus'. Bulgaria in the reign of the Tsar Peter (927-69) was rent by a social and economic crisis: the accumulation of power and wealth in the hands of an oppressive aristocracy was undermining the authority of the state and, as in the Empire, was depriving the peasants of their small holdings. Many of the latter, especially in Macedonia, were falling under the sway of Bogomilism, a new sectarian movement that combined neo-Manichaean dualism and an evangelical and anti-sacramental interpretation of Christianity with an attitude of revolt against the established authorities of Church and State, and which was soon to spread over the whole Balkan peninsula.[121] And, still worse, the Tsar Peter, shortly after his wife's death, committed an error which precipitated the gravest crisis his country had yet experienced. In the winter of 965-6 he sent an embassy to Constantinople to demand further "tribute." This was more than the Emperor Nicephorus Phocas, fresh from his victories of Tarsus and Crete, could endure; Peter's envoys were whipped and dismissed, and Nicephorus moved his army to the Bulgarian border.[122] Reluctant, however, to campaign in that dangerous country, he confined himself to seizing a few frontier forts and sent the *patricius* Calocyros to Russia with instructions to bribe its ruler Svyatoslav to attack Bulgaria. The pagan and warlike son of Olga had the makings of an empire builder: he had recently inflicted a crushing defeat on the Khazars (c.965). He was easily persuaded by the Byzantine ambassador: in 967[123] he crossed the Danube at the head of a large army and rapidly overran the Dobrudja, setting up his residence at Little Preslav (Pereyaslavets), by the river delta. It soon became clear, however, that Svyatoslav had no intention of behaving as Byzantium's hireling; in 968, or early in 969, he returned home at the news that the Pechenegs were besieging Kiev;[124] it is difficult to avoid the surmise that the Emperor, mindful of the precepts of the *De administrando imperio*, had called them in. Before the middle of August 969, having defeated the Pechenegs, Svyatoslav was back in Bulgaria, intending — it seems — to make Little Preslav the capital of his realm.[125] Marching south, he captured Great Preslav, the Bulgarian capital, and stormed Philippopolis; by the end of the year the whole of eastern Bulgaria was in Russian hands. Svyatoslav's ambitions now centered on Constantinople itself: the Pechenegs, the Magyars and, it seems, the Bulgarians themselves

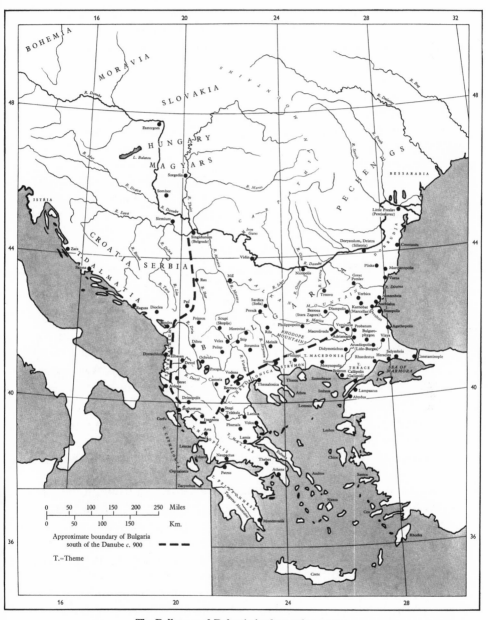

The Balkans and Bulgaria in the tenth century.

59

had joined him in a vast barbarian coalition against the Empire. Calo-cyros himself had turned traitor and was plotting, with the help of the Russians, to seize the Byzantine throne. Conscious of this serious danger, the new Emperor John Tzimisces began negotiations: Svya-toslav's reply was to demand that the Byzantines, if unwilling to pay him an enormous tribute, depart from Europe and cross over into Asia.[126] Not since the days of Symeon had a barbarian ruler dared to address the Emperor of Byzantium in such tones. In the summer of 970 the Russians invaded Thrace, but were defeated at Arcadiopolis by Bardas Sclerus.[127]

In the spring of 971,[128] at the head of a large and well-trained army, John Tzimisces set out on one of the greatest campaigns in the history of Byzantine arms. In April, Great Preslav, furiously defended by Svyatoslav's men, was taken by storm. The Russians, fighting des-perately, fell back on Silistria (Dristra, Dorystolum) where their prince had entrenched himself. For three months packed with heroic epi-sodes, the city was besieged, until finally the Russians, overwhelmed by Tzimisces' iron-clad host, terrified by the fire-shooting ships of the imperial navy that had appeared on the Danube to cut off their retreat, and exhausted by famine, gave up in despair. Svyatoslav undertook to leave Bulgaria, begging only to be allowed to cross the river and to be given some food for the remnant of his army.[129] The Emperor accepted these terms; in July 971 a treaty was signed between the two rulers: the Russian prince pledged himself never again to attack the Empire, Bulgaria, or Cherson, and to fight the enemies of Byzantium,[130] the Emperor renewed the old trading privi-leges of the Russians.[131] After a brief meeting on the banks of the Danube,[132] the two monarchs started on their homeward journeys: Svyatoslav was ambushed by the Pechenegs near the Dnieper rapids and slain in battle (972); John Tzimisces returned in triumph to Con-stantinople, where the Bulgarian Tsar Boris II publicly abdicated his throne. Bulgaria was thus annexed to the Empire. In a single year, John Tzimisces had restored the Empire's northern frontier to the Danube from which Asparuch had evicted the East Romans three centuries earlier, and freed Byzantium from the Russian menace.

Once again, after three centuries, the Empire found itself, across the lower Danube, face to face with the steppes and its denizens. More than ever it needed now a strong and reliable satellite in the north: the Khazar Khanate could fulfill this role no more; it would never recover from the blow dealt to it by Svyatoslav; the Pechenegs had several times proved themselves treacherous allies; the Magyars were increasingly looking to Germany for their culture and religion. Only the prince of Kiev, who now ruled over a vast territory from the Carpathians to the lower Oka and from the gulf of Finland to the lower Dnieper, could stand between the Empire and the chaos of Eurasia. And it was by Christianity alone that Byzantium could hope to secure his abiding loyalty. For all his inveterate heathenism, Svyatoslav, it seems, had not the time nor the inclination to undo his mother's work in Kiev; and all through the tenth century Christianity was slowly filtering into Rus'—from Bulgaria especially, through the Slavonic translations of the disciples of Cyril and Methodius, from Bohemia perhaps, where the vernacular Slavonic culture still survived, and probably also from Germany and Rome. But it was left to the Emperor Basil II to ensure, with the help of his missionaries and diplomatists, the final triumph of Byzantine Christianity in Rus'.

The story of the conversion of Rus' is told at great length by the Russian Primary Chronicle[133] and briefly by the eleventh-century Arab historian Yahya of Antioch.[134] The former, if allowance is made for its peculiar blend of fact and fiction and for probable later interpolations, may be used to supplement the latter, and the following picture then emerges. In the spring of 988, at the most critical moment of his reign, when the troops of the usurper Bardas Phocas stood on the Asian side of the Bosphorus, Basil II was saved by the arrival in Constantinople of six thousand Varangian warriors. The timely assistance of these professional soldiers enabled the Emperor to defeat his rival at Chrysopolis. This expeditionary corps, which was to form the nucleus of the Emperor's celebrated Varangian guard, had been sent by Svyatoslav's son, Vladimir, the prince of Kiev, in fulfillment of an agreement he had contracted with the Empire in the previous winter.[135] For his military assistance Vladimir had been promised the hand of the Emperor's sister, the Porphyrogenita Anna, on condition that he and his people accepted Christianity. But now that the acute danger was past, Basil II seemed in no hurry to honor an obligation so incompatible with the honor and traditions of East Rome.[136] In the summer of 989, in all probability, doubtless to compel Byzantium to send him his promised bride, Vladimir marched to the Crimea and invested Cherson; by the same winter or the early spring of 990 the city was his, and the unwilling princess, sacrificed to the interests of the Empire, was dispatched across the Black Sea. Whether Vladimir became a Christian in Rus' on the conclusion of his agreement with Byzantium, as some Russian sources seem to imply, or whether, as the *Primary Chronicle* prolixly relates, he was baptized in Cherson by the local bishop before his marriage, is a question to which — in the present writer's view — no certain answer can at present be given without ignoring or maltreating part of the evidence. But whichever view is adopted, the role played by Cherson in the conversion of Russia will appear decisive, and this city, so long the focus of missionary work among the northern barbarians, took her captor captive: for after their marriage Vladimir and his imperial bride were escorted from the Crimea to Kiev by members of the local clergy, who began to implant Christianity throughout the Russian realm, while Cherson was returned by Vladimir to the Empire. The new Russian Church was subordinated to the Patriarchate of Constantinople;[137] Vladimir's act of faith and statemanship linked Russia to Byzantine culture and to eastern Christianity; and the East Roman missionaries and diplomatists thus peacefully gained for the Byzantine οἰκουμένη and for Europe a territory which in size exceeded the Empire itself.

The Byzantine government had all the more reason to feel satisfied with the success of its Russian policy, as the situation in the Balkans was rapidly deteriorating. John Tzimisces' conquests, it seems, had been inadequately consolidated; outside the main cities of eastern Bulgaria, Byzantine domination was never secure, and in the west, amid the high lakes and valleys of Macedonia, seems not to have been felt at all. It was there that, on the Emperor's death in 976, the sons of a provincial Macedonian governor, the four Comitopuli, raised the standard of revolt.[138] The rebellion became a war of liberation. By 987, Samuel, the youngest of the four, was the sole ruler of a powerful kingdom, whose capital was first Prespa and later Ohrid, and which comprised by the end of the century most of the former Bulgarian lands between the Black Sea and the Adriatic, with the addition of Thessaly and Epirus, as well as Serbia. In 997 or 998, Samuel proclaimed himself Tsar, and this act, coupled with his restoration of the Bulgarian Patriarchate abolished by John Tzimisces, whose seat was eventually fixed at Ohrid, signified his deliberate assumption of the traditions of the First Bulgarian Empire.

Basil II's first attempt to deal with Samuel ended in disaster: in August 986, returning from an abortive siege of Sardica, his army was ambushed in a mountain pass and slaughtered by the Bulgarians. For the next three years, during which the Emperor was occupied in suppressing the revolts of Bardas Sclerus and Bardas Phocas, Samuel's expansion continued unchecked. By the spring of 991, Basil II was back in Macedonia, where he campaigned for three years with increasing, but still indecisive, success. He was handicapped by having to fight on two fronts, and his wars in Syria and the Caucasus (995-1001) enabled the Bulgarians to thrust at Thessalonica and to invade Greece down to the gulf of Corinth.

But in 1001 the Emperor had made peace with the Fatimids and was back in Constantinople, free to devote all his carefully nurtured powers of mind and body and his military and political genius to what he had come to regard as the main task of his reign. In a series of carefully planned and brilliantly executed campaigns he captured the cities of eastern Bulgaria, including Pliska and the two Preslavs, and advanced deep into Macedonia, seizing fortress after fortress. In four years of this ruthless and methodical strategy Samuel had lost half his Empire. Any hopes he might have had of saving the remainder were dashed in July 1014, when his army was routed in the mountain pass of Kleidion (Cimbalongus) near the Strymon valley. Basil had all the Bulgarian captives — numbering, it was said, fourteen thousand[139] — blinded, save for one in every hundred who was left with one eye to lead his comrades back to the Tsar. At the sight of this gruesome procession Samuel fell to the ground in a fit. Two days later, on 6 October 1014, he was dead.

The end was very near. It was hastened by the chaos that engulfed the remnant of Bulgaria. Samuel's son and successor, Gabriel Radomir, was murdered by his cousin John Vladislav (1015). In vain did the new Bulgarian Tsar, like his predecessor, promise obedience to the Byzantine Emperor; Basil pursued his systematic conquest of Macedonia. Early in 1018, when the news reached him in Constantinople that John Vladislav had been killed in a vain attack on Dyrrachium, the Emperor set out on his last campaign of the war. It was a bloodless and triumphant procession. At the gates of Ohrid he received the formal submission of the late Tsar's family. After a last tour of the conquered territory, his work completed, the "Bulgar-Slayer" paid a visit to Athens, where, before the more splendid triumph that awaited him in Constantinople, he offered humble thanks to Our Lady of Athens in her church, the Parthenon.

For the first time since the Avaro-Slav attacks of the late sixth century the entire Balkan peninsula, from the middle and lower Danube to the southern tip of the Peloponnese, and from the Black Sea to the confines of Istria, now lay in the unchallenged possession, or under the sovereignty, of East Rome. In 1018, the three traditional sectors of the Empire's northern front—the Danube, the Crimea and the south-western approaches to the Caucasus—were more firmly than ever under its sway. In the steppes a favorable balance of power seemed assured for the future, and further north the boundless expanses of Rus' had been brought within the orbit of the Byzantine οἰκουμένη.

List of abbreviations used in the notes to Chapter II

AB	*Analecta Bollandiana*
B	*Byzantion*
BS	*Byzantinoslavica*
BSOAS	*Bulletin of the School of Oriental and African Studies*
BZ	*Byzantinische Zeitschrift*
CMH	*Cambridge Medieval History*
CSHB	*Corpus scriptorum historiae Byzantinae*
D	*Δελτίον τῆς Ἱστορικῆς καὶ Ἐθνολογικῆς Ἑταιρείας τῆς Ἑλλάδος*
DAI	Constantine Porphyrogenitus, *De administrando imperio*
DOP	*Dumbarton Oaks Papers*
DR	Dölger, *Regesten der Kaiserurkunden des oströmischen Reiches*
EB	*Etudes byzantines*
EHR	*English Historical Review*
EO	*Echos d'Orient*
FHG	C. Müller, *Fragmenta historicorum graecorum*
GR	V. Grumel, *Les Regestes des Actes du Patriarcat de Constantinople*
HUS	*Harvard Ukrainian Studies*
JRAS	*Journal of the Royal Asiatic Society of Great Britain*
MGH	*Monumenta Germaniae Historica*
MPG	Migne, *Patrologia Graeca*
MPL	Migne, *Patrologia Latina*
PO	*Patrologia Orientalis*
RH	*Revue historique*
RHSE	*Revue historique du sud-est européen*
SEER	*Slavonic and East European Review*
Sem. Kond.	*Seminarium Kondakovianum*
SP	*Speculum*
VV	*Vizantijskij Vremennik*

FOOTNOTES ON CHAPTER II

[1] The "Patzinaks" of the Greek sources.

[2] See the remarks of Polybius on the exposure of ancient Byzantium to attacks by land, *Hist.* iv, 45; ed. T. Büttner-Wobst (Leipzig, 1889), pp. 57-8 and above ch. I.

[3] The origin, ethnic character and geographical distribution of the Antes still raise some puzzling questions. The main contemporary authorities are Jordanes, *Getica*, v, 32-7 (*MGH Auct. ant.* v. I, pp. 62 ff.) and Procopius, *History of the Wars*, VII, 14, 22-30 and VIII, 4, 9: ed. J. Haury (Leipzig, 1905), pp. 354 ff., who regard them as Slavs, ethnically and linguistically related to the Sclaveni. The former locates them along the Black Sea coast, between the Danube and the Dniester, and as far as the Dnieper; the latter mentions them in the region of the Donets, north of the Sea of Azov. Several different tribes were originally ruled by a non-Slav, possibly Iranian, minority, but slavicised, at least in Bessarabia, by the sixth century. See G. Vernadsky, *Ancient Russia* (New Haven, 1944), pp. 104-8, 155-60 and *passim;* F. Dvornik, *The Making of Central and Eastern Europe* (London, 1949), pp. 279-82.

[4] *Hist. of the Wars*, VII, 29, 1-3; (*op. cit.* p. 423).

[5] E. Stein, *Histoire du Bas-Empire*, II, p. 310.

[6] A number of modern authorities identify the Avars who migrated to Europe with the Juan-juan of the Chinese: J. B. Bury, *History of the Later Roman Empire*, II (London, 1923), pp. 314-16; G. Vernadsky, *Ancient Russia*, pp. 178-9; E. Stein, *op. cit.* II, pp. 541-2. In the view of some scholars, the distinction made by Theophylactus Simocatta (*Hist.* VII, caps 7-8, ed. C. de Boor (Leipzig, 1887), pp. 256 ff. between the 'true Avars' (the Juan-juan) and the 'pseudo-Avars' (who alone migrated to Europe) rests on somewhat fragile foundations: see V. Minorsky, *Hudūd al-'Ālam* (London, 1937), pp. 447-8; R. Grousset, *L'empire des steppes* (Paris, 1939), pp. 226-7. For a different view, see E. Chavannes, 'Documents sur les Tou-Kiue occidentaux', *Sbornik Trudov Orkhonskoj Ekspeditsii*, VI (St. Petersburg, 1903), pp. 229-33; C. A. Macartney, 'On the Greek sources for the history of the Turks in the sixth century', *BSOAS*, XI (1943-6), pp. 266-75; see also H. W. Haussig, 'Theophylakts Exkurs über die Skythischen Völker', B, XXIII (1953), pp. 275-462; A. Kollautz, 'Die Awaren', *Saeculum*, V (1954), pp. 129-78.

[7] *Excerpta de legationibus*, ed. C. de Boor, I (Berlin, 1903), p. 443.

[8] On Justin II's new policy towards the barbarians see E. Stein, *Studien zur Geschichte des byzantinischen Reiches, vornehmlich unter den Kaisern Justinus II und Tiberius Constantinus* (Stuttgart, 1919), pp. 3 ff.

[9] On the Avar embassy of 565 see Menander, *op. cit.* p. 446 and the vivid description of Corippus, *In laudem Iustini*, III. lines 231-407 (*MGH, Auct. ant.* III. pp. 143-7). Cf. H. Howorth, "The Avars", *JRAS*, XXI, 4 (1889), pp. 732-4.

[10] Dölger, *Regesten*, 34.

[11] On the different forms of this name, see J. B. Bury, "The Turks in the Sixth Century", *EHR*, XII (1897), p. 418 n. 2.

[12] Menander, *op. cit.* I, p. 452. Some historians believe that the Byzantine government, while expressing "benevolent interest" in the Turkish proposals, was unwilling to commit itself to a formal alliance in 568: N.H. Baynes, *CMH*, II, pp. 269-70; S. Vailhé, "Projet d'alliance turco-byzantine au VIᵉ siècle", *Echos d'Orient* XII (1909), 206-14; C. Diehl and G. Marçais, *Le monde oriental de 395 à 1081* (Paris, 1944), pp. 128-9. Yet Menander seems to imply that the Turkish offer of ὁμαιχμία was accepted by the Emperor; and an agreement about silk may be inferred both from the embassy's terms of reference and from the fact that ten porters carrying this commodity accompanied the Byzantine envoys on their return journey from Silzibul's capital to Constantinople. Cf. N. V. Pigulevskaya, "Vizantijskaja diplomatiya i torgovlya šelkom v V-VII vv.", *VV*, n.s. I (1947), pp. 184-214.

[13] E. Chavannes, *Documents*, pp. 235-7.

[14] The form Τούρξαθος, which occurs in a sixteenth-century manuscript of Menander in the library of Trinity College, Cambridge (O. 3. 23: πρεσβεία ἐκ τοῦ ὀγδόου λόγου Μενάνδρου, ff. 3-5) is preferred by G. Moravcsik to the habitual Τούρξανθος: "Zur Geschichte der Onoguren", *Ungarische Jahrbücher*, x (1930), 63; *Byzantinoturcica* II, p. 328 (2nd ed.).

[15] Menander, *op. cit.* I, pp. 205-6.

[16] Cf. Dölger, *Regesten*, 46.

[17] The contemporary sources and secondary authorities dealing with these invasions are listed by H. Grégoire, "L'origine et le nom des Croates et des Serbes", *B*, XVII (1944-5), pp. 104-10, and by A.

Bon, *Le Péloponnèse byzantin* (Paris, 1951), pp. 31-2.

[18]*Hist. eccl.* VI, 25; Engl. transl. R. Payne Smith (Oxford, 1860), pp. 432-3.

[19]Menander, *op. cit.* I, pp. 220-1, I, p. 476; H. Howorth, "The Avars", *JRAS,* XXI (1889), pp. 744-9; L. Hauptmann, "Les rapports des Byzantins avec les Slaves et les Avares pendant la seconde moitié du VIᵉ siècle", *B,* IV (1927-8), pp. 137-70; P. Lemerle, "Invasions et migrations dans les Balkans depuis la fin de l'époque romaine jusqu'au VIIIᵉ siècle", *RH,* CCXI (1954), pp. 289-90.

[20]Theoph. Simocatta, I, caps. 5-6, ed. C. de Boor, pp. 48-52; Howorth, *op. cit.* pp. 749-52.

[21]Much learned controversy has been aroused by the statement in the *Chronicle of Monemvasia,* confirmed by a tenth-century scholium of Arethas of Caesarea and echoed in a letter of the Patriarch Nicholas III (1084-1111), that in 587 the Avars and the Slavs conquered and settled the Peloponnese, and that only Corinth, the Argolid and the eastern part of the peninsula remained in Byzantine hands after that date. The reliability of this evidence is strongly and convincingly supported by P. Charanis ("The Chronicle of Monemvasia and the Question of the Slavonic Settlements in Greece", *DOP,* V (1950), 139-66; "On the Question of the Slavonic Settlements in Greece during the Middle Ages", *BS,* X [1949], 254-8). The source references and other works on this controversial topic are cited in A. Bon, *Le Péloponnèse byzantin,* pp. 32-5. See also P. Charanis, "On the Slavic Settlement in the Peloponnesus", *BZ,* XLVI (1953), pp. 91-103.

[22]Miracula S. Demetrii, *MPG,* CXVI, 1284-93. A. Tougard, *De l'histoire profane dans les Actes grecs des Bollandistes* (Paris, 1874), pp. 88 ff. P. Lemerle, *Les plus anciens recueils des Miracles de Saint Démétrius,* I (Paris, 1979), pp. 130, 134. The Avaro-Slav army is here said to have arrived before the city walls on Sunday 22 September, in the reign of Maurice. This gives two possible dates — 586 and 597; opinion is divided as to which of these years is to be accepted.

[23]*DR,* 131.

[24]The chronology of Maurice's Avaro-Slav wars of 592-602, as reconstructed from the evidence of Theophylactus Simocatta, remains confused and controversial.

[25]N.H. Baynes, "The Date of the Avar Surprise", *BZ,* XXI (1912), 110-28.

[26]*Chronicon,* MPL, LXXXIII, 1056.

[27]*Chronicon Paschale,* I, pp. 719ff. (*CSHB*); Theophanes, *Chronographia,* I, pp. 315ff. (ed. C. de Boor); George Pisides, *Bellum Avaricum,* pp. 47-68 (*CSHB*); and the account of an anonymous eye-witness of the siege: Περὶ τῶν ἀθέων Ἀβάρων (A. Mai, *Nova Patrum Bibliotheca* (Rome, 1853), VI, pp. 423 ff.; see also *Izvori za Bŭlgarskata Istoriya = Fontes Historiae Bulgaricae,* VI [Sofia, 1960], pp. 41-55; and F. Barišić, "Le siège de Constantinople par les Avares et les Slaves en 626", *B,* XXIV [1954], pp. 371-95).

[28]*De administrando imperio,* caps. 31, 32, *DAI,* I, pp. 146-60. The reliability of Constantine's account of the southward migration of the Croats and the Serbs in the seventh century has been the subject of a long controversy which is still not finally resolved. However, scholars are increasingly inclined to accept this account as substantially true. See the discussions of this problem by G. Ostrogorsky (*History of the Byzantine State,* 2nd ed. (Oxford, 1968), pp. 104-5, n. 5, F. Dvornik (in *DAI,* II, pp. 94-101, 114-16), and B. Ferjančić(*Vizantijski Izvori za istoriju naroda Jugoslavije,* II [Belgrade, 1959], pp. 37-58).

[29]Nicephorus, *Opusc. hist.* p. 12 (ed. C. de Boor).

[30]G. Moravcsik, "Zur Geschichte der Onoguren", *Ungar. Jahrbücher,* X (1930), pp. 53-90 and the bibliography in *Byzantinoturcica,* I, pp. 65 ff. (2nd ed.)

[31]Nicephorus, *op. cit.,* p. 24. The Onogur ruler who visited Heraclius in 619 was probably Kovrat's uncle Organa (Orchan).

[32]*The Chronicle of John, Bishop of Nikiu,* trans. R. H. Charles (London, 1916), p. 197. Kovrat is certainly identical with Kurt, who according to the eighth-century list of Old Bulgar rulers reigned for sixty years, i.e. according to V. Zlatarski (*Istoriya na bŭlgarskata dŭržava prez srednite vekove* [Sofia, 1918], I, 1, pp. 84-96, 353-82) from 584 to 642. Cf. S. Runciman, *A History of the First Bulgarian Empire* (London, 1930), pp. 272-9.

[33]K.M. Setton has tried to prove that "some time after 641-2" the Onogur Bulgars 'under, conceivably, one of the sons of Kovrat, or under some other lieutenant, attacked and captured Corinth" ("The Bulgars in the Balkans", *SP,* XXV [1950], pp. 502-43; "The Emperor Constans II and the capture of Corinth by the Onogur Bulgars", *ibid.* XXVII [1952], pp. 351-62). His arguments have failed to convince the present writer. Cf. their criticism by P. Charanis, "On the Capture of Corinth by the Onogurs", *SP,* XXVII (1952), pp. 343-50.

[34]The origin of the Khazars, who in the late sixth and early seventh centuries were subject to the Western Turks, is still a matter for debate. Cf. D. M. Dunlop, *The History of the Jewish Khazars*

(Princeton, 1954), pp. 3-40; W. B. Henning, "'A Farewell to the Khagan of the Aq-Aquatärān", *BSOAS*, XIV (1952), pp. 501-2.

³⁵The form "Isperich" occurs in the List of Old Bulgar Rulers; the Greek form Ἀσπαρούχ ("Aspar-hruk" in Armenian: see H. Grégoire; *B*, XVII [1944-5], p. 115, n. 34) is used here, as the more familiar.

³⁶Theophanes, pp. 356-9 (ed. C. de Boor); Nicephorus, *Opusc. hist.* pp. 33-5 (ed. C. de Boor). Theophanes places all these events, the Bulgar "Landnahme" and the foundation of the First Bulgarian Empire, in A.M. 6171 = A.D. 679-80: so V. Zlatarski, *Istoriya*, I. 1, pp. 146-8; S. Runciman, *op. cit.* p. 27; but J. Kulakovsky (*Istoriya Vizantii*, III, p. 249) had already drawn attention to a piece of evidence (Mansi, XI. 617) which shows that the war still continued during part of 681. Cf. G. Ostrogorsky, *History of the Byzantine State*, p. 126, n. 4.

³⁷Contrary to V. Zlatarski, *op. cit.* I. 1, pp. 142-5, who argues that the Slavs entered into a contractual agreement with Asparuch, I. Dujčev has convincingly shown ("Protobulgares et Slaves", *Sem. Kond.* X [1938], pp. 145-54) that they were actually subjugated by the Bulgars.

³⁸There is some doubt as to where this ceremony took place. According to Nicephorus (p. 42) it was in Tervel's camp outside the city walls. The *Suda*, on the other hand, states that Tervel addressed the people of Byzantium in the palace of the Chrysotriclinus (more precisely, in the βασιλική: *Suidae Lexicon*, ed. A. Adler, I, p. 459).

³⁹Nicephorus, *Opusc. hist.* p. 42 states that Justinian Τέρβελιν. . .προσκυνεῖσθαι σὺν αὐτῷ ὑπὸ τοῦ λαοῦ ἐκέλευε.

⁴⁰This may be implied from the statement of Theophanes (ed. C. de Boor, p. 374) that Tervel in 705 undertook *vis-à-vis* Justinian πάντα ὑπακούειν καὶ συντρέχειν.

⁴¹See the remarks on the Khazaro-Byzantine trade by S. Runciman, in *Cambridge Economic History*, II, pp. 91-2.

⁴²G. Moravcsik, "Proiskhoždenie slova τζιτζάκιον", *Sem. Kond.* IV (1931), pp. 69-76.

⁴³F. Dvornik, *Les légendes de Constantin et de Méthode vues de Byzance* (*BS*, Suppl. I, 1933), pp. 159-60.

⁴⁴The *Life of St. Abo of Tiflis*, describing conditions in Khazaria in the second half of the eighth century, states: "in terra illa...multae sunt urbes et pagi, qui secundum Christi legem secure vivant" (P. Peeters, "Les Khazars dans la Passion de S. Abo de Tiflis", *AB*, LII [1934], 25 ff., cf. F. Dvornik, *op. cit.* pp. 158-9, 163-5).

⁴⁵Cf. *Menologion Basilii II Imperatoris*, *MPG*, CXVII, 181; *Synaxarium ecclesiae Constantinopolitanae*, ed. H. Delehaye, *Propylaeum ad AASS Novembris* (Brussels, 1902), col. 263.

⁴⁶G. I. Konidares, Ἀι μητροπόλεις καὶ ἀρχιεπισκοπαὶ τοῦ οἰκουμενικοῦ πατριαρχείου καὶ ἡτάξις αὐτῶν. *Texte und Forschungen zur byzant.-neugriechischen Philologie*, no. 13 (1934), p. 100. This is the interpretation given to "Gothic Eparchy" by V. Mošin ("Επαρχία Γοτθίας v Khazarii v VIII-m veke", *Trudy IV-go Sjezda Russkikh Akademičeskikh Organizacij za granitsej*, I (Belgrade, 1929), pp. 149-56; Mošin's conclusions were accepted by G. Moravcsik (*Zur Gesch. der Onoguren*, pp. 64-5), A. Vasiliev (*The Goths in the Crimea*, pp. 97-104), and to a large extent by F. Dvornik (*Les légendes*, pp. 160-8). For different views see G. Vernadsky, "The Eparchy of Gothia", *B*, XV (1940-1), 67-76, and V. Laurent, "L'érection de la métropole d'Athènes et le statut ecclésiastique de l'Illyricum au VIIIᵉ siècle", *EB*, I (1943-4), pg. 59.

⁴⁷See D. M. Dunlop, *The History of the Jewish Khazars*, pp. 116-70.

⁴⁸See below p. 41.

⁴⁹There are two classic texts showing the predominance of the Slavs in the Peloponnese in the eighth century: (1) Constantine Porphyrogenitus states that in 746-7 ἐσθλαβώθη δὲ πᾶσα ἡ χώρα, καὶ γέγονε βάρβαρος (*De thematibus*, p. 91, ed. A. Pertusi); for the term ἐσθλαβώθη see A. Bon, *Le Péloponnèse byzantin*, p. 29, n. 1; (2) between 723 and 728 Willibald, Bishop of Eichstätt, on his way to Palestine stopped at Monemvasia, a city he locates "in Slawinia terra" (*Vita S. Willibaldi, MGH, Script.* XV, 1, p. 93).

⁵⁰Of the immense literature of unequal value that has accumulated since the days of Fallmerayer (d. 1861) on the controversial question of the Slav settlements in Greece most important works are cited in A. Bon, *Le Péloponnèse byzantin*, p. 30, n. 1. Bon himself provides a cautious and balanced analysis of the problem (pp. 27 ff.) See also Lemerle, "Invasions et migrations", *op. cit.* pp. 301-4; and D. Obolensky, *The Byzantine Commonwealth* (Crestwood, N.Y., SVS Press, 1982), pp. 75-85.

⁵¹As G. Ostrogorsky has convincingly shown ("Postanak tema Helada i Peloponez: Die Entstehung der Themen Hellas und Peloponnes," *Zbornik Radova Vizantološkog Instituta Srpske Akadem-*

ije Nauka, XXI, 1 [1952], pp. 644-77), the theme of Hellas was limited to the eastern part of Central Greece.

[52]The Peloponnesian theme used to be considered to have been created after the Byzantine victory over the Slavs at Patras (805). But, as Ostrogorsky has pointed out (*loc. cit.* pp. 71-3; *History of the Byzantine State*, p. 194, n. 2), the existence of this theme before 805, restricted no doubt to the eastern part of the peninsula, can be clearly inferred both from the *De administrando imperio*, cap. 49, *DAI*, I, p. 228, 5), and from the *Chronicle of Monemvasia*, ed. I. Dujčev (Palermo, 1976). For a more cautious interpretation of the evidence see R. J. H. Jenkins, in *DAI*, II, pp. 184-5.

[53]Theophanes, ed. C. de Boor (Leipzig, 1883), p. 503.

[54]Const. Porphyr., *De administrando imperio*, cap. 42, *DAI*, I. pp. 182-4, and II, pp. 154-5.

[55]The identity of the barbarians who threatened the Khazars and Byzantine Crimea in the fourth decade of the ninth century is a matter of considerable dispute. Scylitzes, ed. I. Thurn (1973), p. 73, states explicitly, and Theophanes Continuatus (p. 122, *CSHB*) by implication, that they were the Pechenegs. It has, however, been pointed out (J. Marquart, *Osteuropäische und ostasiatische Streifzüge* [Leipzig, 1903], p. 28) that in 833 the Pechenegs were still east of the Volga; furthermore, recent archaeological work has shown that Sarkel was situated on the left bank of the Don (M. Artamonov, "Sarkel", *Sovetskaya Arkheologiya*, VI [1940], 130-67): "Khazarskaya Krepost Sarkel", *Acta Arch. Acad. Sc. Hungaricae*, VII [1956], 321-41), and this must mean that it was built against attacks from the West. Those scholars who reject the statement of Scylitzes believe in the main that the barbarians in question were either Magyars (C. A. Macartney, *The Magyars in the Ninth Century* (Cambridge, 1930), pp. 74-5) or the Russian Vikings (J. B. Bury, *A History of the Eastern Roman Empire*, pp. 414-18; F. Dvornik, *Les légendes*, pp. 172-4; A. Vasiliev, *The Goths in the Crimea*, pp. 109 ff.).

[56]Cf. J. Marquart, *loc. cit.*; J. B. Bury, *op. cit.* p. 416.

[57]The Khazar envoys to Constantinople about 860 openly professed monotheism: see *Vita Constantini*, cap. 8: *Constantinus et Methodius Thessalonicenses: Fontes*, ed. F. Grivec and T. Tomšič (Zagreb, 1960) (*Radovi Staroslavenskog Instituta, iv*), p. 109; F. Dvornik, *Les légendes*, p. 358. Moreover, the Khan himself told the Byzantine envoys: "we differ from you on this point alone: you glorify the Trinity and we worship one God, having received the Books" (*Vita Constantini*, cap. 9, ed. Grivec and Tomšič, p. 112; Dvornik, *op. cit.* p. 361). Yet the same Khazar envoys said to the Emperor: "the Jews exhort us to embrace their faith and their traditions, but the Saracens on the other hand. . .urge us to accept their beliefs" (*ibid.* cap. 8, ed. Grivec and Tomšič, p. 109: Dvornik, *op. cit.* p. 358).

[58]About 730-40 ("The Hebrew Correspondence": see Dunlop, *op. cit.*, pp. 116-70); in the reign of Hārūn-ar-Rashīd (768-809) (Mas'udi, *Les prairies d'or*, trans. C. Barbier de Meynard, II [Paris, 1863], p. 8).

[59]This partial conversion to Judaism seems to be implied in a passage of the *Life of St. Abo of Tiflis*, where the Khazars are described as being in the late eighth century "agrestes homines. . .qui leg em nullam habent, nisi quod unum Deum creatorem norunt" (P. Peeters, *op. cit.* p. 25).

[60]"una gens. . .[Gazari] circumcisa est, et omnem Judaismum observat." Druthmar, *Expositio in Matthaeum, MPL*, CVI, 1456.

[61]The present writer cannot hence, without the above qualifications, accept F. Dvornik's statement (*Les légendes*, p. 171) that the Khazars already professed Judaism at the time of Constantine's mission, and agrees, with the same qualifications, with the conclusions of G. Vernadsky ("The Date of the Conversion of the Khazars to Judaism", *B*, XV [1940-1], 76-86); for a different view see Dunlop, *op. cit.* pp. 195-6.

[62]*Vita Const.* cap. 11, trans. F. Dvornik, *Les légendes* p. 370.

[63]The two homilies preached by Photius on this occasion, for all their rhetorical exaggeration, give a vivid impression of the city's anguish in the summer of 860: Müller, *FHG*, v, 1, pp. 162-73; see the translation and commentary by C. Mango, *The Homilies of Photius* (Cambridge, Mass., 1958), pp. 74-100. Cf. the brief but clear analysis of the sources in G. Laehr, *Die Anfänge des russischen Reiches* (Hist. Stud. 189, Berlin, 1930), pp. 91-5, and the very full account of A. A. Vasiliev, *The Russian Attack on Constantinople in 860* (Cambridge, Mass., 1946).

[64]The presence in Constantinople of an embassy from the Swedish *Rhos* is attested as early as 839: *Annales Bertiniani, MGH Script.* I, p. 434. Cf. A. Vasiliev, *op. cit.* pp. 6-13.

[65]For the Arabic sources on the Rūs see V. Minorsky, "Rūs, *Encycl. of Islam*, III, 1181-3.

[66]The Viking colonization of the lower Don and Azov areas raises some controversial problems. The present writer believes that Viking bands had very probably reached the Azov region by the

early ninth century, but finds it hard to accept the view of Vernadsky (*Ancient Russia*, pp. 278-86) and Mošin that the Norsemen built an organized and powerful state in this area: see the full discussion in Mošin, "Varyagorusskij vopros", *Slavia*, x (1931), 109-36, 343-79, 501-37; "Načalo Rusi. Normany v vostočnoj Evrope", *BS*, III (1931), 33-58, 285-307.

[67]On this route see D. Obolensky in *DAI*, II pp. 18-61 (with bibliography).

[68] *The Russian Primary Chronicle* (*Povest' Vremennykh Let*), ed. D. Likhačev and V. Adrianova-Peretts (Moscow-Leningrad, 1950), I, pp. 18-19; English trans. by S. H. Cross and O. P. Sherbowitz-Wetzor (Cambridge, Mass., 1953), pp. 59-60. This will be subsequently cited as *The Russian Primary Chronicle* and the English translation of 1953 as "Cross-Sherbowitz."

[69]The much-debated question as to whether the Russian attack of 860 was launched from Kiev or from the Azov region is discussed by A. Vasiliev (*op. cit.* pp. 169-75), whose arguments in favor of Kiev seem to the present writer convincing.

[70]Theoph. Cont. cap. 33, p. 196 (*CSHB*).

[71]Photius, *Epistolae*, *MPG*, CII, 736-7 (τὸ 'Ρῶς. . .ἐν ὑπηκόων ἑαυτοὺς καὶ προξένων τάξει. . . ἐγκαταστήσαντες).

[72]Theoph. Cont. cap. 97, pp. 342-3. Cf. *DR*, 493.

[73]For the probable coexistence, and possible blending, of the Byzantine and the Roman rites in Moravia, see F. Dvornik, *The Slavs, their early History and Civilization* (Boston, 1956), pp. 84-5, 166-7; F. Grivec, *Konstantin und Method, Lehrer der Slaven* (Wiesbaden, 1960), pp. 179-84.

[74]According to P. Mutafčiev, *Istoriya na bŭlgarskiya narod*, I (3rd ed., Sofia, 1948), pp. 171-6, the country round Ohrid and Prespa was part of the Bulgarian realm by 842.

[75]Οἱ δὲ Βούλγαροι. . .καὶ Χριστιανοὶ γενέσθαι καὶ ὑποτάττεσθαι τῷ βασιλεῖ καὶ 'Ρωμαίοις ᾐτήσαντο: Georgius Monachus, p. 824, 19-20 (*CSHB*).

[76]The date of Boris' baptism—864, and not, as V. Zlatarski (*Istoriya*, I, 2, pp. 27-31) and S. Runciman (*First Bulgarian Empire*, p. 104) believed, 865—was established by A. Vaillant and M. Lascaris ("La date de la conversion des Bulgares," *Revue des Etudes Slaves*, XIII [1933], 5 ff.).

[77]*MPG*, CII, 628-96; *Fontes Historiae Bulgaricae*, VIII (Sofia, 1961), 59-99. Cf. I. Dujčev, "Au lendemain de la conversion du peuple bulgare, l'épître de Photius", *Mélanges de Science Religieuse*, VIII (1951), 211-26.

[78]*Responsa ad Consulta Bulgarorum*, *MPL*, CXIX, 978-1016; *Fontes Historiae Bulgaricae*, VII (1960), 60-125. Cf. I Dujčev, "Die Responsa Nicolai I. Papae ad Consulta Bulgarorum als Quelle für die bulgarische Geschichte", *Festschrift zur Feier des Haus-, Hof- und Staatsarchivs*, I (Vienna, 1949), pp. 349-62.

[79]"Graeci. . .diversa requirunt ingenia, munera post munera numerosa mittentes, et sophistica ei argumenta creberrime proponentes": Anastasius Bibliothecarius, *MPL*, CXXVIII, 20.

[80]On Boris' dealings with Rome and Constantinople see F. Dvornik, *The Photian Schism* (Cambridge, 1948), pp. 91-131, 151-8.

[81]Cf. F. Dvornik, *The Making of Central and Eastern Europe*, pp. 18-22, 124-9, 249-53; *The Slavs, Their Early History and Civilization*, pp. 170-4; A.P. Vlasto, *The Entry of the Slavs into Christendom* (Cambridge, 1970), pp. 26-113.

[82]As his treatment of a group of Methodius' disciples who were sold into slavery by the Moravians and redeemed by a Byzantine envoy in Venice shows; see S. Runciman, *op. cit.* p. 125.

[83]V. Zlararski, *Istoriya*, I, 2, pp. 145-51; G. Ostrogorsky, *History of the Byzantine State*, p. 235, n. 1.

[84]The Cyrillic script which, except in Croatia and Dalmatia, rapidly supplanted the Glagolitic, is considered by most present-day authorities to have resulted from an attempt by Methodius' disciples in Bulgaria to adapt Greek uncial writing to the Slavonic tongue. The question of the relative priority of Glagolitic and Cyrillic may, however, still be considered an open one. For an attempt to argue the priority of Cyrillic, see E. Georgiev, *Slavyanskaya pismennost do Kirilla i Mefodija* (Sofia, 1952).

[85]Cf. M. Murko, *Geschichte der älteren südslawischen Litteraturen* (Leipzig, 1908), p. 57 ff.; B. Angelov and M. Genov, *Stara bŭlgarska literatura* (Sofia, 1922).

[86]*Antapodosis*, lib. III, cap. 29 (ed. I. Bekker, p. 87).

[87]John the Exarch, *Šestodnev*, ed. R. Aitzetmüller, *Das Hexaemeron des Exarchen Johannes*, I (Graz, 1958), p. 195.

[88]See G. I. Bratianu, "Le commerce bulgare dans l'Empire byzantin et le monopole de l'empereur Léon VI à Thessalonique", *Sbornik Nikov: Izvestiya na Bŭlgarskoto Istoričesko Družestvo*, XVI-XVIII (1940), pp. 30-6.

[89]G. Kolias, *Léon Choerosphactès* (Athens, 1939 = *Texte und Forschungen zur byzant.-*

neugriechischen Philologie, XXXI); *Fontes Historiae Bulgaricae*, VIII (1961), 185-84; cf. V. Zlatarski, *Istoriya*, I, 2, pp. 302-12.

[90] *The Russian Primary Chronicle*, ed. Likhačev, I, p. 20; trans. Cross-Sherbowitz, pp. 60-1. *The First Novgorod Chronicle*, on the other hand, attributes the capture of Kiev jointly to Igor, Ryurik's son, and to Oleg, Igor playing the leading role: *Novgorodskaya Pervaya Letopis*, ed. A. Nasonov (Moscow-Leningrad, 1950), p. 107.

[91] On the Dnieper rapids and their Scandinavian and Slav names cited in the *De administrando imperio* (cap. 9), see *DAI*, I, pp. 58-60, and D. Obolensky in *DAI*, II, pp. 38-52, and the Soviet commentary to chapter 9 of the *DAI*, ed. G. Litavrin (Moscow, 1989), pp. 291-332.

[92] For the history of this controversy, see V. Mošin, "Varyago-russkij vopros', *Slavia*, X(1931), 109-36, 343-79, 501-37; A. Stender-Peterson, *Varangica* (Aarhus, 1953), pp. 5-20; H Paszkiewicz, *The Origin of Russia* (London, 1954), pp. 109-132; *DAI*, II, pp. 20-3.

[93] For a classic exposition of the "Normanist" view, see V. Thomsen, *The Relations between Ancient Russia and Scandinavia and the Origin of the Russian State* (Oxford, 1877). The "anti-Normanist" theory was until recently chiefly championed by Soviet historians: see, in particular, B. D. Grekov, *Kievskaja Rus*, 4th ed. (Moscow-Leningrad, 1944), pp. 250 ff.; V. P. Šušarin, "O suščnosti i formakh sovremennogo normanizma," *Voprosy Istorii*, VIII (1960), 65-93. Cf. "Varangian Problems", *Scando-Slavica*, Suppl. 1 (1970).

[94] The Old Russian text of the treaty is preserved in the *Russian Primary Chronicle*, ed. Likhačev, I, pp. 25-9; trans. Cross-Sherbowitz, pp. 65-8. The historicity of Oleg's raid on Constantinople, frequently denied in former times, has been convincingly established by Ostrogorsky (L'expédition du Prince Oleg contre Constantinople en 907", *Sem. Kond.* XI [1940], 47-62) and by A. Vasiliev ("The Second Russian Attack on Constantinople," *DOP*, VI (1951), 163-225, where the relevant literature is exhaustively reviewed).

[95] The Russians were granted total exemption from customs, were allotted a special residence in the suburban quarter of St. Mamas, and received free board for six months, a period twice as long as the normal limit of residence allowed to foreign merchants in Constantinople.

[96] On the question of whether this meeting took place within or outside Constantinople the Byzantine tradition is as ambiguous as in the case of Tervel's investiture (see above, note 38); Georgius Monachus (pp. 877-8, *CSHB*) and Theophanes Continuatus (p. 385, *CSHB*) imply that the Patriarch visited Symeon outside the city; but according to Scylitzes (p. 200) Symeon was entertained by the Emperor at a feast in the Blachernae Palace.

[97] This view is argued by Ostrogorsky ("Avtokrator i Samodržac," *Glas*, CLXIV (1935), 121 ff.; "Die Krönung Symeons von Bulgarien durch den Patriarchen Nikolaos Mystikos," *Actes du IVe Congrès International des Etudes Byzantines*, (Sofia, 1935), I, 275-86), and is accepted by P. Mutafčiev (*Istoriya*, I, p. 240). For a different view, see F. Dölger, "Der Bulgarenherrscher als geistlicher Sohn des byzant. Kaisers", *Sbornik Nikov, loc. cit.*, pp. 221, n. 1, and 228., n. 2 (= *Byzanz. u. d. europäische Staatenwelt*, pp. 185, n. 7, and 193, n. 20).

[98] There are some twenty-nine extant letters of Nicholas Mysticus concerned with Bulgarian affairs, all written during his second Patriarchate (912-25), twenty-eight of which are addressed to Symeon: *MPG*, CXI, 40-196; *Fontes Historiae Bulgaricae*, VIII (1961), 185-297; Greek text and English trans. by R.J.H. Jenkins and L.G. Westerink (Washington, D.C., 1973), pp. 16-214. Zlatarski provides a detailed commentary on them in *Sbornik za Narodni Umotvoreniya, Nauka i Knižnina*, x (1894), 372-428; XI (1894), 3-54; XII (1895), 121-211. Cf. *GR*, nos. 614 ff.

[99] *Ep.* 5, *MPG*, CXI, 45-56. Cf. F. Dölger, "Bulgarisches Zartum und byzantinisches Kaisertum," *Actes du IVe Congrès International des Etudes Byzantines*, I, 61-2 (= *Byzanz u. d. europäische Staatenwelt*, p. 147).

[100] *Ep.* 8, *MPG*, CXI, 64; *Ep.* 5, Jenkins-Westerink, pp. 26-39.

[101] Leo the Deacon, p. 123 (*CSHB*): αὐτοκράτορα ἑαυτὸν ἀνακηρύττειν Ῥωμαίοις ἐκέλευεν.

[102] Nicholas Mysticus, *Ep.* 18, *MPG*, CXI, 125; *Ep.* 19, *MPG*, CXI, 128.

[103] Georgius Mon. pp. 900-1; Theoph. Cont. pp. 405-9; Scylitzes, pp. 218-21; Jenkins-Westerink, pp. 121-30. Cf. S. Runciman, *Romanus Lecapenus* (Cambridge, 1929), p. 92, who quotes Romanus' speech to Symeon.

[104] *Ep.* 31, *MPG*, CXI, 188-96; Jenkins-Westerink, pp. 207-214.

[105] According to Romanus Lecapenus (*Epistolae*, ed. Sakkelion, *D*, I, 1883, 658-64, 665-6; *Fontes Historiae Bulgaricae*, VIII, 1961, 298) Symeon entitled himself βασιλεὺς Βουλγάρων καὶ Ῥωμαίων. However, a leaden *bulla* has been discovered with the simple inscription: Συμεὼν ἐν Χρισ[τῷ] βασιλε[ὺς] Ῥομεῶν [*sic*]:T. Gerassimov, *Bulletin de l'Institut Archéol. Bulgare*, VIII (1934), 350-6.

[106]The date of the foundation of the Bulgarian Patriarchate provides a difficult problem: it was probably established by Symeon, and doubtless after the death of Nicholas Mysticus (15 May 925); see S. Runciman, *First Bulgarian Empire*, pp. 163, n. 2, and 174.

[107]*DR*, 612.

[108]F. Dölger, "Der Bulgarenherrscher als geistlicher Sohn des byzant. Kaisers," *Sbornik Nikov* (1940), pp. 219-32 (= *Byz. u. d. europ. Staatenwelt*, pp. 183-96); G. Ostrogorsky, "Die byzantinische Staatenhierarchie," *Sem. Kond.* VIII (1936), 41-53.

[109]See J. Ferluga, *Vizantiska Uprava u Dalmacii* (Belgrade, 1957), pp. 68-86, and *L'amministrazione bizantina in Dalmazia* (Venice, 1978), pp. 165-89.

[110]Scylitzes (p. 239) refers to the two chieftans as Βουλοσουδής and Γυλᾶς: Constantine Porphyrogenitus calls the former Βουλτζοῦς (*De ad. imp.* c. 40, *DAI*, I, p. 178, l. 66); in the Hungarian tradition he is known as Bulscu: cf. B. Hóman, *Gesch. des ungar. Mittelalters*, I (Berlin, 1940), pp. 127-32, 146-7. "Gyula" was, according to Constantine (*loc. cit.* 51-2), a title and not a proper name. Cf. C. A. Macartney, *The Magyars in the Ninth Century*, pp. 117-18.

[111]*De admin. imp.* c. 1, 16-20 and c. 2-8, *DAI*, I, pp. 48-56.

[112]*Russian Primary Chronicle*, ed. Likhačev, I, p. 43; II, p. 285; trans. by Cross-Sherbowitz, pp. 72-3.

[113]*Russian Primary Chronicle* I, pp. 34-9; Cross-Sherbowitz, pp. 73-37; *DR*, 647.

[114]Exemption from customs duties is no longer mentioned, and the Russians were forbidden to buy large silk fabrics higher in price than 50 *nomismata*; cf. R. Lopez, "Silk Industry in the Byzantine Empire," *SP*, xx (1945), 34-5.

[115]The place and date of Olga's baptism provide a controversial problem, for while the *Russian Primary Chronicle* (I, pp. 44-5; Cross-Sherbowitz, pp. 82-3), Scylitzes, p. 240 and Continuator Reginonis (*MGH*, ed. F. Kurze, 1890, p. 170) state that she was baptized in Constantinople, Constantine Porphyrogenitus in his detailed account of Olga's reception in the capital in 967 (*De cerimoniis*, pp. 594 ff., *CSHB*) does not mention her baptism. Accordingly, some historians believe that Olga was baptized in Kiev a few years before her journey to Constantinople (see G. Vernadsky, *Kievan Russia*, New Haven, 1948, p. 40; G. Ostrogorsky, *History of the Byzantine State*, p. 251, n. 2). The present writer does not accept this view and, together with G. Laehr (*Die Anfänge des russ. Reiches*, pp. 103-5) and F. Dvornik (*The Slavs, Their Early History and Civilization*, pp. 200-1), is of the opinion that Olga's baptism took place in Constantinople. For the most recent discussions of this thorny problem, see A.V. Nazarenko, "Kogda zhe Knyaginya Ol'ga ezdila v Konstantinopol'?", *VV*, 50 (1989), pp. 66-84, and D. Obolensky, "Olga's Conversion. The Evidence Reconsidered," *HUS*, 12-13 (1988-9), pp. 145-58.

[116]Continuator Reginonis, pp. 170, 172.

[117]*De cerim.* pp. 686 ff.; cf. G. Ostrogorsky, "Die byzantinische Staatenhierachie," *Sem. Kond.* VIII (1936), 50-2.

[118]*De admin. imp.* c. 10 and 11, *DAI*, I, p. 62 and p. 64.

[119]*De cerim.* pp. 688 f.; cf. G. Ostrogorsky, "Staatenhierarchie," *op. cit.* p. 52.

[120]*De cerim.*, ibid.

[121]Cf. H.-C. Puech and A. Vaillant, *Le traité contre les Bogomiles de Cosmas le Prêtre* (Paris, 1945); D. Obolensky, *The Bogomils* (Cambridge, 1948).

[122]The chronology of the next three years is confused, as the sources give different dates. Thus Leo the Deacon (pp. 61-3) implies that Nicephorus invaded Southern Bulgaria in the spring of 966, while Scylitzes (pp. 276-7) states that the Emperor marched to the frontier in June 967. The present writer finds it hard to agree with Runciman (*First Bulgarian Empire*, pp. 303-5) that these were two separate expeditions: both Leo and Scylitzes assert that Nicephorus' campaign was immediately followed by the dispatch of Calocyros to Russia.

[123]The date of the first Russian invasion of Bulgaria is not easy to determine, in view of the conflicting evidence of the sources. While recognizing the complexity of the problem, the present writer prefers the date 967 which is given by the *Russian Primary Chronicle* (I, p. 47; Cross-Sherbowitz, p. 84), and accepted by S. Runciman (*op. cit.* p. 304), M. Levčenko (*Očerki po istorii russko-vizantijskikh otnošeny*, Moscow 1956, pp. 258-9), and A. D. Stokes ("The Background and Chronology of the Balkan Campaigns of Svyatoslav Igorevich," *SEER*, XL, 94, 1961, 50-7). The date August 968, supplied by Scylitzes (p. 277), is accepted by P. Karyškovsky ("O khronologii russko-vizantijskoj vojny pri Svyatoslave," *VV*, v, 1952, 127-38) and G. Ostrogorsky (*History of the Byzantine State*, p. 292).

[124] *Russian Primary Chronicle*, I, pp. 47-8; Cross-Sherbowitz, pp. 85-6.

[125] *Russian Primary Chronicle*, I, pp. 48-50; Cross-Sherbowitz, pp. 86-7. The Russian chronicler's dating of Svyatoslav's second invasion of Bulgaria (971) is, as all the authorities agree, unacceptable. Here again Scylitzes supplies the accurate date (Scylitzes, pp. 276-2).

[126] Leo the Deacon, p. 105.

[127] Leo the Deacon, pp. 108 ff.; Scylitzes-Cedrenus, II, pp. 384-8; ed. I. Thurn (1973), pp. 288-91. The *Russian Primary Chronicle* (I, p. 50; Cross-Sherbowitz, pp. 87-8) falsely describes this battle as a Russian victory. Cf. G. Schlumberger, *L'épopée byzantine à la fin du X⁰ siècle*, I (Paris, 1896), pp. 46-52.

[128] The date of John Tzimisces' Russian campaign (April-July 971) has been conclusively established by F. Dölger ("Die Chronologie des grossen Feldzuges des Kaisers Johannes Tzimiskes gegen die Russen," *BZ*, XXXII (1932), 275-92); cf. C. Göllner, "Les expéditions byzantines contre les Russes sous Jean Tzimiscès," *RHSE*, XIII (1936), 342-58; H. Grégoire, "La dernière campagne de Jean Tzimiskès contre les Russes," *B*, XII (1937), 267-76.

[129] The *Russian Primary Chronicle* (I, p. 51; Cross-Sherbowitz, pp. 88-9) brazenly implies that the Russians won the war. Cf. the detailed account in G. Schlumberger, *op. cit.* chs. 1-3.

[130] *Russian Primary Chronicle*, I, p. 52; Cross-Sherbowitz, pp. 89-90; *DR*, 739.

[131] Leo the Deacon, pp. 155-6.

[132] *Ibid.* pp. 156-7.

[133] I, pp. 59-83; Cross-Sherbowitz, pp. 96-119.

[134] Ed. I. Kračkovsky and A. Vasiliev (with a French trans.), *PO*, XXIII, 423. The other sources on Russia's conversion are cited in G. Laehr, *Die Anfänge des russischen Reiches*, pp. 110-15.

[135] *DR*, 771.

[136] On the Byzantine attitude to marriages of imperial, and particularly Porphyrogenitae, princesses to foreigners, see G. Ostrogorsky, "Vladimir Svyatoj i Vizantiya," *Vladimirskij Sbornik* (Belgrade, 1938), pp. 34 ff.

[137] The fact, impugned by several recent theories, that Vladimir's Church was from the moment of its foundation placed under the authority of the Byzantine Patriarch has, in the present writer's view, been conclusively established by V. Laurent ("Aux origines de l'Eglise russe," *EO*, XXXVIII (1939), 279-95), E. Honigmann ("The Foundation of the Russian Metropolitan Church according to Greek sources," *B*, XVII (1944-5), 128-62) and M. Levčenko ("Vzaimootnošenija Vizantii i Rusi pri Vladimire," *VV*, n. s. VII (1953), 193-223; *Očerki*, pp. 340-85).

[138] The much-debated problem of the origin and early stages of the Bulgarian revolt is admirably discussed by G. Ostrogorsky, *History of the Byzantine State*, p. 302, n. 1.

[139] Cecaumenus (*Strategicon*, cap. 49, ed. B. Wassiliewsky and V. Jernstedt, St. Petersburg, 1896, p. 18) puts the number at 14,000, Scylitzes, p. 349 at 15,000. These figures are probably exaggerated; cf. G. Ostrogorsky, *op. cit.* p. 310, n. 1.

CHAPTER III

RUSSIA'S BYZANTINE HERITAGE*

The title of this essay[1] might seem to suffer from the measure of ambiguity attached to the term "heritage." A heritage, bequeathed in the past, might still be possessed by its recipient; or it might have subsequently been lost or abandoned. "Russia's Byzantine heritage" might thus mean either a quasi-permanent, and still existing, ingredient of Russian culture, or a set of influences formerly exerted upon Russia by Byzantium which can no longer be detected at the present time. In theory this distinction is somewhat artificial, for on the plane of history no important element in a country's past is ever completely lost, and, if we assume that the "Byzantine heritage" was once an essential factor of Russian culture and if no trace of this heritage were apparent in that culture today, we could not for this reason deny *a priori* that the influence of Byzantium continues to condition the historical background of present-day Russia. In practice, however, the distinction has its importance; and it is implicit in the contrast between two methods by which the problem of "Russia's Byzantine heritage" is sometimes approached today. There are those who, starting from the present, try and work back to the past: there is much in contemporary Russia that seems unfamiliar and puzzling to the modern Western observer — ideas, institutions, and methods of government that seem to run counter to the basic trends of his own culture; and so, wishing to understand the origin and meaning of these strange phantoms, he is tempted to single out those which appear to him most striking and to trace them back as far as possible into Russia's past history. Our observer could scarcely fail to remark that a strong dose of Byzantine influence is a feature that distinguishes the medieval his-

*Oxford Slavonic Papers, I (1950), 37-63.

75

tory of Russia from that of western Europe; and if, furthermore, his reading of East Roman history will have suggested to him some traits of similarity between the institutions of Byzantium and those of Soviet Russia, he will be inclined to conclude that the similarity is a proof of historical filiation. The other method implies a reverse process, from the past towards the present: a study of the culture and institutions of the Byzantine Empire leads to an analysis of the precise character of the influence of Byzantine civilization on medieval Russia; the most important features of this influence are then singled out, and an attempt is made to trace them down the centuries in order to discover how long they remained an effective ingredient of Russian culture.

It seems to me that both these methods are unsatisfactory. The first is based on an essentially unhistorical approach which comes near to begging the whole question and generally results in biased and spurious judgements of value passed on both medieval Russia and Byzantium. The second method conceals dangers of a more subtle kind: if one concentrates mainly upon those aspects of medieval Russian culture which are regarded as a by-product of Byzantium, abstracting them from the wider context of Russian history, there often results a certain lack of proportion, facts of secondary importance being given undue prominence and vice versa. This approach, moreover, is particularly open to the danger, from which historians are never totally immune, of confusing a derivation with an explanation, of forgetting that any set of circumstances or events can never be fully understood except in the whole context of its own development, and of falling a prey to what Marc Bloch has called *l'idole des origines*.[2]

An historically valid approach to the problem of Russia's Byzantine heritage would thus exclude any endeavour to "read back" any features of contemporary Russian culture to a hypothetical Byzantine prototype, and any attempt to isolate the Byzantine features of Russian medieval culture from the whole context of Russian history in order to follow their development and fortune down the ages. It is only, I would suggest, within a wider framework and as part of a larger picture that the problem of Russia's Byzantine heritage can successfully be studied by the historian. Such a wider framework would include not only the history of Russia, of the Byzantine Empire, and of their mutual relations in the field of culture; Russia's connections with the European and Asiatic worlds that surrounded and affected her during different periods of her history should also form part of the picture.

An attempt to approach the problem from all these angles would far exceed the scope of an essay, whose aim can be no more than to suggest a few general topics for reflection. These topics might be expressed in the form of questions: how far can Russian history be adequately studied with special reference to the history and culture of the Byzantine Empire? What would be the implications of such a study from the wider field of view of European history? And these two questions bring a third one in their wake, which, however, briefly and inadequately, must be answered in conclusion: what is the specific nature of Russia's Byzantine heritage?

I believe that today, at least in those countries where scholarship is free from the control of the State, we are witnessing a reaction against the nationalistic interpretation of history. It can no longer be reasonably claimed that the history of any single nation of the modern European world can successfully be studied in isolation from the history of other countries. Those who would wish to apply the notion of the modern sovereign state to the writing of history may paint a flattering and idealized picture of their own nation's past, but it would be a picture bearing but little resemblance to reality. Professor Toynbee has convincingly argued that the national state is not "an intelligible field of historical study" and has illustrated this thesis with special reference to the history of England. In his opinion, the history of an individual nation becomes fully intelligible only if studied as part of a larger whole, a society or a civilization. In the case of English history this civilization is Western Christendom.[3]

Now it seems to me that to illustrate the truth of Professor Toynbee's thesis, Russian history is an equally good test case, and that the results, if we apply here this method of investigation, would be no less revealing. If we survey the course of Russian history the following episodes might be taken to represent its main chapters: (1) the conversion of the Russians from Slavonic paganism to Byzantine Christianity, which began on a large scale in the late tenth century; (2) the Mongol yoke which lay on most of Russia from 1240 to 1480; (3) the growth of the religious nationalism of the sixteenth-century Moscow autocrats, exemplified in the formula "Moscow the Third Rome;" (4) the ecclesiastical schism of the Old Believers in the seventh decade of the seventeenth century; (5) the Westernizing reforms of Peter the Great in the first quarter of the eighteenth century; (6) the liberal reforms of Alexander II in the seventh decade of the nineteenth century; (7) the Bolshevik Revolution of 1917.

It should not be difficult to show that each of these chapters illustrates Russia's close dependence on the outside world; for none of
them is fully intelligible unless we view it against the background of
one or several cultures more extensive than Russia herself. (i) The
conversion of the Russians to Christianity was an event which united
the scattered tribes of the Eastern Slavs into a single state, linked to
Byzantium by a common religion, and made that state a member of
the Christian community of nations. (ii) The period of Mongol domination is generally regarded—and with some justification—as that of
Russia's "withdrawal into the wilderness." Yet Russia was then a
dependency of a Turko-Mongol Empire which was affiliated to the
cultural centres of central Asia, and the Golden Horde has left its
mark on Russian history; nor was Russia's isolation from Europe in
the fourteenth and fifteenth centuries as complete as is commonly
supposed: western and south-western Rus' were then part of a
Lithuanian-Polish State, closely associated with western Europe by
religion and culture; the cities of north-western Russia were commer-
cially linked with Germany through the Hanseatic League; while
Muscovy itself, the most segregated part of Russia, was in those centuries opened to a fresh flow of cultural influences from Byzantium
and the south Slavonic countries. (iii) The great imperial dream of the
sixteenth century and the attribution by Russian clerics to the Tsars
of Muscovy of religious pre-eminence throughout the world were
partly due, no doubt, to factors of Russia's own history: national consciousness and pride were intensified by the territorial expansion of
Muscovy in the late fifteenth and early sixteenth centuries and by the
liberation from the Tatar yoke in 1480. But the new Russian imperialism was also powerfully stimulated by the growth of diplomatic relations with the powers of central and northern Europe and by the
claim of the Muscovite rulers, consciously formulated in the late fifteenth century, to those remaining lands of their ancestral "patrimony"
which formed part of the Lithuanian-Polish State. And it is significant
that the stimulus which created and justified the doctrine of "Moscow
the Third Rome" came from outside: Byzantium had fallen to the
Turks—a just punishment for tampering with the purity of the
Orthodox faith and signing with the Latins the detestable Union of
Florence; the First Rome had long ago lapsed into heresy; the Second
Rome, Constantinople, was in the hands of the infidels: the Imperial
mantle should now fall by every right on Moscow, the Third Rome;
"and a fourth there will not be." So argued the ecclesiastical panegy-

rists of Holy Russia in the sixteenth century. It is surely remarkable that this extreme glorification of Russian religious nationalism was, in one of its aspects, a by-product of an event of world-wide importance—the fall of Byzantium—and that the formula which sustained it was, it would seem, derived from political ideas current in fourteenth-century Bulgaria.[4] Finally, the doctrine of the divinely ordained and universal monarchy, which gave religious justification to the theory of "Moscow the Third Rome," political significance to the Imperial coronation of Ivan IV in 1547, and ecclesiastical sanction to the creation of the Patriarchate of Moscow in 1589, can be traced back in direct line of ascent to the Byzantine theory of the Christian Empire, adapted from the political philosophy of Hellenism in the fourth century of our era.

(iv) The great religious schism of the seventeenth century, due to the revolt of the "Old Believers" against the liturgical reforms of the Patriarch Nikon, was in one sense the result of Russian national exclusiveness: the Old Believers on the stake and in the Tsar's torture chambers were convinced that they were suffering and dying for the ideal of Holy Russia, where alone the true faith shone as brightly as the sun. This, indeed, would seem to be the very essence of religious separativeness, of deliberate cultural isolation; yet in this case also the stimulus came from outside: the Old Believers fought desperately, and unsuccessfully, against foreign influences on Russian life. Nikon, the servant of Antichrist, would impose on his Church the Scriptural texts and liturgical practice of the contemporary Greeks; he had declared himself: "I am a Russian . . . but my faith and religion are Greek."[5] And the Old Believers preferred to rend the Russian Church in two rather than accept these foreign innovations. (v) The reforms of Peter the Great were patently a response to the impact of outside forces, pressing on Russia from the West; their purpose was to transform Russia's military machinery, social structure, and economic life in accordance with Western institutions and with the help of Western technology. (vi) Alexander II's reforms, particularly the emancipation of the serfs, were both a product of Western liberalism and a consequence of the Crimean War; they, too, aimed at giving Russia the efficient machinery of a progressive Western State. (vii) Finally, the Bolshevik Revolution and the Soviet régime to which it gave birth were at least in part the product of forces which arose and developed outside Russia: the two corner-stones of the Soviet State—Marxism and technology—were borrowed by Russia from the West.

These seven examples, taken from the main chapters of Russian history, show quite clearly that at no time was Russia a self-contained unit and that we cannot understand her history in terms of cultural self-sufficiency. "We have," to quote Professor Toynbee, "to think in terms of the whole and not of the parts; to see the chapters of the story as events in the life of the society and not of some particular member; and to follow the fortunes of the members, not separately but concurrently, as variations on a single theme or as contributions to an orchestra which are significant as a harmony but have no meaning as so many separate series of notes. In so far as we succeed in studying history from this point of view, we find that order arises out of chaos in our minds and that we begin to understand what was not intelligible before."[6]

Can we discover a larger "whole," a civilization of which Russia is a part and from whose standpoint her history will become intelligible?

Our survey of the main chapters of Russian history will have suggested that at different periods of her history Russia was more or less closely connected with Asia, western Europe, and Byzantium. Her relations with Asia were maintained through the nomadic and semi-nomadic empires which successive waves of invaders from the dawn of Slavonic history to the fourteenth century of the Christian era established in the Pontic steppes. Some of them — especially the Khazars in the eighth century, the Cumans in the twelfth, and the Golden Horde in the fourteenth—entered into close relations with the Eastern Slavs and undoubtedly affected their destiny. And at least twice in her history Russia seemed on the verge of becoming an Oriental Empire, with her face and policy turned towards the East: the first occasion was in the tenth century, when the Viking rulers of Rus' made an attempt to gain control of the Caspian and Caucasus regions and when Vladimir of Kiev, before deciding to accept Christianity in the name of his people, hesitated for a moment before the beckoning hand of Islam; the second opportunity occurred in the middle of the sixteenth century, when Ivan IV of Moscow captured the Tatar strongholds of Kazan and Astrakhan: this double event, which marked the final victory of the agriculturist and town-dweller over the Eurasian horsemen of the steppe, brought about the incorporation of large regions of Islamic culture into the new Russian Empire, signified the Tsar's assumption of the political heritage of the Tatar khan, and started Russia's career of expansion towards Siberia and the Pacific. Yet the importance of Russia's connections with Asia should not be exaggerated. The recent "Eurasian" school of Russian historians, while holding that the whole territory of the Soviet Union forms a sub-continent separate from both Europe and Asia, has nevertheless laid the main emphasis on the Asiatic, "Turanian," affinities of Russian culture.[7] It is very doubtful whether much evidence could be found to support this interpretation. The Tatars have often enough been held responsible for all the sins of Russia, though historians are still divided on the question of the extent of the influence exerted by the Golden Horde on Russian culture. On the whole, it does not seem that this influence was very considerable.[8] And we must not in any case forget that Russia's conversion to Christianity separated her from Asia by a moral and cultural gulf which not even the thousand-year-long intercourse with her subsequent Asiatic rulers and subjects was able to bridge. It is not to the East that we must look in our search for Russia's parent civilization.

Does "the West"—the Christian and post-Christian countries of western and central Europe—provide a more satisfactory alternative? In our survey of the seven main chapters of Russian history, the last three, covering the period from the beginning of the eighteenth century to the present day, were concerned with the direct effect of Western techniques, institutions and ideas upon Russia. This in itself suggests that Russia's process of "Westernization," which has progressed at an increasing tempo during the past three centuries, has been a more important and vital factor in her cultural history than her connections with Asia. Nor has she been a mere recipient: since the time of Peter the Great Russia has formed an inseparable part of the European state system; for more than a century she has powerfully contributed to European culture, in literature and music, in science and scholarship, and in recent years she has re-exported to the West, in a new and to some extent characteristically Russian form, the creed and practice of Marxist Socialism.

Yet we may hesitate to place modern Russia unreservedly within the pale of that "Western" civilization which originated in the Western territories of the Roman Empire, the ecclesiastical orbit of the Papacy and the political domains of the Carolingian State, and gradually extended its influence over the greater part of the inhabited globe. Resistance and hostility to all forms of Western Christianity are ingrained in a large proportion of Russians, particularly sometimes in those who have ceased to concern themselves greatly about religion. Most educated Russians have long been conscious of a dichotomy in their cultural inheritance; as early as the beginning of the seventeenth century an acute Russian observer remarked: "We are turning our backs to one another: some of us look to the East, others to the West."[9] Among the historical and philosophical problems debated by Russian thinkers in the nineteenth century none was so constantly advanced and led to such passionate searchings of heart as the question of Russia's status and destiny: was she part of Europe or a separate world *sui generis*; should she look to the "West" or the "East?" And the ambiguity in Russia's relations with the West was forcibly apparent in recent times, when a political creed, a social programme, and an industrial technology, all of which are Western in origin, were used from a Russian base of operations to criticize and assail the very foundations of contemporary Western society. It is also significant that the Westernization of Russia in the eighteenth and nineteenth centuries created a cultural dichotomy, a drawback from which Muscovy, for all its social disunity, had not appreciably suffered. The influence of Polish education and manners in the seventeenth century, Peter the Great's cultural reforms, the assimilation of French literature and German philosophy by the intelligentsia, the impact on Russia of the Industrial Revolution, the spread of Socialism and Marxism, these were practically limited in their effects to the upper class and educated minority. The life and outlook of the peasants — the overwhelming majority of the population — remained, at least until the twentieth century, untouched by these alien importations. In the Russian villages life was lived much as it had been for centuries past. The faith and toil of the humble folk, their strong belief in God, their veneration of the holy man, the monk, and the pilgrim, the annual cycle of work and prayer, their legends, costumes, and folk-songs, these had not altered very much since the dawn of Russian history. It may be said, in fact, that in the eighteenth and nineteenth centuries Russia was living under a dual dispensation: the ruling minority — Westernized nobles, technicians, and the intelligentsia — educated in a cosmopolitan spirit, frequently out of touch with the native culture and even with the faith of their fathers, proselytes of the modern West; and, on the other hand, the mass of the peasants who continued to live in strict accordance with the rules and ethos inherited from their remote ancestors. It would thus seem impossible to regard Russia as an offshoot or a part of modern "Western" civilization; for even during the last two centuries, when Western influences in Russia were at their strongest, some important aspects of her life and history cannot be explained in terms of this civilization.

It will be noticed that our attempt to discover a larger cultural unit in whose terms Russian history may become intelligible has so far been reduced to a search for a culture which has exerted a sufficiently profound and lasting influence on Russia to deserve to be considered as Russia's parent civilization. This method of investigation will prove helpful if we shift our attention once more to the medieval chapters of Russian history. There can be no doubt that the influence of Byzantium on Russian history and culture was far more profound and permanent than that of the Turko-Mongol hordes and more homogeneous than that of the modern West. Russia owes her religion and the greater part of her medieval culture to the Byzantine Empire, both directly, through her connections with Constantinople in the ninth and tenth centuries, and indirectly, through the Slavo-Byzantine schools of tenth-century Bulgaria. Much has been written of late on the remarkable and precocious culture of Kievan Rus', but there is still scope for an essay which would fully reveal the extent to which it was indebted to the civilization of East Rome.[10] The eleventh and twelfth centuries, I would suggest, might prove particularly suited to such an investigation: Byzantine civilization was then in its prime, its attractive power still at its height; Russia was a young and growing nation, with no heavy burden of inherited traditions, no very rigid view of herself or her neighbors: such conditions breed tolerance and favor intercourse and could reveal, from behind the often obstructive screen of later importations, some salient features of her original culture. Such an essay might well be devoted to an illustration of Mr. Sumner's comprehensive formula: "Byzantium brought to Russia five gifts: her religion, her law, her view of the world, her art and writing."[11] The spread of Byzantine Christianity to Rus' in the tenth century, the growth of the young Russian Church under the leadership of Constantinople, and the first flowering of Russian monasticism in the eleventh and twelfth centuries; the introduction into Russia of Byzantine law—which was an extension of Roman law—and its fusion, and sometimes clash, with the customary law of the Eastern Slavs; the radiation of Byzantine art of the Macedonian and Comnenian periods to Russia, where it achieved some of its greatest works and informed the first native schools of architecture and painting; the adoption by the Russians, mainly through Bulgaria, of the Slavonic alphabet and vernacular literature, a gift from Byzantium which enabled them at the dawn of their Christian life to produce works of literature which rank high in the history of their culture; and finally, the question of how far the Russians in the Kiev period assimilated "the thought-world of East Rome"[12] — an important but difficult question, where generalizations and hasty conclusions are especially dangerous: these are some of the problems that would be faced in such a study.

A much-needed essay could also be written on the second and more imperfectly known phase of Russia's relations with Byzantium, the period between 1250 and 1450. And here two awkward questions arise: did Russia really "lapse into barbarism"[13] for two centuries after the Tatar invasion? and how far did the Mongol yoke seal her off from the civilizing influence of the Byzantine world? It is not easy to answer these questions precisely, but it may be suggested that the political catastrophe of the Mongol invasion did not break the continuity in Russian culture nor substantially interrupt the flow of Balkan influence into Rus': the latter, indeed, grew particularly strong in the fourteenth and fifteenth centuries; the new literary trends and the theory and practice of contemplative monasticism, two characteristic features of those centuries of Russian history, were imported from Byzantium, Mount Athos, and the Balkan countries; while, in the field of art, the remarkable school of painting of Novgorod in this period was profoundly influenced by the last great phase of Byzantine art, in the age of the Palaeologoi.[14]

It will be observed that the influence exerted by Byzantine civilization on Russia between the tenth and the fifteenth centuries was markedly different in character and scope from the impact of western Europe after the middle of the seventeenth century; the latter, we have seen, split Russian society into two and created a gulf between the ruling and educated minority on the one hand and the peasantry on the other: Byzantine influence, which spread to Russia through the medium of Christianity and the channel of the ruling class, was often slow in filtering down to the other sections of society; but filter down it did, and over the course of the Middle Ages it pervaded in varying degrees the whole of Russian society from the prince to the peasant, leaving practically no aspect of Russian life untouched.[15]

We may thus conclude that Russia's parent civilization was the Byzantine culture of East Rome, in whose terms Russian cultural history remains intelligible at least until the middle of the fifteenth century. Leaving aside for the moment the task of defining and describing this civilization, we must consider how far, after the fifteenth century,

Russia's parent civilization remains the "intelligible field" for the study of Russian history. There can be no doubt that a strong influence of Byzantine culture can be observed in all sections and classes of Russian society, at least until the second half of the seventeenth century. Two examples may suffice to illustrate this fact. In the early sixteenth century an authoritative spokesman of the Russian Church wrote: "By nature the Tsar is like all other men; but in authority he is like the Highest God";[16] this definition of the functions of the sacred and universal Autocrat, so characteristic of the Byzantine conception of imperial sovereignty, reads like a sentence from the pen of Constantine Porphyrogenitus or Eusebius of Caesarea. And in the second half of the seventeenth century the Archpriest Avvakum, who suffered death on the stake for refusing to accept the practice of making the sign of the cross with three as against two fingers, and reciting the triple as against the double Alleluia, and who exhorted his numerous followers to sacrifice their lives rather than accept the reforms of Nikon, signified his faith in the following words: "I hold to this even unto death, as I have received it. . . . It has been laid down before us: let it lie thus unto the ages of ages."[17] Thus did a Russian parish priest, in his heroic refusal to countenance the slightest deviation from the sacred wholeness of the liturgical practice, echo the words of the Byzantine Patriarch Photius, who wrote eight centuries previously: "Even the smallest neglect of the traditions leads to the complete contempt for dogma."[18]

But, for all this persistence of Byzantine traditions, there was already much in late fifteenth- and sixteenth-century Muscovy that indicated a parting of the ways. It is often argued that, after the fall of the Byzantine Empire and the marriage of Ivan III with Zoë Palaeologina in 1472, Russia consciously took over the political heritage of Byzantium and that the theory of "Moscow the Third Rome," erected in the following century as an ideological superstructure on these events, represented the final triumph of Byzantine influence in Russia. Yet it is difficult to accept this conventional picture of a sixteenth-century Russia, Byzantinized afresh, absorbing and continuing the cultural and political traditions of East Rome. Of course, there can be no doubt that some Russian ideologues welcomed the theory that the seat of Imperial sovereignty had migrated to Moscow after the fall of Constantinople. But the political implications of the doctrine of "Moscow the Third Rome" do not seem to have been taken very seriously by the Tsars of that time.[19] All the attempts made by the diplomatists of the Catholic West to entice the sixteenth-century Tsars into an alliance against the Turks were ignored in Moscow, and while Pope and Holy Roman Emperor, and the Greeks themselves, were dangling before their eyes the glittering prospect of a victorious entry into Constantinople and the dream of an Orthodox Empire uniting the power of the Third Rome with the historical inheritance of the Second, the Muscovite rulers turned a deaf ear to those blandishments, and, sheltering behind the modest but authentic title of "Sovereign of All Russia," merely claimed the inheritance of the Russian lands formerly possessed by their Kievan predecessors. Here, it may be suggested, is an early example of Russia's conscious turning away from the historical heritage of Byzantium: here, in the wake of the *Realpolitik* of Ivan III and Basil III and Ivan IV, the Christian universalism of East Rome was transformed and distorted within the more narrow framework of Muscovite nationalism. The really significant fact is that the beginning of Russia's turning away from her Byzantine heritage in the late fifteenth century coincided with the growth of her connections with the West; Ivan III's marriage with Zoë was a harbinger of these connections: for the niece of the last Byzantine Emperor came to Russia from Italy accompanied by a papal legate, and the marriage had been arranged in Rome; the relations then established between Russia and Renaissance Italy were paralleled by the growing Western influences in Novgorod in the late fifteenth century, which soon spread to Moscow.[20] The policy of the Muscovite rulers of that time, of Ivan III, Basil III, and even Ivan IV, has been compared to that of their Western contemporaries, a Louis XI, a Henry VII, or a Ferdinand of Spain; and it is perhaps true to say that in their autocratic policy which relied on a growing national sentiment and on the increasing need for a strong centralized state making for order, and in the means by which they pursued it — the struggle with the great nobles — they resemble more closely the contemporary monarchs of western Europe than the former emperors of East Rome.

We must not, of course, exaggerate the importance of these early connections between Muscovy and the West: until the middle of the seventeenth century soldiers and technicians, rather than ideas and institutions, formed the bulk of the Western exports to Russia. Morever, between 1450 and 1650, with her Byzantine traditions on the wane and Western influences only slowly filtering in, Russia was developing into a world *sui generis* and fast expanding into a Eurasian Empire. Her culture, however, in these two centuries of the late Muscovite period, was still a fairly homogeneous whole and would, I believe, be still partly intelligible in terms of her Byzantine heritage. Yet in her history this was a period of transition: for when Russia, at the close of the fifteenth century, began to emerge from her "Middle Ages," she started to drift away from her Byzantine inheritance and to fall gradually into step with the political, diplomatic, and economic life of western and central Europe.

The rest of the story is better known and needs no emphasis here, save perhaps in one respect. The wholesale and spectacular policy of Westernization carried out by Peter the Great has often obscured the fact that he was merely continuing on a vaster scale and in a more drastic manner a process which had been gaining momentum in the second half of the seventeenth century. About 1650 the manners, literature, and learning of the Muscovites began to be strongly affected by the influence of Poland and of the latinized culture of the Ukraine.[21] The cultural dualism which these Western influences created in Russian society was aggravated by the schism of the Old Believers, which alienated the various streams of popular spirituality and devotion from a now partly secularized ecclesiastical hierarchy; and both these rifts — the cultural and the religious — anticipated and prepared the profounder gulf between the ruling classes and the peasantry brought about by the Westernizing and secularizing reforms of Peter the Great.

I have already suggested that from the early eighteenth century onwards Russia was living, as it were, under a dual dispensation. The upper strata of society had exchanged the Byzantine traditions of Muscovy for the education and ethos of the modern West, while the peasantry still clung to the old way of life. Yet elements of the old Byzantine tradition survived in all classes of Russian society; thus a notable section of the Russian nineteenth-century intelligentsia, the Slavophiles, for example, regarded the Orthodox tradition derived from Byzantium as their surest bulwark against the encroaching rationalism and materialism of Western "bourgeois" culture. Above all, the continuing strength of the Byzantine inheritance in modern Russia has asserted itself again and again in the form of the Orthodox Christian faith to which the peasantry and a section of the educated classes for long remained profoundly loyal; and there is no conclusive evidence to suggest that the recent attempts of their rulers to destroy or subvert this religious allegiance have met with any notable or lasting success. Especially, perhaps, the vitality of the Byzantine heritage in Russia is manifested in the liturgy, which retains a powerful hold on the mind and emotions of all those, both educated and untutored, who have

not succumbed to atheism or religious indifference, and which is one
of the greatest and original creations of Byzantine genius.

This dichotomy in the Russian culture of the eighteenth and nineteenth centuries shows that Byzantium, Russia's parent civilization,
cannot be regarded as the "intelligible field" for the study of Russian
history in this period. We have likewise examined, and rejected, the
possibility that western Europe might fulfill that purpose in respect of
these centuries. Can any other cultural unit be found to take up the
role relinquished by Byzantium?

To answer this question we must attempt a brief definition of
Byzantine civilization in terms of space and time. A compound of the
Roman, Hellenistic, and Christian traditions, it can be described in
terms of the geographical area over which its influence was once pre-
dominant. Originally limited to the territories of the East Roman
Empire, above all to the Balkans and Asia Minor, Byzantine civilization made a thrust northward into Russia shortly before most of Asia
Minor was lost to Islam. The Balkans and Russia remained its main
strongholds during the remaining part of the Middle Ages. Today the
area occupied by "the heirs of Byzantium" is basically the same, with
the addition of the territories won for Orthodox Christianity by Russia's eastward expansion; it comprises the European lands inhabited
by the Serbs, the Albanians, the Greeks, the Bulgarians, the Rumanians, and the Russians. The history of these six peoples reveals a
striking similarity which to some extent overshadows their ethnic and
linguistic differences; they are united by a common membership of the
Eastern Orthodox Church and by the powerful influence exerted by
Byzantium on their medieval culture; moreover, they were all subjected for several centuries to the rule of Asiatic empires—the Balkans
to the Ottoman, Russia to the Mongol—and on emerging from their
political servitude succumbed, gradually in the case of Russia, more
rapidly in the case of the Balkans, to the influence of west European
ideas and institutions.

It is less easy to define the limits of Byzantine civilization in time.
Its beginning can be plausibly dated from the first half of the fourth
century, for Professor Baynes has cogently argued that the distinctive
elements of this civilization were first brought together into the
melting-pot in the age of Constantine.[22] The difficulty of discovering a
corresponding *terminus ad quem* became apparent when we considered the case of Russia, where elements of Byzantine culture have
survived in various forms to the present day. It seems, however, that

these elements are too isolated from the other forms of social life to allow us to extend the effective hegemony of Byzantine civilization in Russia beyond the beginning of the eighteenth century. In the Balkans Byzantine civilization survived longer and, strange though it may seem, this was due to the Turkish conquest. No more than the Mongol rule in Russia did the *Pax Ottomanica* in the Balkans undermine the Byzantine culture of the subject peoples. In a book bearing the suggestive title of *Byzance après Byzance*,[23] the late Professor Iorga has shown the extent to which the Byzantine inheritance was kept alive among the Christian subjects of the Ottoman Empire: the Orthodox Church, the preciously guarded symbol of their former greatness, presided over by the Patriarch of Constantinople, who was recognized by the Sultan as the spiritual overlord and temporal chief of all his Orthodox Christian subjects[24] and was thus able at last to vindicate his ancient title of "Oecumenical"; the political inheritance of the former East Roman Basileis, taken over partly by the Sultans themselves, partly by the Rumanian princes of the sixteenth and seventeenth centuries who steeped themselves in the imperial tradition of Byzantium to a greater extent than their Russian contemporaries, the Muscovite Tsars; the preservation of Greek literature and Byzantine learning, fostered in the Danubian courts of the Rumanian *Domni* and the schools of the Phanariot Greeks in Constantinople— this survival of Byzantium under the Ottoman rule is a further example of the astonishing vitality and continuity of its civilization. It was not until the late eighteenth century that the East Roman heritage began to decline in the Balkans, undermined by Western influences of the Age of Enlightenment, and in the early nineteenth century, under the impact of the ideas of the French Revolution and modern nationalism, occurred what Iorga called "the death of Byzantium". Yet even then Byzantine memories continued to influence the new Balkan statesmen, and the appeal of Orthodox Christianity remained as strong among the peoples of these countries as it did in Russia.

Our attempt to determine the limits of Byzantine civilization in space and time has thus led us to conclude that Russia and the Balkan Orthodox countries, which share a common inheritance from Byzantium and whose history, despite many local differences, is similar in several important respects, can be regarded as part of one larger cultural area. It is this area that would appear to constitute the wider "Whole", the "intelligible field" against the background of which Russian history should be studied. The name "Byzantium civilization" is clearly inadequate to describe this field over the whole course of medieval and modern history, for, as we saw, the term is not applicable to Russia beyond the late seventeenth century, nor to the Balkans after the early nineteenth, in view of the more complex and heterogeneous culture of these countries in modern times.

As a term to describe this area I would suggest "Eastern Europe". At first sight it has certain disadvantages: the Balkans, from a geographical point of view, are in south-eastern rather than in eastern Europe; but this argument could be met by observing that the Iberian Peninsula, though geographically in south-western Europe, is generally included in the European "west"; the criterion in both cases is cultural rather than geographical. It might also seem unjustifiable to exclude from eastern Europe a country like Poland, which in certain periods of her history has played a prominent role in the destinies of Russia and of the Balkans; yet Poland, since the dawn of her Christian history, has derived her civilization from the Western, and particularly the Latin, world, and her cultural associations with both Russia and the Balkans have been far less intimate; indeed, there would seem to be a strong case for including Poland in central, rather than in eastern, Europe.[25]

More serious objections could be raised against the attempt to group the modern histories of Russia and the Balkans within a single unit, at least after the beginning of the eighteenth century, when Byzantine civilization, still paramount in the Balkans, had already ceased to be the "intelligible field" of Russian history. Indeed, in spite of the close relations between Muscovy and the Balkan Slavs[26] and of Russia's championship, since Peter the Great, of the cause of the Balkan Orthodox peoples, the two regions would seem to have followed divergent lines in their recent political history. Their cultural backgrounds, moreover, are far from identical, for apart from the ethnic and linguistic differences that divide the Russians from the Greeks and both from the Rumanians, the two regions have not always been subjected to the influence of the same foreign cultures. But any distinction between a "north-eastern" and a "south-eastern" Europe, however legitimate, must not obscure the essential fact that, in so far as their culture has been decisively moulded by the influence of Orthodox Christianity and Byzantine civilization and the history of their peoples has, since the Middle Ages, followed a similar pattern (subjection to an Asiatic yoke, followed by political emancipation and increasing Westernization), these two sub-areas constitute a single cultural unit, which may be conveniently termed Eastern Europe.[27]

There is, I would suggest, a further advantage in the term "Eastern Europe," and this brings me to my next point: how far can we really speak of a Byzantine, or East European, world essentially different in culture and historical inheritance from the Christian countries of the Latin and Germanic West? What was, and is, the exact nature of this relationship? Questions such as these only emphasize how inadequate our knowledge is of the relations and interdependence between different regions of Europe, particularly in the Middle Ages. If our discovery and assessment of Russia's parent civilization have any meaning, this must imply that her cultural inheritance was different in some degree from that of the countries of western and central Europe whose historical fountain-head was Rome. It is indeed the fashion today to emphasize the distinction between the cultures of Byzantium and the West, to stress the contrasts between the medieval histories of eastern and western Europe. I do not wish to deny or minimize these differences, yet there seems to be a real danger of interpreting the division between East and West in too rigid and absolute a sense. In the first place, we must not imagine that the Roman and the Byzantine spheres of influence were ever separated by a rigid geographical frontier: the medieval history of the Balkan Slavs and the fate of the Ukraine between the fourteenth and eighteenth centuries provide examples of a close relationship between Byzantine and Western cultures; while medieval Venice was, in many respects, a Byzantine enclave in a Latin world. It is also frequently argued that "the Schism of 1054", which divided Christendom into a Western and Eastern section, forever separated them by the barrier of an *odium theologicum*; and that this Schism was itself only a formal recognition of a gradually increasing rift between Byzantium and the West which began with the very birth of Byzantine civilization. But is this an adequate picture and the whole story? For all the theological disputes between Rome and Constantinople, the rivalry of conflicting jurisdictions, the differences of language, customs, and traditions, in spite even of Charlemagne's coronation as Emperor of the Romans, there is surely no convincing evidence to suggest that, at least until 1054, the majority of the churchmen and statesmen of the East and West were not conscious of belonging to one Christian Society. Would it not be truer to say that at least on two occasions, at Chalcedon in 451 and at the Festival of Orthodoxy in Constantinople in 843, the Byzantine Church triumphantly asserted against the claims of the Asian creeds—

Monophysitism and Iconoclasm—its basic heritage, Roman, Hellenistic and, as it proved, European? The often bitter contentions between the First and Second Rome are more suggestive of a fraternal rivalry for the supreme position in Christendom than of a struggle between two alien civilizations. But we can perhaps go even farther, and ask ourselves whether the consciousness of a united Christendom did not survive the very Schism of 1054. The episcopate of East Rome might have detested what it regarded as Latin innovations in the fields of dogma, ritual and ecclesiastical discipline; though its most enlightened members could still urge their flocks to feelings of charity towards their Western brethren in Christ: some forty years after the Schism the Greek Archbishop of Bulgaria, Theophylact, severely criticized his colleagues for unjustly slandering the customs of the Latin Church.[28] And the simple folk of Byzantium, how would the Schism have appeared to them? When the Roman legates laid the Papal Bull of excommunication upon the altar of Hagia Sophia, could they think that the Church of Christ was being rent in twain for at least nine centuries to come? There had been schisms and excommunications before; the schisms had been healed, the excommunications lifted; was not the Universal Church the very body of Christ? And was not Rome, for all the unorthodox teaching and claims of its pontiffs, a sacred and venerable city, a revered centre of pilgrimage containing the tomb of St. Peter, prince of the Apostles? Anna Comnena is sometimes cited as proof of the hatred and contempt entertained by the East Romans for the Latin West; and she certainly says many bitter things about the ruffians of the First Crusade who caused so much trouble to her father, the Emperor Alexius. But if you reread the *Alexiad* you will probably be struck by the difference in the tones she adopts when referring to the Crusaders and to the Bogomil heretics: these inspire her with horror and loathing; the former, for all their undesirable qualities, are still fellow-Christians. Of course, mutual antipathy and distrust between East and West increased during the twelfth century, and for this the Crusades were largely responsible. But can the picture of two mutually exclusive civilizations be reconciled with the Western influences we find in Byzantine society in the reign of Manuel Comnenus, and with the strongly pro-Latin sympathies of the Emperor, the court, and the aristocracy in the second half of the twelfth century?[29]

As one reads afresh the history of the later Roman Empire in the East one wonders sometimes whether historians have not exaggerated the importance of the events of 1054. If, in the process of gradual estrangement between Byzantium and the West, we sought for an event that seems to mark a real landmark, we could point perhaps with better reason to the climax of the Fourth Crusade; and we would probably conclude that it was then that the people of Byzantium, disgusted at the desecration of their hallowed City by men who called themselves Christians, finally turned away from their society and hardened their hearts to the West. If so, is not 1204 rather than 1054 the real date of the schism in the body of Christendom? Yet on further scrutiny and in the long run the first of these dates may well prove to have as little magical significance as the second. Among the problems of late Byzantine history which require further study there are few more crucial than the nature and scope of the relations between Byzantium and western Europe, especially Italy, in the fourteenth and fifteenth centuries. But there is no doubt that, at least in the fields of learning and art, there was close and constant interpenetration. And if we asked ourselves the question: were the relations between Byzantium and the West in the age of the Palaeologoi any less close than they had been under the Comnenian or the Macedonian dynasties — what would our answer be?

If it be in the negative, the picture we shall have of Byzantium and the medieval West will be of two different but closely interwoven halves of one Graeco-Roman Christian and European civilization. Neither half, on this reading, was in any real sense a self-contained unit or a fully "intelligible field of historical study" at least until the late fifteenth century: and if we were inclined to doubt the truth of this interpretation, we have only to think how much will remain unintelligible in the medieval history of western and central Europe unless we consider the Byzantine contributions to its culture: Anglo-Saxon scholarship of the eighth century, the Carolingian art of the ninth, Otto III's restoration of the Roman Empire, the growth of the Norman kingdom of Sicily, the cultural aftermath of the Crusades, the Italian Renaissance — these and other important events of European history cannot be understood without reference to eastern Europe. The Basilica of St. Mark in Venice, the art of Duccio and El Greco, are these not eloquent signs of how much the Western world owes to the genius of Byzantium?

If from Byzantium we turn to medieval Russia and to her relations with the West, what shall we find — mutual hostility or interpenetration? It would be easy, but hardly necessary, to show that Russia's distrust of and hostility towards the West on the political and religious planes originate in the distant past. Since the thirteenth century she has had to face and repel at least six major invasions from the West, three of which came near to destroying her national existence. It would seem natural to conclude that since the dawn of her history Russia has regarded the West as the hereditary foe, whose weapons are to be borrowed the better to resist its encroachments, and tempting to assume that she inherited this attitude from Byzantium. But the facts of early Russian history lend little support to either of these assumptions. Recent research has revealed the extent to which Rus' in the eleventh and twelfth centuries shared in the common life of Europe: trade relations with Germany, the continued immigration of Scandinavians, intermarriages between members of the Russian dynasty and those of the principal reigning families of Europe, cultural connections with Bohemia and Poland, ecclesiastical contacts with Rome — these facts of Russian history in the pre-Mongol period do not suggest any segregation from or hostility towards the nations of the West.[30] Nor did the Schism of 1054 substantially affect Russia's relations with the West, until the thirteenth century. It is true that her clergy sometimes issued warnings against the doctrinal errors of the Latins, and that anti-Roman polemical literature began to circulate in Rus' in the late eleventh and twelfth centuries. But there is a story that is better evidence of the Russians' friendly attitude to the Westerners at that time. In 1087 some Italian merchants from Bari, sailing home from Antioch, put in at the harbor of Myra, a city in Lycia on the south coast of Asia Minor. By a mixture of cunning and violence they succeeded in carrying off the relics of St. Nicholas from the basilica of the city and sailed home in triumph with this inestimable treasure. In Bari they were treated as heroes, and two years after the perpetration of this robbery the Pope instituted a new feast in the Western Church — commemorating the "translation of the relics of St. Nicholas to Bari," annually celebrated on the 9th of May. It is scarcely surprising that this feast does not occur in the calendar of the Byzantine Church: for the East Romans had every reason to regard themselves as the innocent victims of an act of brigandage. But the Russians had no such inhibitions. St. Nicholas belonged to the common heritage of Christendom; the transfer of his relics to Italy was clearly the work of Divine Providence; Bari was in any case a safer place than Myra, as Asia Minor was devastated by the Turks. It was a cause for rejoicing that one of the greatest saints of Christendom should now, by his posthumous presence, extend his special favor to the West: and so the Russian Church in its turn instituted the annual feast of "the translation of the holy relics of our father among the saints, Nicholas, the Worker of Miracles, from Myra to the city of Bari."[31] The Russian liturgical hymns of this feast, composed at the very end of the eleventh century, eloquently express the spirit of united Christendom: "The day has come of brilliant triumph, the city of Bari rejoices, and with it the whole universe exults in hymns and spiritual canticles. . . . Like a star thy relics have gone from the East to the West . . . and the city of Bari has received divine grace by thy presence. . . . If now the country of Myra is silent, the whole world, enlightened by the holy worker of miracles, invokes him with songs of praise."[32] So conscious were the Russians, half a century after the Schism, of the universal nature of the Christian Church; so little did they feel cut off from Western civilization.

We can now perhaps make a distinction in the history of Russia's relations with the West, which I believe to be important. Two different phases in these relations may be detected: the modern phase, which is commonly associated with Peter the Great, but really began in the late fifteenth century, when Russia borrowed from the West first the rudiments of technology and then, on an increasing scale, literary and philosophical trends, social ideas, and political institutions; these borrowings, as we saw, only affected a small section of the Russian people, at least until recent generations; and the early phase, in the eleventh and twelfth centuries, when the Russians were conscious of an organic link between themselves and Western Christendom. Sir John Marriott has written: "Russia is not, and has never been, a member of the European family."[33] The first of these statements may seem justified in part by recent events; the second is, I submit, a serious misrepresentation. The two phases in the history of Russia's association with the West are separated by two and a half centuries of Mongol yoke, which, by virtually severing the relations between Muscovy and western Europe, was an important cause of their long estrangement. And another turning-point in Russia's relations with the West occurred simultaneously: in the same years of the thirteenth century, when the Tatars, after their devastation and conquest of central Russia, were establishing their rule in the Ukraine, the Prince of Novgorod, Alexander Nevsky, fought back the attacks of the Swedes and the Crusading Orders of the Livonian and Teutonic Knights against the Russian Baltic frontier lands. It was now for the first time that the

West faced Russia no longer as an associate, but as a hostile force carrying eastwards its double threat of territorial conquest and militant Catholicism.

The use of the term "Eastern Europe" to describe the area over which Byzantine civilization held sway in the Middle Ages has at least the merit of emphasizing the underlying unity of the history of European Christendom. And if it be objected that this unity was broken by the incorporation of Russia and the Balkans into Asiatic empires, and that these regions were for many centuries lost to Europe, it may be said in reply that not only was the Byzantine heritage in these countries preserved intact under an alien yoke, but that the Orthodox peoples of Russia and the Balkans remained Europeans at least in so far as they successfully defended their Christian civilization against their Islamic overlords, and, by bearing the full brunt of the Asiatic conquest, made possible the cultural and material progress of their fellow-Christians in the West.[34]

A closer integration of the history of Eastern Europe into our text-books of European history — especially in regard to the Middle Ages — is, I would suggest, a matter of great importance. Unconsciously influenced perhaps by the legacy of Gibbon's contempt of Byzantium, or by the picture of Slavonic barbarism painted by some German nineteenth-century historians, are we not sometimes apt to regard western and central Europe — France, England, Germany, and Italy — as the true centers of European civilization, the primary objects of a medievalist's study? On this reading, the countries east of the Carpathians and south of the Danube seem to play the part of an appendage, or at least of an isolated and self-contained unit, in either case admitted only grudgingly and sparingly into our manuals of European history. There can be no doubt that the writing of history has suffered from this one-sided presentation. Nor are the dangers of cultural parochialism limited to the sphere of the technical historian. In the countries of the West the general public is beginning to appreciate how much our common European inheritance has been obscured, and the international life of modern Europe perverted, by the fact that history has so often during the past century been written from a nationalistic point of view. But the tendency to an egocentric reading of history may conceal dangers of a more subtle kind: the view entertained by present leaders of the Western world that in resisting aggressive totalitarianism they are defending the true values of European civilization has much to commend it; yet it may be asked whether this view would not acquire greater force and conviction if it were rid of two widespread assumptions: the notion that Western culture is identical with European civilization *tout court*, and the belief that there is something perennial and almost predetermined in the present schism in the body of Europe.

The theme of this essay was expressed in the form of three questions. Two of them we have now attempted to answer. We have examined the basic trends of Russian history in terms of Byzantine civilization and found that, at least until the end of the fifteenth century and to a more limited but still notable extent until the late seventeenth, this approach provided us with a guiding thread which made our subject "intelligible." From the eighteenth century, however, Russia's Byzantine heritage, overlaid with influences from the contemporary West, ceased to be the primary source of Russian culture, and the "intelligible field" of Russian history in this period should be widened to include the greater part of Europe. In any case the realm of Byzantine civilization, which in geographico-cultural terms, can both in medieval and modern times, be largely described as Eastern Europe, was never a self-contained unit, but should be regarded as an integral part of European Christendom. We must now, in conclusion, consider briefly our third question—the specific character of Russia's Byzantine heritage.

"Russia's Byzantine heritage" is the title of a chapter in Professor Toynbee's book *Civilization on Trial*.[35] The author stresses the continuity in Russian history and argues that, for all the sweeping changes introduced by Peter the Great and Lenin, the Russia of today still preserves some salient features of her Byzantine past. It is well that we should be reminded of this continuity, which underlies the changing pattern of revolution and reform, and preserved, even in the Russia of Stalin, something at least of the thought-world of Byzantium. Yet I believe that not all students of Russian history will be able to accept Professor Toynbee's view as to the nature of Russia's Byzantine inheritance. In his opinion the rulers of Soviet Russia have inherited from Byzantium a state of mind and an institution: the conviction that they are chosen to inherit the earth and are hence always in the right; and the structure of the totalitarian state. I shall not here discuss in detail the origin of this outlook and this institution, both of which undoubtedly exist in the Soviet Union today. But Professor Toynbee's thesis is so relevant to our present subject that I feel impelled to cite some of my reasons for believing that, at least without serious qualification, it is likely to mislead.

A totalitarian state, for Professor Toynbee, is one "that has established its control over every side of the life of its subjects"; the proof of the totalitarian nature of the Byzantine polity lies in the fact that its emperors succeeded in making the Orthodox Church of the Empire "virtually a department of the medieval East Roman state"; this enslavement of the spiritual by the temporal he calls "Caesaro-papism." Caesaro-papism, in his view, had the disastrous effect of stunting and crushing Byzantine civilization and transmitted to medieval Russia the seeds of totalitarianism; cultivated in the political laboratory of the rulers of Muscovy, these seeds later yielded a harvest under the Soviet régime. Professor Toynbee has argued his conception of Byzantine "Caesaro-papism" at considerable length in the fourth volume of his *Study of History*;[36] the problem is clearly of the greatest importance, for the view we take of the relationship between Church and State in Byzantium will inevitably color some of our basic notions of East European history, both in the Middle Ages and in more recent times.

It would be impossible, within the span of two paragraphs, to attempt a detailed criticism of Professor Toynbee's thesis. But I venture to suggest that neither of these formulae—Caesaro-papism or totalitarianism—is an adequate description of the complex relations that existed in Byzantium between the Emperor and the Church. It is true that: (1) in the Byzantine society the Emperor occupied a supreme and sacrosanct position; (2) the canons and rules of the Church required his sanction before they became effective; (3) he could generally in the last resort depose a recalcitrant patriarch; (4) some emperors claimed the authority of defining ecclesiastical dogma; and (5) the freedom of the Church frequently suffered from their heavy-handed patronage. But each of these statements has its own significant counterpart: (1) the conception of the Emperor as "the living law" and of his sovereignty as the earthly reflection of divine wisdom and power, borrowed by Eusebius from the Hellenistic pagan philosophers, was accepted in Byzantium, but it was generally infused with a Christian interpretation, so that the notion of the Emperor as vicegerent of God, without losing any of its original force, shades off — through the idea of his duty as Defender of the Faith — into the obligation generally assumed after the sixth century by the Emperor at his coronation to preserve untainted the Orthodox faith, and later, to "remain the faithful and true servant and son of Holy Church."[37] (2) The canons of the Church were drawn up and issued by the ecclesiastical Councils: the Basileus only sanctioned and enforced them. (3) On the occasions of conflict with the Church authorities, the emperors often seemed victorious on the surface; but usually in the end, and increasingly so from the ninth century onwards, the Church would vindicate her inner freedom and her right to impose the moral law on the Emperor. Professor Toynbee himself admits that "every famous Western champion of the rights of the Church has his counterpart and peer in Orthodox Christendom."[38] (4) The Imperial claims to define dogma, occasionally asserted, were in general regarded by the Church as an intolerable abuse and, in the long run, successfully resisted; and (5) it is significant that these attempts, due not so much to the emperors' desire to enslave the Church as to their wish to enforce compromise solutions with a view to preserving peace and unity within the State or securing military aid from the West, were always in the end defeated by the refusal of the Church to tamper with the purity of the Orthodox faith. The antithesis between these two sets of propositions constitutes perhaps the crucial problem in any study of the relations between Church and State in Byzantium. And it may be suggested that the solution of this still controversial question might be approached by an attempt to transcend both Professor Toynbee's interpretation of Byzantine Caesaro-papism and, at the opposite extreme, the recent assertion that "the religious history of Byzantium could be represented as a conflict between Church and the State, a conflict from which the Church emerged unquestionably the victor."[39] Any true solution of this problem, I would suggest, must rest on three essential and often neglected facts: firstly, in spite of the interpenetration of the spiritual and temporal spheres in Byzantine society, there always existed in the mind of the Church an unbridgeable gulf between the competence of the State and the sanctifying and saving functions of the Church; secondly, the Emperor's sovereignty was limited — intrinsically, by its subordination to Divine Law and the duties of "philanthropy" incumbent upon him, and extrinsically, by the spiritual authority of the East Roman bishop and the moral authority of the ascetic holy man;[40] and thirdly, whilst the attitude of the Church to the Christian Empire remained substantially the same, the attitude of the State to the Church appears to have undergone a significant change, from the heavy-handed intervention of the early Byzantine emperors in ecclesiastical affairs, through the bitter struggles of the Iconoclast period, to the ninth-century settlement, expressed in Basil I's *Epanagoge*: "As the Commonwealth consists of parts and members, by analogy with an individual man, the greatest and most necessary parts are the Emperor and the Patriarch. Wherefore agreement in all things and harmony (συμφωνία) between the Imperium and the Sacerdotium bring peace and prosperity to the souls and the bodies of the subjects."[41] "Parallelism" and "symphony" between Church and State — are these formulae not a more faithful reflection of the Byzantine mind than Caesaropapism or totalitarianism?

And in medieval Russia it was the same: here too, in spite of local differences, Church and State remained bound by the same twofold relationship which is implicit in the Byzantine *Epanagoge*:[42] parallelism and virtual equality on the one hand, indissoluble unity of purpose on the other. Sometimes, as in the thirteenth and fourteenth centuries when the secular power was weak and decentralized, the Church assumed a preponderance in public affairs; sometimes, as in the sixteenth century, the State, in the person of the all-powerful monarch, would impinge upon the sphere of ecclesiastical jurisdiction. But generally speaking, after each of these oscillations the pendulum would swing back, and in the end the balance would be restored in accordance with the Byzantine theory. The most autocratic Tsars of Muscovy cannot be described as totalitarian rulers; for they, too, like the Byzantine Basileis, were forced to respect the doctrinal supremacy and moral authority of the Church. The seeds of Russian totalitarianism were sown by Peter the Great. It was he who first began to enforce the State's claim to be recognized as the source of all authority in the realm, the ultimate object of men's loyalty. Inevitably this led to the curtailment of the Church's freedom and to its partial secularization. For two centuries between 1721 and 1917 something akin to Caesaro-papism could be found Russia. But it is significant that this partial subjection of the Russian Church to the imperial power was brought about by Peter's imitation of western Lutheran models, and that to carry out his reforms he was forced to try and break down that Byzantine relationship between Church and State which was Russia's medieval legacy from East Rome.[43]

Professor Toynbee's other thesis—his claim that the Soviet Russians have inherited Byzantium's intolerance of the West— also, I would suggest, requires considerable qualification. There is, of course, a measure of truth in this comparison. It would be hard to deny the resemblance between the messianic *credo* of the Russian Communist party and the belief of the Byzantines in their Universal Empire, destined to unite all the Christians of the earth under the sacred sceptre of the Basileus. Both attitudes reflect something of a mixture of faith and politics. Both are strongly intolerant of rivals and opponents. The Bolshevik party has often reserved its fiercest hatred not so much for the capitalists of the West as for the other Socialist parties who, with programs different from its own, are deviationists and traitors to the Cause. The Byzantines were so deeply repelled by the theological innovations of the Latin West that a few months before the fall of the Empire a high dignitary could publicly declare that he would "rather see ruling over Constantinople the turban of the Turks than the Latin mitre."[44] And when Constantinople fell to the Turks in 1453 and, as it seemed to men of that time, the Imperial legacy of Byzantium was proudly assumed by the autocrats of Russia, it was Moscow, the Third Rome, that became the unique repository of the Orthodox faith and its guardian against the heretical West. It would be difficult to resist the impression that there is at least something in common between the religious messianism of the Second and Third Rome and the belief of the Russian Communist in the exclusive truth of the Marxist Gospel, immortally enshrined in the collected works of Marx, Engels, Lenin, and Stalin. Yet this simile, in my opinion, should not be pushed too far: it may give us some insight into the psychological background of contemporary Russia; if taken as a full explanation, it may become a real obstacle to our understanding of both Russia and Byzantium. Historical continuity, like most other facts, is subject to the laws of change, development, and decline. From Byzantine universalism to Russian religious nationalism, and from the latter to the doctrine of world revolution, the change is very great; some indeed, may be tempted to regard it as a gradual debasement. There is, surely, at least one important difference between the intolerance of Byzantium and that of the Kremlin. The latter brand has, at least so far, expressed itself in hatred and violence: all means can legitimately be employed in pursuit of the final goal. That was not so in Byzantium: hatred of the West could sometimes be found there, no doubt, but it was not a hatred of Western culture nor of the Western way of life, but rather a bitter resentment against the barbarians of the Fourth Crusade, who, under the pretext of securing their advance to the East, had stormed and looted the Imperial capital. Byzantine intolerance was not usually aggressive: rather was it due to the pride felt by the East Romans in their own achievement: for centuries they had resolutely and successfully defended their way of life against the barbarians hammering at the gate, and the purity of their Christian faith against all attempts to tamper with Orthodoxy. The Byzantines were deeply attached to their religion: there could be no compromise in matters of faith; and some of them were doubtless sincere in preferring to see their capital under the heel of the Turk than their Church forced to subscribe to the unacceptable doctrines of the Papacy. It has been well said that "Byzantine intolerance is in its essence an affair of the spirit."[45] It is, I think, important that we should remind ourselves of this difference between Communist Moscow and Christian Byzantium.

It may even be doubted whether any historical connection can really be found between the "intolerance" of Byzantium and that of the contemporary Russian Marxists. It is fashionable today to trace the roots of the Soviet leaders' hostility towards the West back to the distant past, through the anti-Western feelings of a section of the nineteenth-century intelligentsia to Muscovite "messianism" and thence to Byzantine Orthodoxy. But the historian may feel justifiably doubtful of the validity of a method which, as I have suggested, results only too often in a process of "reading back" the origin of modern Russian ideas and institutions to a hypothetical or imaginary Byzantine past. It cannot be the purpose of this essay to discover the origins of the present Soviet attitude towards the West. But one final question may be asked in this connection: was not that criticism of modern "European" culture, which we find in the writings of several prominent Russian thinkers of the nineteenth century, itself largely a Western rather than a Russian, product?

If neither totalitarianism nor a messianic intolerance of the West forms part of Russia's Byzantine heritage, can another formula be found to express the true nature of this inheritance? We have in the course of this essay gained a glimpse at several fields in which Byzantine civilization exerted a deep and lasting influence upon Russia. But there is one feature of this heritage which, I would suggest, informs and epitomizes the rest. This feature is best revealed in Russian history of the Kievan period. Then, as we saw, with her doors open to the influence of Byzantium, Rus' was also closely linked with central and western Europe, by trade, culture, and diplomacy, above all by the consciouness of belonging to one world of Christendom, where, in the main, there was still no Hellene nor Latin, but a common culture and a common faith. It is significant that Russia entered the European family of nations through her conversion to Christianity, for which she is indebted to Byzantium. The heritage of East Rome was not, as it is sometimes suggested, Russia's "mark of the beast" that isolated her from medieval Europe: it was the main channel through which she became a European nation. Byzantium was not a wall, erected between Russia and the West: she was Russia's gateway to Europe.

FOOTNOTES ON CHAPTER III

[1] Based on two lectures delivered at Oxford in February, 1949.

[2] Marc Bloch, "Apologie pour l'histoire ou métier d'historien," *Cahier des Annales*, no. 3 (Paris, 1949), pp. 5-9.

[3] Arnold J. Toynbee, *A Study of History* (2nd ed., London, Oxford University Press, 1948), i. 17-26.

[4] Cf. M. de Taube, "À propos de 'Moscou, troisième Rome,'" *Russie et Chrétienté*, nos. 3-4 (Paris, 1948), pp. 17-24.

[5] William Palmer, *The Patriarch and the Tsar*, (London, 1873), ii., 175.

[6] Toynbee, *op. cit.*, i., 23.

[7] On the "Eurasians," see the provocative article by D. S. Mirsky, "The Eurasian Movement" (*Slavonic Review*, vol. vi, no. 17 (1927), pp. 311-19) and the more balanced account by B. Ishboldin, "The Eurasian Movement" (*Russian Review*, vol. v, n. 2 (1946), pp. 64-73).

[8] See the discussion of the Mongol impact on Russia by G. Vernadsky (*The Mongols and Russia*, New Haven, 1953, pp. 333-90), who makes the interesting and plausible suggestion that "in some respects, the direct Tatar influence on Russian life increased rather than decreased after Russia's emancipation" (p. 335).

[9] Ivan Timofeev, in S. F. Platonov, *Drevnerusskiya skazaniya i povesti o smutnom vremeni XVII veka, kak istoricheski istochnik* (2nd ed., St. Petersburg, 1913), p. 206; *Vremennik Ivana Timofeeva*, ed. O. A. Derzhavina and V. P. Adrianova-Peretts (Moscow, 1951), p. 162.

[10] For the culture of Kievan Rus' and its Byzantine foundations see: André Mazon, "Byzance et la Russie," *Revue d'histoire de la philosophie et d'histoire générale de la civilisation*, fasc. 19 (Lille, 1937), pp. 261-77; G. P. Fedotov, *The Russian Religious Mind: Kievan Christianity* (Cambridge, Mass., 1946); B. D. Grekov, *The Culture of Kiev Rus* (Moscow, 1947) (in English); G. Vernadsky, *Kievan Russia* (New Haven, 1948); A. Meyendorff and N. H. Baynes, "The Byzantine Inheritance in Russia," in *Byzantium*, ed. N. H. Baynes and H. St. L. B. Moss (Oxford, 1948), pp. 369-91, and the bibliography on pp. 417-21; D. Obolensky, *The Byzantine Commonwealth* (St. Vladimir's Press, 1982), pp. 309-52.

[11] B. H. Sumner, *Survey of Russian History* (2nd ed., London, 1947), p. 178.

[12] The expression is borrowed from Professor Norman Baynes, whose two lectures, *The Hellenistic Civilization and East Rome* (London, Oxford University Press, 1946) and *The Thought-world of East Rome*(ibid., 1947), form an admirable introduction to the study of medieval Russian culture. They are reprinted in Baynes' *Byzantine Studies and other Essays* (London, 1955).

[13] The expression "relapse into barbarism" is used by Professor Toynbee to describe the consequences of the shift of Russia's political centre from Kiev to the upper Volga region, an event which he dates to the last quarter of the eleventh century, i.e. some 150 years prior to the Mongol conquest (*A Study of History*, vi. 309). Apart from the fact that he antedates this shift by at least half a century, it is scarcely justifiable to speak of a "relapse into barbarism" in the north-eastern region of pre-Mongol Rus'. The whole of this area was closely connected with the southern civilization of Kiev, and the twelfth- and early thirteenth-century architecture of the Suzdal' and Vladimir region remains one of the finest achievements in the history of Russian art. Cf. Vernadsky, *Kievan Russia*, pp. 259-61; N. Voronin, "Kul'tura Vladimiro-Suzdal'skoy zemli XI-XIII vekov," *Istoricheski Zhurnal*, vol. iv (Moscow, 1944), pp. 35-43; *Pamyatniki Vladimiro-Suzdal'skogo zodchestva XI-XIII vekov* (Moscow, 1945); D. R. Buxton, *Russian Medieval Architecture* (Cambridge, 1934), pp. 24-7.

[14] For an account of Russian thirteenth-century literature see V. M. Istrin, *Ocherk istorii drevnerusskoy literatury domoskovskogo perioda* (Petrograd, 1922), pp. 199-248; for the Balkan influences on Russian fourteenth- and fifteenth-century literature see N. K. Gudzy, *History of Early Russian Literature*, trans. by S. W. Jones (New York, 1949), pp. 232-43; cf. P. Kovalevsky, *Manuel d'histoire russe* (Paris, 1948), pp. 94-102, for an attempt to justify the term "Russian Renaissance of the fourteenth century." For the spiritual tradition of medieval Russia see N. Zernov, *St. Sergius— Builder of Russia* (London, n.d.); *A Treasury of Russian Spirituality*, ed. G. P. Fedotov (London, 1950), pp. 50-133. For the Novgorod painting of the fourteenth and fifteenth centuries see N. P. Kondakov, *The Russian Icon*, trans. by E. H. Minns (Oxford, 1927), pp. 71-100; L. Réau, *L'Art russe des origines à Pierre le Grand* (Paris, 1921), pp. 136-95; C. Diehl, *Manuel d'art byzantin*, vol. ii (Paris, 1926), pp. 836-40, 870-2. See now J. Meyendorff, *Byzantium and the Rise of Russia* (Cambridge, 1981).

[15]Professor Vernadsky, on the contrary, suggests a sociological parallel between the Kievan and the "Imperial" periods of Russian history; he compares the rift which the reforms of Peter the Great helped to create between the Westernized upper classes and the conservative peasantry to the cleavage caused by Russia's conversion to Christianity between the Christian and the pagan sections of the community; both process, he maintains, "affected first the upper classes of society and accentuated the cultural cleavage between the élite and the masses" (*Kievan Russia*, pp. 241-2). It is true that in Russia the eleventh and twelfth centuries were to some extent a period of "cultural dualism," but the comparison should not be pressed too far. The cleavage created in Russian society by the increasing Westernization after the middle of the seventeenth century proved deep and permanent, at least until the present century. Christianity, on the other hand, "gradually enveloped more and more of the various social strata," as Vernadsky himself admits. Nor was the distinction between Christianity and paganism in medieval Russia a distinction between the upper classes and "the masses," even in the Kievan period: the former retained something of the pagan ethos at least as late as the end of the twelfth century, as is evident in the *Lay of Igor's Campaign*; and, on the other hand, Christianity seems to have spread fairly rapidly among the peasantry soon after Vladimir's conversion, partly, no doubt, owing to the Slavonic liturgy and translation of the Scriptures.

[16]Joseph, Abbot of Volokolamsk: *Prosvetitel'* (4th ed., Kazan, 1904), p. 547.

[17]Avvakum, *Zhitie*, ed. by N. K. Gudzy (Moscow, 1934), pp. 138-9; cf. *The Life of the Archpriest Avvakum by himself*, trans. by Jane Harrison and Hope Mirrlees (London, 1924), p. 132; *La Vie de l'Archiprêtre Avvakum, écrite par lui-même*, traduite par Pierre Pascal (Paris, 1938), p. 185.

[18]Photius, Ep. 13, Migne, *Patrologia Graeca*, vol. cii, col. 724D; quoted in Baynes, *The Thought-world of East Rome*, p. 10.

[19]D. Likhachev goes as far as to claim (*Kul'tura Rusi epokhi obrazovaniya russkogo natsional'nogo gosudarstva* (Moscow, 1946), p. 32), that in no extant official Russian document, or even diplomatic correspondence, of the fifteenth or sixteenth centuries, is Moscow described as the heir of Byzantium. Yet in the Paschal Tables compiled by the Metropolitan Zosima in 1492 the Grand Duke of Moscow, Ivan III, is described as "the new Emperor Constantine of the new City of Constantine—Moscow" (see M. D'yakonov, *Vlast' moskovskikh gosudarey* (St. Petersburg, 1889), pp. 64-6; D. Stremoou-khoff, "Moscow the Third Rome: Sources of the Doctrine," *Speculum*, vol. xxviii, 1953, p. 91). However, the political implications of the doctrine of "Moscow the Third Rome" seem to have been ignored by the Russian statesmen of the time: cf. N. Chaev, "'Moskva—Treti Rim' v politicheskoy praktike moskovskogo pravitel'stva XVI veka," *Istoricheskie Zapiski*, vol. xvii (Moscow, 1945), pp. 3-23; G. Olšr, "Gli ultimi Rurikidi e le basi ideologiche della sovranità dello Stato russo," *Orientalia Christiana Periodica*, vol. xii (Rome, 1946), pp. 322-73.

[20]The relation between the growth of Western influence and the decline of Byzantine traditions in fifteenth- and sixteenth-century Muscovy is discussed by Fr. George Florovsky in *Puti russkago bogosloviya* (Paris, 1937), pp. 414-29; Engl. transl. in his *Collected Works*, V (Belmont, Mass., 1979).

[21]L. R. Lewitter, "Poland, the Ukraine and Russia in the 17th century," *Slavonic Review*, vol. xxvii, no. 68 (Dec. 1948), pp. 157-71; no. 69 (May 1949), pp. 414-29. See now "The Kiev Mohyla Academy," *Harvard Ukrainian Studies*, VIII, 1-2 (1985).

[22]N. H. Baynes, *The Byzantine Empire* (Home University Library, London, 1939), pp. 7-10; *Byzantium*, pp. xv-xx.

[23]N. Iorga, *Byzance après Byzance* (Bucharest, 1935). Cf. S. Runciman, *The Great Church in Captivity* (Cambridge, 1968).

[24]With the temporary exception of the Serbs, who preserved an independent ecclesiastical organization until 1459, and again between 1557 and 1766, and of the Bulgarians, whose autonomous Archbishopric of Ohrid was abolished in 1767.

[25]Professor O. Halecki's book *The Limits and Divisions of European History* (London and New York, 1950) deals with several problems touched upon in this chapter, particularly with the relationship between western and eastern Europe. The author argues convincingly that "Eastern Europe...is no less European than Western Europe" (p. 121), but his definition of eastern Europe is far from clear. He suggests two different methods of dividing Europe into geographico-cultural areas. The first method is based on a twofold division between a "western" and an "eastern" Europe, the latter including Poland, Hungary, Rumania, the Balkans, and the land of the Eastern Slavs in "those periods of their past which are definitely European" (p. 110): these would consist of Kievan Rus' of the eleventh and twelfth centuries and of the west Rus' lands of the Ukraine and White Russia which were incorporated in the fourteenth century into the Grand Duchy of Lithuania. The second method involves a fourfold distinction between western, "west-central," "east-central," and eastern Europe.

"East-central" Europe is taken to consist of Czechoslovakia, Hungary, Poland, Finland, Rumania, and the Balkan peninsula; eastern Europe, in this classification, should be equated either with the Ukraine and White Russia (but only when they are liberated from the political control of Soviet Russia) or with Great Russia, "if and when Russia is considered part of Europe" (p. 137). Both these methods of classification result in the exclusion from Europe of Muscovy, the Russian Empire, and the Soviet Union, and in a complete cultural separation between these successive epiphanies of a Eurasian Empire on the one hand and the essentially "European" regions of the Ukraine and White Russia on the other.

Professor Halecki's interpretation of Russian history is undoubtedly the weakest part of his valuable book. In the first place, his attempts to justify the exclusion of Muscovite and Imperial Russia from European civilization (pp. 92-9) are far from convincing, and he himself seems to experience some doubts as to the validity of his thesis when applied to the eighteenth and nineteenth centuries. Moreover, the opposition between a "European" Ukraine and a Great Russian "Muscovia," so favored by modern Ukrainian historians and now by Professor Halecki, rests on several historical misinterpretations which have often been pointed out by leading Russian historians. It is astonishing to find the opposite view, which includes the history of the Ukraine and of White Russia in the general course of Russian history, summarily dismissed by the author as a theory held only by "some Russian scholars" (p. 137). To try and trace the frontier of Europe along an imaginary borderline between the Ukraine and White Russia on the one hand and Muscovite Great Russia on the other is to do violence to historical facts. Finally, it is surely inconsistent to claim, as Professor Halecki does, that while Russia was permanently "cut off from Europe" by the Mongol conquest (p. 93), the Christian nations of the Balkans, similiarly placed outside Europe by the Turkish invasion, were "reunited with Europe" after their liberation from the Ottoman yoke (p. 120). In fact, the Ottoman rule in the Balkans lasted twice as long and was considerably more effective than the Mongol domination of Russia. In both cases, as I have suggested, the Christians of eastern Europe preserved their faith, their Byzantine heritage, and their essentially European culture under the Asiatic yoke; and their political liberation was accompanied and followed by an influx of influence from Western Europe.

[26]M. N. Tikhomirov, "Istoricheskie svyazi russkogo naroda s yuzhnymi slavyanami s drevney-shikh vremen do poloviny XVII veka," *Slavyanski Sbornik* (Moscow, 1947), pp. 125-201.

[27]The problem of defining the notion of Eastern Europe has led to some controversy, in which Czech and Polish historians have played a leading role. See: J. Bidlo, "L'Europe orientale et le domaine de son histoire," *Le Monde Slave* (Paris, 1935), tome iv, pp. 1-20, 204-33; "Ce qu'est l'histoire de l'Orient européen, quelle en est l'importance et quelles furent ses étapes," *Bulletin d'Information des sciences historiques en Europe Orientale* (Warsaw, 1934), tome vi, pp. 11-73; M. Handelsman, "Quelques remarques sur la définition de l'histoire de l'Europe orientale," ibid., pp. 74-81; O. Halecki, "Qu'est-ce que l'Europe orientale?", ibid., pp. 82-93; G. Vernadsky, *Kievan Russia*, pp. 9-12; and other articles by Halecki cited in his book *The Limits and Divisions of European History*, p. 205.

[28]Theophylact, Archbishop of Ohrid, *Liber de iis quorum Latini incusantur:* Migne, *Patrologia Graeca*, vol. cxxvi, cols. 221-49; Theophylacti Achridensis *Opera*, ed. P. Gautier (Thessalonica, 1980), pp. 247-85; D. Obolensky, *Six Byzantine Portraits* (Oxford, 1988), pp. 41-5. Cf. B. Leib, *Rome, Kiev et Byzance à la fin du XIᵉ siècle* (Paris, 1924), pp. 41-50.

[29]Cf. N. Iorga, *Relations entre l'Orient et l'Occident* (Paris, 1923), pp. 168-81; C. Diehl, *La Société Byzantine à l'époque des Comnènes* (Paris, 1929), pp. 75-90.

[30]See F. Dvornik, "The Kiev State and its Relations with Western Europe," *Transactions of the Royal Historical Society*, vol. xxix (1947), pp. 27-46; *The Making of Central and Eastern Europe* (London, 1949), pp. 236-61; Vernadsky, *Kievan Russia*, pp. 317-47.

[31]For the "Translation of the Relics of St. Nicholas" see Leib, *Rome, Kiev et Byzance à la fin du XIᵉ siècle*, pp. 51-74. For the possible role played by Russian Varangians in south Italy as intermediaries between Bari and Rus', see Vernadsky, op. cit., pp. 345-6.

[32]*Menologion der orthodox-katholischen Kirche des Morgenlandes*, ed. Rev. A. v. Malzew, ii (Berlin, 1901), 281-22. Cf. Leib, op. cit., pp. 70-2.

[33]Sir J. A. R. Marriott, *Anglo-Russian Relations, 1689-1943* (2nd ed., London, 1944), p. 1.

[34]Since this paper was written, my views on the European foundations of Russian culture have been reinforced by the remarks in Mr. W. Weidlé's admirable book *La Russie absente et présente* (Paris, 1949) (English transl.: *Russia, Absent and Present*, London, 1952, pp. 1-14), and by the arguments of Mr. Sumner ("Russia and Europe," *Oxford Slavonic Papers*, II, 1951, pp. 1016).

[35]Arnold J. Toynbee, *Civilization on Trial* (London, Oxford University Press, 1948), pp. 164-83 (first published in *Horizon*, August 1947).

[36] Toynbee, *A Study of History*, iv. 320-408, 592-623.

[37] Ps.-Kodinos, *Traité des Offices*, ed. J. Verpeaux (Paris, 1966), p. 253. Cf. L. Bréhier, *Les Institutions de l'Empire Byzantin* (Paris, 1949), pp. 9-10.

[38] Toynbee, op. cit., iv., 594.

[39] Henri Grégoire, in *Byzantium* (ed. Baynes and Moss), p. 130.

[40] On this point I am indebted to Fr. Gervase Mathew's course of lectures on "Church and State in the Byzantine Empire," delivered at Oxford in the autumn of 1949.

[41] *Epanagoge*, tit. iii, cap. 8; Ed. Zachariae von Lingenthal, *Collectio librorum juris graeco-romani ineditorum* (Leipzig, 1852), p. 68.

[42] For the influence of the *Epanagoge* in Russia see V. Sokol'sky, "O kharaktere i znachenii Epanagogi," *Vizantiiski Vremennik* (St. Petersburg, 1894), i., 17-54; G. Vernadsky, "Die kirchlich-politische Lehre der Epanagoge und ihr Einfluss auf das russische Leben im XVII. Jahrhundert," *Byzantinisch-Neugriechische Jahrbücher* (Athens, 1928), vi. 119-42; W. K. Medlin, *Moscow and East Rome* (Geneva, 1952), pp. 69-71, 109-12, 133, 171, 177-9, 191, 232-3.

[43] In two footnotes in his *Study of History* (iii, 283, n. 2, and iv., 398, n. 2) Professor Toynbee admits the Western origin of Peter's ecclesiastical reform ("Peter borrowed his 'totalitarian state,' 'Caesaro-papism' and all, from the contemporary West"), but in his *Civilization on Trial* this essential fact is ignored.

[44] Ducas (*Historia Turcobyzantina*, (Bucharest, 1958), p. 329) ascribes these words to the Grand Duke Lucas Notaras. Their authenticity, however, is impugned by Professor C. Amantos (*La Prise de Constantinople*: in "Le Cinq-centième anniversaire de la prise de Constantinople" (*L'Hellénisme Contemporain*, fascicule hors série) Athens, 1953, pp. 10-11).

[45] Henri Grégoire, in *Byzantium* (ed. Baynes and Moss), p. 132.

CHAPTER IV

BYZANTIUM, KIEV AND MOSCOW:
A STUDY IN ECCLESIASTICAL RELATIONS*

Among the many still unresolved problems that confront the historian of medieval Eastern Europe is that of the precise nature of the relationship between the Church of Russia and the Patriarchate of Constantinople. This gap in our knowledge is due to the scantiness and vagueness of the relevant sources: Byzantine writers, at least before the fourteenth century, show themselves singularly uncommunicative about the Russian Church; while the early Russian chroniclers are almost equally reticent on the ecclesiastical affairs of their country, and especially on the relations of their Church with the Byzantine Patriarchate.

One fact stands out, uncontroverted and well-known: from 1039, when a Byzantine prelate is mentioned in Kiev,[1] to 1448, when the Russian bishops, severing their dependence on the Unionist Patriarch of Constantinople, elected their own primate, the Russian Church was a metropolitan diocese of the Byzantine Patriarchate. Was this so from the beginning, and can this direct subordination of the Russian Church to Byzantium be traced during the half-century that followed the official acceptance of Christianity by Prince Vladimir of Kiev in 988 or 989?[2] In the absence of explicit and contemporary evidence on this point, controversy has raged, and some of the advocates in this *cause célèbre* are still in the field. It is not the purpose of this article to discuss the conflicting theories of those scholars who have sought to prove—unsuccessfully in my opinion—that Vladimir's church was dependent on the Bulgarian Patriarchate of Ohrid; subject to Rome; or autocephalous.[3] The ingenuity and learning with which these

---

Dumbarton Oaks Papers, XI (1957), 23-78.

hypotheses have sometimes been argued cannot gainsay the circumstantial evidence which strongly suggests that the Russian Church was
from the beginning directly subordinated to the Patriarchate of
Byzantium: the statement of the eleventh-century Arab historian
Yahya of Antioch that the Emperor Basil II sent to Vladimir of Rus'
"metropolitan and bishops" who baptized him and his people;[4] the
role played by the Greek clergy of the Crimea in the christianization
of Rus', the building of Vladimir's first stone church in Kiev by
Byzantine architects, his marriage with Anna, the Emperor's sister,[5]
his assumption at baptism of the name Basil, doubtless a symbol of
his spiritual adoption by the Emperor:[6] surely these facts create a
strong presumption in favor of the view that Vladimir's church was
placed under East Roman authority.[7]

This contemporary, if indirect, evidence is confirmed by the
explicit testimony of a fourteenth-century Byzantine historian whose
relevance to the problem under discussion does not seem to have been
justly appreciated. Nicephorus Gregoras, in the thirty-sixth book of
his Ἱστορία Ῥωμαϊκή, in which he deals at length with the past and
contemporary history of the Russian Church, writes: "from the time
when this nation [i.e. the Russians] embraced holy religion and
received the divine baptism of the Christians, it was laid down once
for all that it would be under the jurisdiction of one bishop . . . ; and
that this primate would be subject to the See of Constantinople, and
would receive from it the laws of the spiritual authority."[8]

This text is so clear and explicit that its neglect by historians seems
at first surprising. Yet the evidence of so late a writer must clearly be
treated with considerable caution; it is possible, moreover, that, by
appealing to a tradition of so venerable an antiquity, Gregoras was
concerned in this passage to support the claims over the Russian
Church which were being pressed with renewed vigor by the Byzantine Patriarchate toward the middle of the fourteenth century; and at
least one expression in this passage seems inspired by the ecclesiastical
polemics of the time.[9] Yet there do not appear to be adequate grounds
for refusing all credence to this statement of Gregoras. Biased as he
sometimes is, his knowledge of Russian affairs is, as will be shown
below, extensive and on the whole accurate; and, in this case at least,
his testimony on the earliest organization of the Russian Church is
supported by the evidence already cited.

In a passage of the thirty-sixth book of the Ἱστορία Ῥωμαϊκή
which immediately follows the one quoted above, Nicephorus Grego-

ras makes an even more remarkable statement. Referring to the primate (ἀρχιερέα) of the Russian Church and to the time when the Russians were converted to Christianity, he writes: "it was laid down that he would be taken alternately now from that nation [i.e.from the Russians], now from those who were both born and brought up here [i.e. in Byzantium], each primate always being raised to the throne there, after the death of the previous incumbent, by alternate succession, in order that the link between the two nations, thus secured and ratified, might forever preserve the unity of faith pure and undefiled, and find an increased stability for its existence and its strength."[10]

The language of this passage may be rather involved and pleonastic, but its meaning is clear beyond doubt: Gregoras is asserting that when the Russians were officially converted to Christianity—that is in 988 or 989 — an agreement was concluded between the authorities of Constantinople and Kiev — in other words between the Emperor Basil II and Vladimir I — by the terms of which the primates of the Russian Church — i.e. the metropolitans of Kiev — were for all times to be appointed according to the principle of alternate nationality, a native Russian succeeding a Byzantine, and vice-versa. This alternation is explicitly referred to three times in this short passage and is emphasized by the terms ἀμοιβαδόν and παραλλάξ.[11]

The importance of this passage was perceived as early as 1851 by V. Parisot, the first editor of the thirty-sixth book of Gregoras' *History*.[12] He accepted Gregoras' statement as true, but his insufficiently critical approach to this passage, and his somewhat sketchy knowledge of Russian history did not lead him to any very clear or positive conclusions.[13] In 1889 the Russian historian M. D'yakonov quoted this passage as something of a curiosity and, in the absence of corroborative evidence to support Gregoras' statement, was cautious in assessing its historical value.[14] Finally in 1913 another Russian scholar, P. Sokolov, ridiculed the attempt to read into this passage any reference to an alternation in the nationality of the metropolitans of Kiev.[15] As far as I am aware, in no subsequent work of scholarship was this passage discussed.

The negative attitude of Sokolov, and the silence of recent historians are understandable, for Parisot's edition of the sixth book of Gregoras' *History*, from which this passage has been quoted, was superseded in 1855 (four years later) by the Bonn edition of the third volume of the complete *History*, which contains this passage in a mutilated form; six words are missing, and they are precisely the crucial words which refer to the alternation in the nationality of the primates of the Russian Church; Parisot's edition reads: εἶναι δ᾽ αὐτὸν καὶ νῦν μὲν ἐκ τοῦ γένους ἐκείνου, νῦν δ᾽ ἐκ τῶν τῇδε φύντων ὁμοῦ καὶ τραφέντων. The Bonn edition reads: εἶναι δ᾽ αὐτὸν καὶ νῦν μὲν ἐκ τῶν τῇδε φύντων ὁμοῦ καὶ τραφέντων.[16]

It is not surprising that historians, who since 1855 have tended to read the thirty-sixth book of the *History* in the Bonn edition rather than in Parisot's earlier version, have, with the exception of D'yakonov, failed to realize the true meaning of Gregoras' words; indeed, the defective text of the Bonn edition, in spite of such patent clues alluding to the alternation as the correlative clause νῦν μέν and the words ἀμοιβαδόν and παραλλάξ, could at first glance be read to mean that the Russian primates were to be chosen solely from among those who had been born and brought up in Byzantium.[17] In Migne's edition of the *History*, published in 1865, the passage in question is printed in the same, defective form.[18]

The omission of the crucial words which refer to the alternation in the nationality of the primates of Russia from all editions of the thirty-sixth book subsequent to Parisot's is undoubtedly due to an error of I. Bekker, the editor of the third volume of the Bonn text of Gregoras' *History*: for the printed text of this passage in Bonn (as indeed of the entire thirty-sixth book) is derived from a single manuscript, the Par. Gr. 3075 in the Bibliothèque Nationale, which is a copy made in the year 1699 of the fourteenth-century Vat. Gr. 1095 in the Vatican Library;[19] and both manuscripts contain the crucial words in full.[20] I know of no other manuscript containing the thirty-sixth book of Gregoras' *History*. Omont is wrong in stating that it is also to be found in the Par. Gr. 1276 in the Bibliothèque Nationale,[21] an error repeated by R. Guilland in his book on Nicephorus Gregoras.[22] So we are left ultimately with a single manuscript, the Vat. Gr. 1095, on the basis of which this passage, defectively printed in the Bonn edition, should be corrected.[23]

What are we to think of this statement of Gregoras? In no other source is such an agreement between Byzantium and Russia, regulating the nationality of the metropolitans of Kiev, so much as mentioned; the view currently held by scholars of the methods by which the Russian primates were appointed is far removed from the notion of any such working compromise between Rus' and the Empire; and these facts, when added to the lateness of Gregoras' evidence, might well suggest that his statement was a product of fantasy or misinformation. Yet, so long as Gregoras' statement is not directly contradicted by other, more reliable, sources, it is surely worth inquiring whether any evidence, however indirect, can be found to support it, and whether, generally speaking, his testimony might provide adequate grounds for reconsidering the problem of the ecclesiastical relations between Byzantium and medieval Russia. The first step in such an inquiry must be an attempt to ascertain the general reliability of Gregoras' statements about the Russian people and their Church.

In his *History* Gregoras discusses the affairs of Russia at considerable length, in a passage of book twenty-eight which relates how the Grand Duke of Moscow sent, *ca.* 1350, a large sum of money to the Emperor John Cantacuzenus for the repair of the church of St. Sophia,[24] and especially in book thirty-six, in which he describes the struggle carried on before the authorities in Constantinople between 1353 and 1356, by the rival candidates of the Grand Dukes of Moscow and Lithuania, for the jurisdiction over the whole Russian Church.[25] The latter account contains several statements that are tendentious and inaccurate. Gregoras' bias is revealed whenever he touches, however lightly, on the subject of Hesychasm: since 1347, when the accession of John Cantacuzenus secured the triumph of the hesychast doctrines of Gregory Palamas, Gregoras had been in opposition, and in the course of the next few years emerged as the leader of the anti-Palamite party in Byzantium. As such, and as one who had suffered for his convictions, he entertained a particularly violent dislike for the Palamite Patriarch Philotheus,[26] who in June 1354 appointed the Muscovite candidate, Alexius, bishop of Vladimir, to the post of "metropolitan of Kiev and all Russia." Gregoras' dislike of Philotheus undoubtedly colored his judgment of the Patriarch's nominee; and the portrait he draws of Alexius, behaving like some villain of melodrama and securing the metropolitan see by distributing enormous bribes in Constantinople[27] — a picture which flatly contradicts the evidence, not only of Russian sources, but of Byzantine documents as well[28] — shows that his judgment of Russian affairs was apt at times to be clouded by partisan bias. The same desire to blacken the Patriarch Philotheus appears in Gregoras' account of Alexius' unsuccessful rival Roman, a candidate of Olgerd, Grand Duke of Lithuania, who later in the same year 1354 was appointed by the Patriarch "metropolitan of the Lithuanians." Gregoras extolls the virtues of Roman as vigorously as he castigates the vices of Alexius,[29] and, contrary to the evidence of all the other sources, he makes

Roman come to Constantinople and receive the Patriarch's consecration before Alexius' arrival.[30] His aim is clearly to suggest — though,
doubtless to salve his historian's conscience, he does so with disingenuous ambiguity — that the Patriarch Philotheus, out of deference for
the Muscovite gold, unlawfully appointed Alexius to the same post—
the metropolitan see of Kiev and All Russia — to which he had just
nominated Roman.[31]

There can thus be no doubt that, in discussing the contemporary
affairs of the Russian Church, Gregoras, carried away by his hatred of
Hesychasm and of the Patriarch Philotheus, was apt at times to select
and twist the facts to conform with his polemical aims. Even here,
however, he seems reluctant to indulge in downright invention or falsi-
fication.[32] But whenever Gregoras' partisan passions were not involved,
his treatment of Russia was full, careful and well-informed. His
remarks on the geography, climate, and economy of the country,[33] on
the transfer of the metropolitan's residence from Kiev to Vladimir
because of the devastation of South Russia by the Mongols,[34] on the
division of the realm into three or four states or principalities,[35] are
clearly the work of a conscientious and accurate recorder. His remarks
on the Grand Duchy of Lithuania, whose rulers had, by the middle of
the fourteenth century, conquered the greater part of western and
south-western Russia, are equally valuable and precise. He mentions
the paganism of their rulers and their successful resistance to the Tatars;[36] makes some penetrating observations on the ecclesiastical policy
of the Grand Duke Olgerd[37] (1345-77) who, though a pagan himself,
sought to extract from the Byzantine authorities the appointment of
his candidate Roman as metropolitan of Kiev, as a means of further-
ing his political designs on the Muscovite lands; and supplies us with
information, clearly obtained at first hand, on the age and physical
appearance of Roman, and on his kinship with Olgerd's wife.[38]

If Gregoras' information on the history and politics of Lithuania
was obviously obtained from Roman, whom he must have met in
Constantinople, it seems likely that much of his knowledge about
Russia was derived from Theognostus, metropolitan of Kiev and All
Russia from 1328 to 1353. Theognostus was a native of Constantino-
ple, and Gregoras writes of him with affectionate admiration, partly
because of the prestige and influence he is said to have wielded in
Russia,[39] and especially because of the vigorous opposition he dis-
played, on Gregoras' showing, to the doctrines of Gregory Palamas.[40]
There is no proof that Gregoras and Theognostus actually met, but it

is hard to believe that the leader of the anti-Palamite party did not make the acquaintance of so distinguished an ally during one of the latter's visits to Constantinople, or that he failed to obtain from him first-hand information on the current conditions and past history of the land over which he exercised the supreme spiritual authority.[41]

Gregoras' testimony on the Russo-Byzantine agreement regulating the nationality of the metropolitans of Kiev should not be regarded as suspect *a priori*: it occurs not in the later chapters of the thirty-sixth book, where the author, yielding to his anti-Palamite bias, seeks to discredit the Patriarch Philotheus and the Emperor John Cantacuzenus, but in the first part of the same book, near the beginning of the section dealing with Russia, where Gregoras' information is at its most accurate and reliable. At the time he was writing the thirty-sixth book — shortly after his release in 1355 from imprisonment in the Monastery of the Chora[42] — he was in Constantinople, and, through the high connections that he had previously enjoyed, and doubtless to some extent still maintained, at Court, in the Church, and in the office of the Logothete of the Dromos, must have been able to acquire first-hand information on the problem of the appointment of the metropolitans of Kiev, particularly since this problem had been recently reviewed, and no doubt widely debated, in Constantinople in connection with the appointment, in June 1354, of Alexius to the primatial see of Russia.[43] Gregoras is known to have had access to documents which are no longer extant.[44] His leading modern biographer, R. Guilland, has observed that the most reliable parts of his *History* are the later books, including the thirty-sixth.[45] And there is no reason to tax Gregoras with too much exaggeration when, in another part of his work, he asserts that of the events he describes he has personally seen or heard the greater part, relying for the remainder on the exact account of eye-witnesses.[46]

We may thus conclude that Gregoras' statements relating to Russia deserve to be taken seriously, since our author, generally speaking, treats the subject in an accurate and well-informed manner. At the same time, his remoteness, in time and distance, from the events he recounts, and his occasional lapses into partiality, make it impossible to accept unquestioningly his evidence on the Russian Church, unless it is supported by the testimony of other sources. This applies in particular to his assertion that Russia's conversion to Christianity was accompanied by a Russo-Byzantine agreement, according to which the metropolitans of Kiev were to be appointed alternately from among Byzantines and Russians.

One of the purposes of this article is to discover whether, in the absence of direct corroborative evidence, the relevant sources, Byzantine and Russian, provide any indication that such an agreement may, in fact, have existed. Its other, and more general, aim is to reconsider, in the light of Gregoras' testimony, the problem of how the primates of the Russian Church were, from the eleventh to the mid-fourteenth century, actually appointed. These two aims may best be achieved by an attempt to answer three separate questions:

1. Can any regular alternation in the nationality of the metropolitans of Kiev be detected in this period?

2. Is the existence of an agreement such as the one attested by Gregoras consistent with our knowledge of the ecclesiastical relations between Byzantium and medieval Russia?

3. Is there any evidence suggesting that those primates of the Russian Church who, in this period, were not directly nominated by the authorities of Constantinople, were elected in Russia by the Russians themselves?

I propose to consider these questions with reference to two successive periods covered by the evidence of Gregoras: the two and a half centuries that elapsed between the final conversion of Rus' to Christianity in 988 or 989 and the Mongol invasion in the fourth decade of the thirteenth century; and the following century, from 1237 to 1354. And, for reasons of convenience which will become apparent in the course of this discussion, I will consider the second period first.

I

1. With regard to the period 1237-1354, the first question can be answered in the affirmative: the alternation referred to by Gregoras is strikingly evident; with complete regularity Byzantine and Russian candidates were appointed, in turn, to the metropolitan see of Kiev and All Russia: Joseph (1237-?), a Byzantine; Cyril (*ca.* 1249-81), a Russian; Maximus (1283-1305), a Byzantine; Peter (1308-26), a Russian; Theognostus (1328-53), a Byzantine; Alexius (1354-78), a Russian: the list is complete and speaks for itself.[47]

2. Was this alternation fortuitous? Historians of the Russian Church have shown a singular reluctance to ask themselves this question. Golubinsky, for example, regarded the appointment of the Russian candidates in this period as due to a historical accident — the unwillingness of Byzantine prelates to face the rigors and dangers of a

prolonged residence in Kiev, devastated by the Mongols in 1240; this, in his opinion, caused the East Roman authorities to agree to the appointment of a Russian primate *ca.* 1249, and subsequently to accept on several occasions a repetition of this precedent.[48] Quite apart, however, from the lack of any evidence that the Byzantine churchmen of the period were quite so pusillanimous,[49] Golubinsky's explanation by-passes the main issue — the regular alternation in the nationality of the metropolitans of Kiev for nearly a century and a half. Another Russian historian, T. Barsov, facing the problem more squarely, expressed the view that this alternation was not adventitious, but was due to the desire of the Byzantine authorities to retain their hold over the Russian Church without offending the national susceptibilities of the Russians.[50] He did not, however, raise the question as to whether this arrangement was the outcome of a self-perpetuating agreement, or the result of a series of *ad hoc* concessions made by the Byzantines to the Russian authorities. The connection between the alternation in the nationality of the primates of the Russian Church from 1237 to 1378 and Gregoras' statement is obvious. It is possible, of course, that our historian, or the source he used, was merely inferring, from the fact that for the previous century and more Byzantines and Russians had regularly succeeded one another as metropolitans of Russia, the existence of a formal agreement between the two countries, rationalizing, in other words, a *de facto* situation. Yet it does not seem likely that an arrangement that operated so regularly and for so long was the result of chance, or even of a series of *ad hoc* agreements between the authorities of Byzantium and Russia. It is thus probable that Gregoras was right in postulating the existence of a special agreement between the two countries which was effective during the period from 1237 to 1378.

It will be remembered that Gregoras asserts that this agreement was concluded at the time of Russia's conversion to Christianity in the late tenth century. The reliability of this part of his evidence will be discussed later. It may, however, be stated here that the apparent absence of any regular alternation in the nationality of the metropolitans of Kiev before 1237 raises the question whether this agreement between Byzantium and Russia could have been concluded in the first half of the thirteenth century. There exists no direct evidence on this point, but it is tempting to assume a connection between the regular practice of appointing Russians to the metropolitan see of Kiev and the policy of granting wide ecclesiastical concessions to the other Slavonic satellites of the Empire, a policy pursued by the Byzantine authorities during their residence in Nicaea, and exemplified by the foundation of the autocephalous Archbishopric of Serbia in 1219 and the recognition of the Patriarchate of Bulgaria in 1235.[51]

3. It is natural to inquire whether the circumstances in which the metropolitans of Kiev and All Russia were appointed in this period can shed any light upon the problem under discussion. Nothing of particular interest is known about the appointment of the Byzantine prelates, Joseph, Maximus, and Theognostus, who were sent to Russia by the Patriarch, the first from Nicaea, the other two from Constantinople.[52] But on the election of the Russian candidates, Cyril, Peter, and Alexius, we are better informed; and the conclusions we can draw from contemporary sources are not without interest.

Cyril, who was probably a monk of West Russian origin, was chosen by Prince Daniel of Galicia, the most powerful of the Russian rulers of his time, was sent to Nicaea *ca.* 1246 to be consecrated by the Patriarch as metropolitan of Kiev and All Russia, and returned, duly invested, a few years later.[53] There is no suggestion in the sources that the appointment of a native candidate, nominated by a Russian sovereign, was in any way unusual, or that the Patriarch opposed it on canonical or other grounds.

The election, and subsequent career, of the Metropolitan Peter provide us with a few more significant facts. Upon the death of the Greek Metropolitan Maximus in 1305, the Russian abbot Gerontius went to Constantinople, hoping and expecting to be consecrated metropolitan of All Russia by the Patriarch. There is no doubt that Gerontius was the candidate put forward for this office by the senior Russian ruler, Prince Michael of Tver', who at that time held the title of Grand Duke of Vladimir.[54] Simultaneously Prince George of Galicia sent a candidate of his own to Constantinople, with the request that he be consecrated metropolitan of Galicia: this was the Abbot Peter, a native of Western Rus'. The Patriarch Athanasius decided otherwise: he rejected Gerontius' candidature, and instead consecrated Peter metropolitan of Kiev and All Russia (1308).[55] A curious, yet significant, interpretation of the attitude of the Byzantine authorities to these two Russian candidates can be found in the *Vita* of the Metropolitan Peter (who was subsequently canonized by the Russian Church) composed by Cyprian, Metropolitan of All Russia (1390-1406). According to to Cyprian, the Patriarch rejected the candidature of Gerontius because he had been chosen by the Russian secular authorities: "It is unlawful," he is said to have declared, "for laymen to make elections to the episcopate."[56] If the right of "election" is taken to mean the right (of the Russian rulers) to put forward their own candidates for the office of metropolitan, it is probable that the Patriarch said no such thing. His acceptance of Peter's candidature shows that he recognized this right. It has long been clear that Cyprian's account of these events is biased, since during his tenure of the metropolitan office he fought, with only partial success, the very practice whereby the Russian rulers submitted their own candidates for the primatial see.[57] His bias appears further in his account of Peter's consecration: on Peter's arrival in Constantinople, he states, the Patriarch "summons the synod of the most holy metropolitans and proceeds to elect [Peter] in the customary manner."[58] This is a perfectly accurate description of the formal election of a metropolitan by the Patriarchal Synod in Constantinople, the σύνοδος ἐνδημοῦσα, and it conforms to the practice current in the Byzantine Church in the Middle Ages.[59] But in this case the formal election by the supreme authorities of the Byzantine Church was preceded by Peter's nomination (though to a see different from the one to which he was eventually appointed) by a Russian sovereign, and Cyprian is clearly at pains to reconcile Peter's free election by the Patriarchal Synod with the distasteful fact that he was recommended by a secular ruler.[60] Further, it is curious that Cyprian himself involuntarily suggests that the right of the Russian princes to put forward their own candidates for the office of metropolitan was widely recognized at the time: Gerontius, he tells us, "went to Constantinople, as if he already had what he expected."[61] The same conclusion emerges from the subsequent relations of the Metropolitan Peter with the Byzantine See. On his return to Russia Peter became the friend and supporter of the Prince of Moscow, George (1304-25), an association which led the metropolitan, in the last years of his life, to transfer, at the instigation of George's successor Ivan I (1325-41), his residence from Vladimir to Moscow. Peter's close collaboration with the Prince of Moscow brought him into conflict with the latter's rival and enemy, Michael of Tver', who, about 1311, wrote to the Patriarch of Constantinople, requesting that Peter be brought to judgement for infringing ecclesiastical discipline.[62] The Patriarch Niphon wrote back to Michael, suggesting that the Russian metropolitan be tried in Constantinople, and, if found guilty, dismissed; in such a case, the Patriarch states, "we will appoint another [metropolitan], whomsoever your Piety desires."[63] If the Byzantine Patriarchate, always so anxious to maintain a strong hold over the Russian Church, could make so explicit an offer, we may conclude that it did not regard the nomination of a native candidate by the Russian sovereign as outrageous or unusual.

Peter seems to have weathered this storm successfully,, and his position grew stronger when Michael of Tver' met his death at the Golden Horde in 1319. The next Russian to be appointed as metropolitan of Kiev and All Russia was Alexius.[64]

The circumstances that accompanied the nomination, election and appointment of Alexius are so curious, and their relation to the testimony of Nicephorus Gregoras is so suggestive, that they warrant a fairly detailed discussion.[65] The son of a Russian nobleman of high rank, himself the godson of the Grand Duke of Moscow Ivan I Kalita, Alexius had lived as a monk in a monastery in Moscow for over twenty years when he was appointed, in 1340, by his sovereign and by the Metropolitan Theognostus as the latter's coadjutor, with the prospective right of succession to the primacy. In 1352 Theognostus, whose health had deteriorated, consecrated him bishop of Vladimir, again on the understanding that Alexius would succeed him as metropolitan of All Russia. In the meantime, Theognostus and the Grand Duke of Moscow, Symeon, had sent an embassy to Constantinople to request the Patriarch and the Emperor to sanction Alexius' candidature. When the embassy returned to Moscow in July 1353, Theognostus and Symeon were both dead. Thereupon Alexius left for Constantinople, expecting, as the Russian sources imply, to be appointed metropolitan.

Alexius remained in Constantinople for a whole year; during much of this time, one is led to suppose, the Byzantine authorities scrutinized his credentials and discussed his suitability. Finally, on June 30, 1354, a decree of the Synod of the Church of Constantinople, signed by the Patriarch Philotheus, formally appointed him metropolitan of Kiev and All Russia. It is a remarkable document.[66] After a preamble which states that the Church of Constantinople holds the metropolitan diocese of Kiev and All Russia in particular honor because of Russia's numerous inhabitants, the preeminence of the power of its king (ὑπεροχῇ ῥηγικῆς ἐξουσίας), and the presence near its borders of a large pagan population,[67] the decree hints rather darkly at "the ways, diverse and most appropriate to the needs of its administration" (κατὰ τοὺς πολυειδεῖς καὶ ἀρίστους τρόπους τῶν οἰκονομιῶν αὐτῆς), in which the See of Constantinople had in the past appointed (ἐγκατέστησε) the primates of the Russian Church; "similarly" (ὁμοίως) it had now attempted to find a suitable candidate for this post among the clerics of Constantinople; its choice, however, had fallen upon Alexius, who "was born and brought up" in Russia (ἐκεῖσε γεννηθεὶς καὶ τραφείς),[68] because of his piety and virtue, and also because he had been recommended for this office by the late Metropolitan Theognostus. This final decision of the Patriarch and his synod, reached after a careful examination lasting a whole year (ἐξετάσει δεδωκότες ἀκριβεστάτῃ ἐπὶ ὁλόκληρον ἤδη ἐνιαυτόν), was influenced by favorable reports on Alexius obtained from Byzantine visitors to Russia and Russian visitors to Constantinople, and also by the fact that "the great King" (ὁ μέγας ῥήξ) of Russia, i.e. the Grand Duke of Moscow, Ivan II, wrote to the Emperor, John Cantacuzenus, in support of his candidature. The decree then adds the following comment: "although this is by no means customary nor safe for the Church, yet in view of these trustworthy and commendatory reports, and of his virtuous and godly mode of life, we have decided that this shall be, but in respect only of the Lord Alexius; and we by no means permit nor concede that any other person of Russian origin should in the future become the primate (ἀρχιερέα) in that country; on the contrary [the primates of Russia are to be chosen] from [among the clergy of] the . . .city of Constantinople."[69] The Patriarch interposes a recommendation to his successors to abide, when making future appointments to the see of Kiev and All Russia, by this ruling, and declares that Alexius, appointed in full conformity with the canons and laws of the Church, will take possession of his new see "just as though he were from here."[70]

One is immediately struck by two features of this synodal decree: the Patriarch's obvious desire to satisfy the demands of the Muscovite authorities; and his assertion that Alexius' appointment to the see of Kiev and All Russia "is by no means customary nor safe for the Church." The first feature can be easily explained by the political and ecclesiastical situation in eastern Europe in the middle of the fourteenth century. Moscow, which after the death of Metropolitan Peter in 1326 had become *de facto* the ecclesiastical capital of Russia, was at that time emerging as the one political center east of the Lithuanian border capable of acting as an effective rallying point for the rising national consciousness of the Russian people and, as events were soon to prove, of successfully challenging the hitherto impregnable power of the Golden Horde. Its princes, who had embarked with the blessing of the Church and the support of their *boyars* on the policy of "gathering" the whole of eastern Russia under their sway, were becoming increasingly powerful and rich. It is not surprising that the Byzantine authorities, whose realm, weakened by the civil war between John Palaeologus and John Cantacuzenus, hemmed in on land by its enemies, the Turks and the Serbs, and disabled on sea by the encroachments of the Genoese and Venetians, faced financial ruin, were ready in 1354 to lend a favorable ear to the demands of an allied and satellite state from which military and economic assistance could be expected — the Grand Duchy of Moscovy and its μέγας ῥήξ.[71] The policy of granting concessions to Russia was further necessitated by the ecclesiastical situation. Now that the political fabric of the Byzantine state was shattered, the Patriarch of Constantinople was the only force capable of championing the traditional claims of the East Roman Empire to hegemony over the whole of Eastern Christendom.[72] But in 1354 the position of the Byzantine Patriarchate in Eastern Europe was gravely compromised: the Serbian Church, since the establishment of the Serbian Patriarchate by Stephen Dušan in 1346, was in open revolt against the mother Church of Constantinople; the Church of Bulgaria was likewise challenging its authority; its patriarch had recently enabled the monk Theodoretus to gain possession of the see of Kiev, in open defiance of the Patriarch of Constantinople; and Olgerd, Grand Duke of Lithuania, was threatening to subject the Orthodox population of his realm to the jurisdiction of the Pope.[73] The Patriarch Philotheus was fully alive to this danger and to his responsibilities; and during his first tenure of the patriarchal office (1353-5) and especially during the second (1364-76), he strove, with singular energy and remarkable success, to reunite the Orthodox peoples of eastern Europe by a common loyalty to the See of Constantinople.[74] It is hence not surprising that, in appointing the Russian candidate Alexius to the see of Kiev and All Russia in 1354, Philotheus was concerned to placate the Grand Duke of Moscow who was virtually the only sovereign in eastern Europe to remain, at that time, in communion with the Byzantine Church.

Why, then, this grudging acceptance of Alexius' candidature, and the Patriarch's observation that his appointment "is by no means customary nor safe for the Church" (εἰ καὶ οὐδὲν ἦν σύνηθες διόλου οὐδὲ ἀσφαλὲς τοῦτο τῇ ἐκκλησίᾳ)? This question can best be answered by considering Philotheus' views on the government of the Church. By upbringing and conviction Philotheus — like Callistus who both preceded and followed him on the patriarchal throne (1350-3; 1354-63) — belonged to the party of "zealots" in the Byzantine Church, which, in opposition to the "politicians" or "moderates," had fought for centuries against state interference in ecclesiastical affairs.[75] As a leading hesychast and a former monk of Mount Athos, Philotheus rose to prominence among the "zealots," who gained a decisive and lasting victory over their opponents when the teaching of Gregory Palamas was officially recognized by the Byzantine Church in the middle of the fourteenth century. An important feature of the zealots' program was their insistence on the freedom of ecclesiastical appointments: and Philotheus himself was elected to the patriarchate in 1353 after his party had wrested from the Emperor John Cantacuzenus a public apology for having, in the past, engineered the election of his own nominees to the patriarchal throne, and an implied condemnation of the majority of the former emperors for doing the same.[76]

Now from the standpoint of the zealots the appointment of the Metropolitan Alexius suffered from specific and obvious defects. Their nature can be inferred by considering three documents issued by the patriarchal chancellery between 1397 and *ca.* 1401, which contain a particularly clear exposition of the zealots' view on ecclesiastical appointments. In the first, the Patriarch Antony IV roundly rebukes a monk of Thessalonica for allowing the clergy and civil authorities (κληρικῶν καὶ ἀρχόντων) of that city to petition the Patriarch to appoint him as their metropolitan. The Patriarch objects not to the candidate as such, but to the attempt of the authorities of Thessalonica to bypass the rules of canonical election.[77] These rules are stated more clearly in the second document, in which the Patriarch Matthew censures the clergy of Anchialus for asking him to appoint as archbishop of their city a candidate of their own choice. Canon law, he reminds them, requires that the election be made by the bishops of the synod of Constantinople; they are to select three names, of which the patriarch chooses one, and he then consecrates the elected person; the patriarch has no right to suggest any name to the synod before the election; as for the clergy of Anchialus, all they may legitimately do is to recommend a given candidate to the synod and to the Patriarch; the Patriarch concludes this somewhat casuistic exhortation by promising to appoint their candidate, provided he is one of those elected by the synod.[78] The third document is a reply of the Patriarch Matthew to the Emperor of Trebizond who had requested him to appoint a local candidate as metropolitan of the city. The synod, the Patriarch

writes, decided, after a careful study of the Emperor's petitionary letter, to send it back; out of "friendship and love" for the Emperor of
Trebizond and respect for the candidate's qualities, it is prepared to
grant the request, but only on condition that the Emperor send
another letter, in which he would recommend the candidate in general
terms, without mentioning the see of Trebizond; for a recommendation for a specific see *pro persona* (περὶ προσώπου) is contrary to a
strict interpretation of the canons (παρὰ τὴν κανονικὴν ἀκρίβειάν
ἐστιν).[79]

These curious documents suggest that at the end of the fourteenth
century, the "zealot" party in the Byzantine Church was finding considerable difficulty in reconciling its principle of free elections to high
offices with the opposing claims of the sees dependent on Constantinople, and in attempting to eradicate the tendency of local authorities,
secular and religious, to propose their own candidates to these offices,
in accordance with a practice which the Byzantine Patriarchate, for
reasons of expediency, had countenanced in former times.

We may safely assume that the same difficulty faced the Patriarch
Philotheus in 1354. Alexius had been explicitly recommended for the
post of metropolitan of Russia by the Muscovite authorities to Philotheus' predecessor Callistus and to the Emperor John Cantacuzenus.
He had further been nominated as prospective metropolitan by his
predecessor Theognostus, an act which came dangerously near to
infringing canon law.[80] And the pressure which had clearly been
exerted on the Byzantine authorities by the Grand Duke of Moscow
in support of Alexius could scarcely commend itself to a patriarch
who headed the party which insisted on strictness (ἀκρίβεια) in the
application of canon law, and was opposed to the interference of the
secular power in ecclesiastical appointments.

It remains to consider the last objection voiced by Philotheus to
Alexius' candidature: the fact that he was a Russian by birth and
education. It is probable that the Patriarch, in stressing this fact, was
moved, not by ethnic or national prejudice, but by the realization that
a Russian candidate implied the patronage of a Russian sovereign and
hence a capitulation to outside, secular pressure. This is hinted at in
the synodal decree of 1354, which states that future appointments to
the see of All Russia are to be made without outside assistance (μηδε-
νὸς ἑτέρωθεν προσδεόμενον).[81] The decision not to tolerate the election
of any more Russian metropolitans after Alexius was to prove quite
ineffectual, for during the six years that elapsed after the death of

Alexius in 1378, the Byzantine Patriarchate agreed on three different occasions to the appointment of a native metropolitan of Russia.[82] Philotheus' appeal to the past was equally unfortunate: for, since for the past hundred years there had been as many Russian as Byzantine occupants of the see of Kiev and All Russia, his assertion that the appointment of a native Russian to this post was "by no means customary," was, to say the least, an exaggeration. The acts of the fourteenth-century synods of Constantinople are, to be sure, sometimes at variance with historical fact; and one cannot but suspect that in the decree of 1354, couched in the expert phraseology of East Roman diplomacy, Philotheus and his synod, in their desire to safeguard the freedom of ecclesiastical elections, and to retain a strict hold over the Muscovite Church, were trying to introduce a new principle in the appointment of the metropolitans of Russia by willfully ignoring the realities of the past.

What, then, were these realities of the past? It will be observed that the testimony of the Patriarch Philotheus and that of Nicephorus Gregoras, which are almost exactly contemporary, contradict each other on at least one essential point: the Patriarch, in defiance of historical truth, writes of the appointment of a native metropolitan of Russia as if it were a dangerous innovation; Gregoras asserts that the Byzantine authorities had formally agreed in the past to alternate elections of Greek and Russian prelates to the see of Kiev; he does not, it is true, tell us explicitly that this agreement was kept, but the context and tenor of his words suggest that he still regarded it, at the time of writing, as at least theoretically in force.

Because Philotheus made a false statement, it does not of course necessarily follow that Gregoras was speaking the truth. However, if the contradiction in their evidence is related to their opposing views on ecclesiastical matters, we may discover an added reason for giving credit to the latter. It was not only on the theological issue of Hesychasm that Gregoras was strongly opposed to the Palamite Patriarch who had convened the Synod of June, 1354, and appointed Alexius to the see of Kiev. Their views on Church administration seem to have differed as sharply. Philotheus, it has been shown, was a leading member of the "zealot" party in the Byzantine Church, which resisted state interference in ecclesiastical affairs, and fought for freedom of appointments. Gregoras occupied an equally prominent position in the opposing party of "moderates" or "politicians" who were inclined to accept Imperial patronage in the affairs of the Church and, in accordance with the accommodating principle of economy (*oiko-voμía*), believed that the Church, in its relations with the state, should not intransigently reject all concessions and compromises. If the Byzantine authorities had ever conceded the principle that every other metropolitan of Kiev was to be a native candidate, selected by the Russian authorities, secular and ecclesiastical, it is not surprising that the "zealot" party, obliged by the force of circumstances to sanction Alexius' appointment in 1354, should have desired to "hush up" this agreement, just as they suppressed the fact that for the past century Byzantines and Russians had regularly succeeded each other as primates of the Russian Church. For the "moderates," however, the existence of such an agreement would have been a vindication of their program, and a proof that the continued loyalty of the Russian Church to the See of Constantinople was the result of a policy of conciliation and reasonable concessions pursued by the former patriarchs and emperors of East Rome. Thus it seems at least possible that Gregoras, who had no reason to feel well-disposed towards the instigators of the Synod of 1354, countered its attempt to suppress the true facts by drawing attention to the existence of an agreement between Russia and the Empire, concluded, as he himself states, "in order that the link between the two nations, thus secured and ratified, might forever preserve the unity of faith pure and undefiled, and find an increased stability for its existence and its strength."

This survey of the ecclesiastical relations between Byzantium and Russia in the thirteenth and fourteenth centuries may therefore lead us to the following conclusions: From 1237 to 1378 the alternate succession of Byzantine and Russian metropolitans of Kiev is regular and striking. No direct evidence, however, can be found to corroborate Gregoras' assertion that there existed a formal agreement between the two countries, regulating this succession. However, the willingness of the Byzantine authorities in this period to recognize the right of Russian princes to nominate, from time to time, native candidates for this office, the evasive language of the Synod of 1354, Gregoras' knowledge and experience of ecclesiastical affairs, his well-informed interest in the Russian Church, and his sympathy for the policy of diplomatic concessions may be regarded as arguments indirectly supporting his clear and categorical statement.

II

Let us now bring Gregoras' evidence to bear on the two and a half centuries prior to 1237, and attempt to answer, for the Kievan period of Russian history, the three questions we have considered for the thirteenth and fourteenth centuries.

1. Can any regular alternation between Byzantine and native primates of the Russian Church be detected from Vladimir's conversion in the late tenth century to 1237?[83] The answer to this question can only be a negative one. In the first place, the list of these primates that can be collated from contemporary documents and later catalogues[84] is almost certainly incomplete, and the exact dates of the tenure of office of more than half of them are unknown. Furthermore, of the twenty and more primates of the Russian Church of the Kievan period whose names have come down to us,[85] there are only three whose nationality is explicitly attested in contemporary sources; of these two were Russians, one a Byzantine.[86] The origin of several others, as we shall see, can be inferred, but often without assurance and generally only with the help of later and sometimes questionable documents. Finally, in view of the chequered history of Russo-Byzantine relations in the eleventh and twelfth centuries it seems unlikely that a regular method of alternate succession could have operated successfully, even for limited periods. This in itself does not, of course, invalidate the evidence of Gregoras. Our historian, it will be recalled, merely states that an agreement regulating this succession was concluded between Byzantium and Russia. He does not say that it was kept.

2. Could such an agreement have been concluded at any time between Russia's conversion to Christianity and the beginning of the thirteenth century? A positive answer to this question seems unlikely to find ready acceptance by those historians who assume that the patriarchs of Constantinople, in their desire to keep the Russian Church under their control, invariably insisted, in the eleventh and twelfth centuries, on appointing their own candidates to the see of Kiev. This widely-held assumption would seem to rest on three arguments:

(a) Contemporary sources, both Russian and Byzantine, appear to take it for granted that the metropolitans of Kiev were generally, in this period, chosen, appointed, and sent to Russia by the Patriarch of Constantinople.

(b) Since Russia was a metropolitan diocese of this Patriarchate, canon law, in its contemporary Byzantine interpretation, required that the primates of Russia be nominated and consecrated by the Patriarch.

(c) The only metropolitans of Kiev of this period who, from contemporary evidence, are known to have been Russians, i.e. Hilarion and Clement, were elected in circumstances which might suggest that the Russians on these two occasions defied the authority of the Byzantine Patriarch.

I believe, however, that the first of these arguments is inconclusive, and that the other two, if examined without preconceived notions, do not justify the assumption that the Byzantine authorities in the eleventh and twelfth centuries vetoed, on principle, the appointment of Russian candidates to the see of Kiev.

The Russian chronicles, in relating the accession of a metropolitan of Kiev, frequently state that "he came" (*pride or prishel*) to Russia, generally adding "from Byzantium" (*iz Grek* or *iz Tsaryagrada*).[87] Similar assertions can be found in Byzantine sources: Nilos Doxapatres wrote in 1143 that "a metropolitan is sent [στέλλεται] to Russia by the Patriarch of Constantinople;"[88] the Patriarch Lukas Chrysoberges, writing *ca.* 1161 to the Russian Prince Andrew Bogolyubsky, states even more explicitly: "we appoint from time to time [*pro vremenom*] the holy metropolitans of All Russia . . . , we appoint and send them thither;"[89] and John Cinnamus likewise asserts that Kiev, the metropolitan see of All Russia, is governed by a bishop from Byzantium (ἀρχιερεὺς . . . ἐκ Βυζαντίου).[90] What is the exact meaning of these expressions? It is possible — and, in the Russian documents, probable — that the fact of "coming" or "being sent" from Byzantium to Russia implies no more than a journey from Constantinople to Kiev, and that these words would have applied equally well to a native prelate, elected in Rus', and dispatched to Constantinople to be consecrated by the patriarch, who would then send him back to govern his new metropolitan diocese. The Greek statements, on the other hand, seem to imply more than this, and to reflect a claim, put forward by the Patriarchate of Constantinople at various times in the twelfth century, to the exclusive right of nominating a Byzantine candidate to the see of Kiev. How little such protestations could sometimes accord with the true state of affairs is evident from the Patriarch Philotheus' synodal decree of 1354; and the suspicion that such statements, to which the zealot party in the Byzantine Church was apt to resort, may have served to justify claims that could not always be made good, scarcely warrants the assumption that the appointment of a native Russian as primate of Kiev would in this period have been disallowed on principle by the East Roman authorities.

How far could the Patriarch of Constantinople claim the right to nominate the metropolitan of Kiev on grounds of canon law? The question is complicated by the scarcity of unambiguous canonical rules prescribing the methods of election of metropolitans in the Byzantine Church, by the observable discrepancy between the ecclesiastical canons and the Imperial laws regulating episcopal elections, and by the peculiar interpretation given to both by the twelfth-century Byzantine canonists.

The provisions of canon law relating to the appointment of bishops were supposed, in Byzantium, to derive their origin and authority from the first Apostolic Canon: ἐπίσκοπος χειροτονείσθω ὑπὸ ἐπισκόπων δύο ἢ τριῶν.[91] In view of the interest which this canon aroused in Russia, where, as we shall see, it was on several occasions quoted, or misquoted, by those who held that the metropolitan of Kiev could be appointed by the Russian bishops, it is worth noting that, as late as the twelfth century, expert opinion in Byzantium was divided as to whether the verb χειροτονείσθω referred, in this context, to election or to consecration; Zonaras and Balsamon holding the latter view—with which modern scholars concur—but citing the opposite opinion, based on the fact that the term χειροτονία in the early Church generally meant "election."[92]

The canons of the Church councils which are concerned with episcopal appointments—notably the fourth and the sixth canons of the First Oecumenical Council, the nineteenth canon of the Synod of Antioch of 341, and the twelfth canon of the Synod of Laodicea—further emphasize and define the corporate nature of the electoral process:[93] a bishop is to be appointed by the bishops of the ecclesiastical province in which his future see is situated; the presence of at least three of them is required at the election, the others signifying their agreement by letter; the elected candidate is to be consecrated (χειροτονεῖσθαι) by the bishops; while the metropolitan of the province must ratify their decision, in accordance with his right of giving his endorsement (τὸ κῦρος) to, or withholding it from, the election and the consecration.

Although these canons allow the metropolitan the right to exercise a general supervision over the appointment of a bishop, his essential prerogative remains that of ratifying the action of the bishops. He does not himself consecrate the elected candidate.[94] However, in the course of time, the Byzantine Church deviated from this canonical norm; and in the twelfth century we find the official commentators of these canons, Zonaras and Balsamon, attempting to reconcile the cur-

rent Byzantine practice of having the newly-elected bishops consecrated by metropolitans with the canon law of the early Church by
resorting to a philological device: the terms χειροτονία and κῦρος, they
claimed, refer in the canons cited above to election and consecration
respectively. This equivocal interpretation enabled them to claim
canonical authority for the practice followed in episcopal appointments in the centralized Byzantine Church of their time: the electoral
body of bishops selected three candidates, one of whom was chosen
by the metropolitan of the province, who gave his endorsement to the
election, issued a declaration (τὸ μήνυμα) naming the bishop-elect, and
finally bestowed on him the sacramental consecration (ἡ χειροθεσία).[95]

Alongside the canons of the Church, a number of laws issued by
the emperors of East Rome prescribed the form of episcopal elections.
One of their features is the part they ascribe to laymen in these elections. The foundation of this Imperial legislation is to be found in the
123rd and 137th novels of Justinian, which decreed that whenever a
bishop is to be appointed, "the clergy and the leading citizens of the city"
(τοὺς κληρικοὺς καὶ τοὺς πρώτους τῆς πόλεως) for which the bishop is
to be consecrated are to elect three persons (ἐπὶ τρισὶ προσώποις
ψηφίσματα ποιεῖν), the final choice of candidate resting with "the prelate conferring the ordination" (ἵνα . . . ὁ βελτίων χειροτονηθῇ τῇ
ἐπιλογῇ καὶ τῷ κρίματι τοῦ χειροτονοῦντος).[96] And the 123rd novel
adds: "If, as happens in certain places, three eligible persons are not
found, it will be in the power of the electors to elect two or even one
person."[97]

Although Justinian's legislation on the election of bishops was
included in the Byzantine *Nomocanons*, the discrepancy between the
secular laws which envisaged the participation of laymen in these elections, and the ecclesiastical canons which restricted the right to
bishops (and, indeed, in one case expressly forbade secular rulers to
make elections to ecclesiastical offices)[98] tended in the course of time
to undermine the authority of the former, in virtue of the principle,
upheld by the medieval canonists, that in cases of conflict a canon
takes precedence over a law. Thus the twelfth-century canonists, Aristenes and Balsamon, asserted that the ordinance providing for the
election of bishops by "the clergy and the leading citizens of the city"
was no longer valid.[99] Nevertheless, there is evidence that Justinian's
legislation on episcopal elections was at that time neither forgotten
nor wholly discredited. It is remarkable that the provision relating to
the election of bishops by "the clergy and the leading citizens of the

city" was retained in the laws of the Macedonian emperors—in the *Procheiron*[100] and the *Epanagoge*,[101] as well as in the *Basilica*.[102] And in the twelfth century the authority commanded in Byzantium by Justinian's legislation was still sufficiently great to enable a Patriarch of Constantinople to press, albeit unsuccessfully and against his own synod, for the application of another clause of the 123rd novel, included in the *Nomocanon*, but not in the *Basilica*.[103]

Such conflicts between canon law and Imperial legislation could be resolved in different ways. Canonists such as Balsamon argued that, in the event of a conflict, the canon, possessing the double sanction of ecclesiastical authority and Imperial ratification, was to be preferred to the secular law.[104] The Emperor Leo VI, on the other hand, expounded in his seventh novel the view that when a secular law ($τῆς$ $πολιτείας$ $ὁ$ $νόμος$) clashes with a canonical prescription ($ὁ$ $ἱερὸς$ $νόμος$) preference must be accorded to the one which is "more useful to the good order of things" ($λυσιτελέστερον$ $τῇ$ $εὐταξίᾳ$ $τῶν$ $πραγμάτων$).[105] This conflict between the rigorist and the empirical attitudes to Canon Law only reflects the perennial antagonism between the principles of $ἀκρίβεια$ and $οἰκονομία$, championed in the Church and in the office of the Logothete of the Dromos by the "zealots" and the "politicians" respectively; an antagonism expressed, as we have seen, in the different ways in which the Patriarchate of Constantinople responded in the fourteenth century to the periodic attempts of the Russian authorities to put forward their own candidates for the post of metropolitan of Kiev. It seems fair to assume, therefore, that in the period under discussion Justinian's law providing for the election of bishops by the local ecclesiastical and secular authorities, though discounted by the canonists and condemned to gradual obsolescence, could yet, by virtue of its inclusion in the *Nomocanon* and especially in the *Basilica*, be cited by those who supported the policy of $οἰκονομία$.

Byzantine canon law recognized no difference in principle between elections of bishops and of metropolitans: canonically speaking the two processes are essentially analogous. The sixth canon of the Council of Sardica stipulated that "the appointment" ($ἡ$ $κατάστασις$) of metropolitans was to be made by the bishops of the same, and also of the neighboring, dioceses.[106] However, the twelfth-century commentators of this canon, Aristenes, Zonaras and Balsamon, state that in their time the practice was different: according to Aristenes, metropolitans are elected by other metropolitans, while Balsamon asserts that they are no longer "appointed" ($ἐγίνοντο$) by bishops, but by the Patriarch of Constantinople.[107] However, the most important ecclesiastical document on this subject is the twenty-eighth canon of the Council of Chalcedon; the relevant passage states: "the metropolitans of the Pontic, Asian and Thracian dioceses, and they only, and further those bishops of the aforesaid dioceses who are among barbarians (ἐν τοῖς βαρβαρικοῖς), are to be consecrated (χειροτονεῖσθαι) by the . . . most holy throne of the most holy Church of Constantinople . . . ; the metropolitans of the aforesaid dioceses, as has been stated, are to be consecrated by the Archbishop of Constantinople, after agreed elections have been held in the customary manner and reported to him" (ψηφισμάτων συμφώνων κατὰ τὸ ἔθος γενομένων καὶ ἐπ' αὐτὸν ἀναφε-ρομένων).[108] In their highly interesting commentaries on this canon, Zonaras and Balsamon explain the electoral procedure followed in their time: the electoral body consisted of metropolitans, members of the patriarchal synod; they submitted three names to the patriarch, who chose one of them, whom he then consecrated; and Zonaras adds significantly that the intention of the canon is to prevent the patriarch from doing as he pleases in the matter of appointing metropolitans.[109] The dioceses of Pontus, Asia, and Thrace, where the metropolitans were elected in the manner prescribed by this canon, are defined by Balsamon as follows: Pontus extends along the Black Sea coast as far as Trebizond, Asia embraces the territory around Ephesus, Lycia, and Pamphylia, Thrace includes the western lands as far as Dyrrhachium. But the bishoprics within these dioceses which, in terms of the canon, are "among barbarians" extend, according to Balsamon and Zonaras, much further afield: Balsamon, with small regard for historical verisimilitude, includes among them Alania and Rus', "the Alans," he asserts, "belonging to the Pontic diocese, the Russians to the Thracian;" while Zonaras, who also holds that the Alans and the Russians pertain to this group, states, with only slightly more respect for geography, that these two peoples are respectively "adjacent to" (συμπαρά-κεινται) the diocese of Pontus and the diocese of Thrace.[110] One may doubt whether the legalistic fiction that Rus' formed part of the diocese of Thrace was taken very seriously by church circles in twelfth-century Byzantium, but Balsamon's exegesis provides curious evidence of the casuistry to which contemporary canonists were forced to resort in order to justify the right claimed by the Patriarch of Constantinople to consecrate the metropolitans of Rus'.

Imperial legislation offers little material on the general rules governing the appointment of metropolitans. It is significant, however, that the evidence obtainable from this source emphasizes the prerogatives both of the provincial ecclesiastical authorities and the Emperor, at the expense of the Patriarch of Constantinople. Justinian's 123rd novel contains a clause which shows that metropolitans could be consecrated either by the patriarch or "by their own Synod." (i.e. presumably by bishops of their ecclesiastical province),[111] and it is noteworthy that this paragraph passed into the *Basilica*.[112] On the other hand, the creation of new metropolitan sees, or more precisely the promotion of episcopal sees to metropolitan status, was a traditional prerogative of the emperor, a prerogative supposedly founded on the twelfth and the seventeenth canons of the Council of Chalcedon,[113] reaffirmed in an edict issued in 1087 by Alexius Comnenus,[114] reiterated in the fourteenth-century *Syntagma* of Matthew Blastares,[115] and frequently resorted to in the Macedonian and Comnenian periods.[116] This is reason enough for believing that the emperors often exerted considerable influence in the election of metropolitans, especially in the twelfth century, when many of the patriarchs appear to have submitted rather easily to Imperial control.[117]

One is forced to the conclusion that the practice prevailing in the Byzantine Church in the eleventh and twelfth centuries with regard to the election of metropolitans contravened the intention, if not the letter, of canon law on at least one essential point. Canon law stipulated that a metropolitan was normally to be "appointed" (i.e. both elected and consecrated) by the bishops of his ecclesiastical province, with the assistance of bishops from neighboring districts; while in the case of appointments to sees situated in Pontus, Asia, and Thrace, the Patriarch of Constantinople had the right to consecrate the candidates who had been elected "in the customary manner" by the provincial bishops. In practice, however, as a result of the centralizing policy of the Byzantine Church, the electoral powers had by this time been transferred from the council of local bishops to the patriarchal synod in Constantinople, the σύνοδος ἐνδημοῦσα, composed of metropolitans and bishops, appointed by the patriarch, of the higher ranks of the patriarchal secretariat and of Imperial representatives.[118] It was this body that elected three candidates for the vacant metropolitan see, of whom the patriarch chose and consecrated one.[119] However, the old canonical prescriptions, which gainsaid the current policy of ecclesiastical centralization, were never abrogated; and it is curious to observe that Imperial legislation, embodied in the clauses of Justinian's novels which were included in the Basilica, similarly recognized the rights of the local authorities: bishops, it stipulated, were to be elected both by the clergy and by the civil authorities of the city, while metropolitans, in certain cases, could be consecrated by the bishops of their province. And it seems reasonable to suppose that, however much these prescriptions of the Empire's civil law were discountenanced by those who insisted on strictness (ἀκρίβεια) in the interpretation of canon law, the emperors of Byzantium, who were recognized as having a legitimate concern in the appointment of metropolitans, could when reasons of diplomacy demanded it impose on their patriarchs a moderate and conciliatory policy towards the local authorities, who could be allowed a voice in the choice of their own metropolitan, in accordance with the principle of οἰκονομία.

3. We must now consider, in the light of these facts, whether the Russians ever claimed, on the grounds of canon law, the right to elect their own metropolitan, and, if so, whether in the period under discussion they succeeded in so doing.

The first Apostolic Canon and the canons of the church councils relating to espiscopal appointments were certainly known in Rus' in the Kievan period, and were included in the Slavonic translations of the Byzantine "Nomocanons," notably of the *Nomocanon XIV titulorum*, the earliest extant Russian manuscript of which was copied in the eleventh or twelfth century.[120] The sixth canon of the Council of Sardica, and the twenty-eighth canon of the Council of Chalcedon, relating to the appointment of metropolitans, are likewise cited in it.[121] The early Russian *Kormchaya* also contains the clauses of Justinian's 123rd and 137th novels prescribing the election of three candidates for a vacant bishopric or, if need be, of two or even one, by "the clergy and the leading citizens of the city."[122]

There is no doubt that, on a number of occasions, the Russians did claim the right, not only to elect their own metropolitan, but also to have him consecrated by the Russian bishops, and that they based this right on their interpretation of canon law. The most unequivocal evidence of this is found in the sources of the fourteenth and fifteenth centuries. About 1378 the Russian archimandrite Michael, renouncing his original intention of going to Constantinople in order to be consecrated metropolitan of Russia by the Patriarch, is said to have observed to his sovereign, the Grand Duke of Moscow, that such a journey was unnecessary, because he could be consecrated by Russian bishops by virtue of the Apostolic Canon which decreed that a bishop was to be ordained by two or three bishops.[123] In 1415 the Orthodox bishops of the Grand Duchy of Lithuania, in a formal statement declaring that they had elected and consecrated Gregory Tsamblak as metropolitan of Kiev — an act performed against the express orders of the Patriarch of Constantinople—attempted to justify their behavior by misquoting the same Apostolic Canon: "Two or three bishops," they maintained, "consecrate a metropolitan."[124] In 1441 Basil II, Grand Duke of Moscow, in a letter to the Patriarch complaining of the former metropolitan Isidore who had been rejected by the Russians on account of his Unionist behavior at the Council of Florence, requested the authorities of Constantinople to send him a written authorization to have the next metropolitan of Russia elected and consecrated in Russia by the Russian bishops, "according to the sacred canons," and with reference to "the holy and divine Greek canons."[125] Eleven years later, writing to the Emperor Constantine XI to inform him that the Russian bishops had, without permission from Constantinople, elected and consecrated a native candidate as metropolitan, Basil II justified this action by appealing to the canons of the apostles and of the Church councils.[126] Finally, the candidate so elected, the Metropolitan Jonas, declared in an encyclical letter written in 1458-9 that the legality of his consecration was founded on the first Apostolic Canon, the fourth canon of the First Oecumenical Council, and on "many other canonical rules."[127]

It will be observed that in all these cases the Russian authorities seem to have applied to the appointment of their own metropolitan the provision of Byzantine canon law which regulated the appointment of ordinary bishops. They can probably be cleared of the suspicion of having acted in bad faith.[128] In the first place, the canon law of the Eastern Church recognized no fundamental difference between the two electoral processes: bishops and metropolitans were to be elected by a council of bishops, the right possessed by the patriarch of giving his endorsement to, or withholding it from, the election of a metropolitan being in every way analogous to the prerogatives granted to a metropolitan in the case of an episcopal election.[129] Futhermore, it would seem that the claim made by the Russian bishops that they could rightfully not only elect, but actually consecrate (i.e. formally appoint) their own metropolitan could find some justification in the ambiguous meaning of several technical terms used in the canons. In the texts to which reference has just been made, the Russians asserted that canon law gave them, in respect of the metropolitan, the right of *postavlenie*; now the term *postavlenie* (from the verb *postavlyati*) is

generally used in the Slavonic *Nomocanon* to translate either of the
two Greek words κατάστασις and χειροτονία, which are the technical
terms most commonly found in the canons relating to the appointment of bishops and metropolitans: ἡ κατάστασις (from καθιστᾶν,
καθίστασθια) generally means the whole process of appointment to an
ecclesiastical office, including the election (ἡ ψῆφος) and the consecration (ἡ χειροτονία, ἡ χειροθεσία) of the successful candidate; while the
term χειροτονία, which, as we have seen, retained a measure of ambiguity at least as late as the twelfth century, gradually shifted during
the first six centuries of the Christian era its principal meaning from
"election" to "consecration."[130] The ambiguity of the Russian term
postavlenie is particularly apparent in the Slavonic version of the
fourth canon of the First Oecumenical Council which was cited by the
Russian Metropolitan Jonas in support of the contention that he had
been canonically appointed. The Greek text of this canon reads:
Ἐπίσκοπον προσήκει μάλιστα μὲν ὑπὸ πάντων τῶν ἐν τῇ ἐπαρχίᾳ καθί-
στασθαι· εἰ δὲ δυσχερὲς εἴη τὸ τοιοῦτο, ἢ διὰ κατεπείγουσαν ἀνάγκην ἢ
διὰ μῆκος ὁδοῦ, ἐξάπαντος τρεῖς ἐπὶ τὸ αὐτὸ συναγομένους, συμψήφων
γινομένων καὶ τῶν ἀπόντων καὶ συντιθεμένων διὰ γραμμάτων, τότε τὴν
χειροτονίαν ποιεῖσθαι· τὸ δὲ κῦρος τῶν γινομένων δίδοσθαι καθ᾽ ἑκάστην
ἐπαρχίαν τῷ μητροπολίτῃ.[131] In the Slavonic version the terms καθίστασθαι and χειροτονία are rendered by the verbal and nominal forms
of the same root: by *postavlenu byti* and *postavlenie* respectively;
while the term which refers to ratification given to the election by the
metropolitan is translated as *vlast'*.[132] The twelfth-century Byzantine
canonists, interpreting this canon, claimed that καθίστασθαι and χειροτονία refer here to the election of a bishop by other bishops, and that
τὸ κῦρος means, in this context, not only the endorsement of the election, but also the consecration of the elected candidate by the metropolitan.[133] This inference, dubious enough in Greek, cannot possibly
be drawn from the Slavonic text of the canon: for *postavlenie* can
signify either the whole process of appointment (including election and
consecration) or simply consecration, but not election alone.[134] As for
vlast' dayati (τὸ κῦρος δίδοσθαι), it cannot by any stretch of imagination be taken to mean "to consecrate." The usual Slavonic equivalent
of τὸ κῦρος was *blagoslovenie* (literally "the blessing"); and we may
therefore conclude that the Russians, who assumed that the appointment of a metropolitan was essentially analogous to that of a simple
bishop, were sincerely convinced that they were acting in full conformity with the fourth canon of the First Oecumenical Council by

claiming the right to elect and to consecrate their own metropolitan (the right of *postavlenie*), while admitting that, to be valid canonically, these acts required the patriarch's ratification (*blagoslovenie*). Thus Basil II of Muscovy, in his above-mentioned letter to the Emperor Constantine XI, after justifying the election and consecration of the Metropolitan Jonas by the Russian bishops, declared: "Our Russian Church requests and seeks the blessing (*blagoslovenie*) of the holy, divine, oecumenical, catholic, and apostolic Church of Saint Sophia, the Wisdom of God, is obedient to her in all things, . . . and our father, the Lord Jonas, Metropolitan of Kiev and All Russia, likewise requests from her all manner of blessing (*blagoslovenie*) and union."[135]

It is improbable that the Russians discovered only in the fourteenth century that their natural desire to have their metropolitan elected by their own bishops in Russia was in full accordance with canon law, and that even the right claimed by the patriarch to consecrate him (if he was not already in episcopal orders) rested on no firmer foundation than a casuistic interpretation of the twenty-eighth canon of the Council of Chalcedon. It now remains to inquire whether the Russian authorities put forward the same claims in the eleventh and twelfth centuries, and, if so, how far these claims were recognized by the Byzantine Patriarchate. A further aim of this investigation will be to consider whether, in the absence of any proof that the agreement between the Empire and Rus' concerning the nationality of the primates of Kiev, attested by Gregoras, was concluded at any time between the late tenth and the early thirteenth century, the Russian authorities succeeded in this period in appointing native candidates to their own metropolitan see. These two aims are not necessarily identical, for the candidates put forward by the Russian authorities might conceivably in certain cases have been of Byzantine nationality, and, conversely, the patriarch of Constantinople may on occasion have selected a Russian as his nominee. But such cases, if they occurred at all, are not likely to have been frequent. It has been shown in the early part of this study that those metropolitans of Kiev who were appointed by the patriarch between 1237 and 1378 at the request of the Russian authorities were in fact of Russian nationality. Thus our two remaining problems may best be approached by an attempt to ascertain the nationality of as many as possible of the primates of Rus' in the Kievan period, and the circumstances in which they were appointed.

The difficulties of such an investigation have already been pointed out. The nationality of only three primates of Russia in the pre-

Mongol period is known with certainty: these are the Russians Hilarion (1051-*ca.* 1054) and Clement (1147-55), and the Byzantine Cyril II (1224-33).[136] The first two are the only metropolitans of Kiev in this period whose appointment is described in any detail in contemporary Russian sources; in most cases the documents either fail to record the accession of the primates, or confine themselves to a monotonous repetition of the formula "he came" (from Byzantium).[137] Byzantine sources, with one possible exception,[138] do not so much as mention the appointment of any metropolitan of Russia in this period. We must, therefore, in attempting to discover the nationality of other metropolitans of Kiev and the circumstances in which they were appointed, resort to the use of circumstantial evidence and later documents.

Some of these primates may be considered, with some probability, to have been of Byzantine nationality. Thus the Metropolitan George, mentioned in the Russian Primary Chronicle under the years 1072 and 1073, is said to have had doubts as to the sanctity of Boris and Gleb, the martyred sons of Vladimir I.[139] It is highly improbable that a native primate would have dissociated himself, even for a time, from the nation-wide cult of the country's earliest canonized saints which had been spreading in Russia for several decades.[140] John II, who became metropolitan not later than 1077, and died in 1089, was in all probability the uncle of the celebrated Byzantine poet Theodore Prodromus.[141] Nicephorus I, who occupied the see of Kiev from 1104 to 1121, can probably be regarded as a Byzantine on the grounds that one of his sermons opens with the following words: "Many homilies, my cherished and beloved children in Christ, ought I to preach to you with my tongue and to water your good earth, I mean your souls, with this water; but the gift of tongues, as the divine Paul would say, is not given to me, wherewith I might . . . carry out my commission, and for that reason I stand before you voiceless and am much silent." In spite of the rhetorical ambiguity of his language, we can probably conclude that the metropolitan, being ignorant of the Russian tongue, wrote his sermon in Greek, and had it translated and read out by someone else.[142] Finally, the Metropolitan John IV (1164-6), on evidence which will be assessed later, can with some probability, in my opinion, be considered a Byzantine.[143] These, together with Theophylactus of Sebasteia, who in the opinion of some scholars was appointed metropolitan of Russia in the reign of Basil II (976-1025),[144] exhaust the list of the primates of the Russian Church in this period whose Byzantine origin seems probable.

We must now consider whether any evidence can be found to support the view that a number of other primates of Kiev in the pre-Mongol period were native Russians and, if so, whether the circumstances in which they were appointed suggest that their nomination was the result of an agreement between the Byzantine and the Russian authorities. It is the quasi-unanimous belief of modern historians that, at least after 1039 — the date at which the subordination of the Russian Church to the See of Constantinople is first unequivocally attested in the *Primary Chronicle*[145] — and until the Mongol invasion in the thirteenth century, all save two of the metropolitans of Kiev were Byzantine prelates, appointed, consecrated, and sent to Russia by the patriarch. The two exceptions are Hilarion and Clement, appointed by the Russian authorities in 1051 and 1147 respectively. The appointments of the two native primates, Hilarion and Clement, are seen as exceptions which prove the rule, and as rebellious attempts of the Russian Church to shake off the tutelage of Byzantium.

In my opinion these views are not warranted by the evidence, and there are grounds for believing that in the period under discussion the Byzantine authorities agreed on a number of occasions to sanction the appointment of a native candidate, elected and perhaps even consecrated in Russia. To support this submission it will first be necessary to re-examine the evidence on the appointments of Hilarion and Clement.

Hilarion's elevation to the see of Kiev is described in two contemporary sources. The *Primary Chronicle*, in an entry dated 1051, states: "Yaroslav appointed (*postavi*) the Russian Hilarion as metropolitan in St. Sophia having assembled the bishops."[146] The term *postavi* is here used by the chronicler in a somewhat loose sense: for the verb *postavlyati*, as has been shown, served to render the terms καθίστασθαι and χειροτονεῖν,[147] neither of which, in the meaning they then possessed, would have been appropriate to the act of a secular ruler, in this case the Prince of Kiev Yaroslav. Yet the chronicler's meaning seems clear enough: Hilarion was chosen for the office of metropolitan by the Russian sovereign, who then caused him to be formally elected and consecrated in the Cathedral of St. Sophia in Kiev by his bishops.[148] The other contemporary evidence comes from Hilarion himself; his "Declaration of Faith" (*Ispovedanie Very*) concludes with the words: "I, by the mercy of . . . God the monk and priest Hilarion, was by His will consecrated and enthroned (*svyashchen bykh i nastolovan*) by the pious bishops in the great and God-protected city of Kiev, to be the metropolitan in it . . . This occurred in the year 6559 [A.D. 1051], in the reign of the pious Prince (*Kagan*) Yaroslav."[149] The verb *svyatiti* (from which the passive participle *svyashchen* is derived) is equivalent to χειροτονεῖν, while *nastolovati* corresponds exactly to ἐγκαθίδρυσθαι, a term used to signify the solemn installation (ἐγκαθίδρυσις) of a newly appointed prelate.

Scholars in recent years have generally asserted that, in causing Hilarion to be appointed, the Russian ruler Yaroslav was trying to assert his Church's independence from Constantinople.[150] Apart from the underlying assumption that the Byzantine authorities were in no circumstances prepared in this period to countenance the appointment of a native metropolitan of Kiev—the accuracy of which has been questioned above — this view seems to rest largely on the fact that Hilarion's election was preceded by a war between Russia and the Empire. This war broke out in 1043, was decided by a fierce naval encounter in the Bosphorus in which the Russians were defeated, and ended in the same year.[151] The suggestion that Hilarion was appointed as a result of these hostilities was already made in the sixteenth-century Russian *Nikon Chronicle*.[152] Yet this view is not supported by the evidence. In the first place, peace was restored between Byzantium and Russia in 1046, and, probably at the same time, a treaty was concluded, by the terms of which Vsevolod, the son of Yaroslav of Kiev, was to marry a close relative, probably the daughter, of the Emperor Constantine IX Monomachus; the child of this marriage, the future prince of Kiev Vladimir Monomakh, was born in 1053.[153] It is unlikely that the friendly relations between the dynasties and governments of Byzantium and Kiev, restored by this marriage, were broken before 1051, the year of Hilarion's appointment; and supporting evidence of relations between the two countries in that same year is provided by the *Nikon Chronicle*, which tells of the arrival in Russia from Constantinople, in 1051, of three experts on church singing together with their families, who were to instruct the Russians in the Byzantine chant.[154]

Further grounds can be found for the view that Hilarion's appointment was neither preceded nor followed by a rift between Kiev and Byzantium. Referring to this event, the *Primary Chronicle* observes: "God inspired the prince, and he appointed him metropolitan"[155] — a significant comment, if the deference generally shown by the compilers of this document for the Byzantine Church is borne in mind. The *Nikon Chronicle* is even more explicit: "Yaroslav," it tells us, "took counsel with his Russian bishops, and they judged according to the sacred canon and the apostolic commandment as follows: the first canon of the holy Apostles [rules]: let two or three bishops consecrate a bishop; and in conformity with this sacred canon and commandment of the divine apostles, the Russian bishops, having assembled, consecrated (*postavisha*) Hilarion, a Russian, metropolitan of Kiev and of the whole Russian land, neither severing themselves from the Orthodox Patriarchs and from the piety of the Greek religion, nor disdaining to be consecrated (*postavlyatisya*) by them."[156] It is possible, of course, that the sixteenth-century chronicler was merely attempting in this passage to justify the action of Yaroslav and of the eleventh-century Russian bishops in gratuitously ascribing to them this appeal to the first Apostolic Canon, by analogy with the arguments used by the Russians in the fourteenth and fifteenth centuries to justify the conse-cration of the metropolitan by the local bishops.[157] Yet the same Apostolic Canon was, as we shall see, invoked by the Russians in similar circumstances in the twelfth century, and there seems to be no valid reason for distrusting the chronicler's statement that the Russian bishops in 1051 had no desire to sever their canonical dependence on the Byzantine Church, and that no such severance did in fact take place. The same view is expressed even more explicitly by the seventeenth-century Ukrainian chronicler Zacharias Kopystensky, who asserted in his *Palinodiya* — a compilation based upon an encyclopaedic, if at times uncritical, use of earlier sources—that Hilarion obtained "the blessing" (*blagoslovenie*) and the ratification (*stverzhenie*) of his election from the Patriarch of Constantinople.[158]

All this evidence strongly suggests, in my opinion, that the election and consecration of Hilarion in Kiev by the Russian bishops at the instigation of Prince Yaroslav were accepted as valid by the Patriarch of Constantinople, and were ratified by him. A supporting argument is provided by the fact that the later catalogues of the primates of Rus', based on the official diptychs of the Church of Kiev, contain the name of Hilarion, whereas the Metropolitan Clement, who, as we shall see, was appointed a century later in defiance of the Byzantine authorities and contrary to their wish, does not figure in them.[159]

We do not know whether the Patriarchate of Constantinople gave its approval to Hilarion's appointment before or after the event. If before, the concession granted to the Russian authorities in 1051 might perhaps be regarded as an outcome of the negotiations between Byzantium and Kiev that followed the war of 1043 and which led, as we have seen, to a political *rapprochement* between the two countries.

Next to the agreement that the son of the prince of Kiev was to marry a Byzantine princess, the permission given to the Russians to elect and consecrate their own metropolitan would have served the interests of the Empire's foreign policy; to placate the Russians by these concessions, to prevent the recurrence of their attack of 1043, and to reconcile them to the spiritual jurisdiction of the Patriarch of Constantinople — these aims would have commended themselves to the diplomatists in the government and Church of Byzantium who favored the policy of οἰκονομία. On the other hand, it is not impossible that the Russian authorities, convinced that they were acting in conformity with canon law, requested the Patriarch to ratify Hilarion's consecration *post factum*.[160]

The appointment, nearly a century later, of the Russian monk Clement of Smolensk as metropolitan of Kiev is usually considered an event analogous to the consecration of Hilarion — that is, as a second, and equally unsuccessful, attempt by the Russians to shake off Byzantine ecclesiastical control. In my opinion, the two events differed radically in their nature, their causes, and their results. Clement was appointed by the Prince of Kiev Izyaslav II, and consecrated by an assembly of Russian bishops in July 1147, after the previous metropolitan, Michael, had for unknown reasons laid the cathedral church of Kiev under an interdict and departed for Constantinople. Clement's consecration was preceded by a stormy discussion among the bishops as to whether this act was legal. A minority, led by Nifont, Bishop of Novgorod, and Manuel, Bishop of Smolensk, took the view that it was not, and refused to recognize Clement as their primate. The Russian *Hypatian Chronicle*, our principal contemporary source in this matter, gives the following account of this discussion: "The bishop of Chernigov said: 'I know that it is lawful for bishops, having assembled, to consecrate (*postaviti*) a metropolitan.'" The protests of the opposition are recorded as follows: "it is not in accordance with [canon] law for bishops to consecrate (*staviti*) a metropolitan without the Patriarch, but the Patriarch consecrates (*stavit*) a metropolitan"; and, addressing Clement, the opposing bishops added: "we will not recognize your authority, nor will we concelebrate with you, because you have not obtained the blessing (*blagoslovenie*) of St. Sophia [of Constantinople] nor of the Patriarch: if you remedy [this omission], and obtain the Patriarch's blessing (*blagoslovishisya ot patriarkha*), we will then recognize your authority."[161]

This remarkable text clearly shows the difficulty of the problem that faced the Russian bishops in 1147. The majority party, doubtless briefed by Clement himself, a man of great learning and a recognized authority on ecclesiastical matters,[162] based their view on canon law: bishops, they claimed, have the power to consecrate a metropolitan. It is generally thought that they were referring — albeit wrongly — to the first Apostolic Canon. This at least was the belief of the Lithuanian bishops in 1415, who misapplied this canon to the appointment of metropolitans, and quoted Clement's consecration as a precedent justifying their own consecration of Gregory Tsamblak.[163] But it is possible that the bishop of Chernigov was also appealing to canon law in a wider sense; for the most searching study of the *Nomocanon* would have revealed no stronger argument against his contention that the Russian bishops were empowered to consecrate Clement than the twenty-eighth canon of the Council of Chalcedon, whose relevance to Rus' was, to say the least, doubtful; while the same *Nomocanon* contained several clauses — drawn from the sixth canon of the Council of Sardica and from Justinian's 123rd novel — which could be interpreted to mean that an assembly of bishops had the right to consecrate a metropolitan.[164]

The minority party, which denied the legitimacy of Clement's appointment, and which included such an expert canonist as Nifont of Novgorod,[165] agreed with their opponents on one point: they found nothing abnormal or improper in the fact that Clement was a Russian and that he had been elected by the Russian bishops, at the instigation of the prince of Kiev. It is obvious from the text of the *Hypatian Chronicle* that they disapproved solely of the refusal, or inability, of the metropolitan-elect to obtain the patriarch's ratification (*blagoslovenie* = τὸ κῦρος) of his election; and they made it clear that such a ratification would confer immediate validity on the whole proceedings. These facts not only suggest that the method of Clement's election was recognized by the entire Russian episcopate as being in full agreement with the canonical rules of the Eastern Church; they also imply that the appointment of native metropolitans by the Russian authorities, subject to the patriarch's confirmation, was a practice not unknown at the time.

This last conclusion is corroborated by evidence from an unexpected and hitherto neglected source. The eighteenth-century Russian historian V.N. Tatishchev, who is known to have had access to medieval documents that have since perished, quotes in his *History of Russia* the words spoken by Izyaslav II of Kiev to the Russian bishops just before Clement's election. They are, if genuine, of considerable importance. "The metropolitan of Russia," the prince declared, "is now dead, and the Church is left without a shepherd and a spiritual head and governor; whom formerly the Grand Princes [of Russia] used to elect and send to Constantinople to be consecrated; and now it is in my power to elect [a metropolitan], but it is not possible to send him to the Patriarch in Constantinople on account of the current disturbances and abundant strife; moreover, owing to this method of consecrating metropolitans, great and unnecessary expense is incurred [by us]; and above all, through this authority held by the patriarch in Rus', the Byzantine emperors seek to rule and command us, which is contrary to our honor and advantage. According to the canons of the holy Apostles and of the Oecumenical Councils, it is laid down that two or three bishops, having assembled, should consecrate one [bishop], and there are more [than three] of you here; for this reason elect a worthy [candidate], and consecrate him metropolitan of Rus'."[166]

It must be admitted that the uncorroborated evidence of an eighteenth-century historian, who used sources which are no longer extant, may be dangerous to handle, and that Tatishchev's reliability in such cases is a matter on which Russian scholars have not always agreed. Yet his scholarly honesty and conscientiousness are generally acknowledged today, and few historians would now venture to suggest that he was ever guilty of fabricating evidence. In several cases, Tatishchev's previously unconfirmed statements were proved to be true by subsequently discovered documents, and present day scholars are coming more and more, whenever his evidence seems inherently credible, to rely on him as a primary source.[167] In the present case, there appear to be several reasons for regarding Tatishchev's account as trustworthy, in substance if not in form. In the first place, even if we make allowances for possible rhetorical embellishments, it is highly improbable that he invented this speech of Izyaslav. It is much more likely that here, as in many other cases, he was quoting from a medieval source which has not come down to us. Secondly, if we compare the accounts of Clement's appointment given by the *Hypatian Chronicle* and by Tatishchev, we shall easily observe that the latter is the clearer and the more consistent, while the chronicle is on certain points confused, self-contradictory,[168] and shows obvious signs of doctoring; this is probably due to the fact that the chronicler felt obliged to expurgate the prince's indiscreet speech. Thirdly, the content of Izyaslav's speech, as quoted by Tatishchev, accords well both with the national policy of the prince of Kiev and with the political situation of the time: his blunt denunciation of the Byzantine Emperor's intervention in the internal affairs of Russia is an obvious allusion to the efforts which the government of Manuel Comnenus was making at that very time to extend its influence in eastern Europe, and to draw its rulers into the net of Byzantine diplomacy. In his attempts to play off the different princes of Rus' against each other, the Emperor was then supporting Yuri Dolgoruky of Suzdal' against Izyaslav of Kiev.[169] It is no wonder, therefore, that Izyaslav was anxious to shake off the embarrassing tutelage of this powerful overlord of the Byzantine metropolitans of Kiev, and to ensure that the primate of the Russian Church should not act in his realm as an agent of Byzantine imperialism.

Izyaslav's assertion that in former times the princes of Kiev chose their own metropolitans, and sent them for consecration to Constantinople, might, in view of his hostility to Byzantium, be regarded as a piece of special pleading. Yet the Russian bishops seem to have taken their right to elect their own metropolitan, subject to the patriarch's confirmation, for granted, and certainly there is nothing in the sources to suggest that this right was a novelty at the time. The remarkable, and possibly novel, feature of the events of 1147 was the intention of the Prince of Kiev to dispense with the patriarch's ratification. The open revolt of Izyaslav II and of the majority of the Russian episcopate against the See of Constantinople placed the Russian Church in a state of schism for eight years, at the end of which time communion was restored in circumstances which, for our present purpose, are highly instructive.

On Izyaslav's death at the end of 1154, his rival Yuri of Suzdal', the ally of the Emperor Manuel Comnenus, became Prince of Kiev. One of Yuri's first acts was to depose Clement, thus restoring the authority of the Patriarch of Constantinople over the Russian Church. In 1156, a new metropolitan, Constantine I, appointed by the patriarch, arrived in Russia from Constantinople.[170] His origin and nationality are not mentioned in any contemporary source. Tatishchev, however, tells us that Constantine had formerly been bishop of Chernigov, and that, after Clement's deposition, he was elected by Yuri and several Russian bishops, and sent to Constantinople in order to be invested by the patriarch with the dignity of metropolitan of Kiev.[171]

Constantine's career as metropolitan was brief. In 1158, after Yuri's death, the sons of Izyaslav II occupied Kiev. Personal sympathies and family loyalty alike prompted them to reinstate Clement, and Constantine abandoned his see, escaping to Chernigov. But, in their ecclesiastical plans, the new masters of Kiev met with the stubborn resistance of their uncle Rostislav, whom they had invited to reign in Kiev. Rostislav flatly refused to accept Clement as metropolitan, "because," he stated, "he did not receive the blessing from St. Sophia and from the Patriarch."[172] But the sons of Izyaslav declined to reinstate Constantine. In the long and acrimonious discussion that ensued between uncle and nephews, one of the latter, Mstislav, according to Tatishchev, argued that Clement had been lawfully appointed by his father and the Russian bishops, and stood in no need of the patriarch's consecration; for the patriarch himself, he asserted, is chosen by the emperor and consecrated by bishops and metropolitans, his ecclesiastical inferiors, "and is not sent anywhere to be consecrated."[173] Eventually a compromise was reached, and it was decided to ask the patriarch to appoint another primate; this was the Metropolitan Theodore, who arrived from Constantinople in 1161. The *Hypatian Chronicle* notes his accession in terms which might be taken to imply that his candidature had been suggested to the patriarch by the Prince of Kiev: "Prince Rostislav," it states, "had sent for him."[174]

The Metropolitan Theodore died about 1163. Meanwhile the deposed Clement had for some unknown reason gained the favor of Rostislav, who now sent an embassy to the Emperor Manuel Comnenus with the request that he be acknowledged metropolitan. But the Russian envoy was forestalled by the arrival in Kiev of a Byzantine embassy, together with a new metropolitan John IV, sent from Constantinople. The *Hypatian Chronicle* tells us that Rostislav at first refused to accept the patriarch's nominee, but was eventually induced to do so by the Emperor's lavish gifts and by the persuasion of the Byzantine ambassador. The text of the chronicle is, in this place, obviously defective: in all the manuscripts the speech made by the Byzantine envoy breaks off at the very beginning — in one manuscript a blank space was left — but the words that remain clearly show that he was conveying to Rostislav some offer from the Emperor: "The Emperor says to you: 'if you accept with love the blessing of St. Sophia. . . .'"[175] There can be little doubt that the envoy's speech was followed by Rostislav's reply which the chronicler, or perhaps a later copyist, felt obliged to suppress. The reply, however, is cited by Tatishchev, in a passage which in other respects closely follows the chronicle; it must indeed have seemed to the pious, law-abiding Russian scribe too embarrassing to quote: "The Grand

Prince replied: 'This metropolitan [John IV], for the sake of the honor and the friendship which the Emperor has shown [me], I will now accept, but if in the future the patriarch should, without our knowledge and decision and contrary to the canons of the holy Apostles, consecrate a metropolitan for Rus', not only will I not accept him, but we will make a law for ever [prescribing] that [the metropolitans of Kiev] be elected and consecrated by the Russian bishops by order of the grand prince.'"[176]

Historians have differed in their assessment of the historical value of Tatishchev's evidence on this point. Some have dismissed Rostislav's speech as the product of Tatishchev's fantasy or misinformation, and have cast doubts on its authenticity.[177] Others have accepted it as a wholly, or substantially, true record.[178] The sceptics have, in my opinion, failed to produce a single convincing argument in favor of their view. Here again Tatishchev's testimony is not only inherently plausible; it clarifies and completes the account given by the *Hypatian Chronicle* of the Byzantine embassy to Russia; this was probably identical with the embassy sent by the Emperor to Kiev in 1165 which brought about a treaty between Manuel Comnenus and Rostislav, and which is described by Cinnamus.[179]

Rostislav's speech, which, I submit, should be accepted as genuine, at least in substance, sheds some additional light on the problem of appointments to the see of Kiev in the twelfth century. (*a*) In the first place, the Russian sovereign claimed that the patriarch had no right to consecrate a metropolitan of Kiev without his previous knowledge and consent. Now Rostislav, in matters of canon law, was not an irresponsible person; he had himself in the past refused to recognize Clement on the grounds that he had not obtained the patriarch's confirmation.[180] And if the Prince of Kiev considered himself entitled to exercise his right of "decision" in choosing a candidate and then requesting the patriarch to consecrate him, it is probable that some precedent existed on which this claim could be based — the same precedent, in fact, as was invoked in 1147 by Izyaslav II.[181] (*b*) Secondly, in threatening to promulgate a new law prescribing that metropolitans of Kiev should, in the future, be elected and consecrated in Rus', presumably without reference to Byzantium, Rostislav implied that he recognized that the patriarch still possessed the right to endorse or veto the election, and doubtless also to consecrate the elected candidate, a right so tactlessly questioned by Izyaslav II. (*c*) Finally, his appeal to "the canons of the holy Apostles" is yet another reference to the canon law of the Eastern Church; its provisions on episcopal appointments — laid down in the first Apostolic Canon and in other clauses of the Byzantine *Nomocanon* — were, as we have seen, from time to time invoked by the authorities of the Russian Church in support of the right they claimed to elect and consecrate their metropolitan.

It is remarkable, furthermore, that the Byzantine authorities seem to have accepted, in practice if not in principle, Rostislav's first contention; for as soon as the Prince of Kiev agreed to recognize the new metropolitan nominated by the patriarch, a treaty was concluded between him and the Emperor Manuel. This treaty, as several scholars have pointed out, must have included an ecclesiastical settlement;[182] and it is surely significant that John IV's successor as metropolitan of Kiev, Constantine II, was, according to Tatishchev, a Russian bishop chosen by Rostislav, and sent by him to Constantinople where he was confirmed by the patriarch who dispatched him back to Russia in 1167.[183]

The circumstances in which Hilarion and Clement were elected and consecrated metropolitans of Kiev can thus, if they are examined without preconceived notions, lead us to the following conclusions:

(a) The elevation of Clement to the see of Kiev in 1147 was an event essentially different from Hilarion's appointment to the metropolitanate in 1051; the former act was performed in defiance of the Byzantine authorities, and led to a temporary schism between the Churches of Kiev and Constantinople; the latter act was sanctioned, either before or after the event, by the Byzantine Patriarch.

(b) The circumstances and the aftermath of Clement's appointment cannot, any more than Hilarion's consecration, be used as an argument for the view that all the primates of Russia between 1039 and the middle of the thirteenth century were, with these two exceptions, Byzantine prelates, elected in Constantinople and consecrated and sent to Russia by the patriarch. The evidence of the sources adduced above suggests, indeed, the opposite. Both in 1051 and in 1147-65 the leaders of the Russian Church and State seem to have been genuinely convinced that canon law and, at least in the second case, historical precedent, entitled them to elect their own candidate, subject to the patriarch's confirmation; and on several occasions the Byzantine authorities appear to have accepted this contention and to have ratified their choice.

(c) The real difficulty seems to have arisen over the question of whether the consecration of the metropolitan-elect was the prerogative of the Patriarch of Constantinople or the Russian bishops. The East Roman authorities, who at that time held the view that the power of consecrating metropolitans was the visible symbol of the patriarch's spiritual jurisdiction over them, were naturally most reluctant to concede this right to the Russian bishops. Their acceptance of Hilarion's consecration in Kiev is the only well authenticated case prior to the fifteenth century when they may, in practice, have conceded this privilege. The Russians, on the other hand, seem, in this period, to have held conflicting opinions on whether their metropolitan could be consecrated by his own bishops. The majority appear to have recognized the claims of the Byzantine Patriarchate in the matter and to have believed that the rights of their own bishops were confined to electing the primate. However, the provisions of canon law on the appointment of bishops and metropolitans, which in several respects conflicted with the centralized administration of the medieval Byzantine Church, the ambiguity of the Slavonic term *postavlenie* which served to render both the Greek words κατάστασις and χειροτονία,[184] and the desire of their rulers to gain as much independence as possible from Byzantine control, contributed to the rise of another, and more nationalistic, current of opinion; the conflict between these two schools of thought goes far toward explaining the passionate discussions that arose in Russia over the legitimacy of Clement's consecration, as well as Prince Rostislav's angry appeal, when confronted with a Byzantine metropolitan unilaterally appointed by the patriarch, to "the canons of the holy Apostles."

Our investigation has also revealed some grounds for believing that, apart from Hilarion and Clement, several other metropolitans of Kiev in this period may have been selected by the Russian authorities: Constantine I (1156-8) and Constantine II (1167-?) were, according to the evidence of Tatishchev, candidates selected by the Princes Yuri I and Rostislav I respectively, and sent to Constantinople to receive the Patriarch's consecration or confirmation.[185] It is quite possible that both were Russians by birth. Moreover, the Metropolitan Theodore (1161-*ca.* 1163) may perhaps also have been a candidate of Rostislav.[186] Two further metropolitans of the Kievan period were, according to Tatishchev, nominated by Russian rulers: Nicetas (1122-6), he claims, was sent as a bishop to Constantinople by the Prince of Kiev, Vladimir Monomakh, and was there appointed by the Patriarch metropolitan of Russia.[187] Tatishchev maintains that Nicetas, on his journey from Kiev to Byzantium in 1122, accompanied Vladimir's granddaughter who was going to contract an Imperial marriage. From other sources we know that she was to marry Alexius, the son of the Emperor John II Comnenus, in accordance with an agreement recently concluded between Russia and the Empire. Several details supplied by Tatishchev on this marriage, which supplement the evidence of other sources, have been accepted as reliable by modern historians,[188] and there seems to be no valid reason for rejecting his testimony on the metropolitan Nicetas. We may well have here a further example of an ecclesiastical concession made to the Russians by the Byzantine authorities within the framework of a wider political settlement. The other metropolitan on whom Tatishchev provides original information is Matthew (†1220), who, he asserts, was appointed by the Grand Prince of Suzdal', Vsevolod III.[189]

The list of metropolitans of Kiev nominated, on Tatishchev's evidence, by the Russian authorities could perhaps be extended by the addition of another name. In 1089, the *Primary Chronicle* tells us, Yanka, the daughter of Prince Vsevolod of Kiev, returning from Constantinople, "brought back [to Kiev] the Metropolitan John." Historians have generally concluded from this text that this metropolitan, John III (1089-90), was chosen for his Russian post either by Yanka herself or by her father.[190]

This reconstruction of the list of possible Russian nominees to the see of Kiev in the eleventh, twelfth, and early thirteenth centuries relies heavily on the evidence of Tatishchev. His testimony has been doubted or impugned by reputable historians, and the highly critical attitude adopted by such scholars as E. Golubinsky toward his unconfirmed evidence on the nomination of several metropolitans of Kiev by the Russian authorities has tended to relegate it to the lumber-room of groundless hypotheses or preconceptions. This scepticism provides a strange contrast to the reliance that modern historians are increasingly placing on Tatishchev's evidence on other matters, evidence which has often been found to rest on medieval documents no longer extant. It would doubtless be rash to assume that every time Tatishchev asserts that a certain metropolitan was nominated by the Russian authorities, his statement is necessarily true. On one occasion at least, when his testimony appears to contradict the evidence of an earlier source, it should be treated with reserve.[191] However, his evidence on the Kievan metropolitans accords well, in my submission, with the history of the ecclesiastical relations between medieval Russia and Byzantium, which has formed the theme of this article. The speeches of Izyaslav II to the

Russian bishops, and of Rostislav I to the Byzantine ambassador, if they are not forgeries, must be regarded as illuminating contributions to the subject under discussion. They show that at least in the middle of the twelfth century a tradition existed in the ruling circles of Rus' that the metropolitans of Kiev could be, and were from time to time, elected by the ecclesiastical and civil authorities of the country.

One last piece of evidence can perhaps be adduced to support this view. In 1441 the Grand Duke of Moscow, Basil II, in a letter to the Patriarch of Constantinople, after reminding his correspondent of the circumstances of Russia's conversion to Christianity, made the following statement: "strengthened and confirmed by piety, the sons, grandsons and great grandsons [of St. Vladimir] . . . received from time to time the most holy metropolitans in their country from the Imperial City [of Constantinople], sometimes a Greek, sometimes a Russian from their own land, consecrated by the most holy Oecumenical Patriarch."[192] It is possible, of course, that this alternation of Byzantine and native primates, so vividly described by the words "sometimes . . . sometimes" (*ovogda. . .inogda*), should be taken to refer to the regular succession of Greek and Russian metropolitans of Kiev, which we observed between 1237 and 1378. Yet the general terms in which Basil II's statement is couched, and his mention of the immediate descendants of Vladimir I, seem to suggest that he was alluding to a tradition which was thought in his time to go back to the Kievan period.

III

The results of our inquiry must now be briefly summarized. It has been shown that the text of Nicephorus Gregoras which mentions the Russo-Byzantine agreement stipulating that the metropolitans of Kiev were to be appointed in accordance with the principle of alternate nationality—a text accidentally omitted from the Bonn edition of the Ἱστορία Ῥωμαϊκή, and consequently neglected by historians — deserves to be restored to its proper place in the thirty-sixth book of Gregoras' work, and should be considered as a source providing fresh evidence on the ecclesiastical relations between the Empire and medieval Russia. The attempt to assess the reliability of this evidence has led us to reconsider, within a somewhat wider framework, several aspects of these relations between the early eleventh and the late fourteenth centuries. Although no direct evidence has come to light to corroborate Gregoras' statement that a formal agreement concerning the alternate nationality of the primates of Russia was actually concluded between the authorities of Byzantium and Kiev, circumstantial evidence tends to support his testimony, especially in the period between 1237 and 1378, when Byzantine and Russian prelates were appointed in turn with striking regularity to the metropolitan see of Kiev by the Patriarch of Constantinople.

The lack of any similar observable alternation in the nationality of the metropolitans of Kiev in the earlier, pre-Mongol, period of Russian history has led us to investigate in some detail the methods and machinery by which the primates of Rus' were then appointed. This investigation has called in question two widely held assumptions: the belief that the patriarchs of Constantinople in the eleventh and twelfth centuries invariably insisted on selecting their own candidates for the see of Kiev, and the view that all the primates of the Russian Church in this period, with the exception of Hilarion and Clement, were Byzantine nominees of the patriarch. The evidence of contemporary sources, and in some cases of later authorities, notably the testimony of Tatishchev, suggests, in my opinion, that a number of metropolitans of Kiev in this period had, prior to their consecration or confirmation by the patriarch, been nominated in Russia by the local authorities of Church and State, and that the Byzantine Patriarchate, no doubt for reasons of expediency, accepted and tolerated this practice.

We also considered the grounds, ecclesiastical and political, on which this practice was founded. The canon law of the Eastern Church, in its prescriptions concerned with the appointment of bishops and metropolitans, envisages the active participation of the local episcopate in the election and consecration of these dignitaries. Even the twenty-eighth canon of the Council of Chalcedon, which granted to the Patriarch of Constantinople the power to consecrate the metropolitans of certain specified ecclesiastical provinces — and which twelfth-century Byzantine canonists took, with some casuistry, to apply to Rus' as well — stipulated that the metropolitans of those provinces were to be elected by the local bishops. However, by the time the Russians were converted to Christianity, the growing centralization of the Byzantine Church had caused the prerogative of electing metropolitans to be transferred to the Patriarchal Synod in Constantinople. In these circumstances the Byzantine Patriarchate, in accordance with a new interpretation of canon law, officially held that the primate of the Russian Church should, strictly speaking, be elected, appointed and consecrated in Constantinople — should be, in other words, an ἀρχιερεὺς ἐκ Βυζαντίου.[193] The Russians, however, challenged this view on a number of occasions — recorded in the sources of the eleventh, twelfth, fourteenth, and fifteenth centuries—and claimed the right to have their metropolitan elected and consecrated by their own bishops, in accordance with their interpretation — often a forced one — of canon law.

These conflicts between the Russian episcopate and the Byzantine Patriarchate were further complicated by the intrusion of political factors and the intervention of the secular authorities. The princes of Kiev and Moscow, for all the deference most of them felt for the unique position occupied by the Byzantine emperor and patriarch in Orthodox Christendom, were naturally anxious to have a controlling influence on the selection of the primates of their Church; and some of them, notably in the twelfth century, are known to have chafed under the distant, but quite overt, hegemony of the Imperial overlord of their Byzantine metropolitans. The Byzantine emperors, for their part, regarded the metropolitans of Kiev as valuable diplomatic agents, capable of using their considerable moral and spiritual authority to ensure the docility and secure the alliance of the powerful Russian realm; and alliance with Russia was for the Imperial government, so frequently faced in this period with military and economic crises, a prime necessity.

And yet, just because Russia was a country whose military and economic resources commanded the respect of Byzantine statesmen, the emperors could not fail to realize that their aim of building up a favorable balance of power in the steppes and forests of eastern Europe could best be achieved by the use of tactful diplomacy. The most clear-sighted of them still knew the wisdom, which their predecessors had gained through long experience of negotiating and fighting with the barbarians, of acquiring useful allies and appeasing potential foes by timely concessions to their national susceptibilities. And, as the history of the Empire's relations with its northern neighbors, and particularly with the Balkan Slavs, so clearly illustrates, these concessions were apt to include the granting to the satellite states of a measure of ecclesiastical self-government; the recognition by the Emperor Basil II about 1020 of the autonomy of the Bulgarian Church, whose primate, the archbishop of Ohrid, was to be consecrated by his own suffragan bishops, the Emperor reserving for himself the right of appointing or nominating him, is an outstanding and contemporary example of this ecclesiastical diplomacy.[194] It would be surprising if the Imperial government had not been prepared to concede a somewhat more modest privilege to the Russians, and to permit them, from time to time, to nominate their own candidate for the metropolitan see of Kiev. Such a concession would have been all the more justified, since Justinian's legislation on the appointment of bishops and metropolitans — which was included in the *Nomocanon* and in the *Basilica* — allowed the local authorities a leading part in the electoral process, a clause of his 123rd novel even recognizing the right of the provincial bishops to consecrate their metropolitans, and since the appointment to vacant metropolitan sees was acknowledged in Byzantium to lie within the emperor's legitimate sphere of interest.

The often competing interest of the four different parties concerned in the appointment of the metropolitan of Kiev — the Russian bishops, the Patriarch of Constantinople, the Russian princes, and the Byzantine Emperor — could, it seems, have been reconciled in the following manner: whenever the requirements of Imperial diplomacy demanded it, the Russians were allowed to select their own candidate; this choice, however, amounted simply to nomination, and was not considered by the authorities of the Byzantine Church to constitute a canonical election; the election — in this case a pure formality — was made by the Patriarchal Synod in Constantinople, the σύνοδος ἐνδημοῦσα; finally, the candidate thus "elected" was consecrated by the Patriarch, or, if he already possessed episcopal orders, was formally proclaimed by him as the appointed metropolitan of Kiev. This procedure, which was resorted to during the appointment of the Russian Metropolitan Peter in 1308,[195] and which the Byzantine Patriarchate actually recommended to the local authorities of Anchialus and Trebizond in the early fifteenth century,[196] must have been employed on a number of other occasions. While satisfying the desire of the Russian authorities to have their own candidate appointed, it enabled the Church and government of the Empire to achieve a compromise between the demands of canonical rigidity (ἀκρίβεια) and a policy of reasonable concessions (οἰκονομία).

The working compromise on the nationality of the primates of Russia, described by Gregoras, would have fitted well into this pattern of ecclesiastical diplomacy. Whether the agreement between the Empire and Russia, embodying this compromise, was made, as Gregoras himself believed, at the time of Vladimir's conversion to Christianity in the late tenth century, or whether, as seems more likely, it was concluded in the first half of the thirteenth century when the

Imperial authorities resided in Nicaea,[197] its existence, which the evidence cited above tends, in my submission, to confirm, may provide a further example of that genius for combining a program of Imperial hegemony with a policy of concessions to the national aspirations of Byzantium's satellites, which was displayed on so many occasions by the Church and Empire of East Rome.[198]

FOOTNOTES ON CHAPTER IV

[1] *The Russian Primary Chronicle (Povest' vremennykh let)*, ed. V. P. Adrianova—Peretts (Moscow, 1950), I, p. 103—English translation by S. H. Cross and O. P. Sherbowitz-Wetzor (Cambridge, Mass., 1953), p. 138. In subsequent references to this document in this chapter the original will be cited as "Povest'," and the translation as "Cross."

[2] The acceptance of one or the other of these two dates depends on the relative value attached to the different sources relating to Vladimir's baptism. See G. Laehr, *Die Anfänge des russischen Reiches* (Berlin, 1930), pp. 110-15.

[3] For the "Bulgarian" theory, see M. D. Priselkov, *Ocherki po tserkovno-politicheskoy istorii Kievskoy Rusi X-XII vekov* (St. Petersburg, 1913), pp. 35-76; H. Koch, "Byzanz, Ochrid und Kiev 987-1037," *Kyrios*, III (1938), pp. 272-84. For the "Roman" theory, see N. de Baumgarten, "Saint Vladimir et la conversion de la Russie," *Orientalia Christiana*, 27, pt. 1 (1932); M. Jugie, "Les origines romaines de l'Eglise russe," *Echos d'Orient*, 36 (1937), pp. 257-70. For the view that Vladimir's church was autocephalous, see E. Golubinsky, *Istoriya russkoy tserkvi*, I, part 1 (2nd ed., Moscow, 1901), pp. 264-9; G. Vernadsky, "The status of the Russian Church during the first half-century following Vladimir's conversion," *Slavonic Review*, 20 (1941), pp. 298-314.

[4] *Histoire de Yahya-Ibn-Saïd d'Antioche*, ed. and transl. by I. Kratchkovsky and A. Vasiliev, *Patrologia Orientalis*, XXIII, fasc. 3 (1932), p. 423.

[5] *Povest'*, s.a. 988, 989, pp. 76-7, 80-3; Cross, pp. 112-3, 116-9.

[6] Iakov, Monk, *Pamyat' i pokhvala knyazyu ruskomu Volodimeru*: Golubinsky, *op.cit.*, I, 1, p. 239.

[7] The view that the Russian Church was from the time of its foundation placed under Byzantine authority is strongly and convincingly argued by V. Laurent, "Aux origines de l'Eglise russe," *Echos d'Orient*, 38 (1939), pp. 279-95; E. Honigmann, "Studies in Slavic Church History," *Byzantion*, 17 (1944-5), pp. 128-62; F. Dvornik, *The Making of Central and Eastern Europe* (London, 1949), pp. 169-79; and M. V. Levchenko, "Vzaimootnosheniya Vizantii i Rusi pri Vladimire," *Vizantiisky Vremennik*, 7 (1953), pp. 194-223. See now V. Vodoff, *Naissance de la Chrétienté russe* (Paris, 1988), pp. 81-99.

[8] Τοῦτο τοίνυν τὸ ἔθνος, ἀφ' οὗ τῇ εὐσεβεῖ προσερρύη θρησκείᾳ καὶ τὸ τῶν χριστιανῶν θεῖον ἐδέξατο βάπτισμα, ὑφ' ἑνὶ τυποῦσθαι τέτακται καθάπαξ ἀρχιερεῖ. . .καὶ εἶναι τὸν πρῶτον τούτου ἀρχιερέα τῷ τῆς Κωσταντινουπόλεως ὑπείκοντα θρόνῳ, καὶ ὑπὸ τούτου τὰ νόμιμα δέχεσθαι τῆς ἀρχῆς τῆς πνευματικῆς. Nicephorus Gregoras, *Historiae Byzantinae*, xxxvi, cap. 22-3, ed. I Bekker (Bonn, 1855) III, 512-13.

[9] The words ὑφ' ἑνὶ τυποῦσθαι τέτακται καθάπαξ ἀρχιερεῖ, in their emphasis on the ecclesiastical unity of all the Russian lands under the jurisdiction of the metropolitan of Kiev, are doubtless intended to justify the abolition by the Emperor John VI Cantacuzenus in August 1347 of the separate Russian metropolitan diocese of Galicia, established in 1303 by Andronicus II. At that time Gregoras was still on good terms with John Cantacuzenus, and thus probably approved of the ecclesiastical re-unification of Russia. In several public documents issued in 1347 in Constantinople the abolition of the metropolitan diocese of Galicia is held to be justified by the creation, at the time of Russia's conversion to Christianity, of a single ecclesiastical organization for the whole of the country, under the metropolitan of Kiev. See the chrysobullon of John VI reuniting the metropolitanate of Galicia with that of Kiev: K. E. Zachariae von Lingenthal, *Jus Graeco-Romanum*, III (Leipzig), pp. 700-3, and the edict of the Patriarch Isidore, confirming this decision: *Acta Patriarchatus Constantinopolitani*, ed. F. Miklosich and I. Müller, I (Vienna, 1860), p. 267. In a letter written in the same year to Prince Lyubart of Volynia, the Emperor states that the jurisdiction of the metropolitan of Kiev over the whole of Russia was established at the time of the country's conversion "by custom and law" (αὐτόθι ἔθιμον ἦν καὶ νενομισμένον): ibid., p. 265. Finally, an edict of Patriarch Antony, issued in 1389, reiterates this statement, in terms reminiscent of Gregoras' words: ἡ τῆς Ῥωσίας ἐπαρχία πᾶσα ὑφ' ἕνα μητροπολίτην ἀπ' ἀρχῆς ἐτάχθη ποιμαίνεσθαί τε καὶ διευθύνεσθαι: Ibid., II, p. 116.

[10] Εἶναι δ' αὐτὸν καὶ νῦν μὲν ἐκ τοῦ γένους ἐκείνου, νῦν δ' ἐκ τῶν τῇδε φύντων ὁμοῦ καὶ τραφέντων, ἀμοιβαδόν, τὴν ἐκεῖ προεδρίαν ἀεὶ διαδεχομένων μετὰ τὸν προτέρου θάνατον παραλλάξ, ὡς ἂν τὸ τοῖν δυοῖν γενοῖν συναφὲς οὑτωσὶ βεβαιούμενον καὶ κυρούμενον βεβαιοτέραν ἐς τὸ ἀκήρατόν τε καὶ ἀκραιφνὲς καὶ τὴν τῆς πίστεως σύμπνοιαν ἔχῃ φυλάττειν ἀεὶ καὶ μονιμωτέραν τὴν οὐσίαν καὶ δύναμιν. Val. Parisot, *ivre XXXVII de l'Histoire Romaine de Nicéphore Gregoras. Texte grec complet donné pour la première fois, traduction française, notes philologiques et historiques* (Paris, 1851), p. 68.

[11]"Passer d'un prélat russe à un prélat grec, c'est nommer παραλλάξ, peu importe qu'après le Grec on prenne d'autres Grecs ou que l'on revienne à un Russe: si l'on y revient, les choix se feront ἀμοιβαδόν; mais, tant qu'on ne dit pas ἀμοιβαδόν, on ne sait pas si les choix mettent alternativement un Russe et un Grec sur le siège primatial. Qu'on ne croie donc pas παραλλάξ synonyme d'ἀμοιβαδόν; il y a entre eux la même différence qu'entre *varier* et *alterner*. . . Nous disons parfaitement en français *l'alternative dans la variation*." *Ibid.*, pp. 281-2.

[12]See note 10. Parisot called this book the thirty-seventh, but his numeration has been superseded by that adopted by the Bonn editors.

[13]Parisot asserts, in particular, that in the course of the eleventh century this alternation in the nationality of the metropolitans of Kiev "fut consacrée et devint comme officielle" (*ibid.*, p. 281), but adduces no conclusive evidence for this statement.

[14]*Vlast' moskovskikh gosudareĭ* (St. Petersburg, 1889), pp. 6-7.

[15]*Russky arkhierey iz Vizantii* (Kiev, 1913), pp. 39-40.

[16]*Historiae Byzantinae* lib. xxxvi, cap. 23, ed. I. Bekker (Bonn, 1855), III, p. 513, lines 2-4.

[17]This conclusion is, in fact, drawn by Sokolov (*Russky arkhierey iz Vizantii*, pp. 39-40, 265).

[18]*P.G.*, cxlix, col. 453.

[19]Parisot, *op.cit.*, pp. 2-3; R. Guilland, *Essai sur Nicéphore Grégoras* (Paris, 1926), p. xviii.

[20]Par. Gr. 3075, fol. 75 r; Vat. Gr. 1095 fols. 255 v-256 r.

[21]H. A. Omont, *Inventaire sommaire des manuscrits grecs de la Bibliothèque Nationale*, I (Paris, 1898), no. 1276.

[22]Guilland, *Essai sur Nicéphore Grégoras*, p. 242.

[23]The omission of the crucial words from the Bonn edition was no doubt accidental: this is shown by the fact that in the Latin translation underneath the Greek text they are given in full: *qui modo ex gente illa, modo ex nostra terra natis educatisque post antecedentis mortem mutuo sedem occupat. Hist. Byz.*, Bonn, III, p. 513.

[24]*Hist. Byz.* lib. xxviii, cap. 34-6, Bonn III, pp. 198-200.

[25]*op.cit.*, lib. xxxvi, cap. 20-51, *ibid.*, pp. 511-26.

[26]Cf. Guilland, *op.cit.*, pp. 34, 40, 51, 97, 226, 289-91.

[27]*Ibid.*, cap. 36-7, p. 519.

[28]The Russian sources referring to Alexius, who was canonized by the Russian Church, are cited and analyzed in Golubinsky, *op.cit.*, II, 1, pp. 171, ff. High praise is meted out to Alexius in the synodal decree of the Patriarch Philotheus, of June 30, 1354 (*Acta Patriarchatus Constantinopolitani*, I, pp. 336-40) and in the synodal decree of the Patriarch Callistus, of July 1361 (*ibid.*, pp. 425-30). Gregoras' picture of Alexius is all the less convincing, since Alexius had been appointed Vicar-General to the metropolitan of Russia and warmly recommended for the post of future metropolitan by his predecessor Theognostus, a prelate for whom Gregoras professes the highest regard (*Hist. Byz.* lib. xxxvi, cap. 24, 27-30, Bonn, III, p. 513-516).

[29]*Ibid.*, cap. 34-5, p. 518.

[30]The sequence of events, and the exact chronology of Alexius' and Roman's two journeys to Constantinople remain, admittedly, rather uncertain, as the different sources do not always agree. Cf. Golubinsky, *op.cit.*, II, 1, pp. 177-87, 190-3; A. M. Ammann, *Abriss der ostslawischen Kirchengeschichte* (Vienna, 1950), pp. 94-5. It is clear, however, that Alexius was already in Constantinople in 1353, and that Roman could not have arrived before the following year.

[31]The true facts are stated in the synodal decree of Patriarch Callistus, of July, 1361. (*Acta Patr. Const.*, I, pp. 425-30). Alexius was appointed μητροπολίτης Κυέβου καὶ πάσης 'Ρωσίας (on June 30, 1354: *ibid.*, p. 340) and Roman "a little later" (μετὰ μικρόν) μητροπολίτης Λιτβῶν. Gregoras, while inverting the chronological order of these appointments, refers to the titles granted to the two prelates in the vaguest possible terms: Εὐθὺς γὰρ χειροτονηθέντος ἐνταῦθα τοῦ 'Ρωμανοῦ, ἀθρόον ἐπεφύη τις ἐκεῖθεν ἕτερος, τοὔνομ' Ἀλέξιος, . . .καὶ αὐτὸς αὐθήμερον . . .ὤφθη μητροπολίτης (*loc. cit.*, cap. 36, p. 519). Previously he had stated that Roman aspired to the metropolitan see of All Russia (τὴν τῆς ὅλης 'Ρωσίας ἐπισκοπὴν καὶ μητρόπολιν; *ibid.*, cap. 34, p. 518), and we are doubtless meant to believe that Roman and Alexius were in turn appointed to the same post.

[32]P. Sokolov (*Russky arkhierey iz Vizantii*, pp. 376-8) plausibly suggests that Gregoras intermingled the facts of Roman's first and second visits to Constantinople (in 1354 and 1355), in order to bolster up his thesis that the Byzantine authorities, in withholding their support from Roman, missed the opportunity of converting the latter's sovereign, Olgerd, to Christianity. In another context, Gregoras has been harshly criticized for stating that a Russian ruler (ἡγεμών) had been granted the Byzantine court title of ὁ ἐπὶ τῆς τραπέζης by the Emperor Constantine the Great (*Hist. Byz.*, lib. vii, cap. 5, ed. L.

Schopenus [Bonn, 1829], I, p. 239). The disregard for chronology is, of course, blatant, but this passage occurs in a much earlier section of the *History*, and may well have been written before Gregoras had begun systematically to collect information about Russia. Moreover, we know from Maximus Planudes that in the late thirteenth or early fourteenth century a Russian ruler did bear the title of ὁ ἐπὶ τῆς τραπέζης. See H. Haupt, "Neue Beiträge zu den Fragmenten des Dio Cassius," *Hermes*, 14 (1879), p. 445. Cf. A. A. Vasiliev, "Was Old Russia a Vassal State of Byzantium?" *Speculum*, 7 (1932), pp. 353-4. Cf. *infra*, note. 41.

[33]*Hist. Byz.* lib. xxxvi, cap. 21-22, Bonn, III, p. 512.

[34]*Ibid.*, cap. 24-30, pp. 513-6. It may seem surprising that Gregoras does not mention Moscow which, by the time he was writing, was already in fact the political and ecclesiastical capital of Eastern Russia. Yet the Byzantine authorities were slow to recognize this fact, and in the middle of the fourteenth century the primate of the Russian Church still held the title of "metropolitan of Kiev and of All Russia," though his predecessors had ceased to reside in Kiev since 1300.

[35]*Ibid.*, cap. 25-6, pp. 513-4. Though it is possible that this is a reference to the political fragmentation of Rus' which began in the twelfth century, it seems more likely that Gregoras is alluding to the "three or four" rival and independent principalities into which Eastern Russia was divided in the middle of the fourteenth century, i.e. Moscow, Tver', Suzdal' and Ryazan'. Cf. G. Vernadsky, *The Mongols and Russia* (New Haven, 1953), p. 206. See now J.L.I. Fennell, *The Emergence of Moscow 1304-1359* (London, 1968).

[36]*Ibid.*, cap. 26, 33-4 pp. 514, 517.

[37]*Ibid.*, cap. 34-5, pp. 517-18.

[38]*Ibid.*, cap. 34-5, p. 518.

[39]*Ibid.*, cap. 24, 27-31, pp. 513-16.

[40]*Ibid.*, lib., xxvi, cap. 47, p. 114. Cf. Golubinsky, *op.cit.*, II, 1, pp. 168-9; Guilland, *Essai sur Nicéphore Grégoras*, pp. 41-2.

[41]One of Nicephorus Gregoras' letters bears the superscription τῷ ἐπὶ τῆς τραπέζης. The editor of this letter, I. C. von Aretin, took this anonymous addressee to be a prince of Russia, on the grounds that the title of ὁ ἐπὶ τῆς τραπέζης was, on Gregoras' own showing, born by Russian rulers. (*Beyträge zur Geschichte und Literatur*, 4 [Munich, 1805], pp. 609-19). Cf. *supra*, note 32. This view is accepted by R. Guilland, the editor of Gregoras' correspondence, who dates the letter between 1325 and 1330 and suggests that it was probably written to the Grand Duke of Moscow, Ivan I Kalita (1325-41) (*Correspondance de Nicéphore Grégoras* [Paris, 1927], pp. 16, 378-9). The contents of the letter are vague and platitudinous, but show that Gregoras entertained a lively correspondence with the addressee, for whom he professed a high regard. It is quite possible that the Byzantine court title of ὁ ἐπὶ τῆς τραπέζης was, at least in the fourteenth century, traditionally in the hands of the Russian princes, as that of κουροπαλάτης was in those of the Georgian princes in the tenth century (see Constantine Porphyrogenitus, *De Administrando Imperio*, cap. 45-6, ed. Gy. Moravcsik and R. J. H. Jenkins [Budapest, 1949], pp. 204-22). Cf. G. Ostrogorsky, "Die byzantinische Staatenhierarchie," *Seminarium Kondakovianum*, 8 (1936), p. 59: A. A. Vasiliev, "Was Old Russia a Vassal State of Byzantium?," *Speculum*, 7 (1932), pp. 353-4. If Gregoras' correspondent was really the Grand Duke of Moscow, another probable source of our author's knowledge of Russian affairs would be discovered. But was ὁ ἐπὶ τῆς τραπέζης the Muscovite sovereign? The identification, however tempting, seems to me still unproved. On the title ὁ ἐπὶ τῆς τραπέζης see J. B. Bury, *The Imperial Administrative System in the ninth century* (London, 1911), pp. 125-6: Constantine Porphyrogenitus, *De Cerimoniis*, ed. Bonn, I, p. 725 (in the tenth century); and Ps.-Codinus, *De Officiis*, ed. Bonn, p. 35: ed. J. Verpeaux (Paris, 1966) index p. 388. (in the fourteenth century).

[42]Guilland, *op.cit.*, p. 245.

[43]Cf. *supra*, pp. 120-5.

[44]Guilland, *ibid.*

[45]*Ibid.*

[46]*Hist. Byz.*, lib. xii, cap. 1, Bonn, II, p. 571.

[47]For the careers of these churchmen, see Golubinsky, *op.cit.*, II, 1, pp. 50-225; Ammann, *op.cit.*, pp. 57-61, 78-84, 92-9.

[48]Golubinsky, *ibid.*, pp. 50-1, 104-5.

[49]It is noteworthy that according to Byzantine Canon Law, a bishop who refuses to minister to the spiritual needs of the diocese entrusted to his care falls under the sentence of excommunication for as long as he persists in his refusal (36th Apostolic Canon: G. Rhalles and M. Potles, Σύνταγμα τῶν θείων καὶ ἱερῶν κανόνων, II [Athens, 1852], p. 48).

[50]*Konstantinopol'sky patriarkh i ego vlast' nad russkoy tserkov'yu* (St. Petersburg, 1878), pp. 461-4.

[51]On the foundation of the Archbishopric of Serbia in 1219 and the establishment of the Bulgarian Patriarchate in 1235, see M. Spinka, *A history of Christianity in the Balkans* (Chicago, 1933), pp. 84-8, 110-2; G. Ostrogorsky, *History of the Byzantine State* (Oxford, 1968), pp. 431, 437.

[52]See Golubinsky, *op.cit.*, II, 1, pp. 50, 90, 146-7.

[53]The sources, and the somewhat uncertain chronology, relating to the election and consecration of the Metropolitan Cyril are discussed by Golubinsky (*ibid.*, pp. 51-4) and Sokolov (*Russky arkhierey iz Vizantii*, pp. 159-63). Cyril's early career is not precisely known: Golubinsky (*ibid.*, p. 53) and Vernadsky (*The Mongols and Russia*, p. 147) take him to have been a monk in the region of Galicia and Volynia: Ammann (*op.cit.*, p. 58) believes, on somewhat inadequate grounds, that he had been the bishop of Chelm (Kholm) in Galicia.

[54]Cf. Golubinsky, *op.cit.*, pp. 99-101; Sokolov, *op.cit.*, pp. 218-24.

[55]Golubinsky, *op.cit.*, pp. 101-5.

[56]*Kniga Stepennaya Tsarskogo Rodosloviya:* in *Polnoe Sobranie Russkikh Letopisey*, 21 (St. Petersburg, 1908), p. 325.

[57]Cf. Sokolov, *op.cit.*, pp. 219, 347, 451, 473; Golubinsky, *op.cit.*, p. 145, note 1.

[58]*Kniga Stepennaya, loc. cit.*

[59]Cf. *supra*, pp. 131-4.

[60]He attempts to do so by suggesting that Prince George of Galicia, concealing from Peter the fact that he had nominated him for the office of metropolitan, sent him to Constantinople ostensibly for a different purpose, and secretly requested the Patriarch and his synod to appoint him. Golubinsky has no difficulty in showing how improbable this suggestion is (*op.cit.*, II, 1, p. 103, note 1).

[61]*Kniga Stepennaya, loc. cit.*, p. 324.

[62]The accusations put forward against the Metropolitan Peter are discussed by Golubinsky (*ibid.*, pp. 113-15).

[63]*Pamyatniki drevne-russkogo kanonicheskogo prava*, part 1 (2nd ed., St. Petersburg, 1908): *Russkaya Istoricheskaya Biblioteka*, vol. 6, 2nd ed., no. 16, col. 149.

[64]A strange, and not well authenticated, action is ascribed to the Metropolitan Peter by the anonymous author of his fourteenth-century *Vita*. Shortly before his death, Peter is alleged to have nominated as metropolitan a certain Archimandrite Theodore (Metropolitan Makary, *Istoriya russkoy tserkvi*, IV [St. Petersburg, 1886], p. 315). Theodore's identity, origin and fate are quite unknown, and, if true, this statement may mean that Peter nominated not his successor (as Golubinsky, *ibid.*, pp. 145-6, believes), but the candidate for the metropolitan see of Galicia. (See Sokolov, *op.cit.*, pp. 262-4).

[65]For an account of Alexius' appointment, see Golubinsky, *ibid.*, pp. 171, ff.; Sokolov, *ibid.*, pp. 285-353.

[66]The text is printed in *Acta Patriarchatus Constantinopolitani*, I, pp. 336-40.

[67]There is a curious similarity between this passage of the synodal decree and some of Gregoras' references to Russia: both Philotheus and Gregoras describe the Russian people as πολυάνθρωπος (cf. Gregoras, *Hist. Byz.*, lib. xxviii, cap. 35, Bonn, III, p. 199; elsewhere, Gregoras calls the Russians ἔθνος πολυανθρωπότατον: lib., xxxvi, cap. 21, *ibid.*, p. 512); both give the Grand Duke of Moscow the title of ῥήξ (Gregoras, *ibid.*, cap. 28, p. 515); both refer to the pagan neighbors of Russia, the Lithuanians, as fire-worshippers (πυρσολάτρας): *Acta Patr. Constant.*, *loc. cit.*, p. 336; γένος πυρσολατροῦν: *Hist. Byz.*, *ibid.*, cap. 26, p. 514).

[68]The words ἐκεῖσε γεννηθεὶς καὶ τραφείς, used in the synodal decree, are strikingly reminiscent of Gregoras' expression ἐκ τῶν τῇδε φύντων ὁμοῦ καὶ τραφέντων, which occurs in the passage referring to the alternate nationality of the metropolitans of Russia (cf. *supra*, note 10). They may also be compared to Gregoras' statement that the Metropolitan Theognostus ἔφυ τε καὶ τέθραπται in Constantinople (*Hist. Byz.*, loc. cit., cap. 30, p. 516).

[69] Ἡμεῖς, εἰ καὶ οὐδὲν ἦν σύνηθες διόλου οὐδὲ ἀσφαλὲς τοῦτο τῇ ἐκκλησίᾳ, ὅμως διὰ τὰς ἀξιοπίστους καὶ συστατικὰς ταύτας μαρτυρίας καὶ τὴν ἐνάρετον καὶ θεάρεστον αὐτοῦ ἀγωγὴν διεκρίναμεν τοῦτο γενέσθαι, πλὴν εἰς αὐτὸν δὴ τοῦτον καὶ μόνον τὸν κῦρ' Ἀλέξιον, οὐ μὴν δὴ παραχωροῦμεν, οὐδὲ ἐνδιδόαμεν ὅλος ἕτερόν τινα εἰς τὸ ἐξῆς ἀπὸ τῆς Ῥωσίας ὁρμώμενον ἀρχιερέα ἐκεῖσε γενέσθαι, ἀλλὰ ἀπὸ ταύτης τῆς θεοδοξάστου καὶ θεομεγαλύντου καὶ εὐδαίμονος Κωσταντινουπόλεως. . .: *Acta Patr. Const.*, loc. cit., p. 337.

[70]*Ibid.*, p. 338.

[71]On the financial crisis of the Empire in the mid-fourteenth century, see Ostrogorsky, *History of the Byzantine State*, pp. 449-70. It is not impossible that a connection existed between the Russian support for Alexius' candidature and the money sent *ca.* 1350 by the Grand Duke Symeon of

Moscow for the repair of St. Sophia.

[72]The classic expression of these claims can be found in the letter written in 1393 by Antony IV, Patriarch of Constantinople, to Basil I of Moscow: *Acta Patr. Constant.*, II, pp. 188-92; cf. Ostrogorsky, *History of the Byzantine State*, pp. 553-4.

[73]Cf. Spinka, *A History of Christianity in the Balkans*, pp. 117-8, 141-3; Golubinsky, *op. cit.*, II, 1, pp. 179-81; Sokolov, *op. cit.*, pp. 361-2.

[74]O. Halecki, "Un empereur de Byzance à Rome. Vingt ans de travail pour l'union des Eglises et pour la défense de l'Empire d'Orient, 1355-75," *Rozprawy Historyczne Towarzystwa Naukowego Warszawskiego*, 8 (Warsaw, 1930), pp. 179-80, 235-42; Meyendorff, *Byzantium and the Rise of Russia*, pp. 173-99.

[75]On the "zealot" and the "moderate" parties in the Byzantine Church, see A. Vasiliev, *History of the Byzantine Empire* (Madison, 1952), pp. 659-71.

[76]See the remarkable speech made by the Emperor to the synod of Constantinople: John Cantacuzenus, *Historiae*, lib. iv, cap. 37 (Bonn, 1832), III, pp. 272-5.

[77]*Acta Patr. Const.*, II, pp. 275-6 (March, 1397).

[78]*Ibid.*, pp. 345-7 (February, 1400).

[79]*Ibid.*, pp. 541-3. The letter is undated, but it appears to have been written *ca.* 1401. Cf. the remarks on these three documents by Sokolov, *op. cit.*, pp. 342-4.

[80]The Canon Law of the Eastern Church inhibits a dying bishop from consecrating his successor (*Nomocanon XIV titulorum*, tit. I, cap. 18, citing the seventy-sixth Apostolic Canon: Rhalles and Potles, Σύνταγμα, I, p. 56). Balsamon, commenting on this clause, cites the example of a twelfth-century metropolitan of Philippopolis who wished to resign on condition that the Patriarchal Synod appointed his own candidate as his successor; his request was refused (*Ibid.*, II, p. 99).

[81]*Acta Patr. Constant.*, I, p. 338.

[82]These native metropolitans were Michael (1378-9), Pimen (1380-9) and Dionysius (The last one was not formally appointed.). Cf. *Acta Patr. Constant.*, II, pp. 12-8, 116-29. Golubinsky, *op. cit.*, II, 1, pp. 226-60. The separate metropolitan dioceses of Lithuania and Galicia, created in the reign of Andronicus II (1282-1328), and abolished and restored several times in the course of the fourteenth century, were frequently presided over by local primates, recognized by the Byzantine Patriarchate. Cf. Golubinsky, *ibid.*, pp. 96-7, 125-30, 147, 153-4, 157-62, 190-3, 206-14, 324-4. How powerless Philotheus was to carry out his intention of appointing Byzantines to metropolitan sees situated beyond the confines of the Empire is shown by the fact that a few months after Alexius' appointment he consecrated Roman, the candidate and a relative by marriage of the Grand Duke Olgerd, to the see of Lithuania.

[83]There is some doubt as to the place of residence, and the title, of the primates of the Russian Church before 1037. Contemporary sources imply, without conclusive clarity, that they resided in Pereyaslavl' and that some of them at least bore the title of archbishop. On the first point see Golubinsky, *op. cit.*, I, 1, pp. 328-9; on the second point, see Dvornik, *The Making of Central and Eastern Europe*, p. 176. After 1037, however, the primates of the Russian Church were certainly the metropolitans of Kiev: *Povest'*, *s.a.* 1037, 1039; Cross, pp. 137-8.

[84]On these later catalogues of Russian metropolitans, compiled between the fourteenth and the eighteenth centuries, see Golubinsky, *ibid.*, pp. 284-5, note.

[85]Golubinsky (*ibid.*, pp. 281-9) lists twenty-three primates of the Russian Church up to the year 1237, whose existence he regards as well, or fairly well, authenticated. The names of six or seven others, either ambiguously alluded to in contemporary sources, or mentioned in later and not always reliable documents, could be accepted, or rejected, only after further investigation. A systematic study of the later lists of Russian metropolitans has yet to be made.

[86]The two undubitably Russian metropolitans were Hilarion (1051-*ca.* 1054) and Clement (1147-55); the Byzantine one was Cyril II (1224-33) whose Greek origin is attested by the Laurentian and the Novgorod chronicler: *Lavrentievskaya Letopis'*, *s.a.* 1224: *Polnoe Sobranie Russkikh Letopisey*, I (St. Petersburg, 1846), p. 190. *Novgorodskaya pervaya Letopis'*, *s.a.* 1233, ed. A. N. Nasonov (Moscow, Leningrad, 1950), p. 72.

[87]*Povest'*, *s.a.* 1051, p. 107; Cross, p. 142 (George); *Laurentian Chronicle*, *s.a.* 1089 (John III), 1104 (Nicephorus), 1122 (Nicetas), 1156 (Constantine I); *Hypatian Chron.*, *s.a.* 1131 (Michael), 1161 (Theodore), 1164 (John IV); *First Novgorod Chron.*, *s.a.* 1167, ed. Nasonov, p. 32 (Constantine II).

[88]G. Parthey, *Hieroclis Synecdemus* (Berlin, 1866), p. 297; *P.G.*, CXXXII. col. 1105.

[89]Metropolitan Makary, *Istoriya russkoy tserkvi* (2nd ed., St. Petersburg, 1868), III, p. 298. The original document is not extant, and we have only an old Russian translation of it. Cf. V. Grumel, *Les*

Regestes des Actes du Patriarcat de Constantinople, no. 1052, I, 3, pp. 114-15.

⁹⁰Ioannes Cinnamus, *Histor.*, lib. v, cap. 12, ed. A. Meineke (Bonn, 1836), p. 236.

⁹¹G. Rhalles and M. Potles, Σύνταγμα, II, p. 1.

⁹²*In Can. I Ss. Apost.*, *P.G.*, cxxxvii, cols. 36-7. For the different meanings of the ecclesiastical term χειροτονία in the first six centuries, see the valuable study by M. A. Siotis, *Die klassische und die christliche Cheirotonie in ihrem Verhältnis*, Θεολογία, Bd. 20 (1949), Heft 2-Bd. 22 (1951), Heft 2 [offprint] (Athens, 1951).

⁹³See C. Hefele and H. Leclercq, *Histoire des Conciles*, I, pp. 539-47, 552, 720, 1005.

⁹⁴It is true that the twenty-fifth canon of the Council of Chalcedon appears to suggest that the metropolitans were responsible for the consecration of bishops: ἐπειδήπερ τινὲς τῶν μητροπολιτῶν, ὡς περιηχήθημεν, ἀμελοῦσι τῶν ἐγκεχειρισμένων αὐτοῖς ποιμνίων καὶ ἀναβάλλονται τὰς χειροτονίας τῶν ἐπισκόπων. . .Hefele and Leclercq, II, p. 810. However, the fact that this canon was "deviating from the language used at Nicaea and Antioch" (C. H. Turner, *Studies in early Church History* [Oxford, 1912], p. 91) does not necessarily mean that it envisaged that the metropolitans were actually to consecrate bishops: the canons imply that the metropolitan was generally responsible for seeing that a vacant bishopric was filled in the proper manner, and his presence (παρουσία) at the consecration of a bishop is expressly required by the nineteenth canon of the Council of Antioch (341).

⁹⁵*In Can. IV Conc. Nicaen. I: P.G.*, cxxxvii, col. 236. *In Can. XIX Conc. II Antioch.: ibid.*, col. 1328. *In Can. XII Conc. Laod.: ibid.*, col. 1357-60. The ecclesiastical canons and Imperial laws regulating episcopal appointments in the Byzantine church are cited and discussed by I. I. Sokolov, "Izbranie arkhiereev v Vizantii" *Vizantiisky Vremennik*, 22 (1915-6), pp. 193-252.

⁹⁶*Imp. Iustiniani Novellae quae vocantur sive constitutiones*. Ed. C. E. Zachariae v. Lingenthal, II (Leipzig, 1881 [Teubner]): Nov. 123, cap. 1, pp. 294-5; Nov. 137, cap. 2, p. 409. It is not suggested, of course, that it was Justinian who first gave the laity a voice in the election of bishops. In the post-apostolic age, and at least until the fourth century, the lay community as a whole took an active part in episcopal elections. Justinian confined the electoral rights to the πρῶτοι τῆς πόλεως, i.e. to the leading officials and to the holders of high civic positions. Cf. J. Pargoire, *L'Eglise byzantine de 527 à 847* (Paris, 1905), pp. 57-8.

⁹⁷Nov. 123, cap. 1, *ibid.*, p. 296.

⁹⁸Cf. the third canon of the Seventh Ecumenical Council: Rhalles and Potles, Σύνταγμα, II, pp. 564-6.

⁹⁹Aristenes, *In Can. VI Conc. Sardic.: P.G.*, cxxxvii, col. 1449; cf. Balsamon's commentary on the twenty-third chapter of the first title of the *Nomocanon*: Rhalles and Potles, Σύνταγμα, I, p. 60.

¹⁰⁰*Prochiron Basilii, Constantini et Leonis*, tit. xxviii, cap. 1, ed. C. E. Zachariae von Lingenthal (Heidelberg, 1837), p. 155.

¹⁰¹*Epanagoge Legis Basilii et Leonis et Alexandri*, tit. viii, cap. 3: *Collectio librorum juris Graeco-Romani ineditorum*, ed. C. E. Zachariae v. Lingenthal (Leipzig, 1852), I, pp. 77-8.

¹⁰²*Basilica*, lib. III, tit. 1, cap. 8, ed. G. E. Heimbach (Leipzig, 1833), I, p. 93; ed. J. and P. Zepos (Athens, 1896), I, p. 117-8.

¹⁰³Rhalles and Potles, Σύνταγμα, I, pp. 49-50. Cf. M. Krasnozhen, "Tolkovateli kanonicheskogo kodeksa Vostochnoy Tserkvi: Aristin, Zonara i Val'samon," *Uchenye Zapiski Imperator. Yur'evskogo Universiteta*, 1911, pp. 177-9.

¹⁰⁴Cf. Krasnozhen, *op.cit.*, pp. 241-2.

¹⁰⁵*Les Novelles de Léon VI le Sage*, ed. and transl. by P. Noailles and A. Dain (Paris, 1944), p. 37.

¹⁰⁶Hefele and Leclercq, *Histoire des Conciles*, I, p. 777.

¹⁰⁷*In Can. VI Conc. Sardic.: P.G.*, cxxxvii, cols. 1445, 1448-9. The term ἐγίνοντο, used here by Balsamon, really refers to the whole process of appointment to an ecclesiastical office, which includes both an election and a sacramental consecration, and is generally described as κατάστασις. Cf. Siotis, *op.cit.*, pp. 105-6. Balsamon's use of the term is hence improper, since he himself admits in another passage that metropolitans were consecrated, but not elected, by the Patriarch. Cf. infra, note 109.

¹⁰⁸Hefele and Leclercq, *op.cit.*, II, pp. 815-26.

¹⁰⁹Zonaras (*P.G.*, cxxxvii, col. 489): οὐχ οὓς βούλεται ὁ Κωνσταντινουπόλεως χειροτονήσει μητροπολίτας, ἀλλ' ἡ ὑπ' αὐτὸν σύνοδος τὰς ψήφους ποιήσεται. Balsamon, *ibid.*, col. 485. Cf. T. O. Martin, "The Twenty-Eighth Canon of Chalcedon: a Background Note": *Das Konzil von Chalkedon. Geschichte und Gegenwart*, ed. by A. Grillmeier and H. Bacht, II (Würzburg, 1953), pp. 433-58.

¹¹⁰Balsamon, *ibid.*, col. 485: Ἐπισκοπὰς δὲ εἰπὲ εἶναι ἐν τοῖς Βαρβάροις τὴν Ἀλανίαν, τὴν Ῥωσίαν καὶ ἑτέρας. Οἱ μὲν γὰρ Ἀλανοὶ τῆς Ποντικῆς εἰσι διοικήσεως, οἱ δὲ Ῥώσιοι τῆς Θρακικῆς. Zonaras, *ibid.*, col. 489.

[111]Τοὺς δὲ μητροπολίτας τοὺς ὑπὸ τῆς ἰδίας συνόδου ἢ ὑπὸ τῶν μακαριωτάτων πατριαρχῶν χειροτονουμένους: Nov. 123, cap. 3, ed. Zachariae v. Lingenthal, II, p. 298.

[112]Basilica, lib. III, tit. I, cap. 10, ed. Heimbach, I, p. 95; ed. Zepos, I, p. 119.

[113]Cf. Hefele and Leclercq, II, pp. 800-1, 805-6. Balsamon, in commenting on these two canons (P.G., cxxxvii, cols. 432-3, 499-53), argues that the emperor has the right to promote episcopal sees to the rank of metropolitanates by virtue of the authority given to him by God (col. 432); Zonaras, on the other hand, regards this practice as uncanonical (ibid., col. 436).

[114]P.G., cxxvii, cols. 929-32. Cf. F. Dölger, Regesten der Kaiserurkunden des oströmischen Reiches, II (Munich and Berlin, 1925), p. 37, no. 1140.

[115]Σύνταγμα κατὰ στοιχεῖον: Rhalles and Potles, Σύνταγμα, VI, pp. 274-6.

[116]Cf. N. Skabalanovich, Vizantiiskoe gosudarstvo i tserkov' v XI veke (St. Petersburg, 1884), pp. 269-70, 362; J. M. Hussey, Church and Learning in the Byzantine Empire (London, 1937), pp. 121-2.

[117]Cf. Hussey, op.cit. pp. 121, 133.

[118]Cf. Skabalanovich, op. cit., p. 363; Hussey, op. cit., pp. 125-6; Metropolitan Makary, Istoriya russkoy tserkvi, II, pp. 1-2, n. 1, 214-18. J. Hajjar, "Le synode permanent dans l'église byzantine," Orientalia Christiana Analecta, vol. 164 (1962).

[119]Cf. supra, p. 132.

[120]Published by V. N. Beneshevich, Drevne-slavyanskaya Kormchaya XIV titulov bez tolkovany, I (St. Petersburg, 1906). The relevant canons on episcopal elections are printed on pp. 62,84-5, 261, 269, 319, 345.

[121]Ibid., pp. 284, 125-6. It is interesting to observe that the expression ἐν τοῖς βαρβαρικοῖς in the twenty-eighth canon of the Council of Chalcedon, which the twelfth-century Byzantine canonists extended to include Russia, was translated as "v pogan'skyikh" ("among pagans").

[122]Ibid., pp. 764-6, 800.

[123]Nikonovskaya Letopis', s.a. 1378: Polnoe Sobranie Russkikh Letopisey, XI, p. 37; Cf. Golubinsky, op. cit., II, i, pp. 239-40.

[124]Akty, otnosyashchiesya k istorii Zapadnoy Rossii, I (St. Petersburg, 1846), no. 24, pp. 33-5.

[125]Akty Istoricheskie, I (St. Petersburg, 1841), no. 39, pp. 71-5; Pamyatniki drevne-russkogo kanonicheskogo prava, I²: Russkaya Istoricheskaya Biblioteka, VI (1908), col. 530.

[126]Akty Istoricheskie, I, no. 41, pp. 84-5; Pamyatniki, ibid., no. 71, col. 583. This letter was never sent: cf. Golubinsky, op. cit., II, 1, pp. 487-8.

[127]Akty, I, p. 113, col. 2; Pamyatniki, no. 81, cols. 622-3.

[128]The Lithuanian bishops, it is true, misquoted in 1415 the first Apostolic Canon, by substituting "metropolitan" for "bishop" in its text. They were not, as we shall see (cf. supra, pp. 142-3) the first churchmen to have done so. The suggestion of P. Sokolov that the term "metropolitan" had been fraudulently substituted for "bishop" in the Russian version of the Nomocanon (Russky arkhierey iz Vizantii, p. 71) is quite gratuitous. The bishops would certainly have been better advised to cite the sixth canon of the Council of Sardica.

[129]Cf. Sokolov, Izbranie arkhiereev v Vizantii, loc. cit., p. 251.

[130]See Siotis, op. cit., pp. 82-101, 105-7.

[131]Hefele and Leclercq, Hist. des Conc., I, 539.

[132]Beneshevich, Drevne-slavyanskaya Kormchaya, pp. 84-5.

[133]Balsamon, Zonaras, Aristenes, in Can. IV Conc. Nicaen. I: P.G., cxxxvii, cols. 236-7.

[134]Cf. I. I. Sreznevsky, Materialy dlya slovarya drevne-russkogo yazyka, II (St. Petersburg, 1902), col. 1259.

[135]Cf. note 126.

[136]Cf. note 86.

[137]Cf. note 87.

[138]This is the case of a certain Theophylactus, promoted, according to the fourteenth-century historian Nicephorus Callistus (who used an earlier Greek list of cases of translations of bishops) from the see of Sebasteia to Rus' in the reign of Basil II (976-1025) (P.G., cxlvi, col. 1196: ἐπὶ δὲ τῆς αὐτῆς ἡγεμονίας Θεοφύλακτος ἐκ τῆς Σεβαστηνῶν εἰς Ῥωσίαν ἀνάγεται). Honigmann ("Studies in Slavic Church History," Byzantion, 17 [1944-5], pp. 148-9) takes him to have been, before his transfer to Rus', the metropolitan of Sebasteia in the province Armenia II, and, subsequently, the metropolitan of Russia. Cf. Laurent ("Aux origines de l'Eglise russe," Echos d'Orient, 38 [1939], pp. 293-4). Dvornik, on the other hand, is doubtful of this interpretation and prefers to see in Theophylactus the bishop of Sebasteia under the metropolis of Laodicea, transferred to an episcopal see in Rus'. (The Making of Central and Eastern Europe, p. 179, n. 131). The question remains an open one, though the term

ἀνάγεται, used by Nicephorus Callistus, implying promotion, would seem to favor the view of Honigmann and Laurent. Cf., however, the more sceptical view of Nicephorus' evidence held by M. V. Levchenko ("Vzaimootnosheniya Vizantii i Rusi pri Vladimire," *Vizantiisky Vremennik*, 7 [1953], p. 219).

[139]*Povest'*, *s.a.* 1072, 1073, pp. 121, 122; Cross, p. 154-6. Cf. *Zhitiya svyatykh muchenikov Borisa i Gleba*, ed. D. I. Abramovich (Petrograd, 1916), pp. 21, 56.

[140]Cf. Priselkov, *Ocherki po tserkovno-politicheskoy istorii Kievskoy Rusi*, pp. 123-6; Golubinsky, *op. cit.*, I, 1², pp. 290-1.

[141]For the date of John II's accession see Golubinsky, *ibid.*, p. 286. He is mentioned in the *Primary Chronicle*, *s.a.* 1086, 1088 and 1089 (the last time on the occasion of his death): *Povest'*, pp. 136-7; Cross, pp. 169-70. Theodore Prodromus wrote of himself: Πάππου γὰρ εὐμοίρηκα Προδρομωνύμιου – Καὶ θεῖον ἔσχον Χριστὸν ὠνομασμένον – Γῆς Ῥωσικῆς πρόεδρον ἁβρὸν ἐν λόγοις (Theodori Prodromi *Scripta Miscellanea*, *P.G.*, cxxxiii, col. 1412). V. G. Vasilievsky drew attention to the similiarity between the names Christos and Prodromos which Theodore's uncle must have borne (the first being a personal name, the second a family one), and the superscription "John, metropolitan of Russia, called the prophet of Christ" found in one of the writings of John II (*Trudy*, I [St. Petersburg, 1908], pp. 174-5). Cf. Golubinsky, *op. cit.*, I, 1², p. 266, n. 4.

[142]This is the conclusion drawn from Nicephorus' words by Golubinsky (*ibid.*, pp. 858-9). The text of his sermon is printed in Metropolitan Makary's *Istoriya russkoy tserkvi*, II², pp. 349-52. Ignorance of the Russian language was, it seems, by no means uncommon among the Byzantine metropolitans of Kiev; an example cited in the fifteenth century shows that it could lead to curious results: Basil II of Muscovy, in his letter to the Patriarch Metrophanes, supports his request that the Russians be allowed to appoint their own metropolitan by the additional argument that the necessary discussion of state secrets with the metropolitan must take place, if he is a Greek, in the presence of interpreters, young men whose discretion cannot always be trusted and who thus endanger national security. Cf. note 125.

[143]Cf. See below, pp. 146-8.

[144]Cf. note 138.

[145]Cf. note 1.

[146]*Povest'*, *s. a.* 1051, p. 104; Cross, (p. 139) has mistranslated this passage.

[147]Cf. See above, pp. 135-6.

[148]This is the interpretation given to the passage by the Metropolitan Makary (*op. cit.*, II², p. 300).

[149]*Pamyatniki drevne-russkogo kanonicheskogo prava*, II, 1, ed. V. N. Beneshevich: *Russkaya Istoricheskaya Biblioteka*, xxxvi (1920), p. 103.

[150]So, for instance. G. Vernadsky (*Kievan Russia* [New Haven, 1948], p. 82).

[151]See G. Vernadsky, The Byzantine-Russian war of 1043," *Südost-Forschungen*, XII (Munich, 1953), pp. 47-67; J. Shepard, "Why did the Russians attack Byzantium in 1043?", *Byzant.-neugriech. Jahrbücher*, 22 (1979), pp. 147-212.

[152]*Polnoe Sobranie Russkikh Letopisey*, IX, *s.a.* 1051 (St. Petersburg, 1862), p. 83.

[153]*Povest'*, *s.a.* 1043, 1053, pp. 104, 108; Cross, pp. 138 (who mistranslates "after peace had prevailed for three years thereafter"; the true meaning is: "peace having been concluded three years later"), 142. Vernadsky suggests that after peace was restored in 1046, relations between Kiev and Constantinople were broken off once more, in 1048, and that the final agreement was not concluded till *ca.* 1052 (*op. cit.*, pp. 65-6). This conclusion, however, is, in my opinion, supported by no convincing evidence. For the view that the marriage agreement was reached in 1046 or 1047 see Dölger (*Regesten*, II, p. 7, no. 875) and V. Moshin ("Russkie na Afone i Russko-Vizantiiskie otnosheniya v XI-XII vv.", *Byzantinoslavica*, IX, 1947, pp. 74-5). That the Byzantine princess who married Vsevolod of Russia was the daughter of Constantine IX is stated by the seventeenth-century *Gustin Chronicle* (*Polnoe Sobranie Russkikh Letopisey*, II, *s.a.* 1043 (St. Petersburg, 1843), p. 267.

[154]*Polnoe Sobr. Russk. Let.*, IX, *s.a.* 1051, p. 85.

[155]*Povest'*, *s.a.* 1051, p. 105; Cross, p. 139.

[156]*Polnoe Sobr. Russk. Let.*, IX, p. 83.

[157]Cf. See above, pp. 134-5.

[158]*Pamyatniki polemicheskoy literatury v zapadnoy Rusi*, I: *Russkaya Istoricheskaya Biblioteka*, IV, (1878), cols. 1009-10. The *Gustin Chronicle* goes even further: Hilarion, it asserts, was appointed (*postavlen byst'*) metropolitan of Kiev by the Patriarch Michael Cerularius (*Polnoe Sobr. Russk. Let.*, II, p. 268) — an erroneous statement, since his *postavlenie* (ἡ κατάστασις, ἡ χειροτονία) was carried out by the Russian bishops, but one which may be taken to refer loosely to the Patriarch's ratifica-

tion (τὸ κῦρος) of the appointment.

[159]Cf., for example: *Novgorodskaya Pervaya Letopis'*, ed. A. N. Nasonov (Moscow, 1950), pp. 163, 473; *Voskresenskaya Letopis': Polnoe Sobr. Russk. Let.*, VII (St. Petersburg, 1856), p. 239. Cf. note 84.

[160]This view is put forward by the Metropolitan Makary (*op. cit.*, II², pp. 6-7) and by Golubinsky (*op. cit.*, I, I², pp. 297-300), who suggest, rightly in my opinion, that Hilarion's appointment was recognized in Byzantium.

[161]*Ipatievskaya Letopis'*, *s.a.* 1147: *Polnoe Sobr. Russk. Let.*, II, p. 30.

[162]Cf. Sokolov, *Russky arkhierey iz Vizantii*, pp. 61-3.

[163]Cf. See above, pp. 134-5.

[164]Cf. See above, pp. 131-5.

[165]Cf. Sokolov, pp. 67-8.

[166]*Istoriya Rossiiskaya*, II (Moscow, 1773), p. 301.

[167]On the general value of Tatishchev's evidence, see V. S. Ikonnikov, *Opyt russkoy istoriografii*, I, 1 (Kiev, 1891), pp. 50, 117-9, 123; II, 1 (1908), pp. 333-8; *Russky biografichesky slovar'*, vol. Suvorova-Tkachev (St. Petersburg, 1912), pp. 332-46; N. L. Rubinshtein, *Russkaya istoriografiya* (Moscow, 1941), pp. 77-9.

[168]The confused state of the chronicle's account of Clement's election is noted by Golubinsky (*op. cit.*, I, I², pp. 302-3) and by Sokolov (*op. cit.*, p. 65).

[169]Cf. G. Vernadsky, "Relations byzantino-russes au XIIᵉ siècle," *Byzantion*, 4 (1927-8), pp. 269-76; *Kievan Russia*, pp. 217-8.

[170]*Ipatievskaya Letopis'*, *s.a.* 1156: *PSRL*, II, pp. 79-80.

[171]Tatishchev, *Istoriya Rossiiskaya*, III, pp. 36, 98, 117.

[172]*Ipatievskaya Letopis'*, *s.a.* 1159, *ibid.*, p. 85; cf. Golubinsky, *ibid.*, pp. 312-3.

[173]Tatishchev, *op. cit.*, III, pp. 117-9.

[174]*Ipatievskaya Letopis'*, *s.a.* 1161: *PSRL*, II, p. 89.

[175]*Ibid.*, *s.a.* 1164, p. 92.

[176]Tatishchev, *op. cit.*, III, p. 142.

[177]The sceptics in this matter include Golubinsky (*op. cit.*, I, I², pp. 313-5), M. Hrushevsky (*Ocherk istorii Kievskoy zemli ot smerti Yaroslava do kontsa XIV stoletiya* [Kiev, 1891], pp. 363-4; the earlier opinions of Russian historians are cited here), and Sokolov (*op. cit.*, pp. 122-3).

[178]Apart from the older historians, like the Metropolitan Makary and S. M. Soloviev, who regarded Rostislav's speech as genuine, more recent scholars such as F. Chalandon (*Jean II Comnène et Manuel Iᵉʳ Comnène* [Paris, 1912], p. 482), S. P. Shestakov ("Vizantiisky posol na Rus' Manuil Komnen," *Sbornik statey v chest' D. A. Korsakova* [Kazan, 1913], pp. 366-81, Dölger (*Regesten*, II, p. 77), and Grumel (*Les Regestes des Actes du Patriarcat de Constantinople*, I, 3, no. 1056, p. 118) state that as a result of these negotiations Rostislav accepted John IV, but on condition that in the future no metropolitan of Kiev was to be appointed by the patriarch without his consent. This view implies a positive assessment of Tatishchev's evidence. Cf. M. Angold, *The Byzantine Empire, 1025-1204* (London, 1984), p. 176.

[179]Ioannes Cinnamus, *Histor.*, lib. V, cap. 12 (Bonn, 1836), pp. 235-6.

[180]Cf. See above, p. 146.

[181]Cf. See above, pp. 143-4.

[182]Cf. note 178.

[183]Tatishchev, *op. cit.*, III, pp. 151, 157. Constantine II's arrival in Russia is mentioned in the *First Novgorod Chronicle*, *s.a.* 1167, ed. Nasonov, p. 32.

[184]Cf. See above, pp. 135-6.

[185]Cf. See above, pp. 145-6.

[186]Cf. See above, p. 146.

[187]Tatishchev, *op. cit.*, II, p. 225. On Nicetas' accession to the see of Kiev, see the Laurentian and the Hypatian Chronicles, *s.a.* 1122.

[188]Tatishchev is the only source to give the name (Dobrodeya) of this Russian princess, and to state that the marriage, once agreed upon, was delayed for two years owing to the youthfulness of the bride and bridegroom. Cf. Kh. Loparev, "Brak Mstislavny (1122)," *Vizantiisky Vremennik*, 9 (1902), pp. 418-45; S. Papadimitriou, "Brak russkoy knyazhny Mstislavny Dobrodei s grecheskim tsarevichem Alekseem Komninom," ibid., 11 (1904), pp. 73-98.

[189]Tatishchev, *op. cit.*, III, p. 365.

[190]*Povest'*, *s.a.* 1089, p. 137; Cross, p. 170. Cf. Vasilievsky, *Trudy*, II, 1, p. 36; Priselkov, *op. cit.*, pp. 163-4; Sokolov, *op. cit.*, p. 153.

One might feel tempted to add two more names to this list: (1) the Metropolitan Efrem, mentioned in the *Primary Chronicle s.a.* 1089 (*Povest'*, p. 137, Cross, p. 170), is said in a contemporary source to have been, before his consecration, a member of the household of Prince Izyaslav I of Kiev (Nestor's *Life of St. Theodosius: Chteniya v Moskovskom Istoricheskom Obshchestve*, III [1858,], 3, p. 75): this suggests that he may have been a Russian. (2) According to the seventeenth-century *Gustin Chronicle*, a certain Cyril was consecrated metropolitan of Kiev in 1225, and was a Russian (*Polnoe Sobr. Russk. Let.*, II, *s.a.* 1225, p. 335). Both cases, however, are dubious. Efrem, though the *Nikon Chronicle* calls him "metropolitan of Kiev and of All Russia" (*Polnoe Sobr. Russk. Let.*, IX, *s.a.* 1091, 1095, 1096, pp. 116, 125, 128), in all probability was only the bishop of Pereyaslavl' and bore the honorary title of metropolitan: Cf. Golubinsky, *op. cit.*, I, 1², pp. 287, n. 2, 328-9; Sokolov, *op. cit.*, p. 53. As for Cyril, his very existence is dubious: the *Gustin Chronicle*, followed by the later catalogues of primates of Russia, mentions the appointment in rapid succession of two metropolitans of that name: the first Cyril, a Russian, consecrated in 1225; the second one, of unspecified origin, consecrated in 1230. We know from earlier and unimpeachable sources that between 1224 and 1233 the see of Kiev was occupied by Cyril II, a Byzantine prelate sent from Nicaea (cf. *supra*, note 86).

[191]Thus Tatishchev asserts that in 1096 the prince of Kiev, Svyatopolk II, chose Nicephorus, Bishop of Polotsk, for the office of metropolitan and had him consecrated by the Russian bishops (*op. cit.*, II, pp. 169, 479, n. 421). A Metropolitan Nicephorus is mentioned by the *Nikon Chronicle s.a.* 1097 (*Polnoe Sobr. Russk. Let.*, IX, p. 132), so that Tatishchev's evidence is not *prima facie* incredible. However, in that same year a Metropolitan Nicholas is mentioned in the *Primary Chronicle* (*Povest'*, *s.a.* 1097, p. 174; Cross, p. 191). A confusion between the names Nicholas and Nicephorus is certainly within the bounds of possibility.

[192]Cf. note 125.

[193]Cf. See above, pp. 152-3.

[194]Cf. B. Granić, "Kirchenrechtliche Glossen zu den vom Kaiser Basileios II. dem autokephalen Erzbistum von Achrida verliehenen Privilegien," *Byzantion*, 12 (1937), pp. 395-415; Ostrogorsky, *History*, p. 276, note 1.

[195]Cf. See above, pp. 118-19.

[196]Cf. See above, pp. 123-24.

[197]Cf. See above, pp. 117-18.

[198]Some of the views expressed in this article were put forward in a tentative and preliminary manner in a paper read by the author at a symposium on "Byzantium and the Slavs" held at Dumbarton Oaks in April, 1952; also previously, in a shorter form, at the Eighth International Congress of Byzantine Studies at Palermo in 1951. A brief summary of this communication ("Le Patriarcat Byzantin et les métropolites de Kiev") is printed in *Atti dello VIII Congresso Internazionale di Studi Bizantini*, I (Rome, 1953), pp. 437-8 [*Studi Bizantini e Neoellenici*, 7].

CHAPTER V

BYZANTIUM AND RUSSIA IN THE LATE MIDDLE AGES*

"Russia, as I have said earlier, is a highly populated country; the length and breadth of the land occupied by its inhabitants cannot at all easily be measured; the annual produce harvested from its crops is very large and varied; a considerable amount of silver is produced from there, mined in the country; and because that country is gripped by cold owing to its distance from the sun, nature, as you would expect, breeds a large number of thick-fleeced animals which are hunted and whose hides are exported by the local inhabitants to every other land and city, bringing them much gain. And in the neighboring ocean fishes are caught some of whose bones provide useful enjoyment for satraps and princes and kings and for nearly all those who lead a refined life, and are distinguished men. I forbear to mention how much more abundant wealth the Russians obtain in addition by exporting these objects abroad."[1] This description, written about 1355 in Constantinople by the Byzantine historian Nicephorus Gregoras, illustrates the interest which the Byzantines retained, after four and a half centuries of trade with Russia, in the economic resources of the country, and particularly in the raw materials exported from the steppes and forests north of the Black Sea. Their trade relations with Russia, after a temporary eclipse due to the Mongol invasion and to the Latin conquest of Constantinople, revived in the fourteenth century,[2] though the benefit they brought to Byzantium was reduced by the fact that the Black Sea trade was then controlled by the Genoese and the Venetians. However, food supplies from the northern coast of the Black Sea remained of vital importance

---

*J.R. Hale, J.R.L. Highfield, and B. Smalley (eds.). *Europe in the Late Middle Ages* (London, 1965), 248-75.

to Constantinople, and the expulsion in 1343 of the Genoese and the Venetians by the Tatars from the port of Tana near the estuary of the Don, and the subsequent siege by the same Tatars of the Genoese colony of Kaffa in the Crimea, resulted in an acute shortage of bread and salted fish in the Byzantine capital and other cities of the empire.[3] Russian money was as necessary to Byzantium as Russian raw materials. The authorities of Constantinople, faced with the financial ruin of their state, reduced to pawning the Crown jewels and to using leaden and earthenware goblets at the feast of the emperor's cornation in 1347,[4] were now, for any extraordinary expense, wholly dependent on foreign aid. In 1346 an earthquake seriously damaged the church of St Sophia. The ruler of Muscovy sent a large sum of money for the repair of the building.[5] A further sum was sent in 1398 by the grand prince of Moscow, Basil I, to the aid of Constantinople, blockaded at that time by the Turks; a donation intended, in the words of a contemporary Russian chronicle, as "alms for those who are in such need and misery."[6] Each of these gifts was obtained through the good offices of the primate of the Russian Church who, as an appointee of the patriarch of Constantinople and the representative of the emperor, was expected to promote both the ecclesiastical and the secular interests of the empire in Russia. A further contribution from the Russians was sought in 1400: the patriarch of Constantinople wrote to the primate, the Metropolitan Cyprian, urging him, "as a friend of the Byzantines" (ὡς φιλορρώμαιος ἄνθρωπος) to start another fund-raising campaign; he was to assure his Russian flock that it was more meritorious to contribute money for the defense of Constantinople than to build churches, to give alms to the poor, or to redeem prisoners: "for this holy City," wrote the patriarch, "is the pride, the support, the sanctification, and the glory of Christians in the whole inhabited world."[7]

It was not for economic reasons alone that the Byzantines became, in the second half of the fourteenth century, increasingly aware of the advantages to be derived from their relations with Russia. The military and political situation of Byzantium justified the gravest anxieties. The Ottoman Turks, established in Europe since the middle of the century, took no more than four decades to seize most of what remained of Byzantine territory, conquer Bulgaria, and crush the resistance of the Serbian state. By the end of the century, except for its dependency in the Peloponnese and a few islands in the Aegean, the empire was reduced to Constantinople, and the position of the capital, blockaded by the Turks, seemed desperate. It was clear that only foreign military aid on a massive scale could save the dying empire. The emperors' hopes were mainly focused on obtaining help from the West: John V's visit to Italy (1369-71) failed to achieve anything; Manuel II's journey to Italy, Paris and London (1399-1403) was not more successful; and the Hungarian attempt to reconquer the Balkans from the Turks came to ruin at the battle of Nicopolis (1396). In their desperate search for allies, the Byzantine authorities could not fail to observe the significant changes that were taking place in the second half of the fourteenth century on the confines of eastern Europe. In the Russian lands, which around 1300 had formed a congeries of petty principalities virtually independent of each other and subject to the formidable power of the Golden Horde, two political structures had now emerged, competing for the allegiance of the eastern Slavs: the grand duchy of Lithuania and the principality of Moscow. The territories of the former comprised most of western and south-western Russia, and, since about 1362, included the ancient Russian capital of Kiev; Muscovy, still the smaller of the two, was claiming, with growing conviction and success, to embody the political and cultural traditions of Kievan Rus', a state with which Byzantium had enjoyed particularly close and mutually beneficial relations in the early Middle Ages. The Muscovite princes, thrifty, persistent and unscrupulous, pursuing at first a policy of abject submissiveness to the Golden Horde, had embarked, with the blessing of the Church and the support of their *boyars*, on the task of "gathering" the whole of eastern Russia under their sway. By the end of the fourteenth century the power of Muscovy had greatly increased. Among the many causes of its eventual triumph over its rivals we may single out — next to the support consistently given to its rulers by the Russian Church — the belief which was growing in Russia that the prince of Moscow was alone strong enough to stand up to the Tatars and to achieve one day the long-awaited liberation of the country. This faith acquired substance in 1380, when the Russian troops, commanded by Dimitri, prince of Moscow, defeated a large Tatar army at Kulikovo by the River Don. Contemporary Russian sources hail this victory as a great triumph for Muscovy and for the Christian faith; and although from a short-term point of view Kulikovo proved a Pyrrhic victory — two years later Moscow was sacked by a Mongol vassal of Timur — its effect on the prestige of the principality of Moscow, both inside and outside Russia, was lasting and considerable.

The Byzantine government was well aware of these changes which

were affecting the balance of power in the lands to the north of the
Black Sea, an area which, since the early Middle Ages, the imperial
diplomatists had scrutinized with peculiar care.[8] To ensure the friendship and loyalty of the peoples who dwelt in this area had been a
cardinal principle of the empire's foreign policy during its heyday in
the ninth, tenth and eleventh centuries, when Byzantine influence and
prestige throughout eastern Europe were at their height; in the fourteenth and early fifteenth centuries, when Byzantium was a second-
rate power, fighting for its life, such a policy had become more essential than ever. It was also far more difficult to implement. The
Byzantines, however, still held two trump cards: the fascination
exerted by the city of Constantinople on the minds of the peoples of
eastern Europe; and the unifying force of Orthodox Christianity, of
which the Byzantines were regarded (at least until 1439) as the most
authoritative exponents, and whose administrative centre and spiritual
heart were in Constantinople. In the absence of a foreign policy based
on power, the Byzantines were reduced in the fourteenth century to
playing these cards as best they could. During the period between
1350 and 1453, Byzantine foreign policy in eastern Europe was
increasingly driven to rely on the good offices of the Church, whose
supreme executive organ, the Oecumenical Patriarchate, in striking
contrast to the versatile opportunism of the imperial government, was
assuming the role of chief spokesman and instrument of the imperial
traditions of East Rome. Hence, in practical terms, the authorities of
Byzantium were faced with a double program of action: they were
impelled, on the one hand, to consolidate and extend the spiritual
authority of the Oecumenical Patriarchate over the nations of eastern
Europe; and, on the other, to ensure the loyalty of these same nations
to Byzantium by making diplomatic concessions to their national susceptibilities; and this, particularly in the fourteenth century, meant
granting a measure of self-government to those churches outside the
empire which owed allegiance to the see of Constantinople. The fact
that the empire's foreign policy in eastern Europe was then primarily
directed towards these two goals explains the dominant role played by
ecclesiastical affairs — and to a large extent by ecclesiastical diplomacy — in the history of Russo-Byzantine relations in the period
under review.

The ecclesiastical relations between Byzantium and the Russian
lands in the fourteenth century were mostly concerned with the vexed
problem of the jurisdiction, place of residence, and method of

appointment of the primates of the Russian Church. Until the Mongol invasions of the thirteenth century these dignitaries, who were apppointed by the patriarch of Constantinople, resided in Kiev. In 1300, owing to the political fragmentation of the realm, the devastation of Kiev by the Mongols, and the growing political ascendancy of north-east Russia, the metropolitan moved his residence to Vladimir, whence in 1328 it was transferred to Moscow. These successive moves had as yet no significance *de jure*, and the primate of the Russian Church retained until the mid-fifteenth century his traditional title of "Metropolitan of Kiev and of All Russia." In practice, however, from the early fourteenth century the metropolitans increasingly identified themselves with the policies and aspirations of the princes of Moscow. It was only natural that Moscow's rivals for the still contested political hegemony over Russia sought to deprive their opponent of the considerable moral and political advantages derived from the presence within the city walls of the chief bishop of the Russian Church. Their best hope lay in persuading the Byzantine authorities to set up separate metropolitanates in their respective territories. Throughout the fourteenth century Constantinople was bombarded with such requests — from the princes of Galicia, from the grand dukes of Lithuania and, in one case, from the king of Poland; these demands, usually backed by promises, threats or financial bribes, were often successful; and with bewildering and unedifying frequency the emperors and the patriarchs of Constantinople[9] set up in the fourteenth century separate metropolitanates for Galicia and for Lithuania, only to abolish them a few decades, or years, later.[10] The rise of these splinter churches signified the retreat of the Byzantine authorities before the political or economic pressure of rulers who controlled portions of west Russian territory; while their successive abolitions represented as many concessions made by the imperial government and Church to the wishes of the Muscovite sovereigns who, for political reasons, were anxious to exercise through their own metropolitans an authority over the Russian communities outside the boundaries of the Muscovite state. The Byzantine authorities preferred to see a united Russian Church governed by a single primate: tradition, administrative convenience, and a reluctance to submit to foreign secular pressures, caused them to favor a centralized solution; and in the second half of the fourteenth century this solution became the more acceptable to them, as it coincided with the wishes of the Muscovite rulers, whose power commanded increasing respect, and whose military and economic resources the empire in its dire predicament so desperately needed.

The problem of the extent of the Russian metropolitans' jurisdiction was bound up with the question of how, and by whom, they were to be appointed. On this question the Byzantines and the Russians held strong, and often conflicting, views. The former, who regarded the metropolitans of Russia as valuable diplomatic agents, capable of using their moral and spiritual authority to ensure the loyalty of their Russian flock to the empire, were naturally anxious to retain control over the appointment and consecration of these dignitaries; and, for equally obvious reasons, the Muscovite sovereigns, while accepting the principle that their metropolitans were to be approved and consecrated by the patriarchs of Constantinople, wished to have as much influence as possible on their selection. These conflicting claims were for a long time resolved by compromise: from 1237 to 1378 Byzantine and Russian candidates were, with striking regularity, appointed in turn by the patriarchs to the metropolitan see of Kiev and All Russia. There are grounds for believing that this regular alternation was the result of a special agreement concluded between the Byzantine and the Russian authorities.[11] The problems involved in the appointment of the metropolitans of Russia became the central issue in the diplomatic relations between Byzantium and Muscovy in the late Middle Ages. Its historical importance far transcends the level of the obscure and often discreditable manoeuvres ascribed to both parties in the documents of the time. Behind these dubious operations, affecting their outcome or flowing from their cause, we can discern the diplomatic techniques employed by the Byzantine patriarchate and by the Muscovite experts on foreign affairs; the conflict and alignment of different ecclesiastical programs within Byzantium and Russia; the changing pattern of power politics in eastern Europe; and — the most significant in the long run of these factors — the slow crystallization in Muscovy of a new attitude towards the Byzantine empire, an attitude closely linked with the development of post-medieval Russian nationalism.

All these factors were already present in some degree in the circumstances that attended the appointment in 1354 of the Russian bishop Alexius as metropolitan of Kiev and All Russia. The decree of the Synod of the Byzantine Church, signed by the Patriarch Philotheus on 30th June of that year, states unequivocally that the Synod's decision to appoint Alexius was influenced by the wishes of "the great king" of Russia.[12] But it also claims that the appointment of a native to the metropolitanate of Russia is an unusual and dangerous step, which must not be regarded as a precedent. This synodal decree, at times evasive and disingenuous, clothed in the expert phraseology of East Roman diplomacy, is remarkable for its desire to satisfy the demands of the Muscovite authorities, and for its assertion that the appointment of a native Russian "is by no means customary nor safe for the Church." The first of these features can be explained by the political and ecclesiastical situation in eastern Europe: in 1354, the very year in which the Ottomans established themselves on European soil at Gallipoli, and in which the Venetian ambassador to Constantinople informed his government that the Byzantines would readily submit to any power that would save them from the Turks and the Genoese,[13] the East Roman government was not unnaturally disposed to lend a favorable ear to the demands of a friendly state from which at least economic assistance could be expected — the principality of Moscow and its "great king." The patriarch, too, had his reasons for being conciliatory towards the Muscovite ruler. Philotheus consistently strove to consolidate the authority of the see of Constantinople over the nations of eastern Europe. The Balkan Slavonic churches were in 1354 slipping away from his control; the more reason for making sure of the continued loyalty of the Russians, the most numerous of the foreign proselytes of Byzantium. Yet this concession to the Russian demands must have been costly to the patriarch's conscience: for it involved a betrayal of his conviction that the Church should not submit to any form of secular pressure. Philotheus was a leading member of the party of "zealots" in the Byzantine Church, who, in opposition to the "politicians" or "moderates," insisted on the freedom of ecclesiastical appointments.[14] The acceptance of a candidate for a high ecclesiastical post in deference to the wishes of a secular ruler — and a foreign one at that — was a serious derogation of the principle of "strictness" in the application of canon law and a capitulation to his opponents who, in accordance with the opposite principle of "economy," believed that the Church in its relations with the secular powers, both at home and abroad, should not intransigently reject all concessions and compromises. The painful dilemma in which Philotheus found himself in 1354 no doubt accounts for his cavalier treatment of historical truth: for the Synod's bland assertion that the appointment of a native Russian to the see of Kiev and All Russia was "by no means customary" is contradicted by the fact that for the past 117 years there had been — if Alexius himself is included in the list — three Russian and three Byzantine holders of this post.[15]

The Synod's resolve not to tolerate any more Russian metropolitans proved wholly ineffectual, for during the six years that elapsed after Alexius' death in 1378, the patriarchate agreed on three different occasions to the appointment of a native primate.[16] Its inconstancy was further demonstrated by its failure to give adequate support to Alexius himself, who until 1361 had the greatest difficulty in maintaining his rights over Kiev against Olgerd, grand duke of Lithuania, and his nominee, Roman, whom the patriarch had appointed metropolitan of Lithuania in 1354. In 1373 the Patriarch Philotheus sent an envoy to Russia, to investigate the complaints received from the Lithuanian ruler about Alexius' conduct. Two years later this patriarchal envoy, Cyprian, was appointed by the patriarch metropolitan of Kiev and All Russia, with the proviso that the latter half of his title, which implied jurisdiction over the Muscovite Church, would become effective as soon as the accusations against Alexius could be substantiated. However, as we learn from a Byzantine source,[17] the patriarch's commission of inquiry found these accusations devoid of substance, and was impressed by Alexius' immense popularity in Muscovy. He was allowed to retain his authority over the Muscovite Church.[18]

These dubious manoeuvers were scarcely calculated to enhance the popularity of the emperor and patriarch in Muscovy. The Russians found it hard to forgive the humiliation which the Byzantine authorities had so unjustly imposed on the Metropolitan Alexius, who was not only a highly respected spiritual leader, but something of a national hero. The patriarch's decision to appoint Cyprian as primate of All Russia while the case of Alexius was still *sub judice* — taken in order to please the Lithuanian ruler — was, despite the fact that it was later rescinded, felt to be a bitter humiliation. The Byzantines themselves were impressed by the "great tumult," the "uproar," and the "attitude of revolt" which this affair had provoked all over Russia.[19] And in 1378 Cyprian complained that as a result of these events the Muscovites "were abusing the Patriarch, the Emperor, and the Great Synod: they called the Patriarch a Lithuanian, and the Emperor too, and the most honourable Great Synod.[20]

But worse was to come. In 1379, a year after Alexius' death, his successor-elect, the Russian cleric Michael (Mityai), chosen by the grand prince of Moscow and already accepted by the patriarch, set out from Moscow to Constantinople for his consecration. But as the Russian ships sailed down the Bosphorus, a few miles from his destination, Michael suddenly died. His Russian escort, thoughtfully provided by the prince of Moscow with blank charters adorned with his seal and signature, and with a considerable sum of money, used the former to substitute the name of one of their party, the Archimandrite Pimen, for that of the defunct Michael, and probably distributed the money as bribes to officials in Constantinople. With the help of these forged documents they persuaded the Patriarch Nilus to consecrate Pimen as "Metropolitan of Kiev and Great Russia." This sordid and disreputable deal, for which the Russian envoys and the officials of the Byzantine patriarchate must bear joint responsibility,[21] resulted in a period of extreme confusion in the affairs of the Russian Church, which lasted for twelve years and ended with the acceptance by the Muscovites of Cyprian as metropolitan of Russia (1390).

The Muscovite Prince Dimitri, who on these two occasions (in 1375-6 and in 1379-80) found himself a victim of these machinations of Byzantine diplomacy, could hardly have been expected to entertain feelings of goodwill towards the authorities of Constantinople, and especially towards the emperor, whose influence on the appointment of the metropolitans of Russia was usually only too apparent. It is, however, in the reign of Dimitri's son and successor, Basil I (1389-1425), that occurred the first recorded instance of a revolt by the Russians, not indeed against the authority of the Constantinopolitan Church, but against the claims of the Byzantine emperors to exercise a measure of direct jurisdiction over the whole Orthodox Christian world. In 1393[22] Antony IV, patriarch of Constantinople, sent a letter to Basil I of Moscow, rebuking him for having caused his metropolitan to omit the emperor's name from the commemorative diptychs of the Russian Church.[23] The patriarch reprimanded the Muscovite ruler for having expressed contempt for the emperor and having made disparaging remarks about him. He took a particularly grave view of the fact that the Russian sovereign had declared: "We have the Church, but not the emperor." To acknowledge the authority over Russia of the patriarch but not of the emperor is, as Antony points out, a contradiction in terms: for "it is not possible for Christians to have the Church and not to have the empire. For Church and empire have a great unity and community; nor is it possible for them to be separated from one another." And, in an attempt to save Basil I from the consequences of his grievous error, and in pursuance of his own duty as "universal teacher of all Christians," the patriarch solemnly reiterates the fundamental principle of Byzantine political philosophy: "The holy emperor," he writes, "is not as other rulers and governors of other regions are . . . he is annointed with the great chrism, and is elected *basileus* and *autokrator* of the Romans — to wit, of all Christians." These other rulers exercise a purely local authority; the *basileus* alone is "the lord and master of the inhabited world," the "universal emperor," "the natural king," whose laws and ordinances are accepted in the whole world. His universal sovereignty is made manifest by the liturgical commemoration of his name in the churches of Christendom; and, as the patriarch's letter unequivocally implies, the grand prince of Moscow by discontinuing this practice within his realm had deliberately rejected the very foundations of Christian law and government.[24]

There are few documents which express with such force and clarity the basic theory of the medieval Byzantine state. The Patriarch Antony's letter contains a classic exposition of the doctrine of the universal East Roman empire, ruled by the *basileus*, successor of Constantine and vicegerent of God, the natural and God-appointed master of the *Oikoumene*, supreme law-giver of Christendom, whose authority was held to extend, at least in a spiritual and "metapolitical" sense, over all Christian rulers and peoples. The fact that this uncompromising profession of faith was made from the capital of a state that was facing political and military collapse, only emphasizes the astonishing strength and continuity of this political vision which pervades the entire history of the Byzantine body politic. "The doctrine of one oecumenical Emperor," writes Professor Ostrogorsky, "had never been laid down more forcibly or with more fiery eloquence than in this letter which the Patriarch of Constantinople sent to Moscow from a city blockaded by the Turks."[25]

What significance should we attach to the refusal of the Muscovite sovereign to recognize, in the late fourteenth century, the universalist claims of the Byzantine emperor? This question can best be answered by considering how far, and in what sense, these claims were acknowledged in Russia before and after the reception of the patriarch's admonitory letter by Basil I. Direct evidence on this point is not abundant, and doubtless for good reason: the Russian rulers, however genuine their reverence for the city of Constantinople and its supreme authorities, were always careful to safeguard their own political prerogatives, and anxious, within the scope allowed them by their Mongol overlords, to be seen to exercise their national sovereignty. Some indication of their attitude to the emperor of Byzantium has nevertheless been preserved in the documents of the time. In the late thirteenth or early fourteenth century, a Russian ruler is said to have borne the Byzantine court title of "steward of the Emperor's Household"[26] — a sign of his recognition of the traditional right of the emperor to bestow such titles on distinguished subjects or dependent princes; and the same ruler is said to have sent an envoy to Andronicus II, who conveyed to the emperor "the reverent homage" of his Russian master.[27] The authenticity of this form of address is possibly suspect, and its servility may reflect no more than the wishful thinking of the Byzantine author who records the event. But it is not impossible that the Byzantine title was borne by at least one Russian ruler. The next piece of evidence comes from the mid-fourteenth century. In a letter written in September 1347 to Symeon, the grand prince of Moscow, the Emperor John VI Cantacuzenus stated: "Yes, the Empire of the Romans, as well as the most holy Great Church of God is — as you yourself have written — the source of all piety and the teacher of law and sanctification."[28] This statement clearly implies the existence of an earlier letter — not extant — written by the Russian sovereign to the emperor, in which he explicitly acknowledged the legislative authority of the *basileus* over Russia.[29] And in 1452, the year before the fall of Constantinople, the grand prince of Moscow, Basil II, wrote to the last emperor of Byzantium, Constantine XI, in these terms: "You have received your great imperial sceptre, your patrimony, in order to confirm all the Orthodox Christians of your realm and to render great assistance to our Russian dominion and to all our religion."[30] The idea that the emperor enjoys certain prerogatives in Russia is, though veiled in diplomatic language, clearly apparent in these two texts.[31] His universal authority was further emphasized in the Byzantine collections of canon and imperial law which enjoyed great authority in Russia throughout the Middle Ages.[32] And the teachers and guardians of canonical rectitude in Russia, the primates of the Russian Church, could be expected, especially when they were Byzantine citizens, to instil in their flock an awe-struck reverence for the emperor's supreme position in Christendom. It would be quite misleading to try to interpret the relations between the emperor and the princes of Russia in terms either of medieval suzerainty and vassalage, or of the modern distinction between sovereign and dependent states. The Byzantines themselves sometimes thought of the Christian nations of eastern Europe in terms of Roman administration, and described their relationship to the imperial government with the help of technical terms once used to designate the status of the "foederati" and "socii populi

Romani," autonomous subject-allies of the Roman empire.[33] However, in the last resort, any attempt to define the political relations between Byzantium and medieval Russia in precise legal or constitutional terms will obscure and distort their true picture. It is certain that, in practice, the Russian sovereigns would never have tolerated, except in ecclesiastical matters, any direct intervention of the emperor in the internal affairs of their principalities; and that their relationship to the *basileus* was something different from their very tangible allegiance to the khans of the Golden Horde who, between 1240 and 1480, imposed tribute and conferred investiture upon them.[34] But at the same time it cannot be doubted that from the conversion of Rus' to Christianity in the tenth century to the fall of Byzantium in 1453, the Russian authorities — with the sole recorded exception of Basil I of Muscovy — acknowledged, at least tacitly, that the *basileus* was the supreme head of the Christian commonwealth, that as such he possessed by divine right a measure of jurisdiction over Russia, and that, in the words of the Patriarch Antony, "it is not possible for Christians to have the Church and not to have the empire." The difficulty of reconciling the national aspirations of the Russian sovereigns of the Middle Ages with their acceptance of the emperor's supremacy will largely disappear if Russo-Byzantine connections are viewed not from the standpoint of modern inter-state relations, nor in terms — unhappily fashionable — of a struggle between Russian "nationalism" and Byzantine "imperialism," but in the context of a supra-national community of Christian states — the Byzantine *Oikoumene* of which Constantinople was the centre and the whole of eastern and southeastern Europe the domain. This community, as most Russians thought until 1453, was destined to foreshadow on earth the Heavenly Kingdom, until the last days and the coming of Antichrist.[35]

We have no direct knowledge of the effect which the patriarch's letter had on Basil I. It seems likely that the emperor's name was restored before long to the diptychs of the Russian Church: for already in 1398 the Muscovite government sent a large sum of money to the Emperor Manuel II for the defense of Constantinople.[36] And the tone of profound respect with which, as we have seen, Basil I's successor addressed the *basileus* a year before the fall of Constantinople strongly suggests that, so long as this city remained in Christian hands, the Russians never again revolted against the ordered hierarchy of the Byzantine *Oikoumene*.

The preceding survey will have suggested that the attitude of the

Russians towards Byzantium in the late Middle Ages was to a marked degree ambiguous: thus their strong resentment of the methods employed by the Byzantine authorities in the second half of the four-teenth century in making appointments to the Russian metropolitan see did not prevent them from contributing generous sums of money for the architectural and military needs of Constantinople; and Basil I's ill-tempered gesture of bravado against the emperor's authority should not obscure the fact that both his predecessors and his successor recognized, at least tacitly, the oecumenical jurisdiction of the *basileus*. This emotional polarity in the Russian response to Byzantium, this complex amalgam of attraction and repulsion, is traceable through the entire history of Russia's relations with the empire. The memories of the wars waged by the Russians against Byzantium in the tenth cen-tury, whose more vivid episodes were proudly recorded by Russian chroniclers, contributed to the rise of a national heroic tradition which left its mark on the country's medieval literature; in the struggle for native metropolitans, which began in the eleventh century and reached its climax in the fourteenth, the Russians came to resent the insistence of the patriarchs on selecting their own candidates when they felt strong enough to do so, and to despise the ease with which, whenever the empire was weak, the Byzantine authorities yielded on this issue to Russian secular pressure or to the lure of Muscovite gold. And more generally, the superior skill of the Byzantine diplomatists, whose pol-icy towards Russia was aimed at securing military and economic assistance, and ensuring the loyalty of the Russians to the Church of Constantinople,[37] tended to instill in the victims of this diplomatic game of chess a distrust of Byzantine motives and a conviction that "the Greeks"[38] were political intriguers and much too fond of money. The aphorism "the Greeks have remained tricksters to the present day," coined by a Russian chronicler of the eleventh or early twelfth century,[39] was no doubt frequently and pointedly quoted in medieval Russia.

Yet this accumulated legacy of pride, bitterness and distrust paled before the vision, revealed to the Russians of the Middle Ages, of what Byzantium stood for in the things of the mind and spirit. The immensity of the debt which their country owed to the civilization of the empire was apparent wherever they might look: religion and law, literature and art, bore witness to the fact that the Russians, for all the original features in their cultural life, had been, and still were, the pupils of East Rome. In the fourteenth and early fifteenth centuries

Byzantine cultural influences, after a period of decline due to the Mongol invasions, were reviving in Russia; and the work of the Byzantine painter Theophanes, who lived for some thirty years in Russia and produced his masterpieces in Novgorod and (after 1395) in Moscow, shows how close was the connection between late medieval Russian painting and the Palaeologan art of Constantinople.[40] The devotion of the Russians to the mother Church of Constantinople and to its patriarchs was, despite the frictions over primatial appointments, genuine and profound; and not once, at least until 1439, did they seriously entertain the idea of severing their canonical dependence on the see of Constantinople which went back to the early days of Russian Christianity. For this loyalty there was indeed much justification. The Byzantine metropolitans of Russia were for the most part worthy and zealous men; the emperors and the patriarchs were often genuinely concerned to see the Christian faith flourish in Russia; and Russian monasticism, nurtured in the traditions of Constantinople and Mount Athos, was in the second half of the fourteenth century powerfully reviving under the leadership of St Sergius of the Monastery of the Holy Trinity and in close contact with the contemplative schools of Byzantine hesychasm.[41] But the prevailing attitude of the Russians towards Byzantium was not simply that of pupil to master: it was, in a sense, more simple and spontaneous, and is perhaps best epitomized in their reverence for the city of Constantinople, which, in their own language, they called *Tsargrad*, the Imperial City. In the eyes of the Russians — and indeed of all eastern Christendom — Constantinople was a holy city not only because, being the New Rome, it was the seat of the *basileus* and of his spiritual partner, the oecumenical patriarch. The city's essential holiness lay in the supernatural forces abundantly present within its walls: the many relics of Christ's passion and of the saints; the numerous churches and monasteries, storehouses of prayer and famed shrines of Christendom; and above all the patronage of the city's heavenly protectors, the Divine Wisdom, whose temple was St Sophia, and the Mother of God, whose robe, preserved in the church of Blachernae, was venerated as the city's Palladium.[42] These visible signs of divine favour surrounded Constantinople in the eyes of all eastern Christians with an aura of sanctity which could only be rivalled by the glory of Jerusalem: indeed Constantinople was often thought of as the New Jerusalem. The Russian pilgrims and travellers who visited the city in the late Middle Ages and whose writings have come down to us display, before the number of its relics and the holiness of its sanctuaries, the same open-eyed wonder and religious awe which they reveal in their descriptions of the Holy Land;[43] more than one of them dwells on the breath-taking beauty of the church of St Sophia, and on the loveliness of the liturgical chanting therein; and occasionally they seem to catch an echo of that excitement with which the envoys of Prince Vladimir of Russia are said to have described to their sovereign the public worship in St Sophia in the late tenth century: "We knew not whether we were in heaven or on earth: for on earth there is no such beauty or splendour."[44] For the Russians of the Middle Ages Constantinople was indeed, as it was for its own citizens, "the eye of the faith of the Christians" and "the city of the world's desire."[45]

The vision of Constantinople as the New Jerusalem was tarnished and partially obscured in Russia as a result of the Council of Florence, which marks a decisive turn in the relations between Muscovy and Byzantium. The proclamation on 6th July 1439 of the union between the Greek and the Latin churches was an event of major importance for the whole of Christendom: but it was in Russia that its long-term effects were the most far-reaching and significant.[46] A Russian delegation, headed by Isidore, the Greek metropolitan of Kiev and All Russia, attended the sessions of the Council, and its two bishops, Isidore and Avraamy (Abraham) of Suzdal', signed the Decree of Union. In March 1441 Isidore, now a cardinal and an apostolic legate, returned to Moscow. The Latin crucifix which he caused to be carried before him while entering the city, and his liturgical commemoration of Pope Eugenius IV in the cathedral of Moscow, exacerbated the Muscovites' anger and resentment at their metropolitan's behavior at the Council, which they regarded as a betrayal of the Orthodox faith. By order of the Grand Prince Basil II, Isidore was deposed, arrested and imprisoned in a monastery; six months later he escaped abroad, perhaps with the connivance of the Russian government. Muscovy thus explicitly rejected the Union of Florence.[47]

In the course of the next twenty years a number of works dealing with the Council of Florence were produced in Muscovy; they included a brief and artless travelogue by a member of the Russian delegation to the Council; a slightly longer and far more informative report, later included in several sixteenth-century Muscovite chronicles; two successive versions of an account of the Council and of its reception in Muscovy by the monk Symeon, another member of the Russian delegation; and finally, *A Selection from Holy Scripture against the Latins* and the *Story of the Convocation of the Eighth Latin Council,* a turgid and repetitious pamphlet of uncertain authorship, which appeared in 1461 or 1462.[48]

The historical value of these writings as documents on the Council of Florence is slight. These Muscovite pamphlets are too biased, their special pleading is too crude, their authors' understanding of the discussions at Ferrara and Florence too deficient to make them of much use as independent sources on the Council itself. But their interpretation of this event gave rise to a historical myth which acquired body and consistency in Russia during the decades that followed the Council of Florence, and which, illustrating the changing Russian attitude to Byzantium, is highly germane to the subject of this essay. The premises of this myth were simple in the extreme: the Greeks, by signing the Decree of Florence on terms imposed by the pope, betrayed the Orthodox faith, and the emperor and patriarch fell into heresy; the principal cause of this regrettable lapse was the Greeks' fondness for money, for they had been shamelessly bribed by the pope; by contrast, the Orthodox faith is preserved untainted in Russia, thanks to the Muscovite sovereign Basil II, who exposed the traitor Isidore and confirmed the true religion of his ancestors. The contrast between the tragic inconstancy of the Byzantines and the inspired faithfulness of the Russians is vividly drawn in the two following passages of the *Selection*: addressing the Emperor John VIII, the author exclaims: "O great sovereign Emperor! Why did you go to them [i.e. to the Latins]? How could you have entertained a good opinion of such people? What have you done? You have exchanged light for darkness; instead of Divine Religion you have accepted the Latin faith; instead of justice and truth you have embraced falsehood and error. You who formerly were a doer of pious works, how could you now have become a sower of tares of impiety? You who formerly were illumined by the light of the Heavenly Spirit, how could you now have clothed yourself in the darkness of unbelief?" And in the contrasting tones of exultation in which the author addresses "the divinely enlightened land of Russia," a new and significant note is sounded: "It is right that you should rejoice in the universe illumined by the sun, together with a nation of the true Orthodox faith, having clothed yourself in the light of true religion, resting under the divine protection of the many-splendored grace of the Lord . . . under the sovereignty of . . . the pious Grand Prince Vasily Vasilievich, divinely-crowned Orthodox Tsar of all Russia."[49]

The inversion of the former relationship between Byzantium and

Russia is not less striking here for being implied: the emphasis on the universality of the Orthodox faith, the title of tsar applied — still prematurely — to the Muscovite ruler, and even the imagery of light, with its religious and imperial associations, all suggest that for the author Moscow and not Constantinople was now the providential centre of the true Christian religion. It should be remembered, however, that this passage was written eight or nine years after the fall of Constantinople, in the last years of the reign of Basil II, at a time when Muscovy, having weathered an acute political crisis and a civil war that had lasted through most of the second quarter of the fifteenth century, was fast evolving into a centralized, autocratic monarchy, which during the next twenty years was to impose its sovereignty over the greater part of Russia and gain its final freedom from Mongol domination.[50] This new conception of Muscovite Russia, no longer on the periphery of the Byzantine *Oikoumene*, but now the very centre and the heart of Orthodox Christendom, was later to form the starting point of the theory of Moscow the Third Rome.[51] But the Muscovite ideologues of Basil II were not yet ready to draw the logical conclusions from their view of the Greek sell-out at Florence and from their belief in the historic destiny of their own nation. Hesitantly and ambiguously at first, they groped for new formulae to express the link they felt existed between the Byzantine betrayal of Orthodoxy and Muscovy's mission in the world: and it remains to consider how the Muscovites sought to determine their country's relationship to the empire during the twelve years between Isidore's expulsion from Russia and the fall of Constantinople in 1453.

To the Muscovites, who were consistently opposed to the idea of doctrinal agreement with the Latin Church, the acceptance of the Union of Florence by the supreme authorities of Byzantium came as a severe shock. Four and a half centuries of unwavering loyalty to the Church of Constantinople had left them unprepared for the sudden discovery that — as the primate of the Russian Church expressed it so tersely in 1451 — "the Emperor is not the right one, and the Patriarch is not the right one."[52] Their embarrassment was increased by the urgent need to appoint a successor to Isidore; and so, once again, the question of the appointment of the metropolitan of All Russia became for a while the crucial issue in the relations between Russia and Byzantium.

After Isidore's flight from Moscow in September 1441 three courses of action were open to the Russians: they could break off

canonical relations with the Patriarch Metrophanes, on the grounds
that by accepting the Union of Florence he had become a heretic, and
proceed to elect a new primate; or they could take the latter action
without rejecting the patriarch's jurisdiction, in the hope that the
Byzantine authorities could eventually be induced to sanction the election; or else they could play for time, pretend to ignore the union
between the Greek and Latin churches, and meanwhile seek permission from Constantinople to elect and consecrate their metropolitan in
Russia, hoping that the anti-unionist party in Byzantium, known to be
on the ascendant, would soon triumph over the adherents of the Flo-
rentine agreement. The first course of action was far too drastic and
revolutionary for the conservative and law-abiding Muscovite churchmen, and there is no evidence to suggest that the Russians in 1441
seriously contemplated a move which would have cast them adrift
from their mother Church. In fact they adopted the third, and later
the second, course of action. In 1441 Basil II wrote a letter to the
patriarch, saluting him as the supreme head of Orthodox Christendom, complaining of Isidore's treacherous behavior, and mentioning
the fact that before his appointment as primate of Russia (1436), the
Muscovite authorities had vainly attempted to persuade the emperor
and patriarch to appoint as metropolitan the Russian Bishop Iona
(Jonas). Courteously and with curious diffidence, the Muscovite sovereign then proceeded to ask the patriarch, and through him the
emperor, for a written authorization to have a metropolitan elected in
Russia by a national council of bishops, tactfully avoiding any mention of his own candidate, Bishop Iona, and stating the ostensible
grounds for his request: the authority of canon law; the difficulties of
the long journey between Moscow and Constantinople, made more
hazardous still by the Mongol incursions into Russia and "the disturbances and upheavals in the lands that lie near to ours" (perhaps a
semi-ironical allusion to the parlous state of the Byzantine empire);
and — rather surprisingly — the fact that discussions of state secrets
with the metropolitan must be held, if he is a Greek, in the presence of
interpreters whose discretion cannot always be trusted and who thus
endanger national security. And Basil II concludes his remarkably
shrewd and skilfully argued letter by declaring his intention to maintain the close relations which had always existed between Christian
Russia and "the holy Emperor" and to continue to recognize the spiritual jurisdiction of the patriarch.[53]

The fate of this letter is unknown; there is indeed no certainty that it was even sent. For the next seven years Russia remained without a metropolitan. For Basil II these were difficult years: he had a civil war on his hands, and for several months in 1445 he was a prisoner of the Tatars. The next move to end the ecclesiastical impasse was made in December 1448, when a council of Russian bishops, convoked by Basil II, elected Bishop Iona of Ryazan' as metropolitan of All Russia.

The die was cast; Iona's election and consecration were a direct challenge to the patriarch's authority. It seems that the Russians, even at this late hour, were extremely perturbed by the consequences of their own audacity. An influential minority in Muscovy held that Iona's appointment was uncanonical.[54] For more than three years the Russian authorities awaited the Byzantine reaction in anxious silence. Finally, in 1452 Basil II wrote a last letter to Constantinople, addressed to the new emperor, Constantine XI. It was as respectful in tone as his letter of 1441: indeed, he went as far as to acknowledge that the emperor possessed by virtue of his sacred office certain pre-rogatives in Russia.[55] But, behind the now expert phraseology of Muscovite diplomacy, two new notes are sounded in this letter: self-justification for what, from the Russian as well as from the Byzantine point of view, was an act of ecclesiastical insubordination; and an allusion, veiled yet pointed, to the fact that a considerable section of Byzantine society remained strongly opposed to the government's acceptance of union with Rome.[56] "We beseech your Sacred Majesty not to think that what we have done we did out of arrogance, nor to blame us for not writing to your Sovereignty beforehand; we did this from dire necessity, not from pride or arrogance. In all things we hold to the ancient Orthodox faith transmitted to us [from Byzantium], and so we shall continue to do . . . until the end of time. And our Russian Church , the holy metropolitanate of Russia, requests and seeks the blessing of the holy, divine, oecumenical, catholic, and apostolic Church of St Sophia, the Wisdom of God, and is obedient to her in all things according to the ancient faith; and our father, the Lord Iona, Metropolitan of Kiev and All Russia, in accordance with the same faith, likewise requests from her all manner of blessing and union, except for the present recently-appeared disagreements."[57]

This final attempt of the Russians to square the circle by reconciling their traditional loyalty to the Church of Constantinople with their unwillingness to remain dependent on a unionist patriarch, was soon rendered obsolete by rapidly moving events. On 7th April, 1453, Mehmet II laid siege to Constantinople, and on 29th May the city fell.

The Union of Florence collapsed with the Byzantine empire, and the Church of Constantinople reverted to Orthodoxy. Basil II's letter remained unsent in the state archives of Muscovy.[58] The theological obstacle to Russian ecclesiastical dependence on Constantinople had disappeared, only to be replaced by a political one, which in the eyes of the power-conscious Muscovite rulers proved the more insuperable of the two: the Church of Constantinople was now in the power of a Moslem state, and the patriarch received his investiture from the Ottoman sultan. And so the Russian Church retained the autonomous status it had acquired *de facto* in 1448, a status which in 1589, by common consent of the other Orthodox churches, was converted to that of an autocephalous patriarchate.

Thus at the end of our story, in the final chapter of the history of Russo-Byzantine relations, there comes to light, in the Russian attitude to Byzantium, the same polarity, the same ambiguous blend of attraction and repulsion, which we discerned in the earlier phases of this relationship. A distrust of Byzantine diplomacy and an abhorrence of its works — yet an open-hearted and probably disinterested desire to come to the aid of the holy city of Constantinople; resentment of the emperor's endeavors to control too closely the affairs of the Russian Church — yet a willingness to acknowledge his oecumenical authority, and so his prerogatives in Russia; a dogged and umbrageous striving for political self-determination — yet a perpetual longing for the fruits of Byzantine civilization; scandalized horror at the readiness of the Byzantine authorities to barter the Orthodox faith for the empire's security at the Council of Florence — yet an equally strong reluctance to sever the canonical dependence of their Church on the patriarchate of Constantinople: the two panels of the diptych that was medieval Russia's image of Byzantium seem to be poised in continuous equilibrium.

Yet this last impression is illusory. For the Russian view of Byzantium was in the fifteenth century no longer part of a fixed and incontrovertible vision of reality; it was being subverted and refashioned by the rapidly developing national consciousness of the Muscovites and by a series of violent shocks administered from the outside world; two of these shocks had a traumatic impact on Russia: they were provoked by the Council of Florence and the fall of Constantinople; their effect was both immediate and delayed, and they produced waves of reaction whose repercussions are traceable well into the sixteenth century. The immediate effect of the Council of Florence was, we have seen, one of alarm and consternation; and only gradually did the idea gain ground in some official circles in Muscovy that the Byzantines, by uniting with the Latins, had forfeited their right to be regarded as the leaders of Christendom. As for the fall of Constantinople, it had on the minds of the Muscovites an impact even more powerful; and the Russian reaction to this event was marked by the old and now familiar ambivalence. The more sententious of the Muscovite ideologues proclaimed that the fall of Byzantium was God's punishment for the Greek betrayal of Orthodoxy at Florence, a view which was then fairly current in the eastern Christian world, and indeed among the Greeks themselves.[59] The first to expound it in Russia was the Metropolitan Iona, in these words from a letter he wrote in 1458 or 1459: "As long as its people adhered to Orthodoxy, the Imperial City suffered no ill; but when the city turned away from Orthodoxy, you know yourselves, my sons, how much it endured."[60] And in another letter, written in 1460, the metropolitan was more explicit still: referring to "God's punishment" meted out to Constantinople for its rejection of Orthodoxy, he quotes the words of St Paul: "If any man defile the temple of God, him shall God destroy" (I Cor. III, 17).[61]

But the spontaneous Russian response to the fall of Constantinople did not wholly accord with this factitious, meta-historical theory which seems to have been propagated in ecclesiastical circles close to the Muscovite court. There is reason to believe that the feelings first aroused in Russia by the events of 29th May, 1453, were those of horror and pity. The destruction of the Christian empire, the end of a thousand years of history, the desecration of St Sophia, the sufferings now endured by the Byzantines — these events, whose magnitude it was difficult to comprehend, invited comparison with the greatest calamities of human history and suggested that the end of the world was near.[62] Soon after the fall of Constantinople, a Byzantine writer, John Eugenicus, wrote a lament "on the capture of the Great City."[63] Translated into Russian not later than 1468, it became part of Muscovite literature, and can thus be held to reflect a common attitude of Greeks and Russians to the fall of Byzantium.[64] With impassioned rhetoric and moving despair the author mourns "the glorious and much longed-for City, the mainstay of our race, the splendour of the inhabited world," the church of St Sophia, "that heaven on earth, that second paradise," the schools and libraries now destroyed, and the citizens of Byzantium, "the holy nation," "the people of the universe," now driven from their homes and scattered like leaves in autumn; the

Mother of God, age-long guardian of Constantinople, has now, he says, deserted Her city; and stunned by the magnitude of these disasters, the author can find no analogies save in the great catastrophes of mankind: the destruction of Jerusalem, Christ's death on the cross, and the last days of the world.[65]

Side by side, not always or necessarily in conflict, these two reactions to the fall of Byzantium, the nationalistic and the apocalyptic, are traceable through Muscovite literature of the late fifteenth and early sixteenth centuries. The latter reaction left traces in an account of the siege of Constantinople by Nestor-Iskender, a Russian conscript in the Turkish army who took part in the capture of the city; and in an early sixteenth-century historical compendium, the *Chronograph* of 1512. The former, nationalistic, interpretation became one of the elements in the tradition glorifying Moscow as the Third Rome, which was given substance and form in the sixteenth-century writings of Philotheus of Pskov.[66] Gradually, as the spiritual and emotional shock caused by the fall of Constantinople wore off, and the Muscovites became increasingly conscious of their own national heritage, this interpretation carried the day, and in the sixteenth century there were few Russians left who, from the self-contained, self-satisfied, and power-conscious world of Muscovite nationalism, could still look back with nostalgia to the oecumenical traditions and European horizons of Byzantium.

FOOTNOTES ON CHAPTER V

[1]Nicephorus Gregoras, *Historiae Byzantiae*, lib. xxxvi, cap.21-2, iii (Bonn, 1855), 512. The exact meaning of the penultimate sentence of this passage is hard to discover, owing to the vagueness of Gregoras' language. V. Parisot believed that he is alluding to the ivory obtained from the tusks of walruses and narwhals in the White Sea and the Arctic Ocean, and to objects of luxury (e.g. musical instruments) manufactured from it: *Livre XXXVII de l'Histoire Romaine de Nicéphore Grégoras* (Paris, 1851), 266-78.

[2]For trade relations between Byzantium and Russia in the late Middle Ages, see M.N.Tikhomirov, *Srednevekovaya Moskva v XIV-XV vekakh* (Moscow, 1957), 121-31; "Puti iz Rossii v Vizantiyu," *Vizantiiskie Ocherki*, ed. Tikhomirov (Moscow, 1961), 3-33.

[3]Nicephorus Gregoras, *Hist. Byz.*, lib. xiii, cap. 12: ii, 683-6; cf. W. Heyd, *Histoire du Commerce du Levant au Moyen Âge,* ii (Leipzig, 1936), 187-8.

[4]See G. Ostrogorsky, *History of the Byzantine State* (Oxford, 1956), 469-70.

[5]Nicephorus Gregoras, *Hist. Byz.*, lib. xxviii, cap. 34-6: iii, 198-200.

[6]*Polnoe Sobranie Russkikh Letopisey*, xi (St Petersburg, 1897), 168.

[7]Τὸ γὰρ καύχημα τῶν ἁπανταχοῦ τῆς οἰκουμένης χριστιανῶν, τὸ στήριγμα, ὁ ἁγιασμὸς καὶ ἡ δόξα ἡ πόλις ἐστὶν αὕτη ἡ ἁγία. *Acta Patriarchatus Constantinopolitani*, ed. F. Miklosich and I. Müller, ii (Vienna, 1862), 361. The results of this appeal are unknown.

[8]See above, pp. 1-22.

[9]The prerogative of promoting bishoprics to the rank of metropolitanates was, at least after 1087, generally considered to belong to the emperor. Alexius Comnenus issued a law to this effect: see Migne, *P.G.*, cxxvii, cols. 929-32 (no. 7). Most Byzantine canonists seem to have accepted its propriety: see Balsamon, *In Can. XII Conc. Chalced., P.G.*, cxxxvii, cols. 432-3 (for a contrary view, however, see Zonaras, ibid., cols. 433-6); and in 1335 this imperial prerogative was confirmed once more by Matthew Blastares (Σύνταγμα κατὰ στοιχεῖον), ed. G. Rhalles and M. Potles, Σύνταγμα τῶν θείων καὶ ἱερῶν κανόνων, vi (Athens, 1859), 274-6). Imperial initiative in the creation and abolition of metropolitanates naturally tended, whenever the sees in question were situated outside the empire's confines, to link very closely the decisions taken in Constantinople to organize or reorganize the ecclesiastical administration of these territories with the interests of Byzantine foreign policy.

[10]See E. Golubinsky, *Istoriya russkoy tserkvi*,ii, 1 (Moscow, 1900), 96-7, 101-4, 125-30, 147-8, 153-4, 157-60, 177-87, 190-3, 206-11, 342, 388-9; A.M. Ammann, *Abriss der ostslawischen Kirchengeschichte* (Vienna, 1950), pp. 88-98, 106-10, 120-3· A.V. Kartashev, *Ocherki po istorii russkoy tserkvi*, i (Paris, 1959), 297-9, 303-4, 313-23, 332-3, 338, 346.

[11]See above, pp. 109-165.

[12]The text of the decree is printed in *Acta Patriarchatus Constantinopolitani*, i, 336-40. The Muscovite prince is termed ὁ μέγας ῥήξ, and acknowledgment is made of the pre-eminence of his power (ὑπεροχῇ ῥηγικῆς ἐξουσίας).

[13]See Ostrogorsky, *History of the Byzantine State*, 530-1; cf. D.M. Nicol, *Byzantium and Venice* (Cambridge, 1988), pp. 278-9.

[14]On the "zealot" and the "moderate" parties in the Byzantine Church, see A. Vasiliev, *History of the Byzantine Empire* (Oxford, 1952), 659-70.

[15]On this point, and for an analysis of the Synodal decree of 30th June, 1354, see above, pp. 120-126.

[16]See above, pp. 125, note 82. Later, however, the Patriarchate was more successful in enforcing its will: there were no native metropolitans of Russia between 1390 and 1448.

[17]The decree of the Patriarchal Synod of June 1380: *Acta Patriarchatus Constantinopolitani*, ii, 12-18.

[18]See Golubinsky, op. cit., ii, 1, 182-215; Ammann, op. cit., 95-100; Kartashev, op. cit., i, 317-22.

[19]Θροῦς δ' ἐπιγείρεται μὲν πλεῖστος ἀνὰ πᾶσαν τὴν ῥωσικὴν ἐπαρχίαν καὶ στάσις καὶ ὄχλησις οὐ μικρά: Synodal decree of 1380: *Acta Patriarchatus Constantinopolitani*, ii, 14.

[20]*Russkaya Istoricheskaya Biblioteka*, vi (St Petersburg, 1880), col. 185: the abusive term "Lithuanian" was clearly intended to suggest that by appointing Cyprian the Byzantine authorities had shown favouritism to the Grand Duke of Lithuania, Muscovy's political rival and enemy. Cf. D. Obolensky, *Six Byzantine Portraits* (Oxford, 1988), p. 188.

[21]Our principal sources for the history of this affair are the fourteenth-century acts of the Synods

of Constantinople and the sixteenth-century Muscovite Chronicle of Nikon. Golubinsky (op. cit., ii, I, 242 ff) and Kartashev (op. cit., i, 323-33) suppose, on somewhat inadequate evidence, that this fraudulent deal was initiated by the Byzantine officials. On the other hand, an attempt (likewise unconvincing) to exonerate the Patriarch and to place the entire blame on the shoulders of the Russian envoys, is made by A. Tachiaos (Ἐπιδράσεις τοῦ ἡσυχασμοῦ εἰς τὴν ἐκκλησιαστικὴν πολιτικὴν ἐν Ῥωσίᾳ, 1328-1406 (Thessalonica, 1962), pp. 113-15). Cf. G.M. Prokhorov, *Povest' o Mityae* (Leningrad, 1978).

[22]For the dating of this letter, see J.W. Barker, *Manuel II Palaeologus* (New Brunswick, N.J., 1969), pp. 109-10.

[23]The text is printed in *Acta Patriarchatus Constantinopolitani*, ii, 188-92; cf. *Russkaya Istoricheskaya Biblioteka*, vi, Appendix 40, cols. 265-76; an English translation of about two-thirds of the letter can be found in *Social and Political Thought in Byzantium*, ed. Ernest Barker (Oxford, 1957), 194-7. See, however, a different view of Basil's behavior in Meyendorff, *Byzantium and the Rise of Russia*, pp. 254-6.

[24]"Hear what the prince of the Apostles, Peter, says in the first of his general epistles, 'Fear God, honour the King.' He did not say 'Kings,' lest any man should think that he had in mind those who are called kings promiscuously among the nations; he said 'the King,' showing thereby that the universal King is one." *Acta Patr. Constant*, ii 191; Barker, op. cit., 195.

[25]*History of the Byzantine State*, 554.

[26]A rough English equivalent of ὁ ἐπὶ τῆς τραπέζης.

[27]Ὁ βασιλεὺς τῶν Ῥὼς ὁ ἐπὶ τῆς τραπέζης τῆς ἁγίας βασιλείας σου προσκυνεῖ δουλικῶς τὴν ἁγίαν βασιλείαν σου: H. Haupt, "Neue Beiträge zu den Fragmenten des Dio Cassius", *Hermes, xiv* (1879), 445; see also Nicephorus Gregoras (*Hist. Byz.*, lib. vii, cap. 5, i, 239); cf. A. Vasiliev, "Was Old Russia a vassal state of Byzantium?", *Speculum*, vii (1932), 353-4.

[28]Ἡ βασιλεία γοῦν τῶν Ῥωμαίων, ἀλλὰ δὴ καὶ ἡ ἁγιωτάτη τοῦ θεοῦ μεγάλη ἐκκλησία ἕνι, ὡς ἔγραψες καὶ σύ, πηγὴ πάσης εὐσεβείας καὶ διδάσκαλος νομοθεσίας τε καὶ ἁγιασμοῦ. *Acta Patriarchatus Constantinopolitani*, i, 263. The μεγάλη ἐκκλησία is the Patriarchate of Constantinople.

[29]It may be noted that one of the official titles of John Cantacuzenus was ὁ βασιλεὺς τῶν Ῥώσων: Cantacuzenus, *Historiae*, lib. iv, cap. 14 (Bonn), iii, 94. It can be regarded as certain, however, that no Russian ruler would have dreamt of acknowledging that the *basileus* was "Emperor of the Russians."

[30]*Russkaya Istoricheskaya Biblioteka*, vi, col. 577.

[31]See M. D'yakonov, *Vlast' moskovskikh gosudarey* (St Petersburg, 1889), 13-22: P. Sokolov, *Russky arkhierey iz Vizantii* (Kiev, 1913), 35-9, 305-6; Vasiliev, *Was Old Russia a vassal state of Byzantium?*, loc. cit., 359.

[32]See F. Dvornik, "Byzantine Political Ideas in Kievan Russia," *Dumbarton Oaks Papers*, ix-x (1956), 73-121.

[33]See above, pp. 15-17.

[34]It is noteworthy, however, that the title of *tsar* (the equivalent of *basileus*) was, in general, applied by the Russians in this period only to the Byzantine emperor and to the khan of the Golden Horde.

[35]For the idea of the Byzantine *Oikoumene*, see the following studies by G. Ostrogorsky, "Avtokrator i Samodržac", *Glas Srpske Akademije Nauka*, clxiv (Belgrade, 1953), 95-187; "Die byzantinische Staatenhierarchie," *Seminarium Kondakovianum: Recueil d'Etudes*, viii (Prague, 1936), 41-61; "The Byzantine Emperor and the Hierarchical World Order," *The Slavonic and East European Review*, xxxv (1956-7), 1-14.

[36]See above, p. 168.

[37]See M.V. Levchenko, *Ocherki po istorii russko-vizantiiskikh otnosheny* (Moscow, 1956), 441 and *passim*.

[38]It is noteworthy that in the Middle Ages the Russians, as well as the Balkan Slavs, invariably referred to the Byzantines as "Greeks," and not as *Rhomaioi*.

[39]*The Russian Primary Chronicle (Povest' vremennykh let)*, ed. V.P. Adrianova-Peretts and D.S. Likhachev (Moscow, 1950), i, 50; English translation by S.H. Cross and O.P. Sherbowitz-Wetzor (Cambridge, Mass., 1953), 88.

[40]See V.N. Lazarev, "Etyudy o Feofane Greke," *Vizantiisky Vremennik*, vii (1953), 244-58; viii (1956), 143-65; ix (1956), 193-210; *Feofan Grek i ego shkola* (Moscow, 1961).

[41]For the hesychast influences upon the monastic school of St Sergius, see Tachiaos, op. cit., 42-60. Cf. Meyendorff, *Byzantium and the Rise of Russia*, pp. 119-44.

[42]See N.H. Baynes, *Byzantine Studies and Other Essays* (London, 1955), pp. 240-60.

[43]See *Itinéraires russes en Orient,* translated by Mme B. De Khitrowo, i, I (Geneva, 1889);. G.P. Majeska, *Russian Travelers to Constantinople in the Fourteenth and Fifteenth Centuries* (Washington, D.C., 1984).

[44]*The Russian Primary Chronicle,* i, 75; English translation, 111.

[45]Τῆς Χριστιανῶν ὀφθαλμὸν ὑπάρχουσαν πίστεως: L. Sternbach, "Analecta Avarica," in the *Rozprawy* of the Academy of Cracow, XV (1900), 304.— Ἡ κοσμοπαμπόθητος αὔτη πόλις: Constantine the Rhodian, in *Revue des Etudes Grecques,* IX (1896), 38.

[46]The effect of the Council of Florence on the Russian attitude to Byzantium will be discussed rather briefly, as detailed treatments of the problem are readily available. See, in particular, F. Delektorsky, "Kritiko-bibliografichesky obzor drevne-russkikh skazany o Florentiiskoy Unii," *Zhurnal Ministerstva Narodnogo Prosveshcheniya,* ccc (July, 1895), 131-84: P. Pierling, *La Russie et le Saint-Siège,* i (Paris, 1896), 7-104; E. Golubinsky, *Istoriya russkoy tserkvi,* ii, I (Moscow, 1900), 424 ff.; I. Ševčenko, "Intellectual Repercussions of the Council of Florence,"*Church History,* xxiv (1955), 291-323; M. Cherniavsky, "The Reception of the Council of Florence in Moscow," ibid., 347-59; O. Halecki, *From Florence to Brest (1439-1596)* (Rome, 1958), 42-74; G. Alef, "Muscovy and the Council of Florence," *The American Slavic and East European Review,* xx (1961), 389-401.

[47]Isidore, a trained theologian, had played a leading part in securing Greek agreement to the Decree of Union. His Russian companions at Ferrara and Florence, however, appear to have been poorly equipped for the theological discussions of the Council. See Ševčenko, op. cit., 307-8. However, Father J. Gill's view (*The Council of Florence* (Cambridge, 1961), 361), that "the reasons for Vasili's [i.e. Basil II's] rejection of Isidore and his mission were probably purely political" is scarcely convincing. The Muscovites may not have had very clear views on the *Filioque,* but their opposition to Latin doctrines and customs and to the Papal claims were genuine and long-standing.

[48]The text of the first four of these works is printed in V. Malinin, *Starets Eleazarova monastyrya Filofei i ego poslaniya* (Kiev, 1901), Appendices, 76-127: for a German translation of the travelogue, see "Reisebericht eines unbekannten Russen (1437-1440)," trans. G. Stökl, in *Europa im XV. Jahrhundert von Byzantinern gesehen [Byzantinische Geschichtsschreiber,* hersg. von E. v. Ivánka, ii, Graz, 1954], 149-89. The *Selection* is published in A. Popov, *Istoriko-literaturny obzor drevne-russkikh polemicheskikh sochineny protiv Latinyan (XI-XV v.)* (Moscow, 1875), 360-95. For a discussion of these documents, see the works cited above (note 46) and also H. Schaeder, *Moskau das dritte Rom,* 2nd edn. (Darmstadt, 1957), 21-38.

[49]Popov, op. cit., 372, 394-5. Cf. Cherniavsky, op. cit., 352-3.

[50]For the internal history of the principality of Muscovy in the fifteenth century, see L.V. Cherepnin, *Obrazovanie russkogo tsentralizovannogo gosudarstva v XIV-XV vekakh* (Moscow, 1960), p. 715 ff.

[51]An analysis of the theory of Moscow the Third Rome, which acquired final form in the sixteenth century, lies outside the scope of this essay, which is concerned with the relations between Byzantium and Muscovite Russia until the fall of the empire in 1453.

[52]*Russkaya Istoricheskaya Biblioteka,* vi, col. 559.

[53]*Russkaya Istoricheskaya Biblioteka,* vi, cols. 525-36. The same letter, with appropriate changes, was addressed two years later (1443) to the Byzantine Emperor John VIII. See *Polnoe Sobranie Russkikh Letopisey,* vi (St Petersburg, 1853), 162-7. The arguments of A. Ziegler (*Die Union des Konzils von Florenz in der russischen Kirche* (Würzburg, 1938), 102-7), who regards the letter as spurious and maintains that it was composed in the 1460s, in order to justify *post factum* Basil II's decision to have Iona consecrated metropolitan in Moscow, seem to the present writer unconvincing. For discussions of this letter, see Golubinsky, op. cit., ii, I. 470-8; Kartashev, op. cit., i, 357-9.

[54]See Kartashev, op. cit., i, 360.

[55]See above, p. 177.

[56]The Metropolitan Iona, in a letter written in January 1451, alleged that the only strongholds of the unionist party in Constantinople were St Sophia and the Imperial palace, while the remaining parts of the Byzantine capital (as well as Mount Athos) remained entirely devoted to Orthodoxy: *Russkaya Istoricheskaya Biblioteka,* vi, col. 558. Though probably an exaggeration, this statement shows that the Russians were well informed about the strength of the anti-Unionist group in Constantinople.

[57]*Russkaya Istoricheskaya Biblioteka,* vi, cols. 583-4.

[58]Golubinsky (op. cit., ii, I. 487-8) and Kartashev (op. cit., i, 362) suggest that the letter was never sent off because the Muscovite authorities, having learnt of the solemn proclamation of the Union

by Constantine XI in St Sophia on 12th December, 1452, decided that further negotiations with Constantinople on ecclesiastical matters were useless. This does not seem altogether convincing, as Constantine had for some time past openly displayed his pro-unionist sympathies. Could it be that the Russians were deterred from sending Basil II's letter by news of the growing military isolation of Constantinople, which further increased with the completion, in August 1452, of the Turkish fortress of Rumeli Hisar on the Bosphorus?

[59]See Ševčenko, *Intellectual Repercussions of the Council of Florence*, 300, and n. 60; Gill, *The Council of Florence*, 391.

[60]*Russkaya Istoricheskaya Biblioteka*, vi, col. 623; cf. Ševčenko, ibid. 309; Schaeder, *Moskau das dritte Rom*, 44.

[61]Ibid., vi, cols. 648-9.

[62]For the belief, current in Russia, that the world would end in 1492, see Malinin, *Starets Filofei*, 427-43; Schaeder, op. cit., 49-51; A. Vasiliev, "Medieval ideas of the end of the world: West and East," *Byzantion*, xvi, 2 (1942-3) 462-502.

[63]One of the manuscripts of this work—Τοῦ νομοφύλακος Ἰωάννου διακόνου τοῦ Εὐγενικοῦ μονῳδία ἐπὶ τῇ ἁλώσει τῆς μεγαλοπόλεως—was published by S. P. Lambros in Νέος Ἑλληνομνήμων, v, 2-3 (1908), 219-26. On John Eugenicus, the brother of Mark (the celebrated Metropolitan of Ephesus) see K. Krumbacher, *Geschichte der byzantinischen Litteratur*, 2nd edn. (Munich, 1897), 117, 495-6; Gill, op. cit., *passim*.

[64]The Russian translation is still unpublished. See N. A. Meshchersky, "Rydanie Ioanna Evgenika i ego drevnerussky perevod," *Vizantiisky Vremennik*, vii (1953), 72-86; I. Dujčev, "La conquête turque et la prise de Constantinople dans la littérature slave contemporaine," *Byzantinoslavica*, xvii (1956), 280-3; idem, "O drevnerusskom perevode 'Rydaniya' Ioanna Evgenika," *Vizantiisky Vremennik*, xii (1957), 198-202.

[65]Lambros, loc. cit., 219-226.

[66]For these works, see Schaeder, op. cit., 38-49, 65-81.

CHAPTER VI

MODERN RUSSIAN ATTITUDES TO BYZANTIUM*

In marked contrast to the peoples of Western Europe, the Russians inherited from their medieval ancestors a variety of attitudes towards Byzantium. This inherited tradition was compounded of several elements. It was based, at least in the case of the educated classes, on a considerable body of historical knowledge, derived in part from the excerpts from the works of Byzantine historians — notably John Malalas, George Hamartolos, John Zonaras and Constantine Manasses — which had been incorporated, in Slavonic translations, into medieval Russian chronicles.[1] It implied the view that the history of Byzantium had a special relevance to the destinies of the Russian people, a relevance illustrated by the fact that the dated section of the Russian Primary Chronicle opens and closes with an event of Byzantine history: the accession of Michael III and the death of Alexius Comnenus.[2] And above all it was distinguished by a set of value-judgments, in which the intellectual and emotional attitudes of the medieval Russians towards the Byzantine Empire are most clearly revealed: on the one hand, a deep-rooted loyalty and devotion to Byzantium which had given the Russians their religion and much of their medieval culture, and to Tsar'-grad, the Imperial capital, which for them, no less than for its own citizens, appeared as "the eye of the faith of the Christians," and "the city of the world's desire"; on the other hand, a certain distrust of the Byzantines and a suspicion of the motives of their Imperial diplomacy, coupled after the Council of Florence with the belief held by some Muscovite ideologues that the Greeks had forfeited their right to the spiritual leadership of Christendom, and that the providential center of the Orthodox faith had now been transferred to Moscow, the Third Rome.[3]

*Jahrbuch der Österreichen Byzantinischen Gesellschaft, xv (1966), 61-72.

This emotional polarity in the Russian attitude to Byzantium, this ambiguous blend of attraction and repulsion, survived the Middle Ages and, in altered circumstances and different forms, is reflected in the views expressed by Russian statesmen, ecclesiastics, philosophers and historians of more recent times. The role played by Byzantium in the historical concepts of the Russians since the seventeenth century can perhaps best be considered under three headings, corresponding to three largely successive and partly overlapping periods: firstly, the seventeenth and early eighteenth centuries, when Byzantine history was put to didactic and often highly tendentious use by advocates of particular policies in Church and State; secondly, the nineteenth century, when certain views of Byzantium played a part in the great debate on philosophical, historical and literary subjects conducted by Russian intellectuals; and finally, the academic tradition of Byzantine scholarship which was established in Russia in the 1870's.

The seventeenth century saw a notable widening of the historical horizon of educated Russians. One of its symptoms was a renewed interest in the fate of the Greek Orthodox world, an interest stimulated by the influx of Greek ecclesiastics from the Ottoman Empire who sought financial and moral support for their churches from the Muscovite government. This fresh impact of Greek culture produced conflicting reactions in Muscovite society; and these reactions, in their turn, elicited different views of Russia's Byzantine inheritance. Thus a pro-Greek party in the Church, led by Patriarch Nikon, argued that the spiritual authority was superior to the temporal power by appealing, somewhat inappropriately, to Byzantine precedents: Nikon took his stand, in particular, on the classic definition of the prerogatives of the Emperor and the Patriarch within the Christian Commonwealth contained in the ninth-century Epanagoge: and in 1653 he had Leunclavius' *Jus graeco-romanum*, which contained this text, translated into Slavonic.[4] An opposing, nationalistic, party—the so-called "Old Believers" — resisted Nikon's program of reforming the Russian Church in accordance with Greek models; their leader, the Archpriest Avvakum, later burned at the stake for refusing to accept these reforms, reiterated the doctrine of Moscow the Third Rome, which had been formulated 150 years earlier by Philotheus of Pskov; he declared in 1667 to the Patriarchs of Constantinople and Alexandria: "Oecumenical doctors! Rome fell long ago and lies unregenerate, the Poles have perished with her and have become for ever enemies of the Christians. And in your lands too Orthodoxy has been tainted by the oppression of

Mahomet the Turk."[5]

This tendentious use of Byzantine history in support of power politics or ecclesiastical reforms was resorted to half a century later by Peter the Great. The examples which the Tsar found in this history were distinctly unedifying: thus he maintained that the fate of "the Greek monarchy" was an instructive lesson of how a state is brought to ruin by civil disobedience, treachery and the neglect of warfare.[6] Nor could the past history of the Byzantine Church find much sympathy with so revolutionary and pro-Western a monarch as Peter: his indictment of Byzantine monasticism is worthy of Voltaire or Gibbon. The bigotry of the Byzantine emperors, and even more of their wives, led — Peter claimed — to the gangrenous proliferation of monasteries in the Empire; on the shores of the Bosphorus alone there were some 300 monasteries; consequently, when the Turks laid siege to Constantinople, less than 6000 soldiers could be found to defend the city.[7]

In these polemical utterances by Russian statesmen and churchmen of the seventeenth and early eighteenth centuries there is little evidence of independent historical thinking. Moreover, their use of Byzantine history was highly selective and overtly pragmatic: some particular feature or event of Byzantine history, real or imaginary, was adduced either to stimulate imitation or to provide salutary warning. It was not until the third decade of the nineteenth century that Russian thinkers began to submit the whole of Byzantine history to a critical interpretation and to examine it in the light of their own historical and philosophical conceits. In the passionate debate which raged in Moscow in the eighteen-thirties and forties between the Westerners and the Slavophiles, Byzantium not infrequently appeared as a witness, now for the prosecution, now for the defense. The debate, which owed much to the influence of European romanticism and of German idealist philosophy, was concerned with Russia's mission in the world, and in particular with her relationship to Western Europe. The Westerners held that Russia was and should continue to be an integral part of European civilization. The Slavophiles, by contrast, emphasized the distinctive elements in the Russian national tradition and regarded this tradition, based on the living organism of the Orthodox Church and the social virtues of the peasant community, as superior in every way to the rationalism, materialism and legalism of the West. The most extreme of Russian Westerners, Peter Chaadaev, argued in the first of his famous *Lettres Philosophiques,* written in 1829 and published in 1836, that the sterility of Russian culture was due to the legacy of "la misérable Byzance, objet du profond mépris," which cut off the Russians from the civilized brotherhood of Christian peoples.[8] And in a letter written in 1846, he singled out the subordination of the Church to the imperial power as the most deplorable element in Russia's Byzantine inheritance.[9] Not all the Westerners, however, thought badly of Byzantium. Indeed one of their leaders, Timofei Granovsky, published in 1850 an eloquent apologia of Byzantium and a plea for serious Byzantine studies. Granovsky was a professional historian, and his views on this subject, which seem to bridge the gap between Westerners and Slavophiles, foreshadowed the emergence twenty years later of a genuine tradition of Russian Byzantine scholarship. "We received from Constantinople," he wrote, "the best part of our national inheritance, that is religious beliefs and the beginnings of education. The Eastern Empire brought young Russia into the community of Christian nations." Only Slav scholars, he claimed, are fully qualified to resolve the problems posed by Byzantine history. Indeed, Granovsky declared, "we have in a sense the duty to evaluate a phenomenon to which we owe so much."[10]

The Slavophiles displayed in their attitudes to Byzantium the same Russia-centered bias, the same *penchant* for judgements of value, and the same ambiguity. Thus, while Ivan Kireevsky contrasted in 1852 the artistic, contemplative culture of the Byzantine world with western Catholicism, perverted by Roman legalism and rationalism,[11] the leading Slavophile philosopher and theologian, Aleksei Khomyakov, passed a more ambivalent judgement on Byzantium. He, too, paid glowing tribute to its spiritual achievements, in theology, monasticism and missionary endeavour, of which the Russians were the beneficiaries. But on the debit side he stressed several times — and particularly in an article written in 1852—that the law and the state in the Byzantine Empire were Roman, and as such were open to the charges of paganism, formalism and institutionalism. "Rome's juridical chains," he wrote, "clasped and choked the life of Byzantium."[12]

It was inevitable that the interest in Byzantine history, which began to spread in Russian society after 1850, soon acquired a distinct political flavor. A vague connection between Byzantine studies and the objects of Russia's foreign policy had been established in the eighteenth century. Such events as Peter the Great's campaign of the Pruth (1711) and Catherine II's "Greek Project" (1782) had suggested to a section of public opinion that a knowledge of Byzantine history was a necessary preparation for the task of liberating the Orthodox in the

Balkans from the Turkish yoke. The missing link between "Byzantinism" and the "Eastern Question" was provided by Panslavism, which grew out of Slavophile teaching between 1856 and 1878; it found notorious expression in Nikolay Danilevsky's famous work *Rossiya i Evropa*, published in 1869. He argued that Russia alone had the right to Constantinople and that her historic mission was to restore the East Roman Empire, like the Franks had once restored the Roman Empire in the West; and he proposed the creation of a federation comprising the Slav countries, the Greeks, the Rumanians and the Magyars, under the political leadership of Russia and with its capital in Constantinople.[13]

The influence of Danilevsky is strongly felt in the work of Konstantin Leontiev (1831-91), a writer whose life was dominated by the highly individual vision of Byzantium he had created for himself. He shared Danilevsky's hostility to Western culture, the Slavophiles' belief in the superiority of Russia's indigenous institutions, and the Panslavists' dream of Russian sovereignty over Constantinople. Yet he differed profoundly from Slavophiles and Panslavists in rejecting the concept of Slavonic cultural unity and in opposing the liberation of the Balkan Slavs from Turkish rule. His outlook was a curious blend of romantic aestheticism, transcendental mysticism and political reaction. His thought is best epitomized in his essay "Vizantizm i Slavyanstvo," published in 1875 and partly inspired by the revival of the "Eastern Question." The hope of the world, he believed, lay in the survival of "Byzantinism"; by this concept he meant a peculiar amalgam of political autocracy, social inequality and Orthodox mysticism which flourished in Byzantium and was adopted by the Russians in the Middle Ages. Byzantinism had sustained Russian society in the past; Russia's future was assured by the fact that "the spirit, principles and influences of Byzantium, like the complex texture of a nervous system, pervade the whole of Russia's social organism."[14]

Leontiev, Danilevsky and, to a large extent, the Slavophiles, despite their differing appreciation of "Byzantinism," all injected into this concept a strong dose of positive value-judgement. Their nationalistic aspirations caused them to ascribe to the "Byzantine inheritance" a powerful and constructive role in the growth of Russia's cultural and political self-determination. A startlingly different view of Byzantium and its works was propounded during the last two decades of the nineteenth century by Vladimir Soloviev (1853-1900), the notable philosopher, theologian and poet. His rejection of secular nationalism

and his view of the Roman Church as the providential center of
Christian unity appeared to him valid reasons for condemning Byzan-
tium as harshly as Chaadaev had done sixty years earlier. But while
Chaadaev had confined himself to a few uncomplimentary remarks,
Soloviev delivered himself in two of his works — *La Russie et l'Eglise
Universelle (1889)*[15] and *Vizantizm i Rossiya (1896)*[16] — of a lengthy
and passionate indictment of "l'empire pseudo-chrétien de Byzance."
The Byzantines, he argued, betrayed Christ's legacy to mankind. By
concentrating unduly on the externals of religious observance and by
abdicating their duty to Christianize the social and political order,
they built an empire that was more pagan than Christian; by losing
sight of the universality of the Christian tradition they allowed
churchmen like Photius and Cerularius to lead them into schism; and
their spiritual leaders, by slavishly submitting to the tyranny of the
state, promoted the baneful "Caesaropapism," whose pervasive effects
caused Byzantium to resemble more closely the empire of Nebuchad-
nezzar than that of Christ.[17] In passing final sentence on Byzantium,
Soloviev appealed to the verdict of history: "L'histoire a jugé et con-
damné le Bas-Empire."[18]

None of these nineteenth century writers, with the possible exception of Granovsky, could in their treatment of Byzantium be regarded
as scholars in the modern sense of the word. The significance of their
views lies rather in the interest in Byzantine history which they stimulated in Russian political opinion; in the role played by their concepts
of Byzantium in the development in Russia of historical and philosophical thought and of ideas of national self-determination; and in the
relevance of some of their ideas on Byzantine history to Russia's foreign and domestic politics. A genuine and continuous tradition of
Byzantine scholarship required the fulfillment of three conditions: 1. a
readiness to start not from preconceived "metahistorical" concepts, but
from a critical study of the documents; 2. the appearance of scholars
willing to devote their lives to specialized research in this field; 3. the
readiness of universities and public opinion to recognize Byzantine
studies as an autonomous discipline in their own right.

It was not until the 1870's that all three conditions were fulfilled in
Russia. However, both the study of Byzantine sources and the emergence of devoted and enthusiastic scholars in this field had begun a
hundred years earlier; and we may rightly regard the period from 1770
to 1870 as an important preparatory phase in the history of Byzantine
scholarship in Russia. The leading figures were G. S. Bayer, G. F.

Müller, A. L. von Schlözer and J. G. Stritter in the eighteenth century, J. P. Krug and A. A. Kunik in the nineteenth.[19] Particularly important were the publication, between 1771 and 1779, of a four-volume collection of Byzantine sources concerned with Eastern Europe, translated into Latin and edited by Stritter,[20] and the scholarly contributions of Kunik, who in 1853 read a paper in the Imperial Academy of Sciences under the title: "Why does Byzantium still remain a riddle in world history?" Kunik was an enthusiastic propagandist for Byzantine studies: "Does not the Russian people — he asked rhetorically — owe its Christian faith to Byzantium, and did not this faith give the Russian princes and people the strength for centuries to resist Islam and finally free themselves from its yoke. . . Is it not true, broadly speaking, that the greater part of Russian history is the reflection of the history of Byzantium?" Yet Kunik ends this passage on a cautious and even pessimistic note: "Where — he asks — shall we find enough Byzantinists to enable us to take our stand in this field alongside other nations?"[21]

Kunik's statements exposed the two principal weaknesses of the emergent Byzantine studies in Russia in the middle of the nineteenth century: the lack of qualified *cadres*, and the almost exclusive preoccupation of Russian Byzantinists with the history of their own country: the choice and treatment of their themes, and their approach to their subject, showed that they were interested almost solely in those aspects of Byzantine history which had a bearing on and could illuminate the history and culture of medieval Russia. This intermittent and applied character of Russian Byzantine studies lasted until the 1870's.

The founder of the scholarly tradition of Byzantine historical studies in Russia was Vasily Vasilievsky. Originally a classical scholar and a pupil of Mommsen, he began to teach Byzantine history in the University of St. Petersburg in 1870. By the time he died in 1899 he had contributed works of major importance in the fields of Byzantine social and administrative history, hagiography and Russo-Byzantine relations; had established Byzantine studies in his country as an autonomous and respectable discipline, of growing interest to the educated public; had founded the well-known periodical, *Vizantiisky Vremennik*, whose first volume appeared in 1894; and had so increased the international standing of Russian Byzantine studies that Krumbacher himself found it necessary to learn Russian and to make his pupils do the same. The two central themes of Vasilievsky's work were Russo-Byzantine relations and the agrarian and social history of the Byzan-

tine Empire. The former subject he inherited from his Russian predecessors; while his interest in social history, doubtless stimulated in part
by the contemporary liberal and socialist movements in Europe,
proved of great importance in the subsequent development of Byzantine studies in Russia.[22] It was shared by Vasilievsky's younger contemporary, Fedor Uspensky, a figure of comparable importance in the
history of Byzantine studies.[23] An admirable organizer, Uspensky took
a leading part in the development of this subject in the University of
Odessa (1874-94); directed, from 1895 to 1914, the work of the Russian Archaeological Institute in Constantinople; led the Russian
archaeological expedition to Trebizond in 1916 and 1917; and in the
years between the Revolution and his death in 1928 attempted to sal-
vage what remained of Byzantine studies in Russia.[24] A highly prolific
scholar, he contributed most to the study of the social and economic
history of Byzantium, of Byzantine religious and philosophical thought,
and of Byzantine-Slav relations in the early Middle Ages. His works
on the last topic were, originally at least, influenced by the Slavophile
views of his teacher Lamansky. Uspensky was the most vigorous
champion, before 1917, of the view that the occupation of the Balkan
Peninsula by the Slavs profoundly altered the social and economic
structure of the Empire's European provinces in the seventh and
eighth centuries, and that the peasant commune of the Farmer's Law
was of Slavonic origin. His devotion to pure scholarship did not,
however, prevent him on occasion from seeking in Byzantine history
political "lessons" for his contemporaries. Some of these "lessons"
clearly reveal the influence of Panslavist ideas. In the preface to the
first volume of his "History of the Byzantine Empire," written in 1912,
he declared: "The lessons of history should be carefully considered by
those who, at the present time, are awaiting the partition of the inheritance of 'the sick man' of the Bosphorus." And in the main body of
the book, published in 1914, he wrote: "We would be deceiving ourselves if we thought that we can avoid an active part in the liquidation
of the inheritance left by Byzantium. . . Russia's role in the Eastern
Question has been bequeathed to her by history, and cannot be
changed by arbitrary decision."[25]

Russian Byzantine studies between 1870 and 1917 were marked by
three main characteristics: by their high scholarly quality, probably
unrivalled by any other branch of historical studies in Russia, which
enabled them to equal, and in some fields perhaps to surpass, the
works of contemporary Byzantinists in Western Europe; by their con-

cern with social, administrative and economic history and with the problems of Russo-Byzantine relations; and by the debt which they owed to the great theological "academies" (graduate schools), particularly those of Moscow and St. Petersburg.[26]

It remains to say a few words about the role played by Byzantium in the historical concepts of scholars in the Soviet Union. It is not my intention to attempt a survey of the development of Byzantine studies in the USSR, nor an analysis of the work of individual Soviet scholars in this field. I will confine myself to pointing out the increasingly important position which Byzantine studies have come to occupy in Soviet historical studies since 1939; and to identifying briefly the central problems of Byzantine history selected by Soviet scholars for special study.

The death of Uspensky in 1928 was followed by a decade which witnessed an eclipse of Byzantine studies in his country, during which, in the words of the leading Soviet Byzantinist M. V. Levchenko, "scholarly research in this field of learning was temporarily interrupted."[27] A gradual revival of these studies began in 1939, and gathered momentum after 1944. Its main landmarks were the creation in 1939 of a Byzantine section at the Institute of History of the Academy of Sciences,[28] the simultaneous formation of a Byzantine group in Leningrad,[29] the appearance in 1940 of Levchenko's History of Byzantium,[30] the publication in 1945 of the *Vizantiisky Sbornik* prepared by the Leningrad group,[31] and the reappearance in 1947 — after an interruption of some twenty years — of the *Vizantiisky Vremennik*.[32] These were the principal stages by which Byzantine studies, through the devoted efforts of their genuine practitioners, regained their place as an autonomous historical discipline, and Byzantine history became once more, as it had been between 1870 and 1924, accessible to the Russian educated public.

Soviet Byzantinists inherited from their pre-revolutionary predecessors a dominant interest in two themes: the social and economic history of the Byzantine Empire, and the relations between Byzantium and medieval Russia. Both these themes, of course, are treated by them in the light of Marxist historical concepts. The development of Byzantine feudalism, which they regard essentially as a social and economic phenomenon, and as a term that adequately describes the social relations in Byzantium;[33] the history of cities in the Byzantine Empire;[34] and the role played by the Slav invasions in the development of the social structure of the Byzantine Empire: these are some of the problems of the internal history of the Empire which Soviet Byzantinists have approached from the Marxist point of view. On the problem of the Slav colonization of parts of the Balkans, Soviet Byzantinists today, despite some differences of opinion, seem agreed that, though Uspensky's views suffered from exaggeration, the social structure and customary law of the Slavs influenced the development of the Byzantine commune, and that their invasions contributed materially to the collapse of the "slave-holding formation" and to its replacement by feudalism.[35]

The work of Soviet Byzantinists further suggests that the relations between Byzantium and Russia is a subject that will always loom large in Russian Byzantine scholarship.[36] This problem, of course, is part of a more general one, whose importance and difficulty were so clearly illustrated by the discussions provoked by several papers presented in 1965 at the Congress of historians in Vienna.[37] To recognize that the influence of Byzantine culture on the medieval culture of Russia was pervasive and far-reaching and that, in the words of Karl Marx, "the religion and civilization of Russia are of Byzantine origin;"[38] yet to acknowledge that Byzantine influence was not an omnipotent demiurge, acting on a passive receiver, and that the Russian people often showed a creative response to its challenge by selecting, accepting or rejecting this or that element of Byzantine culture — is to posit in general terms a thesis which would need to be substantiated and empirically verified at every point of investigation. Soviet scholars, I venture to suggest, are in principle well equipped to study this dialectical process. And, in their continued research into the history of Russo-Byzantine relations, they will, we may hope, increasingly bear witness to the fact that Russian Byzantine studies have in former times and at the peak of their achievement derived their vitality from two sources: the sense of continuity with the scholarly tradition of the past; and the willingness to advance the frontiers of knowledge in collaboration with the scholars of other nations.

FOOTNOTES ON CHAPTER VI

[1]F. Ternovsky, *Izuchenie vizantiiskoy istorii i ee tendentsioznoe prilozhenie v drevney Rusi I* (Kiev, 1875), pp. 4-153; V. S. Ikonnikov, *Opyt russkoy istoriografii, II, 1* (Kiev, 1908), pp. 81-96; A. A. Shakhmatov, "Povest' Vremennykh Let i ee istochniki," *Trudy Otdela Drevnerusskoy Literatury* 4 (1940) 41-80.

[2]*Povest' Vremennykh Let*, ed. V. P. Adrianova-Peretts and D. S. Likhachev, Moscow-Leningrad 1950, I, pp. 17, 202.

[3]See above, pp. 178-87.

[4]V. Sokol'sky, O *kharaktere i znachenii Epanagogi, Vizantiisky Vremennik* I (1894) 50; G. Vernadsky, *Die kirchlich-politische Lehre der Epanagoge und ihr Einfluss auf das russische Leben im XVII. Jahrhundert*, in: *Byzantinisch-neugriechische Jahrbücher* 6 (1928-9) 119-42; W.K. Medlin, *Moscow and East Rome* (Geneva, 1952), pp. 177-9, 232-3.

[5]*Zhitie protopopa Avvakuma*, ed. N. K. Gudzy (Moscow, 1960), p. 101.

[6]Ternovsky, op. cit., II (Kiev, 1876), p. 263.

[7]S. M. Soloviev, *Istoriya Rossii s drevneishikh vremen, IX* (Moscow, 1963), p. 506.

[8]P. Ya. Chaadaev, *Sochineniya i pis'ma*, ed. M. Gershenzon, I (Moscow, 1913), p. 85. The *Lettres Philosophiques* were written in French.

[9]Ibid., pp. 271-2.

[10]T. N. Granovsky, *Sochineniya*, 4th ed. (Moscow, 1900), pp. 378-9. Cf. I. N. Borozdin, "T. N. Granovsky i voprosy istorii Vizantii", in: *Vizantiisky Vremennik* II (1956) 271-8.

[11]I. V. Kireevsky, *Polnoe Sobranie Sochineny*, I (Moscow, 1911), pp. 174-222.

[12]A. S. Khomyakov, "Po povodu stat'i I. V. Kireevskogo 'O kharaktere prosveshcheniya Evropy i o ego otnoshenii k prosveshcheniyu Rossii,'" *Polnoe Sobranie Sochineny*, 4th ed., I (Moscow, 1911), p. 217. Cf. P. K. Christoff, *An Introduction to Nineteenth Century Russian Slavophilism. A Study in Ideas I: A. S. Xomjakov* (The Hague, 1961), pp. 150-1, n. 30.

[13]N. Ya. Danilevsky, *Rossiya i Evropa*, 4th ed. (St. Petersburg, 1889), pp. 398-473.

[14]K. Leontiev, "Vostok, Rossiya i Slavyanstvo," *Sobranie Sochineny*, V (Moscow, 1912), pp. 111-260, esp. p. 139. Cf. N. Berdyaev, *Konstantin Leont'ev* (Paris, 1926), pp. 175-219.

[15]V. Soloviev, *La Russie et l'Église Universelle*, 5th ed. (Paris, 1922), pp. xxiv-li.

[16]V. Soloviev, "Vizantizm i Rossiya", *Sobranie Sochineny*, 2nd ed., VII (St. Petersburg,), n.d., pp. 283-325.

[17]*La Russie et l'Église Universelle*, ibid; *Vizantizm i Rossiya*, pp. 286-9, 315-19.

[18]*La Russie et l'Église Universelle*, p. L.

[19]V. Buzeskul, *Vseobshchaya istoriya i ee predstaviteli v Rossii v XIX i nachale XX veka*, I (Leningrad, 1929), pp. 7-16.

[20]*Memoriae populorum, olim ad Danubium, Pontum Euxinum, Paludem Maeotidem, Caucasum, Mare Caspium, et inde magis ad Septemtriones incolentium, e scriptoribus historiae byzantinae erutae et digestae* a I. G. Strittero, I-IV (St. Petersburg, 1771-9). Stritter's great work appeared in an Russian translation in St. Petersburg between 1770 and 1776.

[21]A. A. Kunik, "Pochemu Vizantiya donyne ostaetsya zagadkoy vo vsemirnoy istorii?", *Uchenye Zapiski I-go i III-go Otdeleniya Imper. Akademii Nauk.*, III 3 (1853) 423-444. Cf. F. Uspensky, "Iz istorii vizantinovedeniya v Rossii", in: *Annaly* 1 (1922) 115-16.

[22]On Vasilievsky, see: P. Bezobrazov's obituary notice in *Vizantiisky Vremennik* 6 (1899), 636-52, and the bibliography of Vasilievsky's works, *ibid.*, pp. 652-8; A. A. Vasiliev, Moi vospominaniya o V. G. Vasil'evskom, in: *Annales de l'Institut Kondakov* 11 (1940) 207-14; P. B. Struve, "V. G. Vasil'evsky, kak issledovatel' sotsial'noy istorii drevnosti i kak uchitel' nauki", *ibid.*, pp. 215-26; G. Ostrogorsky, "V. G. Vasil'evsky kak vizantolog i tvorets noveishey russkoy vizantologii", *ibid.*, pp. 227-35; Z. V Udal'tsova in: *Ocherki istorii istoricheskoy nauki v SSSR* II, ed. M. V. Nechkina (Moscow, 1960), pp. 513-15, 521-2.

[23]On Uspensky, see: H. Grégoire, "Les études byzantines en Russie soviétique", in: *Bulletin de l'Académie Royale de Belgique, cl. des lettres*, 5e série, 32 (1946) 194-219; B. T. Goryanov, "F. I. Uspensky i ego znachenie v vizantinovedenii", in: *Vizantiisky Vremennik* I (1947) pp. 29-108; A. G. Gotalov-Gotlib, "F. I. Uspensky kak professor i nauchny rukovoditel'", *ibid.*, pp. 114-26; A. A. Vasiliev, *History of the Byzantine Empire* (Oxford, 1952), pp. 35-8; Z. V. Udal'tsova, in: *Ocherki istorii istoricheskoy nauki v SSSR* II, pp. 515-19; Udal'tsova, "Vizantinovedenie v SSSR posle Velikoy Oktyabr'skoy Sotsialisticheskoy Revolyutsii (1917-1934 gg.)", in: *Vizantiisky Vremennik* 25 (1964) pp. 3-16.

[24]On Byzantine studies in Russia during the first ten years after the Revolution, see G. Lozovik, "Desyat' let russkoy vizantologii (1917-27)", in: *Istorik Marksist* 7 (1928), pp. 228-38.

[25]F. I. Uspensky, *Istoriya Vizantiiskoy Imperii I* (St. Petersburg, 1914), pp. xii, 46.

[26]On the theological academies, see G. Florovsky, *Puti russkogo bogosloviya* (Paris, 1937), pp. 335-90.

[27]M. V. Levchenko, "Zadachi sovremennogo vizantinovedeniya", in: *Vizantiisky Sbornik*, ed. M. V. Levchenko (Moscow-Leningrad, 1945), p. 4.

[28]Levchenko, *ibid.*, p. 6.

[29]N. S. Lebedev, "Vizantinovedenie v SSSR za 25 let", in: *Dvadtsat' pyat' let istoricheskoy nauki v SSSR*, ed. V. P. Volgin, E. V. Tarle and A. M. Pankratova (Moscow-Leningrad, 1942), p. 217; Lebedev, "Vizantinovedenie v SSSR 1936-46", in: *Byzantinoslavica* 9 (1947-8), p. 98.

[30]M. V. Levchenko, *Istoriya Vizantii* (Moscow-Leningrad, 1940). French translation: *Byzance des origines à 1453* (Paris, 1949).

[31]See note 27.

[32]The editorial of the first volume (pp. 3-7) was sharply criticized from a chauvinistic standpoint in the editorial of the second: "Protiv burzhuaznogo kosmopolitizma v sovetskom vizantinovedenii", in: *Vizantiisky Vremennik* 2 (27) (1949) pp. 3-10. Cf. the French translation of the second editorial by M. Canard, "Vizantiiski Sbornik et Vizantiiski Vremennik", in: *Byzantion* 21 (1951), pp. 471-81.

[33]Z. V. Udal'tsova and G. G. Litavrin, "Sovetskoe Vizantinovedenie v 1955—60 gg.", in: *Vizantiisky Vremennik* 22 (1963), pp. 3-17.

[34]*Ibid.*, pp. 18-24. Cf. N. V. Pigulevskaya, E. E. Lipshits, M. Ya. Syuzyumov and A. P. Kazhdan, "Gorod i derevnya v Vizantii v IV-XII vv.", in: *Actes du XIIᵉ Congrès International d'Etudes Byzantines* I (Belgrade, 1963), pp. 1-44.

[35]Goryanov, "F. I. Uspensky i ego znachenie", loc. cit., pp. 39-54; V. I. Picheta, "Slavyano-vizantiiskie otnosheniya v VI-VII vv. v osveshchenii sovetskikh istorikov (1917-47), in *Vestnik Drevney Istorii* 3 (1947) 95-9; Udal'tsova and Litavrin, "Sovetskoe Vizantinovedenie v 1955—60 gg.", loc. cit., pp. 9-11; M. Yu. Braichevsky, "Problema slavyano-vizantiiskikh otnosheny do IX veka v sovetskoy literature poslednikh let", in: *Vizantiisky Vremennik* 22 (1963), pp. 80-99.

[36]See the detailed study by I. Ševčenko, "Byzantine Cultural Influences", in: *Rewriting Russian History. Soviet interpretations of Russia's past*, ed. C. E. Black (London, 1957), pp. 143-97. Cf. Levchenko, "Problema russko-vizantiiskikh otnosheny v russkoy dorevolyutsionnoy, zarubezhnoy i sovetskoy istoriografii", in: *Vizantiisky Vremennik* 8 (1956) pp. 7-25; Udal'tsova and Litavrin, loc. cit., pp. 29-34.

[37]"L'Acculturation", in: *XIIᵉ Congrès International des Sciences Historiques*, Rapports I (Vienna, 1965), pp. 7-93.

[38]K. Marx and F. Engels, *Sochineniya* IX (Moscow, 1933), p. 439. This passage was cited in 1945 by Levchenko in his editorial contribution to *Vizantiisky Sbornik* (p. 4).

CHAPTER VII

STS. CYRIL AND METHODIUS,
APOSTLES OF THE SLAVS*

The aims of this paper[1] are to outline the story of an attempt, made in the second half of the ninth century, to create in Central Europe a Slavonic vernacular Church under the joint auspices of Byzantium and Rome; and to assess the significance of a cultural movement which spread in the early Middle Ages from Moravia to the Balkans and to Rus', and exerted a profound and lasting influence upon the religion and thought-world of the Slavs who lived in these areas. This attempt and this movement are associated with the names of the two great Byzantine missionaries—Cyril and Methodius.

The recorded history of the vernacular Slavonic Christianity begins in 862. That year an embassy arrived in Constantinople, sent to the Emperor Michael III by a Slavonic ruler in Central Europe, the Moravian prince Rastislav. The purpose of this embassy was twofold: the Moravians, whose realm at that time included Moravia, Slovakia and part of present-day Hungary, were hard pressed by their neighbors, the Franks and the Bulgarians and wished to conclude a political alliance with the Byzantine Empire. The second aim of the embassy was destined to be, in the long run, of far greater importance. It was to request the Emperor to send the Moravians a Christian missionary acquainted with their own Slavonic language. Christianity had already spread to Moravia during the first half of the ninth century, but its preachers were German missionaries from Salzburg and Passau. It is possible, as several scholars have recently argued, that Irish missionaries had also worked in Moravia in the late eighth and the early ninth centuries;[2] though the evidence on this point seems to me still inconclusive. Rastis-

---

*St. Vladimir's Seminary Quarterly, VII (1963), 1-11.

lav no doubt realized that the German missionaries threatened the precarious independence he had recently wrested from his overlord, Louis the German, King of Bavaria. To secure for his country a measure of political and cultural autonomy he needed priests who could preach the Gospel to the Moravians in their own Slavonic tongue.

The Byzantine government, mindful of the advantages — spiritual and temporal—to be derived from these distant solicitations, responded readily to Rastislav's request: an alliance was concluded with Moravia, and the choice of ambassadors to head the Moravian mission fell on two brothers from Thessalonica, Constantine and Methodius. They were both at that time famous men, distinguished in the service of Church and State. Their lives and activity, recorded in detail in contemporary Slav and Latin sources, have for more than a century been the subject of careful scrutiny and extensive research.[3]

The younger of the two brothers, Constantine, more widely known under his later monastic name of Cyril, had held a teaching post in the University of Constantinople, and had studied under Photius, the future Patriarch and the greatest scholar of his age. Methodius had been a governor of a Slavonic province of the Empire, and had thus come to know the Slavs early in his life. But both brothers soon experienced a call to the religious life. Methodius abandoned his career and became a monk. Constantine was ordained a priest. Soon the two brothers became known as outstanding missionaries and diplomatists. In 860, for instance, they headed an important and successful Byzantine mission to the realm of the Khazars, north of the Caucasus. But their strongest qualification to lead the embassy to Moravia was their intimate knowledge of the Slavonic language. Thessalonica, their native town, was in the ninth century a partially Greek city with a Slav-speaking hinterland; and according to the Slavonic biography of Methodius, written soon after his death, the Emperor, in urging the two brothers to go as his envoys to Moravia, adduced this argument: "You are both natives of Thessalonica, and all Thessalonicans speak pure Slav."[4]

Before leaving Byzantium, Constantine, according to his ninth century Slavonic biography, invented an alphabet for the use of the Moravian Slavs, his future flock. This alphabet he adapted to a Slavonic dialect of Southern Macedonia, from the neighborhood of Thessalonica. I cannot enter here into a discussion of the difficult and controversial problems raised by the fact that the oldest Slavonic manuscripts are written in two different alphabets, the Glagolitic and the Cyrillic. Over the question as to whether Constantine invented both of them, or if not, which of the two, philologists have argued for well over a century. Most scholars today are convinced, however, that the alphabet invented by Constantine for the Moravians was the Glagolitic, and that the so-called Cyrillic, which bears Constantine's monastic name of Cyril, resulted from an attempt by Methodius' disciples in Bulgaria to adapt Greek uncial writing to the Slavonic tongue.[5] If Cyrillic is very largely an adaptation of Greek, Glagolitic is a highly distinct and original alphabet whose inventor, Constantine, seems to have adapted in a modified form certain Greek, Hebrew and other Oriental letters. Of the two alphabets, Cyrillic was to be historically by far the more important, for the Church books of the Orthodox Slavs are printed in a slightly simplified form of this alphabet to the present day, and the modern alphabets of the Bulgarians, the Serbs and the Russians are all based on Cyrillic. Yet the invention of Glagolitic, which, despite its relative complexity, was admirably adapted to the qualities of the Slavonic tongue, was undoubtedly the work of a linguistic genius, and Constantine must rank among the greatest philologists Europe has ever produced. Before leaving Constantinople, Constantine, with the help of his new alphabet, translated into Slavonic a selection of lessons from the Gospels, intended for liturgical use, starting with the opening words of St. John: "In the beginning was the Word."[6]

Thus was created a new literary language, based on the spoken dialect of the Macedonian Slavs, modelled on Greek, and at first largely ecclesiastical in character. It is known to modern scholars as Old Church Slavonic. In the ninth century the different Slavonic languages were still so similar in structure and vocabulary that Old Church Slavonic was as intelligible to the Slavs of Moravia as, in the course of the next two centuries, it proved to be to the Bulgarian, Serbian and Russian Slavs. It became henceforth and remained throughout the Middle Ages the third international language of Europe and the sacred idiom of those Slavs — the Bulgarians, the Russians and the Serbs — who received their religion and culture from Byzantium. Constantine, still venerated by all the Slavs as St. Cyril, was not only, with his brother Methodius, the greatest of all missionaries who worked among the Slavs; he was also the founder of Slavonic literary culture.

In the autumn of 863 the Byzantine embassy arrived in Moravia, where Prince Rastislav received it with honor. The two immediate tasks that faced the missionaries were to train a new Slav-speaking clergy and to give the Moravians a liturgy in their own language. A few Christian texts had previously been translated from Latin into Slavonic and transcribed in Latin characters — such as formularies of baptism and confession, the Creed and the Lord's prayer.[7] Of these translations, which were current in Moravia during the first half of the ninth century, Constantine and Methodius doubtless made use. But the liturgical offices had so far been celebrated in Latin, with which the Moravians were unfamiliar. Constantine, in the words of his contemporary biographer, soon translated "the whole ecclesiastical office, Matins, the Hours, Vespers, Compline and the Mass."[8]

The question of what rite was used by Constantine for his Old Church Slavonic translation of the liturgical offices has long been debated, and is to some extent still an open one. In the passage from Constantine's *Life* which I have just quoted, the liturgical terminology seems to be Byzantine, to judge at least from the fact that the Slavonic term for "Compline" — *Pavechernitsa* — corresponds to the Greek *Apodeipnon* and not to the Latin *Completorium*.[9] For this and other reasons it seems difficult to doubt that the Slavonic liturgy was first celebrated in Moravia according to the Byzantine rite. It is possible, however, that in the course of time Constantine also translated and adapted the Roman Mass, which the earlier Frankish missionaries had introduced into Moravia. Several distinguished modern authorities, Father Dvornik and Dr. Grivec among them,[10] believe that the oldest Slavonic formulary of the Roman Mass, preserved in part in the Glagolitic *Kiev Leaflets*, is a translation made by Constantine from the Liturgy of St. Peter, itself a Greek adaptation of the Roman Mass. Be that as it may, there are cogent reasons for supposing that both the Roman and the Byzantine liturgies were translated into Slavonic in the second half of the ninth century. And it is quite possible that the liturgical tradition eventually adopted in the new Slavonic Church in Central Europe represented a blending of the Byzantine and the Roman rites.

The translation of the liturgical offices into a vernacular language was, from the Byzantine point of view, natural and legitimate. Constantine himself, when later defending the Slavonic liturgy against its detractors in Venice, cited the example of many nations of Eastern Christendom who praised God in their native languages: among them were the Armenians, the Persians, the Egyptians, the Georgians and the Arabs.[11] But the Western Church, in which Latin was recognized as the only legitimate idiom for sacramental worship, had every reason to look askance at the liturgical experiments of Constantine and Methodius; all the more so, as Moravia was ecclesiastically within the jurisdiction of Rome. It is not surprising that the Frankish clergy in Moravia, whose position was greatly strengthened by the forced submission of Prince Rastislav to Louis the German in 864, viewed the activities of the two Byzantine brothers with hostile suspicion.

But the attitude of the Papacy proved to be different from that of the German clergy. Five years after their arrival in Moravia, Constantine and Methodius travelled to Rome, in response to a summons from Pope Nicholas I. In Rome they were well received. The two brothers could scarcely have chosen a more propitious moment to plead their cause before the Holy See. The Papacy was at that time trying to secure its hold over the Balkan Slavs; it had recently scored a sensational, if ephemeral, triumph in Bulgaria. High hopes were entertained in the Papal Chancellery that the whole Slavonic world would soon join the family of nations that paid homage to the Bishop of Rome. The new Pope, Hadrian II, had every reason to look with favor on the work of Constantine and Methodius: their missionary work among the Slavs had been highly successful; their personal piety and learning were widely admired; and they were strongly backed by the Slavonic rulers of Central Europe — by Rastislav of Moravia and Kotsel of Pannonia. There was only one embarrassing circumstance: they celebrated the Divine Office not in Latin, as the Western custom, now rapidly becoming a fixed tradition, commanded, but in Slavonic. Was the Pope to sanction this innovation which might create a dangerous precedent in the Western Church? Or was he, for the sake of an established custom, to surrender effective control of Moravian and Pannonian Christianity to the Frankish clergy? Hadrian II was a statesman: he accepted the bargain. He gave his unqualified support to the work of Constantine and Methodius, and commanded that the Slavonic liturgical books be placed on the altar of the Basilica of Santa Maria Maggiore and that the Liturgy be celebrated in the Slavonic language in four Roman basilicas. The two Greek brothers from Thessalonica, who barely six years earlier had set out from Byzantium on their mission to Moravia, could not have dreamt that their work would be crowned so soon and so authoritatively. But Constantine soon after fell seriously ill. Feeling the approach of death, he became a monk under the name of Cyril. In 869 he died in Rome and, at his brother's request, was buried in the Basilica of St. Clement. His last words to his brother were to implore him not to abandon their common work for the Slavs, even if it meant never returning to the monastery on Mount Olympus in Asia Minor, where Methodius had received the tonsure. This injunction, recorded by his ninth century biographer, provides a moving illustration of the perennial tension between the missionary calling and the contemplative life: "Behold, my brother, we were both harnessed to the same yoke, ploughing the same furrow. I am falling down by the gate, my day's work finished, but you have a great love for the Mountain. Do not, for the sake of the Mountain, abandon your teaching. For how better can you be saved?"[12]

The rest of Methodius' life was spent in loyal obedience to his brother's last wish. Armed with the pope's approval of the Slavonic liturgy, he returned to Central Europe where, as Archbishop of Pannonia and Papal Legate to the Slavonic nations, he continued the work of building a vernacular Christianity, translating the remaining parts of the Scriptures and training the next generation of Slav-speaking priests. Yet the foundations on which he built were precarious. The East Frankish and Bavarian clergy, whose earlier prerogatives in Pannonia and Moravia were annulled by Methodius' new jurisdiction, took advantage of the increased power of Louis the German in Moravia to secure the arrest of Methodius. Condemned as a usurper of episcopal rights by a local synod presided over by the Archbishop of Salzburg, he spent two and a half years in prison. It was only in 873 that the new pope, John VIII, having learnt at last of Methodius' plight, forced Louis the German and the Bavarian bishops to release him.

But Rome was fast losing interest in the Slavonic liturgy. The Papacy was now showing a growing unwillingness to risk, for the sake of this liturgy, a major conflict with the Frankish Church. John VIII still loyally supported Methodius. But his successors, turning their back on the achievements of Nicholas I and Hadrian II, banned the Slavonic liturgy. In 885 Methodius died in Moravia, his work among the Slavs on the brink of ruin. His principal disciples were arrested and exiled from Moravia; others were sold into slavery.

So ended the life-work of St. Cyril and St. Methodius, apostles of the Slavs and founders of Slavonic Christianity. It must indeed, at the time, have seemed a tragic failure. The Slavonic liturgy and the new Slavo-Byzantine culture appeared to be on the verge of extinction. Yet it took more than two centuries to wipe out the last remnants of the work of Cyril and Methodius in Central Europe — a sure sign of its vitality and appeal. Old Church Slavonic literature and the Slavonic liturgy flourished in Bohemia until the end of the eleventh century, and Croatia in the tenth and eleventh centuries had a strong Slavonic liturgical tradition which went back to the time of Cyril and Methodius. On the coast and on several islands of Dalmatia Slavonic Glagolitic missals are still in use. But in Central Europe the Roman policy of centralization and linguistic uniformity destroyed Slavonic vernacular Christianity in the late eleventh century.[13]

These developments, however, were of secondary importance. The future of Slavonic Christianity lay elsewhere. Expelled from Moravia upon their master's death, the disciples of Methodius found refuge in another land. Their work was saved for Europe and the Slavs by the Bulgarians, whose destiny it was to enrich this vernacular culture and to transmit it to the other Slavs who owed allegiance to the Orthodox Church — the Russians and the Serbs.

The Bulgarian ruler Boris was, together with many of his subjects, baptized into the Byzantine Church in 864, a year after Cyril and Methodius started on their mission to Moravia. By 870 Bulgaria was firmly attached to the Eastern Church and placed within the sphere of Byzantine culture. But Boris and the Bulgarian nobility, while wishing to benefit from their association with the Empire, were yet afraid that the Greek clergy which controlled their Church might prove to be the instrument of Byzantine political domination. Slavonic priests and the Slavonic liturgy would, they must have foreseen, provide an admirable solution to their dilemma. The vernacular tradition of Cyril and Methodius would allow Bulgaria to enjoy the benefits of Byzantine civilization without prejudice to her independence as a Slavonic nation. And so, when the disciples of Methodius, after their expulsion from Moravia, travelled down the Danube valley and arrived in Bulgaria, they were cordially received by Boris. The leading member of this group was Clement, a Byzantine Slav, whose contribution to the history of Slavonic vernacular culture was surpassed only by that of Cyril and Methodius. Clement was sent by Boris to Macedonia; there working among the Macedonian Slavs for thirty years, he was consecrated bishop, preaching the Gospel in Slavonic, celebrating the Slavonic liturgy according to the Byzantine rite, translating Greek religious writings, and training a native clergy.[14] Thanks to St. Clement and to his co-disciple and collaborator St. Naum, Macedonia became for over a century one of the foremost centers of Christian culture in Europe, and its capital, the city of Ohrid by the beautiful mountain lake of that name, was the cradle of Slavonic Christianity in the Balkans. Meanwhile, at the opposite, North-Eastern, extremity of the country, in the Bulgarian capital of Preslav, another school of Slavonic literature was developing under the patronage of Symeon, Boris' son and eventual successor. It was here, probably in the closing years of the ninth century, that the Glagolitic script, invented by Constantine-Cyril, was replaced by the simpler Cyrillic alphabet, more obviously based on Greek. During the next hundred years, the school of Preslav produced a rich crop of translated literature. Theological extracts from the Greek Fathers, Byzantine chronicles and encyclopaedias, and a Byzantine treatise on poetics were thus made accessible to Slavonic readers. It was mostly a literature of translation and adaptation; but some original works were also produced, such as the first grammar of the Slav language, and at least one remarkable poem in Old Church Slavonic. This literary movement has been compared to the vernacular culture of Anglo-Saxon Northumbria which flourished two centuries earlier. But its historical importance, I would suggest, was greater: for, by making Byzantine sacred and secular literature accessible to the Slavs, it fostered for many centuries the cultural life of the peoples of Eastern Europe.[15]

* * *

If one were to attempt a general assessment of the work of Cyril and Methodius, its significance, I suggest, would be seen to lie in its unifying tendency and creative character. In a Christendom that was beginning to feel the growing tension between East and West, they sought to reconcile and to unite three important elements in the civilization of medieval Europe: the Byzantine, the Roman, and the Slavonic.

Cyril and Methodius were citizens of the East Roman Empire, and never ceased to regard Byzantium as their fatherland. As ambassadors of their emperor to Moravia, they loyally performed the mission with which they were entrusted. By training and vocation they belonged to the Byzantine élite of their time. The remarkable revival of monastic culture and secular learning which began in the middle of the ninth century and which some historians have termed "the Byzantine Renaissance" was imprinted on their outlook and activity. Methodius the monk and Cyril the scholar, sometime professor at the University of Constantinople and a friend of Photius, the greatest humanist of the age, embody two of the most striking features in the medieval culture of Byzantium. Typical of this culture was the belief in the one, universal, Christian Empire, the pattern and prefiguration of the Kingdom of God. This view is explicitly ascribed to Cyril by his ninth century biographer: "Our Empire," he declared to the ruler of the Khazars, "is. . .that of Christ, as the prophet said, 'God shall set up a heavenly kingdom, which shall never be destroyed: and the kingdom shall not be left to other people, but shall break in pieces and consume all these kingdoms, and it shall stand for ever.'"[16] The Byzantine authorities, for their part, gave their continued support to the two brothers and to their disciples. In the last years of his life Methodius visited Constantinople, at the invitation of the Emperor Basil I. There, his biographer tells us, he was warmly received and, before returning to Moravia, left behind him a priest and a deacon with the Slavonic liturgical books.[17] The keen interest, which the Byzantine authorities showed in the Slavonic liturgy as a means of evangelizing the Slavs, is seen also in an episode that occurred soon after Methodius' death. An envoy of the Emperor, visiting Venice, noticed a group of slaves, offered for sale by Jewish merchants. On enquiry, he discovered that they were disciples of Cyril and Methodius, whom the Moravians had sold as heretics. He bought them and took them back to Bulgaria to continue their work.[18] This active support given to Slavonic vernacular Christianity by the Byzantine authorities was part of the intense missionary activity then displayed by the Eastern Church, which led to the conversion of the Balkans and of Rus'. And in this too, Cyril and Methodius, the apostles of the Slavs, embody that Christian universalism, which, in their most successful hour, the Church and Empire of East Rome preached to the newly converted nations of Europe.

And the Old Rome, too, welcomed and blessed for a while the work of the two brothers. It was the Frankish clergy, with its urge for cultural domination and political control, that destroyed the Slavonic vernacular Christianity that was planted in Central Europe by the common action of Byzantium and Rome. The persistence of the schism between the Churches of East and West has often distorted the historians' view of the relations between Rome and Byzantium in the ninth century. It is well to remind ourselves that these relations were, on the whole, quite friendly. Their leaders may have engaged at times in violent polemic with each other, their theologians may have begun to differ on the doctrine of the double procession of the Holy Spirit. Yet for the average Byzantine of the time, Old Rome remained the

venerable city of St. Peter, and in its bishop, the Patriarch of the West
— the "Apostolicus," as he is called in the Slavonic biographies of
Cyril and Methodius — was vested the primacy of honor in the whole
of Christendom. I believe that we would fail to grasp the significance
of the work of the two brothers unless we recognized that their attitude to the Roman see and its bishop in no way differed from that of
most of their Byzantine contemporaries.

The debt which the Slavs owe to Cyril and Methodius is great
indeed. A mission, whose original purpose was to preach Christianity
in the idiom of the Moravians, led to the rise of a whole Slavonic
culture. A liturgy, in a language rich, supple and intelligible; the Christian Scriptures, translated into the same vernacular tongue; access to
the treasury of Greek patristic literature and Byzantine secular learning: truly a new world was opened to the Slavs by the work of Cyril
and Methodius. The two brothers were aware of the importance of
their mission. This is apparent in their biographies, in the writings of
their immediate disciples, and especially in a remarkable Old Church
Slavonic poem, which many modern authorities ascribe to Cyril himself, and others to his pupil, Bishop Constantine, who wrote in Bulgaria at the turn of the century. Whether written by Cyril or not, this
poem, which is a Prologue to the Slavonic version of the Gospels,
expresses faithfully and eloquently the ideas prevalent in his circle.[19]
The author compares peoples without sacred books in their own language to a naked body and to a dead soul; and laments the misery of
those who, deprived of letters, can neither hear the peals of thunder
nor smell the scent of flowers. And, turning to the Slavs, the poet
triumphantly exclaims: "Then hear now with your own mind, listen,
all you Slavs: Hear the Word, for it came from God, the Word that
nourishes human souls, the Word that strengthens heart and mind,
the Word that prepares all to know God!"[20] It is perhaps worth noting that this poetic eulogy of the vernacular language has a parallel in
a passage written almost simultaneously at the other end of Europe,
though in sober prose: "For it seems well to me," wrote King Alfred
of England, "that we also change into the tongue that we all know the
books that are most needful to be known by all men" (The passage is
taken from Alfred's preface to his translation of Gregory the Great's
Cura Pastoralis).[21]

This vindication of the vernacular language fostered in its turn,
among the followers of Cyril and Methodius, a particular outlook,
part religious and part national, which is not without interest for the

historian of ideas. A national language was held to be sanctified by being used liturgically, above all through serving as the language of the Mass; and thereby the nation which spoke this language was in its turn raised to the status of a consecrated people. This idea is suggested in the letter sent in 863 by the Emperor Michael to Rastislav of Moravia, and cited by Cyril's biographer: the newly invented Slavonic letters, the Emperor states, are being sent to the Moravians as a priceless gift, "that you too may be numbered among the great nations who praise God in their own language."[22] The same idea is implicit in Cyril's spirited defense of vernacular languages during his disputation with the Venetian clergy.[23] For all tongues are equal in the sight of God; and it is through the language that is man's most intimate possession, through his mother tongue, that God can come into closest contact with the human soul. Thus, in the Cyrillo-Methodian tradition, was the idea of a consecrated nation combined with the concept of a plurality of languages equal in status, and nationalism was sublimated by the notion of an ecumenical society of Christian peoples. It may be said, in other words, that Cyril and Methodius transmitted to the Slavs the idea that underlies the whole of their missionary work: that every nation has its own particular gifts and every people its legitimate calling within the family of the universal Church.[24]

These ideas became the inheritance of those Slavonic nations which accepted the Christian faith from Byzantium. Their influence was particularly felt in Russia, whose medieval writers, for all their indebtedness to Byzantium, soon began to display a native originality, conscious as they were that in the common patrimony of Christendom their own newly baptized nation had its own and not unimportant place under the sun. And upon the humble folk the legacy of Cyril and Methodius had an impact that was no less powerful. For the Slav peoples of Eastern Europe received Christianity in a language that was close to their vernacular. They listened to the Gospel as it was read in church and could grasp something at least of its meaning. Above all was the Slavic liturgy a source of ever renewed inspiration. The liturgy of the Eastern Church is one of the great original creations of Byzantine genius. On the Russians of the Middle Ages it produced an impression of overwhelming beauty: "We knew not whether we were in heaven or on earth," so did the Russian envoys of Vladimir describe to their sovereign the service in St. Sophia in Constantinople in the late tenth century.[25] Translated into Slavonic, this liturgy, with its eucharistic drama, the poetry of its hymns, and the dogmatic symbolism of its setting — the church with its mosaics and frescoes depicting the heavenly hierarchy dominated by the majestic figure of the Pantokrator — Christ the All-Ruler — entered the very core of Slav Christianity. Its role was thus described by the British Byzantinist, the late Norman Baynes, in a lecture delivered in 1945: "Still today it is the common liturgy which is the bond between the separate branches of the Orthodox Church — the liturgy in the vernacular tongue which was the gift of Byzantium. . .that liturgy which may yet even in the Russia of Stalin see a resurrection and reassert its claims against the propaganda of a godless creed."[26]

Such, in brief, are the main achievements of Cyril and Methodius, Byzantine missionaries, apostles of the Slavs and saints of the universal Church.

FOOTNOTES ON CHAPTER VII

[1] Read at St. Vladimir's Seminary on 12 April 1962 and based on one of the Birkbeck Lectures, delivered by the author under the auspices of Trinity College, Cambridge, on 25 April 1961.

[2] See J. Cibulka, "L'architecture de la Grande-Moravie au IX^c siècle à la lumière des récentes découvertes", *L'Information de l'histoire de l'art*, 2 (Paris, 1966), pp. 1-34. J. Poulík, "The Latest Archaeological Discoveries from the Period of the Great Moravian Empire", in *Historica*, I (Prague, 1959), pp. 24-7; Z. R. Dittrich, "The Beginning of Christianisation in Great Moravia", in *The Slavonic and East European Review*, xxxix (December, 1960), pp. 164-73.

[3] See F. Grivec and F. Tomšič, *Constantinus et Methodius Thessalonicenses. Fontes* (Zagreb, 1960). [*Radovi Staroslavenskog Instituta*, 4]. See also the following bibliographies: G. A. Il'insky, *Opyt sistematicheskoi Kirillo-Mefod'evskoi bibliografii* (Sofia, 1934); M. Popruzhenko and S. Romansky, *Kirilometodievska bibliografiia za 1934-1940 god.* (Sofia, 1942); I. Dujčev and others, *Kirilo-metodievska bibliografiya 1940-1980* (Sofia, 1983). The following modern works are of special importance: F. Dvornik, *Les Slaves, Byzance et Rome au IX^c siècle* (Paris, 1926); F. Dvornik, *Les Légendes de Constantin et de Méthode vues de Byzance* (Prague, 1933); *Byzantine Missions among the Slavs* (New Brunswick, N.J., 1970); F. Grivec, *Konstantin und Method, Lehrer der Slaven* (Wiesbaden, 1960). A.P. Vlasto, *The Entry of the Slavs into Christendom* (Cambridge, 1970); P. Dinekov (ed.), *Kirilo-Metodievska Entsiklopediya*, 1- (Sofia, 1985-).

[4] *Vita Methodii*, V, 8 (Grivec-Tomšič, p. 155).

[5] See *Handbook of Old Church Slavonic*, II [by R. Auty] (London, 1960), pp. 1-14.

[6] *Vita Constantini*, XIII, 14 (Grivec-Tomšič, p. 129).

[7] See A. V. Isačenko, *Začiatky vzdelanosti vo Velkomoravskej Ríši* (Turčiansky Sv. Martin, 1948). [With summary in Russian].

[8] *Vita Constantini*, XV, 2 (Grivec-Tomšič, p. 131).

[9] See Grivec, *Konstantin und Method*, pp. 179-84.

[10] See F. Dvornik, *The Slavs, their early History and Civilization* (Boston, 1956), pp. 85, 166-7; Grivec, *op. cit.*, pp. 179-84. Cf. A. Dostál, "The Origins of the Slavonic Liturgy", *Dumbarton Oaks Papers*, XIX (1965), pp. 67-87.

[11] *Vita Constantini*, XVI, 7-8 (Grivec-Tomšič, p. 134).

[12] *Vita Methodii*, VII, 1-3 (Grivec-Tomšič, p. 157).

[13] See F. Dvornik, *The Slavs, their early History and Civilization*, pp. 170-7; K. Onasch, *Der Cyrillo-Methodianische Gedanke in der Kirchengeschichte des Mittelalters*, in *Wissenschaftliche Zeitschrift der Martin-Luther-Universität*, Halle-Wittenberg, VI (1956-7), pp. 27-39.

[14] See N. L. Tunitsky, *Sv. Kliment, episkop slovensky* (Sergiev Posad, 1913); M. Kusseff, *St. Clement of Ochrida*, in *The Slavonic and East European Review*, XXVII (1948), pp. 193-215; D. Obolensky, *Six Byzantine Portraits* (Oxford, 1988), pp. 8-33.

[15] See M. Murko, *Geschichte der älteren südslawischen Litteraturen* (Leipzig, 1908); B. Angelov and M. Genov, *Stara bŭlgarska literatura* (Sofia, 1922); E. Georgiev, *Raztsvetŭt na bŭlgarskata literatura v IX-X v.* (Sofia, 1962).

[16] *Vita Constantini*, X, 52-3 (Grivec-Tomšič, pp. 116-17). Cf. M.V. Anastos, *Political Theory in the Lives of the Slavic Saints Constantine and Methodius*, in *Harvard Slavic Studies*, II (1954), pp. 11-38.

[17] *Vita Methodii*, XIII, 5 (Grivec-Tomšič, p. 163).

[18] *Vita S. Naoum*, ed. M. Kusseff, in *The Slavonic and East European Review*, XXIX (1950-1), p. 142.

[19] See E. Georgiev, *Kiril i Metody, osnovopolozhnitsi na slavianskite literaturi* (Sofia, 1956), pp. 165-90; F. Grivec, *Konstantin und Method, Lehrer der Slaven*, pp. 217-21; R. Jakobson, *Selected Writings*, VI (Berlin-New York-Amsterdam, 1985), pp. 191-205.

[20] Jakobson, loc. cit.

[21] Cited in C. Dawson, *Religion and the Rise of Western Culture* (London, 1950), p. 103.

[22] *Vita Constantini*, XIV, 16 (Grivec-Tomšič, p. 129).

[23] *Vita Constantini*, XVI (Grivec-Tomšič, p. 146).

[24] See R. Jakobson, *The Beginnings of National Self-Determination in Europe*, in *The Review of Politics*, VII (1945), pp. 29-42. See also his *Selected Writings*, VI, pp. 115-28.

[25] *Povest' Vremennykh Let*, ed. V. P. Adrianova-Peretts and D. S. Likhachev (Moscow-Leningrad, 1950), I, p. 75; English translation by S. H. Cross and O. P. Sherbowitz-Wetsor: *The Russian Primary Chronicle* (Cambridge, Mass., 1953), p. 111.

[26] N. H. Baynes, *Byzantine Studies and Other Essays* (London, 1955), pp. 21-2.

CHAPTER VIII

THE HERITAGE OF CYRIL
AND METHODIUS IN RUSSIA*

I

The Russian Primary Chronicle, in a passage describing the measures taken in 1037 by the Russian sovereign Yaroslav to provide his subjects with Slavonic translations of Byzantine books — a passage written in the eleventh or early twelfth century—makes the following observation: "Great is the profit obtained from book learning: for through books we are taught the way of repentance, and from the written word we gain wisdom and self-control. Books are rivers which water the entire world; they are springs of wisdom; in books there is an unfathomable depth; by them we are consoled in sorrow; they are the bridle of self-control. . . . He who reads books often converses with God, or with holy men."[1] Such statements are no doubt a commonplace of medieval literature; yet their conventional character cannot, even today, wholly obscure the genuine emotion with which the chronicler, who was probably a Russian monk, affirms that the life of men can be greatly enriched by the reading of books. And, as the context of this passage plainly shows, the chronicler's emotion is heightened by his knowledge that his compatriots have now been provided with books in their own Slavonic language. This he gratefully attributes to the enlightened action of the rulers of his own land — Yaroslav, Prince of Kiev, and his father Vladimir who converted Rus' to Christianity in the late tenth century. So concerned is the chronicler to extol the virtues of these two Russian sovereigns in promoting the Slav vernacular culture that he fails, in this passage, to mention the fountainhead of this

---

*Dumbarton Oaks Paper, XIX (1065), 47-65.

culture — the work of Cyril and Methodius. Yet, as we shall see, the Russians of the Middle Ages were well aware of the true origins of their vernacular literature, and cherished with gratitude and veneration the memory of the two Byzantine apostles of the Slavs; and the same Russian Primary Chronicle contains other passages which clearly acknowledge that the Russians owe their alphabet, their literature, and their scholarly tradition, to the Moravian mission of Constantine and Methodius. One of the aims of this chapter is to demonstrate that the importance of this mission, and its relevance to the cultural history of the Eastern Slavs, were appreciated in medieval Russia; the second aim is to outline the history of the Cyrillo-Methodian tradition in medieval Rus' and to assess the role it played in the culture and thought-world of the Eastern Slavs: I would emphasize the word "outline"; for it is clear to me that the "Heritage of Cyril and Methodius in Russia" is a problem too vast and complex to be treated, within the scope of a single chapter, in any but a fragmentary and tentative manner.

I propose to approach my subject chronologically. I shall concentrate mainly on the period which begins with the official acceptance of Christianity in the late tenth century and ends in the early twelfth. It was then, notably in the eleventh century, that Russian literature was born; it was then, too, that Russian national consciousness found its first articulate expression. The central part of my theme—the heritage of Cyril and Methodius in eleventh-century Rus'—will be introduced by a brief sketch of its antecedents on Russian soil, and will be followed by an epilogue illustrating its impact on late medieval Russia.

II

Our story begins with a puzzle, which has taxed the ingenuity of many a scholar. The first recorded conversion of the Russians to Christianity took place in the sixties of the ninth century: contemporary Byzantine sources inform us that this conversion closely followed the Russian attack on Constantinople in 860;[2] that by 867 the Russians had accepted a bishop from Byzantium;[3] and that about 874 an archbishop was sent to them by the Patriarch Ignatius.[4] This first ecclesiastical organization on Russian soil seems to have been submerged, later in the century, by a wave of paganism which swept away the pro-Christian rulers of Kiev and replaced them by a rival group of Scandinavians from North Russia. Yet there is little doubt that a Christian community survived, at least in Kiev, attracting a growing number of converts throughout the tenth century, until Russia's final conversion in the reign of St. Vladimir, in 988 or 989 or 990. Some of the Russian envoys who ratified the treaty with the Empire in Constantinople in 944 were Christians, and a Christian church, ministering to a numerous community, existed in Kiev at that time.[5] Some time between 946 and 960 Princess Olga, regent of the Russian realm, was baptized in Constantinople;[6] and in 983, a few years before Vladimir's conversion, two Christian Varangians were martyred in Kiev for their faith.[7]

It is apparent from these facts that the beginnings of Russian Christianity coincide in time with the Moravian mission of Constantine and Methodius and with the conversion of Bulgaria to the Christian faith; and that a Christian community existed in Kiev, continuously or with brief interruptions, for 125 years before Vladimir's baptism. Moreover, the comparatively rapid establishment of a diocesan organization at the end of the tenth century, the perceptive and mature understanding of the Christian life revealed by Russian writers of the next two generations, and the high literary standards attained by some of them in the Slavonic language, strongly suggest that the Russian ecclesiastical leaders and intellectual élite of that time were building on earlier foundations; and it is only natural to suppose that these older foundations were such as to ensure the survival of the Christian community in Kiev as a going concern for more than a century before Vladimir; that this community, in other words, was provided with an effective clergy, intelligible Scriptures, and a liturgy capable of satisfying the spiritual needs of the Slav and Varangian converts to the Christian religion. We would expect, in brief, to find traces in Rus', between 860 and 988, of the Cyrillo-Methodian tradition of Slavonic vernacular Christianity.

These traces, however, are singularly insubstantial. The evidence which scholars have extracted from the sources, or dug out from the ground, amount to a few meagre crumbs: it has been maintained, for instance, that the Slavonic texts of the Russo-Byzantine peace treaties of the tenth century, preserved in the Primary Chronicle, prove that the Russians could by that time read and write in Slavonic, although we do not know for certain when or where these documents were translated from the Greek;[8] the observation that Princess Olga, at the time of her baptism and visit to Constantinople, knew no Greek and relied on the service of interpreters has led to the suggestion that the liturgy may have been celebrated in Slavonic for her benefit in Kiev;[9] the fact that in the eleventh century the Russians had some acquaintance with the Glagolitic script has been taken to mean that they imported, not later than the middle of the tenth century, the Slavonic liturgy and books from Macedonia, where the Glagolitic tradition was still in existence;[10] a Cyrillic inscription, consisting of a single word, was discovered on a clay vessel during excavations near Smolensk in 1949, and was dated by its discoverer, D.A. Avdusin, to the first quarter of the tenth century;[11] all this, in terms of direct evidence, does not amount to very much.

And yet it seems likely enough that well before Vladimir's conversion, by the mid-tenth century at the latest, the Christian community in Kiev was familiar with the Slavonic liturgy, with Slavonic translations of parts of the Scriptures, and with Slav-speaking priests. It is permissible to speculate where these may have come from. Common linguistic and ethnic ties, and the political relations which existed in the tenth century between the Eastern Slavs on the one hand, and the Western and Southern Slavs on the other, may well have facilitated, or even provoked, the spread of Slav priests and books to Rus' either from the former territories of Great Moravia, or else from Bulgaria.[12]

Some of the these priests and books may even have come from Constantinople where, at least in the second half of the ninth century, the Byzantine authorities assembled Slav-speaking priests and stockpiled Slavonic books for the needs of missionary enterprises beyond the Empire's northern borders. We have no direct evidence to show how far, before or after the time of Vladimir, the Byzantine missionaries in Rus' deliberately encouraged the Slavonic vernacular as a means of evangelizing the country; however, the rapid establishment of this tradition in Rus' after Vladimir's conversion, to the virtual exclusion of the Greek language from the liturgy at a time when the Russian Church was governed by prelates appointed by Constantinople, strongly suggests that the East Roman authorities acknowledged that the tradition of vernacular Slavic Christianity, which had already yielded rich dividends in Bulgaria, was the only one that could reasonably be imposed on the numerous population of their powerful and distant northern proselyte.[13]

This introductory survey has rested less on direct information — which is fragmentary and equivocal — than on circumstantial evidence and on later material derived from the eleventh century. It is customary to blame the Russian Primary Chronicle for our inadequate knowledge of the beginnings of the Cyrillo-Methodian tradition in Rus'. It is indeed at first sight surprising that this document, compiled in the eleventh and early twelfth centuries, which treats in such detail of the earliest history of the Russian people and is so plainly concerned with the fate of Russian letters and learning, has nothing precise to say about the channels through which the Slav vernacular tradition came to Rus'. It attributes, as we have seen, the introduction of book learning to Vladimir and his son Yaroslav. Are we then to conclude that the author, or authors, of the Chronicle knew nothing of any earlier beginning, and that they believed that the Christian community in Kiev before Vladimir's time celebrated the liturgy in Greek? Different answers have been given to this question. The Russian scholar N. K. Nikol'sky, in a study of the Russian Primary Chronicle, published in 1930, argued that its compilers were perfectly aware of the Slavonic origin of Russian Christianity, but deliberately avoided any mention of it, in order to give greater prominence to the story of Vladimir's baptism by Byzantine missionaries, to present the conversion as an exclusively Greek achievement, and thus to justify the claims of the Byzantine clergy to ecclesiastical hegemony over Rus'.[14] This thesis should be considered in a broader context: for the past fifty years it has been fashionable to regard the authors of the Primary Chronicle as men moved by political passions and factional loyalties, propagandists not averse to suppressing, twisting, or inventing evidence to gratify their prejudices or to flatter their ecclesiastical or secular patrons. This view is best epitomized in the well-known history of Kievan Russia by M. D. Priselkov, published in 1913, who carried to extreme, and sometimes absurd, lengths the more balanced and cautious conclusions of his teacher Shakhmatov, that unrivalled authority on Russian chronicles.[15] The problem of the reliability of the Primary Chronicle is too large and too complex to be discussed here. I can only express my personal belief that, although the compilers of the Chronicle did at times show a personal bias in the selection and presentation of their material, to maintain or imply that they were wholesale forgers, playing an elaborate game of hide-and-seek with their medieval readers (and with modern scholars as well), is to overestimate their ingenuity, to degrade their sense of history, and to ascribe to them motives which are, to say the least, anachronistic.

What Nikol'sky called "the mysterious silence" of the chronicler about the early introduction of Slavonic letters into Rus' can, it seems to me, be explained more satisfactorily if we suppose that he was ignorant of the facts, rather than that he took part in a conspiracy to suppress them. He had, as we shall see, precise and detailed information on the Moravian mission of Constantine and Methodius; but the circumstances in which the fruits of this mission were first acquired by the Russians must have remained unknown to him. The Soviet scholar V. M. Istrin has plausibly suggested that this ignorance may be explained by the gradual, sporadic, and undramatic way in which the Slav vernacular tradition filtered in to Russia in the tenth century; and by the fact that among its carriers — Slav-speaking priests from the Balkans or the West Slavonic area — no memorable personality emerged of the calibre of Cyril and Methodius and their immediate disciples.[16]

III

It is scarcely possible to doubt that elements of the Cyrillo-Methodian tradition — priests, books, and the liturgy — came to Rus' before the time of Vladimir. It would, however, be unwise to exaggerate the extent and importance of this penetration. It was only after the official conversion of Rus' to Christianity in 988-90, which led to the stregthening of the links with Byzantium and the establishment of a nation-wide ecclesiastical structure under the authority of the Patriarch of Constantinople, that the problem of building a Slav vernacular Church became really urgent.[17] For this new period, which spans and slightly overlaps the eleventh century, we have considerably more information; and much of it comes from the Russian Primary Chronicle.

In an entry dated 898, the Chronicle gives a fairly detailed account of the Moravian mission of Constantine and Methodius; this is preceded by a brief note describing the invasion of Moravia by the Magyars; the introductory section of the Chronicle has a further entry which refers to the earliest history of the Slavs and to their dispersal from their primeval European home.[18] This introductory entry is linked with the later note on the conquest of Moravia by a common emphasis on the ethnic and linguistic unity of the Slav peoples; and both the entry and the note are connected with the account of the Moravian mission by the importance they all ascribe to "Slavonic letters" (*gramota slověnьskaja*) as a force expressive of Slav unity. The scholars who have studied these various entries in the Chronicle — A. Shakhmatov, P. Lavrov, N. Nikol'sky, V. Istrin, and, most recently, Professor Jakobson — are agreed that they are all fragments of a single work, stemming from a Cyrillo-Methodian environment, and brought to Russia from the West Slavonic area.[19] Shakhmatov, who called it *The Tale about the Translation of Books into the Slav language (Skazanie o prelozhenii knig na slovensky yazyk)* — the name has stuck — plausibly suggested that it came to Rus' in the eleventh century; and Professor Jakobson has described it as "a Moravian apologetic writing of the very end of the ninth century."[20]

For our present purpose, the most interesting of these surviving fragments is the account of the Moravian mission. It has long been known to contain four separate quotations from the *Vita Methodii*, and to be generally based on this work, with several borrowings from the *Vita Constantini*.[21] On several points, however, the version of the Russian Chronicle deviates from the *vitae* of the apostles of the Slavs: on none of them is the Russian version reliable; most of the divergences may be ascribed to error or confusion on the chronicler's part: for instance, he states quite wrongly that Kotsel, as well as Rastislav and Svatopluk, requested a teacher from Byzantium, that the Slavonic alphabet was invented in Moravia, and that toward the end of his life Constantine taught in Bulgaria; in one case, however, the Russian chronicler can be suspected of deliberately deviating from his sources: he acknowledges that the work of Constantine and Methodius was supported by the Papacy, but makes no mention of their stay in Rome; this omission, probably due to anti-Roman censorship, suggests the hand of a revisor of the late eleventh or early twelfth century, when hostility to the Latin Church was beginning to gain ground in Russia.[22]

As source material on the Moravian mission, the *Tale about the Translation of Books* is wholly derivative and of no great value to the historian. Yet in other respects this document is of considerable interest: it proves that the Russian chronicler was familiar with the written Lives of Constantine and Methodius; it shows how a West Slavonic work, breathing the authentic spirit of the Cyrillo-Methodian tradition, could be adapted to a specifically Russian situation; and, whether in its original or adapted form, it made, as I shall presently suggest, a small but not insignificant contribution to that tradition.

The emphasis which the *Tale* repeatedly lays on the unity of the Slavonic language; its manifest pride in the "power" and "intelligibility"[23] of the Slavonic letters created by Constantine and Methodius which, it tells us explicitly, are a common patrimony of the Moravians, the Bulgarians, and the Russians; its critical attitude to the "trilingual heresy," that *bête noire* of the Slavonic apostles and of their disciples:[24] these are familiar and characteristic ingredients of the Cyrillo-Methodian thought-world. But in its concluding part, which obviously bears the mark of a Russian revision, the *Tale* breaks new ground, and claims that the heritage of Cyril and Methodius has been acquired by the

Russian people; it bases this claim on a series of syllogistic arguments: the Slavonic letters were brought by Constantine and Methodius to the Moravians; the Russians, like the Moravians, are Slavs, and speak the same Slav language; the conclusion is implied that the Russians, too, are pupils of the Slavonic apostles; furthermore, Moravia and Pannonia, the lands of Methodius' spiritual jurisdiction, had once been evangelized by St. Andronicus, one of Christ's seventy disciples; but St. Andronicus was the disciple of St. Paul, who himself preached in Moravia. Therefore St. Paul is the teacher of the Slavs, and the Russians, by virtue of being Slavs and pupils of St. Methodius, are likewise disciples of St. Paul.[25] By means of these complicated constructions, and by appealing to the current though legendary tradition that Paul and Andronicus preached in northern Illyricum and Pannonia, the Russian chronicler traces the spiritual ancestry of his people back to Cyril and Methodius on the one hand, and to St. Paul on the other. The conjunction of names is significant, for the veneration of St. Paul, the apostle of the Gentiles, is an essential feature of the Cyrillo-Methodian tradition.[26]

There is clearly something artificial in these putative spiritual genealogies; even the syntax of this passage in the Chronicle is awkward: there are eleven causal conjunctions in nine lines. The chronicler's patent embarrassment doubtless stems from his inability to identify the historical channels through which the Cyrillo-Methodian heritage penetrated from Moravia to Rus'; and it confirms the view I expressed earlier that his silence on this point comes from ignorance, not from bad faith. At the same time he is aware, and rightly so, that the Slav vernacular tradition which flourished in Rus' in his day has its roots in the Moravian mission of Constantine and Methodius.

Two Scriptural quotations inserted in the *Tale* seem to me of special interest, and suggest that the chronicler, or his source, did more than just reiterate the classic themes of the Cyrillo-Methodian tradition. The first of them is embedded in the phrase: "The Slavs rejoiced to hear the mighty works of God in their own tongue;" and in a later passage the pope is made to declare: "All nations shall tell the mighty works of God, as the Holy Spirit will give them utterance."[27] The latter citation is taken from Pope Hadrian II's letter to Rastislav, Svatopluk, and Kotsel, as quoted in the eighth chapter of the *Vita Methodii*;[28] and both of these quotations in the Chronicle are also derived, pratically verbatim, from the second chapter of the Acts of the Apostles, verses four to eleven, which describe the descent of tongues of fire upon the Apostles at Pentecost. So far we are on familiar Cyrillo-Methodian ground, for the gift of tongues is a theme closely related to that of vernacular languages, and the pope's citation of Acts II in the *Vita Methodii* implies that the appearance of the Slavonic liturgy and books can be regarded as a second Pentecost. However, these two Pentecostal quotations acquire added significance if we relate them to the introductory part of the Primary Chronicle, which immediately precedes the first fragment of the *Tale*: this introduction, based largely, though not exclusively, on the Slavonic translation of the Byzantine chronicle of George Hamartolos,[29] begins with the story of the division of the earth among the sons of Noah after the Flood, and ends with a brief account of the building of the Tower of Babel. The Russian version of the latter episode, based, it would seem, on the Slavonic version of a lost historical compendium mainly derived from the chronicles of John Malalas and George Hamartolos,[30] states that when the Lord scattered His people over the face of the earth, the pristine linguistic and ethnic unity of mankind gave way to a multiplicity of languages and nations. The Russian chronicler deliberately links this Biblical introduction to his account, which follows immediately, of the early history and dispersal of the Slavs, by placing them both among the heirs of Japheth and among the seventy-two nations which were scattered from the Tower of Babel. The conclusion seems inescapable that the chronicler wished to suggest a contrast between the former multiplicity of tongues and the present unity of the Slavonic languages, a unity to which Cyril and Methodius gave a new significance; and that he did so by implying that the Slavonic letters are an extension of the miracle of Pentecost whereby the Holy Spirit rescinded the confusion of tongues which sprang from the Tower of Babel. This contrast between Pentecost and Babel, which gives a new and more universal dimension to the work of Cyril and Methodius, is not, as far as I know, explicitly drawn in any other work of the medieval Cyrillo-Methodian tradition. One or the other of the two contrasting themes is touched upon occasionally: the Tower of Babel and the confusion of languages are mentioned in Khrabr's celebrated defense of the Slavonic letters, written in Bulgaria in the late ninth or the early tenth century;[31] and, as Professor Jakobson has shown, the Pentecostal miracle is alluded to in a *troparion* of a canon to Cyril and Methodius, dating from the same period, which states that Cyril "received the grace of the Holy Spirit equal to that of the Apostles."[32] It is true that the *Prologue to the Holy Gospels*, an Old Church Slavonic poem attributed by many scholars to Constantine himself, seems to go some way toward implying a contrast between Babel and Pentecost: its third line reads: "Christ comes to gather the nations and tongues;"[33] but only in the Russian Primary Chronicle are the two terms of the contrasting parallel clearly brought out.

The origin of this idea is not hard to find: the contrast between Babel and Pentecost, and the belief that the latter has cancelled the former, are repeatedly emphasized in the Byzantine offices for Whit Sunday. The *kondakion* of the feast makes the point with particular clarity: "When the Most High went down and confused the tongues, He divided the nations: but when He distributed the tongues of fire, He called all men to unity."[34] We do not know whether this idea, which is so succinctly expressed in the Greek and Slavonic service of Pentecost and is also to be found in the writings of several Greek Fathers,[35] was directly applied to the Slavs by the Russian chronicler, or whether he found it in his source, the *Tale about the Translation of Books*; be that as it may, the notion that the Slavonic peoples share in the Pentecostal abrogation of Babel can be regarded as a significant addition to the storehouse of Cyrillo-Methodian ideas.

The chronicler's adaptation of the *Tale about the Translation of Books* shows how close was the connection in his mind between the conversion of the Russians to Christianity and their acquisition of the Cyrillo-Methodian vernacular tradition; by contrast, as we have seen, he did not know when and how this tradition first came to Rus'. He is not much more informative on this point when he comes to the reign of Vladimir. Yet common sense suggests that the establishment of Christianity as the state religion in his reign would have been impossible had not the Slav-speaking clergy preached the Gospel and celebrated the liturgy in the vernacular on a wide scale. But of this we know next to nothing. It is true that the so-called "Chronicle of Joachim," a seventeenth-century compilation, no longer extant, based on medieval sources, and discovered and quoted in part by the eighteenth-century historian Tatishchev, contains several statements which, if true, would give us just the facts we need. After Vladimir's conversion to Christianity, we are told in this source, Symeon, tsar of Bulgaria, sent to Rus' "learned priests and sufficient books."[36] The view that the "Chronicle of Joachim" is a fabrication of Tatishchev has been abandoned by historians generally,[37] and this particular piece of evidence is accepted as genuine by a number of scholars. As early as 1856, P. A. Lavrovsky attempted to explain away the anachronistic connection between Vladimir and Symeon (who died half a century before the former's accession) by referring to the statement of the Byzantine chronicler of Scylitzes that Romanus, son of the Bulgarian Tsar Peter, assumed the name of his grandfather Symeon.[38] Romanus is believed by some historians to have been tsar of Bulgaria between about 979 and 997. However, though Romanus was undoubtedly a contemporary of Vladimir, it is far from clear that he ever reigned in Bulgaria.[39] A further statement in the "Chronicle of Joachim" seems to confirm that Vladimir's clergy was partly of Slavonic origin: the Byzantine authorities, it asserts, sent to Vladimir the Metropolitan Michael, a Bulgarian by nationality, to head the Russian Church.[40] This Michael, we may note, is mentioned as the first primate of Russia in several sixteenth-century sources.[41] However, tempting though it is to accept the statements of the "Chronicle of Joachim" on the penetration of a Slavonic clergy and books into Russia in the late tenth century, there are, in my opinion, too many uncertainties connected with this text to make it possible to regard it as reliable evidence.

The earliest trustworthy account relating to the use of Slavonic in the Russian Church does, however, come from the reign of Vladimir; and it is supplied by the Primary Chronicle. In an entry dated 988, the chronicler tells us that after the Russians had been baptized Vladimir "sent round to assemble the children of noble families, and gave them to be instructed in book learning."[42] It is *prima facie* highly improbable that the teaching in these earliest known Russian schools was conducted in Greek; some knowledge of the Greek language was doubtless imparted to the members of Vladimir's *jeunesse dorée* who were destined for high office in the Russian Church; but there is every reason to believe that by "book learning" (*učenьe knižnoe*) the chronicler meant literary instruction in Slavonic. Evidence that this was so is provided by the chronicler's comment on Vladimir's schools, in a passage which immediately follows the account of their foundation: "When these children were assigned to study books in various places, there was fulfilled in the land of Rus' the prophecy which says: 'In that day shall the deaf hear the words of a book and the tongue of the dumb shall be clearly heard.'"[43] There is, I submit, much significance in this Biblical quotation. It is a composite one, and is drawn from two different chapters of the Septuagint version of the Book of Isaiah, the first half from Isaiah 29:18, the second half from Isaiah 35:6.[44] In its original context it describes the change in Israel's relation to Jahweh, by which the people's blindness and stupidity will give way to knowledge and joy. "The words of a book" (λόγους βιβλίου) are the commands of Jahweh, and these will be accepted when the book is unsealed.[45] These words of Isaiah are in the Primary Chronicle adapted to the Russian people's new relationship to God after their conversion to Christianity; and "the words of a book" (λόγοι βιβλίου), by a translation both semantically accurate and creatively fitted to a new situation, are rendered in Slavonic as *slovesa knižnaja*, an expression which refers to the Christian Scriptures, but is also a technical term for the Scriptures and liturgy translated into the Slavonic tongue.

The idea of applying the words of Isaiah to the Slav vernacular tradition was not an invention of the Russian chronicler. It has not, so far as I know, been observed that his conflation of the two quotations from Isaiah 29:18 and Isaiah 35:6 has an exact parallel in the fifteenth chapter of the *Vita Constantini*, which they are likewise combined and placed in a similar context. This chapter, which describes Constantine's work in Moravia, opens with the following words: "When Constantine arrived in Moravia Rastislav received him with great honor and, having assembled some disciples, he gave them to him to be instructed. He soon translated the whole of the ecclesiastical office, and taught them the services of matins, the canonical hours, vespers, compline, and the sacred liturgy. And, according to the words of the prophet, the ears of the deaf were unstopped, and they heard the words of a book (*kniž'naa slovesa*), and the tongue of the dumb was clearly heard."[46] The similarity between these two passages in the Primary Chronicle and in the *Vita Constantini* is striking: both contain the same composite quotation drawn from two different chapters of the Book of Isaiah; both apply the prophet's λόγους βιβλίου to the Slavonic vernacular; and there is an obvious analogy between Rastislav's and Vladimir's educational measures: both are said to have assembled pupils and to have assigned them for instruction. There can be little doubt that the passage in the Russian Primary Chronicle is directly based on the opening section of the fifteenth chapter of Constantine's Life. And this leads to the following conclusions: firstly, borrowings by the Russian chronicler from the *Vita Constantini* are not confined to the early sections of the chronicle which go back to the *Tale about the Translation of Books*; secondly, the Russian chronicler, by making use of the fifteenth chapter of the *Vita Constantini* and quoting from it, implied a parallel between the introduction of the Slavonic liturgy and Scriptures into Moravia through the combined efforts of Constantine and Rastislav, and their transmission to Russia on the initiative of Vladimir; and thirdly, the chronicler was convinced that Vladimir's educational measures really marked the beginning of the vernacular Slav tradition in Russia: in which belief, as we have seen, he was not altogether correct.

We know regrettably little about Vladimir's Slavonic schools; their beginnings cannot have been altogether smooth, to judge from the chronicler's statement that the mothers of these conscripted pupils "wept over them, as though they were dead."[47] The brighter of these alumni, who must have become adults by the year 1000 at the latest, doubtless formed the nucleus of that educated élite which produced the earliest works of Russian literature in the first half of the eleventh century.[48] This and the following generation of scholars must have taken an active part in the second of Russia's educational reforms, promoted by Vladimir's son Yaroslav and to which I alluded at the beginning of this chapter. This reform is described in the Primary Chronicle under the year 1037. Yaroslav, repeatedly termed a "lover of books," which he is said to have read frequently night and day, "assembled many scribes and had them translate from Greek into the Slavonic language. And they wrote many books." These books, we are told in a subsequent passage, were deposited by Yaroslav in the newly built church of St. Sophia in Kiev, the principal cathedral in the land.[49]

The origin and nationality of Yaroslav's translators are unknown. That some of them were Russians can scarcely be doubted. Others may have been Greeks or Slavs from Byzantium. It is very probable that the group included Bulgarian priests and scholars, some of them perhaps refugees who had fled their land after the Byzantine conquest in 1018. It is not impossible that some were Czechs. It has been suggested that the traces of various Slav languages found in some translations current in Rus' at the time indicate that Yaroslav's translators formed a kind of international commission.[50] Here, however, the historian finds himself on peculiarly slippery ground: he cannot safely venture over it before he has an answer to three questions: What writings of Greek religious and secular literature were available in Rus' in the early Middle Ages? Which of these translations can with reasonable certainty be attributed to Russian hands? And of these Russian translations, which were executed in the reign of Yaroslav, that is between 1019 and 1054? On none of these questions do philologists appear to have reached a consensus of opinion. A. I. Sobolevsky supposed that nearly all the extant translations made in Bulgaria in the ninth and tenth centuries were available in Rus' during the first centuries after the conversion.[51] The same scholar drew up a tentative list of thirty-four of these translations which, in his opinion, were done by Russians in the pre-Mongol period. These include the Life of St. Andrew Salos, the Life of St. Theodore the Studite, the Monastic Rule of Studios, the Christian Topography of Cosmas Indicopleustes, Josephus Flavius' History of the Jewish War, the Romance of Alexander, the Bee (Μέλισσα), the Physiologus, and the *Devgenievo deyanie*, generally regarded as a fragmentary Russian translation of an early version of *Digenis Akritas*.[52] V. M. Istrin, in his monumental edition and study of the Slavonic version of the Chronicle of Hamartolos, has argued that this work was translated in Kiev, in the forties of the eleventh century, by a Russian member of Yaroslav's pool of translators.[53] But this view has been disputed, or at least modified, by several scholars.[54] Philologists are always reminding us how difficult it is to distinguish on linguistic grounds an Old Church Slavonic text written in Rus' from one composed in Bulgaria or Bohemia, so homogeneous, until the end of the eleventh century, was the common Slavonic written tradition.[55] And the historian who seeks to avoid the dangers of overemphasizing the cultural achievements of Kievan Rus' must surely heed these words of caution. He will admit the contribution made by Russian scholars, in the eleventh century and later, to the available store of Old Church Slavonic translations from Greek; he will acknowledge that many, perhaps most, of the translations available in the Kievan period came from Bulgaria; and, to complete the picture, he will also recognize that some literary works stemming from the very area where Constantine and Methodius had worked — Moravia and Bohemia — were brought to Rus' in the eleventh century. Among these works, written in the Czech recension of Old Church Slavonic and available in the Kievan period, were the Martyrdom of St. Vitus, the Martyrdom of St. Apollinarius of Ravenna, and Gumpold's Life of St. Wenceslas of Bohemia — all translations from the Latin; and the original Slavonic Lives of St. Wenceslas and St. Ludmila.[56] The cult of these two Czech saints in Kievan Rus' is a striking but by no means isolated example of the close cultural and religious links which existed between Rus' and Bohemia in the late tenth and in the eleventh century, at a time when Bohemia was still a living repository of the Cyrillo-Methodian tradition.[57]

Evidence of the Cyrillo-Methodian tradition in eleventh-century Russian literature is not confined to Old Church Slavonic writings imported into Rus' from the Balkans and Bohemia. Significant traces of this tradition can also be found in the earliest products of native literature, composed in the Russian recension of Old Church Slavonic. In an anonymous Tale (*Skazanie*), written in the late eleventh or early twelfth century, describing the murder of the saintly princes Boris and Gleb, a parallel is drawn between their martyrdom and that of St. Wenceslas of Bohemia;[58] and, as Professor Chyzhevsky has pointed out, the influence of Gumpold's Life of St. Wenceslas can probably be detected in the approximately contemporary *Vita (Chtenie)* of Boris and Gleb by the monk Nestor, and in the *Vita* of St. Theodosius of the Kiev Monastery of the Caves by the same author.[59] The connection between the cult of St. Wenceslas and that of Boris and Gleb acquires added significance if we recall that relics of these two Russian saints were deposited inside the altar of the Abbey of Sázava in Bohemia, that important center of the Slavonic liturgy and literature in the eleventh century.[60]

It has been suggested by several scholars that the influence of the Cyrillo-Methodian tradition can also be detected in the attempts of some early Russian writers to define the place occupied by their nation within the Christian community. Professor Jakobson, in an essay entitled "The Beginnings of National Self-Determination in Europe," has argued that a distinctive feature of the Cyrillo-Methodian heritage was the idea that a language used for the celebration of the liturgy acquires a sacred character, which is then assumed by the people which speaks it; and the cognate notion that every nation has its own particular gifts and its own legitimate calling within the universal family of Christian peoples. This concept of national self-determination, he suggests, shaped the outlook of the early writers of Kievan Rus';[61] and with this view the late George Fedotov, to judge from his book *The Russian Religious Mind,* would have concurred.[62] If the ideological basis of the Cyrillo-Methodian movement were thus defined, the theme of this study could legitimately be widened to include a discussion of national and patriotic motifs in early Russian literature; and of the attitude of its writers to the Byzantine Empire and to its claims to world supremacy. But these are problems too large and complex to be discussed here. Enough, I think, has been said to show that the Cyrillo-Methodian inheritance was a vital force in eleventh-century Rus'.

IV

We cannot, for lack of information, trace the continuous history of the Cyrillo-Methodian tradition in Rus' after the early twelfth century. It is only in the late Middle Ages that the evidence becomes clearer and more abundant. And this evidence suggests that in the late fourteenth and in the fifteenth century interest in the work of Cyril and Methodius, which may have flagged somewhat after the early twelfth century,[63] began to revive, and that attempts were made in that period to claim that their missionary activity, and particularly that of Constantine, had been directly connected with Rus'. The motive forces behind these unhistorical constructions were probably a renewed interest in Russia's past history and international connections, a nationalistic desire of the Russians to claim some of the brothers' achievement for themselves, and, doubtless, genuine error. Thus, the anonymous Greek "philosopher," who in the Primary Chronicle delivers a speech of inordinate length, and dubious orthodoxy, to persuade Vladimir to accept Byzantine Christianity, is in two fifteenth-century chronicles given the name Cyril;[64] a Greek account of the conversion of Rus' to Christianity, the so-called Banduri Legend, preserved in a fifteenth-century manuscript and partly based on a lost Slavonic source, contains the colorful story of the dispatch by the Emperor Basil I to Rus' of two missionaries, Cyril and Athanasius, who baptized the Russians and taught them the Slavonic alphabet;[65] finally a Russian text, found in a manuscript of the *Tolkovaya Paleya*, copied in 1494 and subsequently inserted in an account of the death of Cyril and the conversion of Vladimir, contains these words: "Be it known to all nations and all men. . .that the Russian alphabet was by God made manifest to a Russian in the city of Cherson; from it Constantine the philosopher learned, and with its help he composed and wrote books with Russian words."[66] The interest of this text, which is clearly based on the eighth chapter of the *Vita Constantini*,[67] lies in the author's attempt to interpret the passage, so hotly debated by modern scholars, which describes how Constantine during his stay in Cherson in the winter of 860-1 discovered a Gospel book and a Psalter written *rusьskymi pismeny*. It is curious to note that the attempt to interpret this passage of the *Vita Constantini* to mean that the Slavs had invented a Slavonic alphabet before Cyril—a view still vigorously championed by some East European scholars[68] — goes back to an anonymous Russian patriot of the fifteenth century.

These belated and factitious claims, and the somewhat antiquarian interest in the work of Cyril and Methodius which they reveal, bear some characteristic marks of the historical thinking of early Muscovite Russia. And yet the Russians of the fifteenth century could, with far better reason, point to a genuine and recent instance which showed that the Cyrillo-Methodian tradition was still a vital and creative force in their country. About 1378 a Russian monk by the name of Stephen went to preach the Gospel to the pagan Zyrians; this East Finnic people, known today as Komi, lived in the northeastern part of European Russia, in the basin of the Vychegda river, and were then subjects of the republic of Novgorod. Before embarking on his mission, Stephen learnt their language, invented a Zyrian alphabet and, with the approval of the Muscovite authorities, translated the liturgical books into Zyrian. He successfully Christianized his flock by preaching and singing the offices in their vernacular, disputing with the pagan shamans, building churches, and training disciples. In 1383 he was consecrated Bishop of Perm', and spent the last fourteen years of his life ably administering his Zyrian diocese. He died in 1396, and was later canonized by the Russian Church.[69]

The striking analogy between the achievements of St. Stephen of Perm' and those of Constantine-Cyril is pointedly emphasized by Stephen's biographer and contemporary, Epiphanius the Most Wise. He calls Stephen "in truth the New Philosopher," and describes him as an accomplished Greek scholar; champions the cause of vernacular liturgies and Scriptures by quoting extensively from the defense of the Slavonic letters by the monk Khrabr, that knight-errant of the Cyrillo-Methodian tradition; and even improves on Khrabr by suggesting that although St. Cyril and St. Stephen were equal in goodness and wisdom, and though they performed tasks of the same importance, Stephen's merit was the greater, for whereas Cyril was assisted by his brother Methodius, Stephen had no help save from God.[70]

Thus, at the end of our story, in the Russia of the late Middle Ages, we find the vitality of the Cyrillo-Methodian inheritance manifested not only in literary reminiscences, but also in the example of a man who in his personal life embodied the ideals and emulated the achievements of the two Byzantine missionaries. But in contrast to their performance the work of St. Stephen proved ephemeral. In the centralized Muscovy of the sixteenth century there was no place for the rights of vernacular languages, and the liturgical books of the Zyrians gradually fell into disuse.[71] Yet Stephen's missionary achievements were applauded by the Russian Church; and, above all, the memory of those who had inspired his life-work — St. Cyril and St. Methodius — continued to be reverently cherished by his compatriots. It is significant that the great majority of the extant manuscripts — complete or fragmentary — of their two biographies come from Russia: forty-four out of fifty-nine for the *Vita Constantini*, fourteen out of sixteen for the *Vita Methodii*.[72] Liturgical offices for Sts. Cyril and Methodius are included in the early Russian *Menaia*, the oldest of which go back to the late eleventh century: one of these early hymns addresses Cyril as follows: "Cyril, glorious teacher of virtue, you taught the Moravians to give thanks to God in their own language, by translating God's religion and its righteousness from Greek into the Slavonic language; therefore the Slavonic nations now rejoice and glorify God."[73]

In concluding this study, I feel impelled to express a feeling of doubt that frequently assailed me during its preparation. I am acutely conscious of the fact that a historian who is not a trained philologist cannot, in discussing the Cyrillo-Methodian heritage in Russia, do justice to what he must surely acknowledge to be an essential, perhaps the essential, component of this heritage. I refer to the Old Church Slavonic language, acquired by the Russians partly in its Moravian but more especially in its Bulgarian recension, which became the medium for their religious expression and the foundation of their medieval literature, sacred and secular. Blending in the course of time with the native vernacular speech, later re-injected several times into the secularized Russian language by dictates of literary fashion, Old Church Slavonic has never ceased to enrich the vocabulary and the thought-world of the Russian people. The vernacular tradition which it created may have acted to some extent as a screen between the Russians and the culture of antiquity, and have been partly responsible for the fact that a good knowledge of Greek was comparatively rare in medieval Russia. Yet we must not forget that Old Church Slavonic was itself modelled on Greek; and that it enabled the Russians to produce an abundant literature of their own, which ranks high in the history of their culture.

One element in this Church Slavonic tradition has proved of peculiar strength and vitality: the Christian liturgy, which so moved the Russian medieval chronicler that he attributed the conversion of his country to the beauty of the public worship in Constantinople,[74] and which, in its Slavonic version, continues even today to bear witness to the undying strength of Orthodox Christianity in the midst of the Soviet atheistic state.

I would justify this concluding reference to a contemporary situation, which some of us may be disposed to view with optimism and hope, by appealing to the very nature of the Cyrillo-Methodian tradition. For surely hope and optimism, and their spiritual counterpart, joy, are a central theme of this tradition: joy which springs from the knowledge that the commands of the Lord are no longer a sealed book, that the Word has been made manifest to men, that the confusion of Babel has been repealed by the Pentecostal gift of tongues, and that "the divine shower of letters"[75] has been sent down upon the Slavonic nations. This sense of triumph is conveyed most powerfully in the opening verses of the thirty-fifth chapter of the Book of Isaiah, the very verses from which the author of the *Vita Constantini*, of the Russian Primary Chronicle and of the Life of St. Stephen of Perm',[76] quoted to describe the bounty of the Slav vernacular tradition: "The wilderness and the dry land shall be glad, the desert shall rejoice and blossom; like the crocus it shall blossom abundantly, and rejoice with joy and singing. . . . Then the eyes of the blind shall be opened, and the ears of the deaf shall be unstopped. Then shall the lame man leap like a hart, and the tongue of the dumb shall be clearly heard. . . . They shall see the glory of the Lord, the splendor of our God."

FOOTNOTES ON CHAPTER VIII

¹*Povest' vremennykh let*, ed. by V. P. Adrianova-Peretts and D. S. Likhachev (Moscow-Leningrad, 1950), I, pp. 102-3; English translation by S. H. Cross and O. P. Sherbowitz-Wetzor (Cambridge, Mass., 1953), p. 137. In subsequent references to this document the original will be cited as "Povest'," and the translation as "Cross."

²Theophanes Continuatus (Bonn), p. 196.

³Photius, *Epistolae*, PG, 102, cols. 736-7.

⁴Theophanes Continuatus, pp. 342-3. Cf. F. Dölger, *Regesten der Kaiserurkunden des oströmischen Reiches*, I (Munich-Berlin, 1924), p. 60.

⁵*Povest'*, I, p. 39; Cross, p. 77. The Russo-Byzantine treaty, dated by the chronicler to 945, was in fact concluded in the previous year. See *Povest'*, II, p. 289; Dölger, *op. cit.*, I, p. 80.

⁶*Povest'*, I, pp. 44-5; Cross, pp. 82-3. The date and place of Olga's baptism, and the time (or times) of her visit or visits to Constantinople, have been the subject of lively controversy during the past twenty-five years. See above, Chapter II, p. 72, note 115.

⁷*Povest'*, I, pp. 58-9; Cross, pp. 95-6.

⁸See D. S. Likhachev, in *Povest'*, II, pp. 257, 278. For the text of these treaties, see *Povest'*, I, pp. 24-9, 34-9, 52; Cross, pp. 64-8, 73-7, 89-90. Cf. S. Mikucki, "Études sur la diplomatique russe la plus ancienne. I. Les traités byzantino-russes du Xᵉ siècle," *Bulletin international de l'Académie Polonaise des Sciences et des Lettres*, cl. de philol., d'hist. et de philos., no 7 (Cracow, 1953), pp. 1-40; I. Sorlin, "Les traités de Byzance avec la Russie au Xᵉ siècle," *Cahiers du monde russe et soviétique*, II (1961), 3, pp. 313-60, 4, pp. 447-75.

⁹Constantine Porphyrogenitus, *De Cerimoniis* (Bonn), I, p. 597. Cf. P.A. Lavrovsky, "Issledovanie o Letopisi Yakimovskoy," *Uchenye Zapiski Vtorogo Otdeleniya Imper. Akademii Nauk*, II, 1 (1856), p. 149.

¹⁰See M. Speransky, "Otkuda idut stareishie pamyatniki russkoy pis'mennosti i literatury?", *Slavia*, VII, 3 (1928), pp. 516-35; B. S. Angelov, "K voprosu o nachale russko-bolgarskikh literaturnykh svyazey," *Trudy Otdela Drevnerusskoy Literatury*, XIV (1958), pp. 136-8. On the Glagolitic tradition in medieval Russia, see V. N. Shchepkin, "Novgorodskie nadpisi Graffiti," *Drevnosti. Trudy Imper. Moskovskogo Arkheologicheskogo Obshchestva*, XIX, 3 (1902), pp. 26-46; G. Il'insky, "Pogodinskie kirillovsko-glagolicheskie listki," *Byzantinoslavica*, I (1929), p. 102.

¹¹D. A. Avdusin and M. N. Tikhomirov, "Drevneishaya russkaya nadpis'," *Vestnik Akademii Nauk SSSR* (1950), 4, pp. 71-9.

¹²On Russia's relations with Bohemia in the tenth century, see A. V. Florovsky, *Chekhi i vostochnye slavyane*, I (Prague, 1935), pp. 1-44. On Russia's relations with Bulgaria in the same period, see M. N. Tikhomirov, "Istoricheskie svyazi russkogo naroda s yuzhnymi slavyanami s drevneishikh vremen do poloviny XVII veka," *Slavyansky Sbornik* (Moscow, 1947), pp. 132-52.

¹³For the Byzantine attitude toward the tradition of Slavonic vernacular Christianity, see F. Dvornik, *Les Slaves, Byzance et Rome au IXᵉ siècle* (Paris, 1926), pp. 298-301; I. Dujčev, "Il problema delle lingue nazionali nel medio evo e gli Slavi," *Ricerche Slavistiche*, VII (1960), pp. 39-60; I. Ševčenko, "Three Paradoxes of the Cyrillo-Methodian Mission," *The Slavic Review*, XXIII (1964), pp. 226-32; D. Obolensky, *The Byzantine Commonwealth* (St. Vladimir's Seminary Press, Crestwood, N.Y., 1982), pp. 200-4. The problem is complex and requires further investigation; in the meantime, it may be tentatively suggested that the farther a given Slavonic country was situated from Constantinople, and the less chance there consequently was of Hellenizing its culture, the more ready the Byzantine authorities were to consolidate its Christianity and to ensure its loyalty to the Empire by encouraging it to acquire and develop the Slav vernacular tradition.

¹⁴N. K. Nikol'sky, "Povest' vremennykh let, kak istochnik dlya istorii nachal'nogo perioda russkoy pis'mennosti i kul'tury," *Sbornik po Russkomu Yazyku i Slovesnosti Akademii Nauk SSSR*, II, 1 (Leningrad, 1930). See the review of this work by G. Il'insky, *Byzantinoslavica*, 2, 2 (1930), pp. 432-6.

¹⁵M. D. Priselkov, "Ocherki po tserkovno-politicheskoy istorii Kievskoy Rusi X-XII vv.," *Zapiski ist.-filol. fak. Imperat. Sankt-Peterburgskogo Universiteta*, CXVI (1913).

¹⁶V. M. Istrin, "Moravskaya istoriya slavyan i istoriya polyano-rusi, kak predpolagaemye istochniki nachal'noy russkoy letopisi," *Byzantinoslavica*, 3 (1931), pp. 327-32, 4 (1932), pp. 51-7.

¹⁷For Russia's conversion to Christianity in the reign of Vladimir, see *Povest'*, I, pp. 59-81; Cross, pp. 96-117, 244-8; Laehr, *Die Anfänge des russischen Reiches*, pp. 110-15; G. Vernadsky, *Kievan Russia* (New Haven, 1948), pp. 60-5. For the establishment of a Byzantine hierarchy in Russia, see D. Obolensky, above, Chapter IV, pp. 109-10. L. Müller, *Zum Problem des hierarchischen Status und*

The Heritage of Cyril and Methodius in Russia 239

der jurisdiktionellen Abhängigkeit der russischen Kirche vor 1039 (Cologne, 1959) (*Osteuropa und der deutsche Osten*, III, 6).

[18] *Povest'*, I, pp. 11, 21-3; Cross, pp. 52-3, 62-3.

[19] A. Shakhmatov, "Povest' vremennykh let i ee istochniki," *Trudy Otdela Drevne-Russkoy Literatury*, IV (1940), pp. 80-92; P. Lavrov, "Kirilo ta Metodiy v davn'o-slov'yans'komu pis'menstvi," *Zbirnik Ist.-Filol. Viddilu, Ukraïns'ka Akademiya Nauk*, 78 (1928), pp. 129-136; Nikol'sky, *op. cit.*; Istrin, *op. cit.*; R. Jakobson, "Minor Native Sources for the Early History of the Slavic Church," *Harvard Slavic Studies*, 2 (1954), pp. 39-47; *Selected Writings*, VI, 1, pp. 159-89.

[20] R. Jakobson, "Comparative Slavic Studies," *The Review of Politics*, XVI, 1 (1954), p. 79.

[21] See Shakhmatov, "Povest' vremennykh let i ee istochniki," *op. cit.*, pp. 87-9; Jakobson, "Minor Native Sources," *op. cit.*, p. 40.

[22] See Jakobson, *ibid.*, p. 41.

[23] For the use of *sila* and *razumъ* in the Cyrillo-Methodian vocabulary, see Jakobson, *ibid.*, p. 41, note.

[24] *Povest'*, I, p. 22: "Certain men rose up against them [i.e. against Cyril and Methodius], murmuring and saying: 'It is not right for any people to have its own alphabet, except for the Jews, the Greeks, and the Latins, according to Pilate's inscription, which he caused to be inscribed on the Lord's cross'." Cf. Cross, 63. The "trilingual heresy," based on the view that Hebrew, Greek, and Latin are the only legitimate liturgical languages, is ascribed by Constantine's biographer to the Latin clerics who opposed Constantine and Methodius in Moravia and who disputed with the former in Venice. See *Vita Constantini*, XV, 5-9, XVI, 1-5, XVIII, 9: *Constantinus et Methodius Thessalonicenses. Fontes*, ed. by F. Grivec and F. Tomšič (Zagreb, 1960) (*Radovi Staroslavenskog Instituta*, 4), pp. 131, 134, 141. Cf. *Vita Methodii*, VI, 3-4, *ibid.*, pp. 156. On the "trilingual heresy," see Dujčev, "Il problema delle lingue nazionali nel medio evo e gli Slavi," *op. cit.; id.*, "L'activité de Constantin Philosophe-Cyrille en Moravie," *Byzantinoslavica*, 24 (1963), pp. 221-3.

[25] *Povest'*, I, p. 23; Cross, p. 63.

[26] Cf. Jakobson, "Minor Native Sources," *op. cit.*, pp. 43-4.

[27] "I radi byša slověni, jako slyšiša veličьja Božьja svoimь jazykomь. . . . Vsi vъzъglagoljutь jazyki veličьja Božьja, jako že dastь imъ Svjatyi Duchъ otvěščevati": *Povest'*, I, p. 22; Cross, p. 63.

[28] *Vita Methodii*, VIII, 13 (Grivec-Tomšič, p. 158).

[29] *Povest'*, I, pp. 9-11; Cross, pp. 51-2. Cf. Shakhmatov, "Povest' vremennykh let i ee istochniki," *op. cit.*, pp. 41-5; *Povest'*, II, pp. 203-13; Cross, p. 231.

[30] Shakhmatov, *ibid.*, pp. 44-5, 72-7.

[31] For the text of Khrabr's treatise *O pismenechъ*, see P. A. Lavrov, *Materialy po istorii vozniknoveniya drevneishey slavyanskoy pis'mennosti* (Leningrad, 1930) (*Trudy Slavyanskoy Komissii Akademii Nauk SSSR*), pp. 162-4; I. Ivanov, *Bŭlgarski Starini iz Makedoniya*, 2nd ed. (Sofia, 1931), pp. 442-6. On Khrabr, see I. Snegarov, "Chernorizets Khrabŭr," *Khilyada i sto godini: slavyanska pismenost, 863-1963. Sbornik v chest na Kiril i Metody* (Sofia, 1963), pp. 305-19; A. Dostál, "Les origines de l'Apologie slave par Chrabr," *Byzantinoslavica*, 24 (1963), pp. 236-46; V. Tkadlčik, "Le moine Chrabr et l'origine de l'écriture slave," *Byzantinoslavica*, 25 (1964), pp. 75-92. The older literature on the subject is listed in G. A. Il'insky, *Opyt sistematicheskoy Kirillo-Mefod'evskoy bibliografii* (Sofia, 1934), pp. 27-8; M. Popruzhenko and St. Romanski, *Kirilometodievska bibliografiya za 1934-1940 god* (Sofia, 1942), pp. 30-1; K. Kuev, *Chernorizets Khrabŭr* (Sofia, 1967).

[32] R. Jakobson, "St. Constantine's Prologue to the Gospel," *St. Vladimir's Seminary Quarterly*, VII, 1 (1963), p. 15. Cf. Lavrov, *Materialy*, p. 113 (no.22).

[33] "Christosь gredetь jezyki sъbrati": Lavrov, *ibid.*, p. 196; Jakobson, *Selected Writings*, VI, 1, pp. 194-5.

[34] "Ὅτε καταβὰς τὰς γλώσσας συνέχεε, διεμέριζεν ἔθνη ὁ Ὕψιστος· ὅτε τοῦ πυρὸς τὰς γλώσσας διένειμεν, εἰς ἑνότητα πάντας ἐκάλεσε (Πεντηκοστάριον Χαρμόσυνον [Rome, 1883], p. 400).

[35] The idea that the Pentecostal miracle, by reuniting the languages of the earth, repealed the confusion of tongues which followed the building of the Tower of Babel, implied by Origen (*In Genesim*, PG, XII, col 112), was explicitly formulated by Gregory Nazianzen (*Oratio XLI: in Pentecosten*, PG, XXXVI, col. 449), John Chrysostom (*De Sancta Pentecoste, Homilia II*, PG, L. col. 467; *In epistolam I ad Cor. Homilia XXXV*, 1, PG, LXI, col. 296), Cyril of Alexandria (*Glaphyra in Genesim*, II, PG, LXIX, cols. 77, 80), Cosmas Indicopleustes (*The Christian Topography*, ed. by E. O. Winstedt (Cambridge, 1909), bk. III, pp. 95-7), and the Emperor Leo VI (*Oratio XII: in Pentecosten*, PG, CVII, col. 128). Cf. A. Borst, *Der Turmbau von Babel, Geschichte der Meinungen über Ursprung und Vielfalt der Sprachen und Völker*, I (Stuttgart, 1957), pp. 236-9, 246, 249-50, 252, 262-3, 302.

Gregory Nazianzen expressed the contrast between Babel and Pentecost in the following terms: Πλὴν ἐπαινετὴ μὲν καὶ ἡ παλαιὰ διαίρεσις τῶν φωνῶν (ἡνίκα τὸν πύργον ᾠκοδόμουν οἱ κακῶς καὶ ἀθέως ὁμοφωνοῦντες, ὥσπερ καὶ τῶν νῦν τολμῶσί τινες)· τῇ γὰρ τῆς φωνῆς διαστάσει συνδιαλυθὲν τὸ ὁμόγνωμον, τὴν ἐγχείρησιν ἔλυσεν· ἀξιεπαινετωτέρα δὲ ἡ νῦν θαυματουργουμένη. Ἀπὸ γὰρ ἑνὸς Πνεύματος εἰς πολλοὺς χυθεῖσα, εἰς μίαν ἁρμονίαν πάλιν συνάγεται (PG, XXXVI, col. 449). An Old Church Slavonic translation of this sermon by St. Gregory on Pentecost, preserved in an eleventh-century manuscript in Russia, existed there in the thirteenth century at the latest. See *XIII slov Grigoriya Bogoslova v drevneslavyanskom perevode po rukopisi Imper. Publichnoy Biblioteki XI veka*, ed. by A. Budilovich (St. Petersburg, 1875), pp. iv, 270-82, esp. p. 281. For an English translation of this sermon, see *A Select Library of Nicene and Post-Nicene Fathers of the Christian Church*, ed. by P. Schaff and H. Wace, VII (Grand Rapids, Michigan, 1955), pp. 378-85.

[36]V. N. Tatishchev, *Istoriya Rossiiskaya*, I (Moscow-Leningrad, 1962), p. 112.

[37]See S. K. Shambinago, "Ioakimovskaya Letopis'," *Istoricheskie Zapiski*, XXI (1947), pp. 254-70; M. N. Tikhomirov, in Tatishchev, *ibid.*, p. 50.

[38]Cedrenus, *Historiarum Compendium*, II (Bonn), p. 455; Scylitzes (1973), p. 346. P.A. Lavrovsky, "Issledovanie o Letopsi Yakimovskoy," *op. cit.*, pp. 147-8. Cf. V. Nikolaev, *Slavyanobŭlgarskiyat faktor v khristiyanizatsiyata na Kievska Rusiya* (Sofia, 1949), pp. 80-8; V. Moshin, "Poslanie russkogo mitropolita Leona ob opresnokakh v Okhridskoy rukopisi," *Byzantinoslavica*, 24 (1963), p. 95.

[39]Romanus, together with his brother Boris (the former tsar of Bulgaria) fled from Constantinople to Bulgaria about 979. Boris was killed on the way, but Romanus succeeded in joining the Comitopulus Samuel, who led the anti-Byzantine revolt in Macedonia. The statement of the eleventh-century Arab historian Yahya of Antioch that Romanus was proclaimed tsar of Bulgaria was accepted by V. N. Zlatarski (*Istoriya na Bŭlgarskata Dŭrzhava*, I, 2 [Sofia, 1927], pp. 647-59) and by N. Adontz ("Samuel l'Arménien, roi des Bulgares," *Mémoires de l'Académie Royale de Belgique*, classe des lettres, XXXIX [1938], p. 16). However, S. Runciman (*A History of the First Bulgarian Empire* [London, 1930], p.221) and G. Ostrogorsky (*History of the Byzantine State*, p. 301) point out, probably with better reason, that Romanus, being a eunuch, was disqualified from occupying the throne.

[40]Tatishchev, *Istoriya Rossiiskaya*, I, p. 112.

[41]*Nikonovskaya Letopis', s.a.* 988: *Polnoe Sobranie Russkikh Letopisey*, IX (St. Petersburg, 1862), p. 57; *Kniga Stepennaya Tsarskogo Rodosloviya, ibid.*, XXI, 1 (St. Petersburg, 1908), p. 102. Both these sources describe Michael as a Syrian. Michael is also mentioned as the first metropolitan of Russia in several fifteenth-century manuscripts of the Church Statute of Vladimir: See *Pamyatniki drevne-russkogo kanonicheskogo prava*, pt. 2, fasc. 1, ed. by V. N. Beneshevich: *Russkaya Istoricheskaya Biblioteka*, XXXVI (Petrograd, 1920), p. 4; cf. E. Golubinsky, *Istoriya russkoy tserkvi*, I, 1, 2nd ed. (Moscow, 1901), pp. 277-81, 621, note 5.

[42]"Poslavъ nača poimati u naročityc čadi děti, i dajati nača na učenьe knižnoe." *Povest'*, I, p. 81; Cross, p. 117.

[43]"Sim že razdajanomъ na učenьe knigamъ, sъbystьsja proročestvo na rusьstěi zemli, glagoljuščee: 'Vo ony dnii uslyšatъ glusii slovesa knižnaja, i jasnъ budetъ jazykъ gugnivychъ'," *ibid.*

[44]Καὶ ἀκούσονται ἐν τῇ ἡμέρᾳ ἐκείνῃ κωφοὶ λόγους βιβλίου (Is. 29:18)... καὶ τρανὴ ἔσται γλῶσσα μογιλάλων (Is. 35:6).

[45]See *The Book of Isaiah, translated from a critically revised Hebrew text with commentary*, by E. J. Kissane, I (Dublin, 1960), p. 320. Cf. Is. 29:11.

[46]"Došьdъšu že jemu Moravy, sъ velikoju čьstiju prijetъ jego Rastislavъ i učeniky sъbravъ i vъdastъ i učiti. Vъskorě že vъsь crьkovnyi činъ priimъ nauči je utrьnici i časovomъ i večer'nii i pavečer'nici i tainěi služ'bě. I otvrъz'ošе se proročьskomu slovese učesa gluchyichъ i uslyšaše kniž'naa slovesa i jezykъ jasьnъ bystъ gugnivyichъ." *Vita Constantini*, XV, 1-3 (Grivec-Tomšič, p. 131). In their translation of this passage Grivec and Tomšič erroneously derive the citations *et apertae sunt... aures surdorum* and *et lingua plana facta est balborum* from Is. 35:5 and Is. 32:4, respectively (*ibid*, p. 202). They have also failed to observe that the words *ut audirent verba scripturae* are a quotation from Is. 29:18.

[47]*Povest'*, I, p. 81; Cross, p. 117.

[48]On the Russian literature of the eleventh century, see M. N. Speransky, *Istoriya drevney russkoy literatury*, 3rd ed., I (Moscow, 1920), pp. 113-345; V. M. Istrin, *Ocherk istorii drevnerusskoy literatury domoskovskogo perioda* (Petrograd, 1922), pp. 118-57; A. S. Orlov, *Drevnyaya russkaya literatura* (Moscow-Leningrad, 1945), pp. 1-193; N. K. Gudzy, *Istoriya drevney russkoy literatury*, 6th ed. (Moscow, 1956), pp. 45-89, 96-104: English translation: *History of Early Russian Literature* (New York, 1949), pp. 84-146; D. Tschiževskij (Chyzhevsky), *Geschichte der altrussischen Literatur im 11., 12. und 13. Jahrhundert* (Frankfurt am Main, 1948), pp. 105-57, 174-99; *id.*, *History of Russian*

Literature from the Eleventh Century to the End of the Baroque (The Hague, 1960), pp. 20-81. The masterpiece of this literature, the *Sermon on Law and Grace* by Hilarion, metropolitan of Kiev, is the subject of an excellent critical edition and study by L. Müller, *Des Metropoliten Ilarion Lobrede auf Vladimir den Heiligen und Glaubensbekenntnis* (Wiesbaden, 1962).

⁴⁹*Povest'*, I, pp. 102-3; Cross, pp. 137-8.

⁵⁰See Chyzhevsky, *Geschichte der altrussischen Literatur*, pp. 69-70, 84.

⁵¹A. I. Sobolevsky, *Perevodnaya literatura Moskovskoy Rusi XIV-XVII vekov* (St. Petersburg, 1903), op. v.

⁵²A. I. Sobolevsky, "Materialy i issledovaniya v oblasti slavyanskoy filologii i arkheologii," *Shornik Otdeleniya Russkogo Yazyka i Slovesnosti Imp. Akademii Nauk*, LXXXVIII (1910), no. 3, pp. 162-77.

⁵³V. M. Istrin, *Khronika Georgiya Amartola v drevnem slavyanorusskom perevode*, 3 vols. (Petrograd, 1920-2, Leningrad, 1930), esp. vol. II, pp. 268-309.

⁵⁴See N. Durnovo, "K voprosu o natsional'nosti slavyanskogo perevodchika Khroniki Georgiya Amartola," *Slavia*, IV (1925), pp. 446-60; P. A. Lavrov, "Georgy Amartol v izdanii V. M. Istrina," *ibid.*, pp. 461-84, 657-83.

⁵⁵See R. Jakobson, "The Kernel of Comparative Slavic Literature," *Harvard Slavic Studies*, I (1953), pp. 37-41.

⁵⁶On these and other works brought from Bohemia to Kievan Russia, see R. Jakobson, "Some Russian Echoes of the Czech Hagiography," *Annuaire de l'Institut de Philologie et d'Histoire orientales et slaves*, VII (1939-44), pp. 155-80; *Id.*, *Selected Writings* VI, 2, pp. 820-45; Chyzhevsky, *op. cit.*, pp. 100-1; F. Dvornik, *The Making of Central and Eastern Europe* (London, 1949), pp. 242-7; Jakobson, *The Kernel of Comparative Slavic Literature*, pp. 41-8.

⁵⁷See Florovsky, *Chekhi i vostochnye slavyane*, I, pp. 11-58, 99-151, 158-99.

⁵⁸*Zhitiya svyatykh muchenikov Borisa i Gleba*, ed. by D. I. Abramovich (Petrograd, 1916), p. 33.

⁵⁹D. Cyževskyj [Chyzhevsky] "Anklänge an die Gumpoldslegende des hl. Václav in der altrussischen Legende des hl. Feodosij und das Problem der 'Originalität' der slavischen mittelalterlichen Werke," *Wiener Slavistisches Jahrbuch*, I (1950), pp. 71-86.

⁶⁰*Ibid.*, p. 84; cf. Florovsky, *op. cit.*, pp. 106-07, 128.

⁶¹R. Jakobson, "The Beginnings of National Self-Determination in Europe," *The Review of Politics*, VII, 1 (1945), pp. 29-42; and *Selected Writings*, VI, 1, pp. 115-28.

⁶²G. P. Fedotov, *The Russian Religious Mind* (New York, 1960), pp. 405-12.

⁶³See N. K. Nikol'sky, "K voprosu o sochineniyakh, pripisyvaemykh Kirillu Filosofu," *Izvestiya po Russkomu Yazyku i Slovesnosti Akademii Nauk SSSR* (1928), I, 2, pp. 400-2.

⁶⁴*Povest'*, I, pp. 60-74, II, pp. 330-5; Cross, pp. 97-110; *Novgorodskaya Chetvertaya Letopis'*, *s.a.* 986: Polnoe Sobranie Russkikh Letopisey, IV, 1 (Petrograd, 1915), p. 61; *Sofiiskaya Pervaya Letopis'*, *s.a.* 986; ibid., V (St. Petersburg, 1851), p. 115. Cf. A. A. Shakhmatov, *Razyskaniya o drevneishikh russkikh letopisnykh svodakh* (St. Petersburg, 1908), pp. 152-3, 231, 558.

⁶⁵The complete text of the "Banduri Legend" was published by V. Regel (*Analecta Byzantino-Russica* [St. Petersburg, 1891], pp. 44-51; cf. *ibid.*, pp. xix-xxxii) and by I. Sakkelion (Διήγησις ἀκριβὴς ὅπως ἐβαπτίσθη τὸ τῶν Ῥώσων ἔθνος, ἐκ πατμιακοῦ χειρογράφου ἐκδιδομένη [(Athens, 1891]). The scorn poured on this work by Golubinsky (*Istoriya russkoy tserkvi*, I, 1², pp. 247-52) is not altogether justified. For a more balanced assessment of its historical value, see I. Dujčev, "Le testimonianze bizantine sui Ss. Cirillo e Metodio," *Miscellanea francescana. Rivista di scienze, lettere ed arti*, LXIII (Rome, 1963), pp. 10-4.

⁶⁶V. Istrin, "Iz oblasti drevne-russkoy literatury," *Zhurnal Ministerstva Narodnogo Prosveshcheniya*, CCCLV (October, 1904), p. 344. Cf. V. Jagić, "Rassuzhdeniya yuzhnoslavyanskoy i russkoy stariny o tserkovno-slavyanskom yazyke," *Issledovaniya po Russkomu Yazyku (Otdelenie Russkogo Yazyka i Slovesnosti Imp. Akademii Nauk)*, I (1885-95), pp. 308-9; Lavrov, *Materialy*, pp. 36-7; B. S. Angelov, "Kirilometodievoto delo i ideayata za slavyansko edinstvo v staroslavyanskite literaturi," *Slavistichen Shornik*, II (Sofia, 1958), pp. 47-8.

⁶⁷*Vita Constantini*, VIII, 15 (Grivec-Tomšič, p. 109). Cf. Shakhmatov, "Povest' vremennykh let i ee istochniki," *op. cit.*, p. 86.

⁶⁸The controversial words are: "I obrět' t' že tu evaggelie i psaltirъ, rusъskymi pismeny [*var.* rosъsky pismenъ] pisano," Grivec-Tomšič, pp. 109, 111. A leading protagonist of the view that the passage refers to "Russian," i.e. Slavonic, letters is E. Georgiev (*Slavyanskaya pis'mennost' do Kirilla i Mefodiya* [Sofia, 1952], pp. 48-52). For earlier attempts to interpret this passage of the *Vita Constantini*, see the bibliographies in Il'insky, *op. cit.*, pp. 66-7, and in Popruzhenko and Romanski, *op. cit.*, p. 56. More convincing is the view of A. Vaillant, who argued that *rusъskymi* is a misspelling for *surъskymi* i.e.

Syriac letters: "Les 'lettres russes' de la *Vie de Constantin,*" *Revue des études slaves*, XV (1935), pp. 75-7. Cf. R. Jakobson, "Saint Constantin et la langue syriaque," *Annuaire de l'Institut de Philologie et d'Histoire orientales et slaves*, VII (1939-44), pp. 181-6; *Selected Writings*, VI, 1, pp. 153-8. For a general discussion of the problem of possible attempts before Constantine to create a Slavonic alphabet, see I. Dujčev, Vŭprosŭt za vizantiisko-slavyanskite otnosheniya i vizantiiskite opiti za sŭzdavane na slavyanska azbuka prez pŭrvata polovina na IX vek," *Izvestiya na Instituta za Bŭlgarska Istoriya*, Bŭlgarska Akademiya na Naukite, VII (1957), pp. 241-67.

⁶⁹*Zhitie sv. Stefana, episkopa Permskogo*, ed. by V. Druzhinin, photomechanic reprint with an introduction by D. Čiževskij [Chyzhevsky] [The Hague, 1959]. Cf. G. Lytkin, "Pyatisotletie zyryanskogo kraya," *Zhurnal Ministerstva Narodnogo Prosveshcheniya*, CCXXX (1883), pp. 275-326; id., *Zyryansky kray pri episkopakh permskikh i zyryansky yazyk* (St. Petersburg, 1889). Golubinsky, *Istoriya russkoy tserkvi*, II, 1, pp. 262-96.

⁷⁰*Zhitie sv. Stefana*, pp. 8, 69, 70-3. The analogy may be carried further by observing that both the Moravian and the Zyrian missions had a political aspect. Cyril and Methodius were ambassadors of the Byzantine Emperor to Moravia; Stephen's work among the Zyrians enjoyed the active support of the Muscovite secular authorities, who seized this opportunity for extending their influence over the Novgorodian lands along the Vychegda river, which they annexed in the fifteenth century. For the relations between Stephen and Prince Dimitri of Moscow, see *Zhitie sv. Stefana*, p. 59; for the political significance of the Zyrian missions, see *Ocherki Istorii SSSR, Period Feodalizma, IX-XV vv.*, 2 (Moscow, 1953), pp. 455-9.

⁷¹As early as the fifteenth century Slavonic began to replace Zyrian in the liturgy of St. Stephen's diocese. However, the Zyrian vernacular was still used in monastic offices in the Komi region in the eighteenth century. See G. Lytkin, *Pyatisotletie zyryanskogo kraya*, pp. 296-9; V. I. Lytkin, *Istoricheskaya grammatika komi yazyka*, I (Syktyvkar, 1957), pp. 40-1; Id., *Drevnepermsky yazyk* (Moscow, 1952), pp. 50-9, 63, 75.

⁷²See B. S. Angelov, "Slavyanski izvori za Kiril i Metodi," *Izvestiya na Dŭrzhavna Biblioteka "Vasil Kolarov" za 1956 g.* (Sofia, 1958), pp. 181-6. Angelov's list includes incomplete manuscripts and nineteenth-century copies.

⁷³Lavrov, *Materialy*, p. 115. Cf. R. Jakobson, "The Slavic Response to Byzantine Poetry," *Actes du XIIᵉ Congrès international d'études byzantines*, I (Belgrade, 1963), pp. 261-2; id., *Selected Writings*, VI, i, p. 253.

⁷⁴*Povest'*, I, p. 75; Cross, p. 111.

⁷⁵"Trěbujušče dьžda Božii bukvь": *Prologue to the Holy Gospels*, in Lavrov, *Materialy*, p. 197.

⁷⁶Like the author of the *Vita Constantini* and the Russian chronicler, Epiphanius, in his biography of St. Stephen, combines the two quotations from Isaiah 35:6 and Isaiah 29:18: *Zhitie sv. Stefana*, p. 66. See *supra*, notes 43 and 46. Ševčenko has pointed out further parallels between the *Vita Constantini* and the Life of St. Stephen, which strongly suggest that Epiphanius made use of the former document (*Three Paradoxes of the Cyrillo-Methodian Mission*, p. 225, note 19).

CHAPTER IX

STS. CYRIL AND METHODIUS
AND THE CHRISTIANIZATION OF THE SLAVS*

The 1100th anniversary of the mission of Sts. Cyril and Methodius to Moravia was celebrated in 1963; this celebration was marked
in many countries by the publication of symposia and commemorative volumes concerned with the historical work of the two apostles to
the Slavs. Two things appear clear in these works: the almost inex-
haustible richness of the present-day bibliography on this subject and
the complexity of a number of historical and philological problems
posed by this Byzantine mission to modern scholarship. In a paper on
so general a theme, it is clearly impossible to mention more than a few
of these problems. Furthermore, it does not seem very useful simply
to summarize the principle events of the lives of Cyril and Methodius;
or to attempt a study in depth of one or another detail of this mission
as presented in the sources in order to suggest some new solution. My
intention here is rather to follow a middle course between these two
extremes, and to attempt a kind of compromise between the methods
of synthesis and analysis. I would like to single out some of the main
events and results of the Cyrillo-Methodian mission not in the form of
a continuous narrative, but by grouping and studying them under two
headings which can be formulated in two questions: 1) What was the
attitude of Byzantium — of the Church authorities and of public opinion in the empire — towards the work of Cyril and Methodius?
2) What were the reactions of the medieval Slav peoples to the
Byzantine mission, of which they were the immediate beneficiaries? I
propose therefore to posit the problem in the dialectical form of 'challenge and response,' and to consider the Cyrillo-Methodian tradition

* Translated from the French. Settimane di studio del Centro italiano di studi sull' alto medioevo,
XIV (Spoleto, 1967), 587-609.

in the context of an encounter between Byzantine civilization and the cultural aspirations of the Slav peoples, an encounter which was both tension and synthesis. This method, I hope, will permit us to see our theme more clearly from a threefold point of view: religious, political, and cultural.

The first thing to remember is that Cyril and Methodius were both missionaries and diplomats. This double role resulted from the close relationship which existed, especially from the sixth century onwards, between the evangelical ideal of the Byzantine Church and the foreign policy of the empire. The last was established by identifying the Pax Romana and the Pax Christiana, and found expression in the belief, held by the Byzantines, that they alone, the Rhomaioi, had been consecrated to the service of Christ by the emperor Constantine, and were therefore the new chosen people who had the duty to bring the Gospel to the barbarians of the whole world. This explains the Byzantine missionary's dual role: as an apostolic figure sent to extend the boundaries of the kingdom of God and an ambassador of East Roman imperialism. To such an ambassador was naturally attached something of the pomp and majesty of his political sovereign. Missionaries and diplomats of Byzantium, Cyril and Methodius were also Byzantines of their time, typical representatives, no matter how eminent, of the cultural elite of their period.[1] The revival of monastic spirituality and of humanistic scholarship in the ninth century, which some historians have termed the "Byzantine renaissance," remained imprinted on their thought and their careers. Methodius the monk and Cyril the scholar, professor at the University of Constantinople and pupil of Photius, the greatest humanist of the age, admirably personified these two aspects of Byzantine civilization of the ninth century. This was a period in which the intellectuals and statesmen of Byzantium believed more than ever in their empire's world-wide mission. The Slavonic *Vita* of Constantine (Cyril's name before his monastic profession) shows that its hero was very much aware of his role as a spokesman for the Byzantine imperial traditions. To the Arab Khalife, to whom he was sent as ambassador about 855, Cyril proudly declared that "it is from us that all the arts have come."[2] And in 861 at the court of the Khazar ruler, he proclaimed his faith openly in the universality of the Christian empire whose representative he was: "Our empire is that of Christ, as the prophet said: 'The God of heaven shall set up a kingdom which shall never be destroyed: and the kingdom shall not be left to other people, but it shall break in pieces and consume all these kingdoms, and it shall stand forever.'"³ Later, during their mission to the Slavs and until the end of their lives, Cyril and Methodius loyally served their temporal sovereign, the emperor of Byzantium; on the eve of his monastic profession in Rome, fifty days before his death in 869, Cyril, according to his *Vita*, considered himself to be the "servant of the emperor."⁴ Similarly, Methodius sent his solemn blessing to the same emperor two days before his death in 885.⁵

Since the missionary activity of Cyril and Methodius tallied so well with the goals of Byzantine foreign policy in the second half of the ninth century, we would expect to see their mission supported by the state authorities: this is indeed what we find in the sources, especially in the Slavonic biographies of the two missionary brothers, written in the ninth century. The *Vita Constantini* tells us that the emperor and his counsellors asked Cyril to undertake the mission to the Moravians after their prince Rastislav had sent a request to Constantinople in 862 asking for a missionary who could preach in the Slavonic language. However, the essential instrument required for the success of the mission, an alphabet, had not yet been developed. According to the emperor Michael III, his two predecessors, Theophilus and Michael II, had sought in vain for such an alphabet.⁶ After the invention by Cyril of the Slavonic letters, i.e. the Glagolitic alphabet, the emperor showed himself very conscious of the value of this instrument for the evangelization of the Slav peoples. He wrote: "Accept a gift greater and more precious than any gold or silver, than any precious stones or any treasure — so that you can be counted among the great peoples who glorify God in their own language."⁷ Unfortunately, we have no information on the relations of Cyril and Methodius with Byzantium during the years that followed their arrival in Moravia in 863. Ecclesiastically, Moravia was in the Roman sphere of influence, while politically it was in the Frankish orbit; this situation obliged the brothers to turn to the pope, and resulted in their journey to Rome where they received the full support of Hadrian II for the use of the Slavonic liturgy. After Cyril's death, Methodius was appointed archbishop of Pannonia and papal legate to the Slavonic nations. It is possible that these two servants of the papacy were estranged for a while from their Byzantine homeland, especially during the conflict which, between 863 and 877, divided the churches of Rome and Byzantium over the affair of the patriarch Photius. It may be that this cooling of relations explains the rumors which the Frankish priests, Methodius' sworn enemies, were spreading about him in

Moravia. "The emperor," they alleged, 'is angry with Methodius, and if he is found he will not escape alive."[8] In the event these rumors were shown to be false: about 882 Methodius went to Constantinople at the invitation of the Emperor Basil I. His biography tells us that Basil as well as the Patriarch Photius received him well. Before his return to his central European diocese, Methodius left two of his disciples in Constantinople along with the liturgical books that he and his brother had translated into Slavonic from Greek.[9] The lively interest which the Byzantine authorities at this time showed in the Slavonic liturgy as a means of evangelizing the Slavs appears in another episode which took place soon after the death of Methodius in 885. A number of Methodius's disciples, arrested by the Moravian authorities hostile to the Slavonic liturgy, and sold into slavery, were redeemed in Venice by an agent of the emperor and sent to Constantinople, where they obtained positions in the Church.[10]

It is clear therefore that in the second half of the ninth century the Byzantine government gave the widest support to the work of Cyril and Methodius; and it is worth noting that this support was part of the intense missionary effort which enabled the Byzantine Church in the second half of the ninth century to convert the Bulgarians, the Serbians, and the Russians to Christianity. So in this sense it may truly be said Cyril and Methodius embodied a Christian universalism which, in a period of unsurpassed cultural expansion, the church and the empire of Byzantium brought to the new nations of Europe.

We should, however, avoid the danger of idealizing this Byzantine universalism. It can scarcely be doubted that the support given by the Byzantine government to the Slavonic liturgy was motivated in good part by political interest. Byzantine diplomatists knew from long experience the wisdom of ensuring the loyalty of the satellite peoples toward the empire by timely concessions to their national sensivities. It seems, moreover, that when Cyril invented the Slavonic alphabet a group of influential people in Byzantium were firmly opposed to this linguistic and liturgical experiment. The *Vita Constantini* tells us that the emperor considered the translation of the Greek liturgy to be an innovation without recent precedent; and even Cyril himself feared that in undertaking this work, he might be accused of heresy.[11] This passage of the *Vita Constantini* suggests that there were at this time in Byzantium two opposing camps: the emperor, his prime minister Bardas, a group of imperial advisers, as well as Cyril and his disciples; and on the other hand opponents of the Slavonic liturgy, whom the biographer, for reason of tact or prudence, does not name, but who presumably belonged to the clergy of Constantinople. We may assume that this second group supported a doctrine, especially popular in the West, that the divine office could be celebrated only in three languages: Hebrew, Greek, and Latin. Cyril and his disciples called this attitude "the three languages heresy;" he strongly attacked it during his spirited defense of the Slavonic liturgy against its detractors in Venice.[12]

In Byzantium, during the second half of the ninth century, there were then two opposing attitudes: one accepting and the other contesting the legitimacy of the Slavonic liturgy. On what were these two opinions based, and who were their advocates? It is not easy to answer these questions. In the first place, it seems to me, we should consider them in a larger context and distinguish the Byzantine attitudes to vernacular liturgical languages adopted at different times. It is remarkable that these views display the same dualism, ambiguity, and tension between rigorism and liberalism that we have detected in the Byzantine attitudes toward the use of the Slavonic language in the liturgy. In principle, the Byzantines, who regarded themselves as citizens of a supra-national empire, recognized the right of every people to pray and glorify the Lord in its own language. Thus in a sermon preached in Constantinople, St. John Chrysostom rejoiced in the fact that the Gothic community of the capital could preach Christianity in its own language, and affirmed the right of barbarian peoples to become members of the great Christian family.[13] This sermon by the great doctor of the eastern Church was not forgotten in Byzantium; and it is possible, as Professor Ševčenko has suggested, that Cyril had it in mind during his controversy with the "trilingualists" in Venice.[14] Trilingualism, moreover, appears in a list of doctrinal errors imputed to the Latin Church in a Byzantine work probably dating from the eleventh or twelfth century; the author claims that the Latins teach that "the Divinity is to be honored in three languages only, Hebrew, Greek, and Latin."[15] From this same twelfth century we have two other Byzantine statements approving of liturgies in non-Greek languages. The celebrated canonist Theodore Balsamon, in reply to the patriarch of Alexandria who asked of him whether the Syrian and Armenian priests in Egypt should be required to celebrate the liturgy in the Greek language, stated: "Those who are wholly ignorant of the Greek language may celebrate in their own languages provided they have exact copies of the usual sacred prayers written clearly on scrolls in Greek letters."[16] At about the same time, Eustathius, metropolitan of Thessalonica, declared that the word of the Lord could be preached in any language.[17] The educated Byzantine knew very well that the principle of non-Greek liturgical languages had been recognized in eastern Christendom for a long time. In his discussions in Venice, Cyril rightly cited the example of nations "who possess writing and render glory to God, each in his own tongue;" in this list we find among others, Armenians, Persians, Georgians, Goths, Khazars, Arabs, and Egyptians.[18]

Do these statements allow us to postulate, as Professor Dujčev does, "a fundamental Byzantine conception in favor of national languages?"[19] This concept, in my view, calls for some qualification. We should not forget how convinced the cultivated Byzantine was of the superiority of Greek over all other languages; for him these 'barbarian' languages remained impenetrable to true civilization: and the notorious Byzantine snobs, such as Anna Comnena or Theophylact of Ohrid, felt obliged to apologize from time to time to their Greek readers for using proper names of 'barbarian' origin.[20]

Even Latin aroused the contempt of some Byzantines; thus the emperor Michael III, the very man who sent Constantine-Cyril to Moravia, declared in a letter to the pope that Latin was a barbarian and 'Scythian' language;[21] and in the early thirteenth century, Michael Choniates, the learned metropolitan of Athens, proclaimed that asses would more readily perceive the melodious sound of the lyre and dung-beetles perfume, than the Latins comprehend the harmony and elegance of the Greek language.[22] This linguistic snobbery could very well co-exist with the belief, at least theoretical, that the barbarian could lose his barbarian nature by becoming a Christian and a member of the Byzantine community.[23] However, there existed even on the religious level an ambiguity and tension between the superiority complex of literate Byzantines and their belief that in Christ there is neither Greek nor Gentile. This *double-think* no doubt reflected the tension between the Hellenic and Christian traditions which was never wholly overcome in Byzantium.

The enthusiasm of some modern historians who lavish praise on the Byzantines for having favored the Slavonic liturgy should be accepted with some reservations.[24] In the first place it should not be forgotten that in all the provinces of the empire which were occupied by the Slavs and later recolonized by the Byzantines in the ninth and tenth centuries—especially Greece and the Peloponnese—the Slavs were not only Christianized but hellenized. The emperor Leo VI tells us that his father Basil I was able to assimilate the Slavs into the empire by three means: he imposed Byzantine governors on them; he baptized them; and he made Greeks of them (*graikoʹsas*).[25] There was never any question, it seems, of giving them the right to celebrate the liturgy in Slavonic; and the recent attempt of Professor Dujčev to show that the evidence of the *Vita Constantini* concerning the efforts of Michael III's two predecessors to discover a Slavonic alphabet applies to the Slavs within the empire seems to me unconvincing.[26]

The passage from the *Vita* which I have already quoted shows that on the eve of the Moravian mission there were persons in Byzantium, probably belonging to the clergy, who were opposed in principle to the Slavonic liturgy. Thirty years later this same opposition showed itself in a foreign mission field, Bulgaria. After the death of Methodius in 885, an important group of his disciples, exiled by the Moravian government, found refuge in Bulgaria. Recently converted to Christianity by Greek missionaries, Bulgaria had been firmly attached to the Byzantine Church in 870. It seems, however, that Boris of Bulgaria and a section of the Bulgarian aristocracy, though anxious to absorb Byzantine civilization, feared that the Greek clergy who administered their Church might become the instruments of Byzantine political control. The experience of neighboring Moravia must have suggested one way out of this dilemma: the best way to enable Bulgaria to accept Byzantine Christianity and culture without prejudice to its political independence was to obtain a Slavonic clergy and a liturgy in the vernacular. It is understandable then that the disciples of Methodius were warmly welcomed by the Bulgarian ruler. Thus, in the classic words of Fr. Dvornik, the work of Cyril and Methodius was "saved by the Bulgarians."[27] This salvaging was accompanied by a remarkable flowering of literature in Old Church Slavonic, especially in Macedonia and in Preslav, the Bulgarian capital. This literary work was inspired by Clement and Naum, two disciples of Methodius, and encouraged by the new ruler Symeon, Boris' son. It was in large part a literature of translations, though some original works were also composed. This corpus of writings constitutes an important chapter in the history of the transmission of Byzantine culture to the Slavs. Thanks to this literature, mostly written in Cyrillic, Slavonic became, after Greek and Latin, the third international language of Europe, and remained during the Middle Ages the sacred language of all those Slavs — the Bulgarians, the Russians, and the Serbs — who received their religion and the foundation of their culture from Byzantium.[28]

One of the most original works of this body of literature is a short treatise on the Slavonic alphabet, written at the end of the ninth or the beginning of the tenth century by the monk Khrabr. It is a moving defense of the Slav alphabet which, the author considered, was superior to the Greek alphabet for a very medieval reason: it was invented all at once by a saint, Cyril; in contrast, the Greek alphabet was created in several stages by pagan Greeks. Khrabr's treatise is a clearly polemical work directed against those whom Cyril, Khrabr's master, called trilingualists. It is clear from the content of this work that this Slavic monk had personal disputes with them, presumably in Bulgaria. There can be little doubt that Khrabr's treatise was an attempt to justify and exalt the work of Cyril and Methodius in the eyes of the Greek missionary clergy in Bulgaria, a section of which was hostile to the Slavonic liturgy.[29]

In the second half of the ninth century, Slavonic was not the only non-Greek liturgical language which provoked the hostility of the Byzantine trilingualists. An episode in the *Life of St. Hilarion of Iberia* written in Georgian no later than the end of the tenth century, shows that even the Georgian tongue, one of the oldest liturgical languages of the East, was scorned by these extreme philhellenes: a group of Georgian monks led by St. Hilarion was brutally treated by the abbot of a Greek monastery on Mt. Olympus in Bithynia. These monks obtained justice only through the intervention of the Virgin Mary who appeared to the abbot and said to him: "Wretched man! Why have you acted so harshly toward these strangers? Do you think that only the Greek language is pleasing to God? Do you not know that all who love him and glorify him are pleasing to the Lord?" The story has a remarkable ending: after the death of St. Hilarion in 875, his relics were deposited in a monastery in Constantinople where, by permission of the emperor Basil I, Georgian monks were settled. Not content to give them his personal protection, the emperor placed his two sons, Leo and Alexander (both future emperors), in their care and asked the monks to teach them "the sacred letters" and the Georgian language.[30].

The public support accorded by Basil I to the Georgian liturgical language reminds us of the similar support given by his predecessor Michael III to the Slavonic liturgy; and the linguistic liberalism of the imperial authorities contrasts markedly with the attitude of part of the Byzantine clergy in the second half of the ninth century in Constantinople, Bulgaria and Asia Minor. For them Greek was the only acceptable liturgical language in the eastern Church. The governmental point of view was no doubt based in part on diplomatic considerations: the best way to ensure the political and ecclesiastical loyalty of the Christian neighbors of the empire was to make concessions to their desire for cultural autonomy. As for the "opposition" party, they no doubt raised arguments of a practical and professional nature. For the conservative circles of the Byzantine clergy, the Slavonic liturgy represented a break with tradition, threatened their monopoly of liturgical expertise, added to the practical difficulties of their missionary work, and perhaps offended their aesthetic sensitivities. Here again we lack precise data, but it is tempting to assume that the "liberal" and "rigorist" groups who fought over the legitimacy of the Slavonic liturgy were related respectively to the "moderates" and "extremists," whose disputes figure prominently in the history of the Byzantine Church.[31] In such a context we can perhaps best understand why, at least in the ninth century, the imperial power pursued towards the Slavs outside the empire a pragmatic policy based on the principle of *oikonomia*, while the conservative sections of the clergy were hostile to all concessions. These conservatives stood for traditional rigorism based on the opposite principle of *akribeia*.

We should not, to be sure, oversimplify matters. There were no doubt supporters of the Slavonic liturgy among the Byzantine clergy, and it is certain that the Patriarch Photius supported and encouraged these missionary efforts. On the other hand, some Byzantine ecclesiastics seem to have had an equivocal position on this question: the famous archbishop of Ohrid, Theophylact, is a good example. At the end of the eleventh century, while expressing at times the deepest scorn for his Bulgarian flock, he wrote a *Vita* of St. Clement of Ohrid based in part on a previous Slavonic *Vita*, in which he heaped the most lavish praise on Cyril and Methodius.[32]

It is probable that the attitude of the Byzantines toward the indigenous Slavic traditions varied with the distance of a given country from Constantinople; in Russia, for example, whose geographic remoteness from the capital rendered any consistent effort at hellenization impossible, the Byzantine clergy appear to have encouraged the use of Slavonic as a liturgical and literary language. In respect of the Slavs within the empire, there was no question of such linguistic liberalism.

To sum up the results of this inquiry into the Byzantine attitudes towards the work of Cyril and Methodius, this attitude in the last resort appears complex and ambiguous. For my part, on this still controversial question, I am inclined to take an intermediate position between the view of Father F. Dvornik and I. Dujčev who insist on the generosity of Byzantium toward the Slav national tradition, and the opposite point of view expressed by D. Angelov[33] and I. Ševčenko who tend to stress the cultural imperialism of the Byzantines. It seems to me that these contradictory attitudes co-existed and sometimes clashed in the religious policy of Byzantium. In the final analysis, this ambiguity has it roots in the tension which was never wholly resolved in Byzantium between the classical heritage and the Christian ideal.

Passing now from the giver to the receiver, from Byzantium to the Slavs, what attitudes can be detected towards the work of Cyril and Methodius among its immediate beneficiaries? In order to attempt an answer to this question, we must first measure the extent of the debt the Slavs owe to these two Byzantine missionaries: a task which obviously goes far beyond the framework of the present discussion. To attempt this task we would have to consider how a mission, whose limited goal was to preach Christianity to the Moravians in their own language, ended by giving the Slavs the foundation of their medieval culture: its principal elements were a Slavonic liturgy in a rich, flexible, and intelligible language; the Christian scriptures translated into this same tongue; access to the Greek patristic tradition; and a language—Old Church Slavonic—at once modeled on Greek and close to the native spoken tongue, which became the common literary idiom of the Bulgarians, the Russians, the Ukrainians and the Serbs. A whole new world was opened to the Slavs by the work of Cyril and Methodius. The task which I propose to undertake is more modest. I would like to show by three examples how the Orthodox Slavs, who built up a veritable cult around the work of Cyril and Methodius, displayed in their appreciation of this work a certain creative originality.

The first example relates to the concept of national self-determination. This concept was founded on the idea that a language used in the liturgy becomes a sacred language, and that the people who speak it share in its sacred nature. Hence every Christian nation which has its own linguistic culture has a special place and mission in the universal family of Christian people.[34] Of course, this idea was never formulated, at least in the medieval period, in so general and abstract a manner. Nonetheless, applied to the Slavs, the concept appears in several literary works belonging to the Cyrillo-Methodian tradition: especially in the *Vita Constantini*, in the poetic Prologue (the *Proglas*) to the Slavonic Gospel Book which many scholars attribute to Cyril himself,[35] and in the Russian Primary Chronicle. It is apparent in the notion that the Slavs, converted to Christianity and endowed with an alphabet of their own, became a "new people" — an expression we find in several classic works of the Cyrillo-Methodian tradition: in the panegyric to the two brothers, written in Moravia soon after 885;[36] in the Alphabetical Prayer of Constantine the Priest, composed in Bulgaria at the end of the ninth century;[37] in the Sermon on Law and Grace by the Russian metropolitan Hilarion in the eleventh century;[38] and in the Russian Chronicle. In order to show that these "new people," though late-comers, occupy a position in the community of Christian nations in no way inferior to that of the others, several writers of the Cyrillo-Methodian tradition cited the parable in St. Matthew's Gospel of the householder who hired workers to work in his vineyard; those who were hired at the eleventh hour received the same salary as those who had worked from the beginning. This parable was applied to the Slavs by the anonymous author of the panegyric to Cyril and Methodius,[39] to the Bulgarians by Theophylact of Ohrid[40] (more probably by the Slavonic source he used), to the Russians by Nestor in his *Vita of Boris and Gleb*,[41] and to the Zyrians of northern Russia who were converted in the fourteenth century and given a liturgy in their own language; this last story is told in a biography of St. Stephen of Perm' by Epiphanius the Wise who compares his hero to St. Cyril.[42] This concept of self-determination, in which the national feeling of the Orthodox Slavs was sublimated by the notion of a community of Christian peoples, marks an attempt by the Slavs to define the place they occupied in this community; and they did this by appealing to the tradition of Cyril and Methodius.

My second example will show that these same Slavs attempted to justify their self-determination in a wider context and by means of more ambitious arguments. The text of a letter by Pope Hadrian II to the princes Rastislav, Svatopluk, and Kotsel in which the bishop of Rome authorized the use of the Slavonic liturgy in Moravia and in Pannonia is cited in a Slavonic translation in the *Vita Methodii*; the pope quotes a passage from the second chapter of the Acts of the Apostles where we read about the descent of the Holy Spirit in the form of tongues of fire on the apostles at Pentecost.[43] This text clearly implies that for the pope and for the author of the *Vita Methodii* the appearance of the Slavonic liturgy and the Cyrillic alphabet was equivalent to a second Pentecost. The same idea is expressed, though less clearly, in this verse of the Prologue to the Slavonic Gospel Book: "Christ comes to gather the nations and tongues."[44] But the apologetic intention of the Cyrillo-Methodian tradition went further still, and in one of its writings the theme of Pentecost, applied to the Slavonic literature, acquired a more universal dimension. In a passage of the medieval Russian Chronicle, a contrast is drawn between the present unity of the Slavonic languages and the ancient multiplicity of human tongues which was born of the Tower of Babel. This contrast appears in the fact that the chronicle's account of Cyril and Methodius is preceded by an introduction (based largely on the Slavonic translation of the Byzantine chronicles of John Malalas and George the Monk) which begins with the story (based on the Book of Genesis) of the division of the earth among the sons of Noah after the Flood, and ends with a brief account of the building of the Tower of Babel. It states that when the Lord scattered His people over the face of earth, the original unity of mankind gave way to a multiplicity of languages and nations. The chronicler follows this biblical introduction with the story of the origins and dispersal of the Slavonic peoples; and he includes the Slavs among the seventy-two nations who were scattered from the Tower of Babel. The conclusion seems to me inescapable that for the Russian chronicler the invention of the Slavonic vernacular writing was an extension of the miracle of Pentecost by which the Holy Spirit abolished the confusion of tongues which sprang from the Tower of Babel.[45] The idea that Pentecost abolished the results of Babel was not new in Christian literature; we find it in the *kondakion* of the office of Pentecost in the eastern Church; as Arno Borst has shown in his book *Der Turmbau von Babel*, it appears in the writings of several Greek Fathers, including St. Gregory of Nazianzus and St. John Chrysostom.[46] However, the notion that the Slavonic peoples share in the Pentecostal abrogation of Babel seems to be an invention either of the Russian chronicler or the source he used; we can therefore consider it as an original contribution to the tradition of Cyril and Methodius: a contribution which allowed the Slavs to interpret the work of the two brothers in the universal context of the history of human salvation.

I am aware that the method I have just used to interpret these passages of the Russian Chronicle must be applied with prudence: it is not always safe to attempt to reconstruct the latent thought of a medieval author by examining the context of his biblical references and of his scriptural quotations. But in the present case, where we can detect in his thinking the triple relation between the Slavonic liturgy, Pentecost, and the Tower of Babel, the method, in my opinion, leads to valid results.

I propose to apply the same method to my third example which will serve as a conclusion to my paper. Here we will be dealing neither with the self-determination of the Slavs within the Christian community nor with the role of the heritage of Cyril and Methodius in the universal history of human salvation, but with an exegesis at once more immediate and more spontaneous: we shall witness an attempt by medieval Slavonic authors, anchored in the tradition of Cyril and Methodius, to exalt this heritage by seeing in it an element of the transfiguration of the whole creation by the advent of the kingdom of God. Their exegesis was based on two passages of the prophet Isaiah: "In that day shall the deaf hear the words of the book" (Is. 29:18), and "the tongue of the dumb shall be clearly heard," (Is. 35:6). In the Septuagint version the two passages read as follows: Καὶ ἀκούσονται ἐν τῇ ἡμέρᾳ ἐκείνῃ κωφοὶ λόγους βιβλίου. . .καὶ τρανὴ ἔσται γλῶσσα μογιλάλων. The first of these passages is paraphrased in the anonymous panegyric of Cyril and Methodius,[47] and is quoted in the Prologue to the Slavonic Gospel Book;[48] in these two cases, the apologetic intention is obvious: the miraculous healing of the deaf and the dumb was achieved by the Slavonic letters. The second passage is applied by metropolitan Hilarion of Kiev to the conversion of the Russians.[49] The full scope of this exegesis, however, is apparent only in three other works of the Cyrillo-Methodian tradition, whose authors combine the two quotations from Isaiah: the ninth century *Vita Constantini*, the Russian Primary Chronicle, compiled at the end of the eleventh century or the beginning of the twelfth, and the *Vita of St. Stephen of Perm'* by Epiphanius, written at the end of the fourteenth century.[50] The first two authors took the words of Isaiah, which in their biblical context were applied to the change in the relation established in the first place by the Slavs, and in the second case by the Russian people, with God after their conversion to Christianity and their acquisition of the Slavonic letters. The expression "the words of a book" (*logoi bibliou*) which in the Book of Isaiah referred to the commandments of the Lord, was translated in both cases into Slavonic by *slovesa knizhnaya*, an expression which means both the Christian scriptures and the scriptures and liturgy translated into Slavonic.

It is thus in the context of the thirty-fifth chapter of the Book of

Isaiah, from which these verses are in part taken, that these scriptural passages acquire the importance that the Slavic exegetes attributed to them. In the last analysis, it is in the context of cosmic joy and triumph that the Slavonic apology for the work of Cyril and Methodius received its metaphysical justification. The whole of this chapter of Isaiah could be applied to the transformation in the life of the Slavonic peoples brought about by the work of the two apostles of the Slavs. I will confine myself to citing this passage: "The wilderness and the dry land shall be glad, the desert shall rejoice and blossom; like the crocus it shall blossom abundantly, and rejoice with joy and singing. . . Then the eyes of the blind shall be opened, and the ears of the deaf shall be unstopped. Then shall the lame man leap like a hart, and the tongue of the dumb shall be clearly heard. . . . They shall see the glory of the Lord, the splendor of our God."

FOOTNOTES ON CHAPTER IX

¹F. Dvornik, *Les Légendes de Constantin et de Méthode vues de Byzance* (Prague, 1933).
²Vita Constantini, VI, 53: F. Grivec and F. Tomšič, *Constantinus et Methodius Thessalonicenses, Fontes* (Zagreb, 1960), p. 105; English translation by M. Kantor and R. S. White, Michigan Slavic Materials no 13 (1976), p. 19.
³ *Vita Constantini*, X, 52-3 (Grivec-Tomšič, pp. 116-7; Engl. transl., p. 31).
⁴*Ibid.*, XVII, 3 (G-T., p. 165; Engl. transl., p. 55).
⁵Vita Methodii, XVII, 7 (G-T., p. 165; Engl. transl., p. 91).
⁶ *Vita Constantini*, XIV, 10 (G-T., p. 129; Engl. transl., p. 45).
⁷*Ibid.*, XIV, 18 (G.-T., p. 129; Engl. transl., p. 45).
⁸Vita Methodii, XIII, 1 (G.-T., p. 163; Engl. transl., p. 87).
⁹*Ibid.*, XIII, 5 (G.-T., p. 163; Engl. transl., p. 87).
¹⁰Vita S. Naoum, ed. M. Kusseff, *The Slavonic and East European Review*, XXIX (1950), p. 142.
¹¹ *Vita Constantini*, XIV, 11 (G.-T., p. 129; Engl. transl., p. 45).
¹²*Ibid.*, XV, 5-9, XVI, 1-5, XVIII, 9 (G.-T., pp. 131, 134, 141). For the "trilingual heresy" see I. Dujčev, "Il problema delle lingue nazionali nel medio evo e gli Slavi," *Ricerche Slavistiche*, VIII, 1960, pp. 39-60; *id.*, "L'activité de Constantin Philosophe-Cyrille en Moravie," *Byzantinoslavica*, XXIV (1963), pp. 221-3.
¹³Migne, PG, LXIII, cols. 500-1, 506, and 509.
¹⁴I. Sevčenko, "Three Paradoxes of the Cyrillo-Methodian Mission," *Slavic Review*,XXIII (1964), p. 230, n. 37.
¹⁵J. Hergenröther, *Monumenta graeca ad Photium ejusque historiam pertinentia* (Ratisbonae, 1869), p. 68, no. 19. This text is wrongly attributed by its editor to patriarch Photius, and in reality is from a later period: see J. Davreux, Byzantion, X, 1935, p. 105; J. Darrouzès, *Revue des études byzantines*, XXI, 1963, p. 63; Sevčenko, *op. cit.*, p. 228, n. 30.
¹⁶Theodore Balsamon, *Responsa ad Interrogationes Marci, Patriarchae Alexandriae*, Migne, PG, CXXXVIII, col. 957B.
¹⁷Eustathii Metropolitae Thessalonicensis *Opuscula*, XV, 34, ed. T.L.F. Tafel, (Frankfurt, 1832), p. 133, 91-4; quoted by Sevčenko, *op. cit.*, p. 227, n. 25.
¹⁸ *Vita Constantini*, XVI, 7-8 (G.-T., p. 134; Engl. transl., p. 49).
¹⁹I. Dujčev, "Il problema delle lingue nazionali," *ibid.*, p. 59.
²⁰K. Lechner, *Hellenen und Barbaren im Weltbild der Byzantiner* (Munich, 1954), p. 89; D. Obolensky, *Six Byzantine Portraits* (Oxford, 1988), pp. 58-9.
²¹Nicholas I, Pope, Epistola VI, M.G.H., p. 459.
²²Lechner, p. 85.
²³*Ibid.*, pp. 100-4.
²⁴On this matter, see the perspicacious study by Sevčenko, *Three Paradoxes*.
²⁵*Leonis imperatoris Tactica*, XVII, 101, Migne, *PG*, CVII, col. 969.
²⁶I. Dujčev, "Vŭprosŭt za vizantiisko-slavyanskite otnošeniya i vizantiiskite opiti za sŭzdavane na slavyanska azbuka prez pŭrvata polovina na IX vek," *Izvestiya na Instituta za Bŭlgarska Istoriya*, VII (1957), pp. 241-67.
²⁷Dvornik, *Les Slaves, Byzance et Rome au IXᵉ siècle* (Paris, 1926), pp. 282ff.
²⁸G. C. Soulis, "The Legacy of Cyril and Methodius to the Southern Slavs," *Dumbarton Oaks Papers*, XIX (1965), pp. 19-43; D. Obolensky, "The Heritage of Cyril and Methodius in Russia," *ibid.*, pp. 45-65 and above, p. 252.
²⁹For the text of the treatise of Khrabr, *O pismenekh*, see P. A. Lavrov, *Materialy po istorii vozniknoveniya drevneishey slavyanskoy pismennosti* (Leningrad, 1930), pp. 162-4; I. Ivanov, *Bŭlgarski Starini iz Makedoniya*, 2nd edition (Sofia, 1931), pp. 442-6. See also I. Snegarov, "Chernorizets Khrabŭr, *Khilyada i sto godini: slavyanska pismenost, 863-1963.*" *Sbornik v chest na Kiril i Metody* (Sofia, 1963), pp. 305-19; A. Dostál, "Les origines de l'Apologie slave par Chrabr," *Byzantinoslavica*, XXIV (1963), pp. 236-46; V. Tkadlčík, "Le moine Chrabr et l'origine de l'écriture slave," *Byzantinoslavica*, XXV (1964), pp. 75-92; K. Kuev, *Chernorizets Khrabŭr* (Sofia, 1967).
³⁰See P. Peeters, "Saint Hilarion d'Ibérie," *Analecta Bollandiana*, XXXII (1913), pp. 236-69; I. Dujčev, *Note sulla Vita Constantini-Cyrilli, Cyrillo-Methodiana*, ed. M. Hellmann, R. Olesch, B. Stasiewski and F. Zagiba (Cologne-Graz, 1964), pp. 76-80.
³¹On the parties of the "liberals" and the "zealots," see A. Vasiliev, *History of the Byzantine Empire* (Madison, 1952), pp. 659-71.

[32]Ed. A. Milev (Sofia, 1955).

[33]D. Angelov, "Kiril i Metody i vizantiiskata kultura i politika," *Khilyada i sto godini*, pp. 53-68.

[34]See R. Jakobson, "The Beginning of National Self-Determination in Europe," *The Review of Politics*, VII, 1 (1945), pp. 19-42; *Selected Writings*: VI, 1 (Berlin, New York, Amsterdam, 1985), pp. 115-128.

[35]A. Vaillant, "Une poésie vieux-slave: La Préface de l'Evangile," *Revue des Etudes Slaves*, XXXIII (1956), pp. 10-13; R. Jakobson, "St. Constantine's Prologue to the Gospel," *St. Vladimir's Seminary Quarterly*, VII, 1 (1963), pp. 14-19; *Selected Writings*: VI, 1, pp. 191-206.

[36]A. Teodorov-Balan, *Kiril i Metodi* I (Sofia, 1920), pp. 125 and 127.

[37]R. Nahtigal, "Rekonstrukcija treh starocerkvenoslovanskih izvirnih pesnitev," *Razprave Akademije Znanosti in Umetnosti in Ljubljani*, I (1943), pp. 45-73.

[38]L. Müller, *Des Metropoliten Ilarion Lobrede auf Vladimir den Heiligen und Glaubensbekenntnis* (Wiesbaden, 1962), pp. 86-7.

[39]Teodorov-Balan, p. 124.

[40]*Life of St. Clement of Ohrid*, ed. A. Milev (Sofia, 1955), p. 42, 1.15-19.

[41]D.I. Abramovich, *Zhitiya svyatykh muchenikov Borisa i Gleba i sluzhby im* (Petrograd, 1916), pp. 3-4.

[42]*Zhitie sv. Stefana episkopa Permskogo*, ed. V. Druzhinin (The Hague, 1959), pp. 12-13.

[43]*Vita Methodii*, VIII, 13 (G.-T., p. 158; Engl. transl., pp. 79-80).

[44]Lavrov, *Materialy*, p. 196; Jakobson, *Selected Writings*, VI, 1, p. 194.

[45]*Povest' vremennykh let*, ed. V.P. Adrianova-Peretts and D.S. Likhachev (Moscow-Leningrad, 1950), I, pp. 10-11; cf. D. Obolensky, *The Heritage of Cyril and Methodius in Russia*, above, p. 254.

[46]A. Borst, *Der Turmbau von Babel. Geschichte der Meinungen über Ursprung und Vielfalt der Sprachen und Völker*, I (Stuttgart, 1957), pp. 236-9, 246, 249-50, 252, 262-3, 302.

[47]Teodorov-Balan, p. 127.

[48]Vaillant, p. 10. Jakobson, *op. cit.*, p. 194.

[49]Müller, p. 92.

[50]*Vita Constantini*, XV, 103 (G.-T., p. 131; Engl. transl., p. 47); *Povest' vremennykh let*, I, p. 81; *Zhitie sv. Stefana*, p. 66.

CHAPTER X

THE BOGOMILS*

The history of the Bogomil sect in the Balkans is a subject whose importance greatly transcends its historical and geographical setting. The student whose preliminary investigations have convinced him that Bogomilism was not simply an obscure heresy which flourished in a distant corner of the Balkan peninsula some time in the Middle Ages may be justly astonished at the number and versatility of its implications. To scholars and experts in widely different subjects Bogomilism still offers many an unexplored, or half-explored, gold-mine. Thus, for example, the theologian and the philosopher can find in the Bogomil sect one of the most interesting examples of the growth on European soil in the early Middle Ages of a system of thought and a way of life which may be termed "dualistic." The specialist in the history of Eastern Europe—Byzantinist and Slavist alike—will grant to Bogomilism an important place in the ecclesiastical, political, social and literary heritage, and even in the contemporary folklore, of the Balkan peoples. A detailed study of Bogomilism should help a Western medievalist to shed new light on the still obscure problem of the historical connections between Asiatic Manichaeism and the medieval dualistic movement of Western Europe, particularly of the Italian Patareni and the Cathari or Albigenses of Southern France. This connection, if successfully established, would in its turn enable church historians to regard the Bogomil sect as the first European link in the thousand year-long chain leading from Mani's teaching in Mesopotamia in the third century to the Albigensian Crusade in Southern France in the thirteenth. While, more generally, the study of the Bogomil movement has its own, and by no means negligible, part to play in the investiga-

*Eastern Churches Quarterly (October-December, 1945), 1-23.

tion of the relations, cultural and religious, between Eastern and Western Europe, the urgency of which is increasingly perceived at the present time, not only from the standpoint of European history, but also with the practical view to rapprochement or reunion between Western and Eastern Christianity.

It is hoped that this survey of a very wide problem might serve as a contribution to the knowledge of a subject which so far has been almost entirely neglected in this country and thus improve on the conclusions of Gibbon who, in his *Decline and Fall*, dismisses the Bogomils in a single footnote with the remark: "a sect of Gnostics, who soon vanished."

Among the ever-recurring problems which have confronted human reason throughout the ages one of the most complex is that of the nature and origin of evil. Whenever man seeks to support his religious faith by rational thinking, sooner or later he is led to the problem of reconciling the absolute qualities he attributes to God with the obviously limited and contingent character of the world he lives in. The metaphysician and the theologian must explain the possibility of any relation between the Infinite and the finite, between the perfection of the Creator and the imperfection of the creature, between God and the world; and those men who, without being philosophers, believe that God is the source of all perfection and that He has created the world, cannot but recognize that in this world moral and physical evil—suffering, cruelty, decay, death—is abundantly present. How then can God, the Supreme Good, be the cause of evil?

Behind the many solutions to the problem of evil attempted by human reason we may distinguish two main attitudes of mind, radically opposed to each other. The first is based on the belief in a fundamental relation between God and the world created by Him. It was above all the faith of the Jewish people, so clearly mirrored in the Book of Genesis, that the world, created by God, is good. Judaism, throughout its history, emphasized the profound nature of the relation between the Infinite and the finite, which, though to the human reason it remains a mystery, has yet all the reality of a fact willed by God; thus it recognized the work of Divine Providence in the world by stressing the positive importance of human history in preparing the Kingdom of God on earth and proclaimed its belief in the ultimate value of this life. The Judaic view received a supreme and all-embracing confirmation by the Incarnation of the Word, whereby God became flesh and entered human history. Christianity, by teaching the reality of God-man, recognized that the gulf between the Infinite and the finite had been finally bridged and that the created world into which the Creator Himself had entered was not only of positive value but even capable of sanctification. Henceforth to those who on account of the incommensurability of God and the material world denied the possibility of contact between them Christianity was able to reply that God created the world, became man and will raise up the flesh.

In complete contradiction to the Christian view of evil, which follows from the belief in the hypostatic union and the consequent value attributed to this life and to the body, we find another conception which, in some respects, is older than Christianity. This conception is based on a fundamental opposition between good and evil and on the denial that God, who is essentially good, can be the author or the cause of evil. The origin of evil is outside God, and must be sought in the visible, material world, where disorder and suffering are dominant. The origin of evil lies in matter itself, whose opaqueness and multiplicity are radically opposed to the spirituality and unity of God. This view, which attributes to evil the same positive and ultimate quality as possessed by good, thus leads to an inevitable *dualism* between God and the opposite principle of matter. Man himself in a microcosmic form mirrors this cosmological dualism: his soul is of divine origin, his body ineradicably evil. The body is "the tomb of the soul," the instrument whereby the powers of evil seek to imprison light in the darkness of matter and to prevent the soul from ascending back to the heavenly spheres. Every consistent dualist must see the origin of all misfortune in life in this world: for the birth of man is the imprisonment of a divine or angelic soul in an unredeemable body. The only final redemption is in death—in the escape of the soul from its prison and the return of a particle of light to the one uncreated light. This redemption does not lie in repentance for the moral evil committed by man: man cannot be really responsible for the guilt of sin if evil is not due to the abuse of his free will but is rooted in his material body and is thus the inevitable concomitant of life itself. But though he is not responsible for the existence of evil and has thus ultimately no free will, man can and must collaborate in the work of God in striving by his knowledge and his actions to purify his soul from the contagion of its material envelope. Purification as understood and practised by the consistent dualist implies forbearance from all actions which further the soul's imprisonment in the body—especially from marriage and the procreation of children which strengthen the power of matter in the world — and a rigid asceticism, based not on the desire to discipline the flesh, but on a radical hatred of the body.

In the history of Europe and the Christian Church dualism has played an important part. It was largely the necessity of refuting the doctrines of the dualists that led the Christian theologians to formulate, in a precise and comprehensive manner, their own teaching on the problem of evil. Moreover, dualism gave rise to a number of sects which during the whole of Christian antiquity and until the very end of the Middle Ages were fierce and dangerous enemies of the Church, and against which both in Eastern and Western Europe Church and State were compelled to wage an almost ceaseless war.

It has hitherto been customary among most historians and theologians to trace systematic dualism back to the Zoroastrian tradition of Persia. Although this problem lies outside the scope of the present study, it may be stated that our present knowledge of Zoroastrian doctrines derived from the results of recent Iranian scholarship makes such a historical filiation appear very doubtful, since it would seem that Zoroastrianism, in some important respects, was incompatible with true dualism.[1] There seems to be little doubt to-day that the origin of systematic dualism must be sought above all in Gnosticism, which arose in Asia Minor in the first century of our era, and, in its most developed and classical form, in Manichaeism, invented in Babylonia in the middle of the third century by the Persian Mani. Mani's celebrated teachings[2] which, in the course of the thousand years after their first appearance, spread over large parts of Europe and Asia, from the Pacific to the Atlantic oceans, have in recent years been the subject of renewed interest and study owing to two important discoveries of original Manichaean sources: the first—between 1899 and 1907 in the oasis of Turfan in Chinese Turkestan,[3]—the second in 1930 in Egypt.[4]

Manichaean dualism penetrated into Europe in two waves, separated by an interval of some three centuries. The first wave, that of primitive Manichaeism, spread between the third and seventh centuries over the whole of the Mediterranean world, from Syria, Armenia and Asia Minor to Egypt, North Africa, Spain, Southern Gaul, Italy, and penetrated into the two centres of Roman Christian civilization— Rome and Byzantium. The second wave was that of a revived and in many respected modified Manichaeism, often known as "Neo-Manichaeism." It appeared in South Eastern Europe with the dawn of the Middle Ages and, between the ninth and fourteenth centuries, swept over all southern and part of central Europe, from the Black

Sea to the Atlantic and the Rhine.

It is not surprising that, whereas the first spread of Manichaeism in Europe has already been studied in some detail,[5] a comprehensive history of the Neo-Manichaean movement as a whole has yet to be written: for before this can be attempted, it will be necessary to study in greater detail than has yet been done its origin, character and development in each of the European countries where it found a home, particularly in Bulgaria, Greece, Serbia, Bosnia, Northern Italy and Southern France. A study of Bogomilism in Bulgaria and in the Byzantine Empire forms an indispensable first chapter in such an investigation.

A complete study of the origins of the Bogomil movement must presuppose an attempt to establish the exact connections — historical and doctrinal — between primitive Manichaeism and the different dualistic sects which may be termed Neo-Manichaean. Such an attempt, however, would far exceed the scope of this study. But a few indications seem necessary. There can be no doubt today that the scepticism shown by some scholars regarding the existence of any historical connection between Manichaeism and Neo-Manichaeism is not justified. It is true that the religious history of the Near East in the first nine centuries of our era offers, to the despair of historians, a bewildering picture of numerous movements and sects, some features of which frequently suggest points of contact with the teaching of Mani, but whose exact relation to Manichaeism and to each other can seldom be proved directly. It is also true that, in default of a proven historical connection between these movements and primitive Manichaeism, it is sometimes more satisfactory to regard them as successive and more or less independent manifestations of the same spiritual tendency — towards either cosmological dualism or extreme moral asceticism. Nevertheless, a careful study of the development of dualism in the Near East in the first nine centuries of our era reveals a thread which leads from Mani's teaching in Mesopotamia in the third century to the rise of Bogomilism in Bulgaria in the middle of the tenth. The thread may best be followed by a study of those factors which enabled Manichaeism to survive and spread in the Near East for several centuries after the death of its founder. The most important of these factors seems to have been the partial — though essentially artificial — contact between Manichaeism and Christianity, due on the one hand to the appeal of Manichaeism to various heretical movements within the Christian Church (for example, to Encratism,

Montanism, Novatianism and to certain distorted forms of Christian monasticism) and, on the other hand, to the increasing practice among the followers of Mani of borrowing Christian concepts and terms in their attempt to adapt their dualistic teaching to the dogmas of the Church. It seems, moreover, significant that these sectarian movements within Christianity were particularly widespread in those very regions which in the fourth century had witnessed a powerful extension of Manichaeism, and which, between the seventh and the ninth centuries, became the strongholds of Neo-Manichaeism — particulary in Armenia and Asia Minor. It was those two countries that nurtured the two most powerful Neo-Manichaean sects which in the course of the ninth and tenth centuries were to spread into Europe from their Asiatic homes and directly influence the growth of Balkan Bogomilism: these were the sects of the Paulicians and of the Massalians.

The Paulician sect arose in Armenia and Asia Minor in the second half of the seventh century. In the seventh and especially in the ninth centuries the Paulicians suffered violent persecution from the Byzantine authorities, due not so much to the fact that from the standpoint of the Byzantine Church they were heretics, as to the military and political menace which they were to the Empire: forming turbulent military colonies on the Eastern borders of the Asiatic themes and frequently allied with the Arabs, the Paulicians were a source of constant irritation to the authorities in Constantinople. Matters came to a crisis in 867 when, after a series of spectacular raids on Byzantine fortresses which carried them to the shores of the Aegean Sea, the Paulicians proudly demanded the Imperial provinces East of the Bosphorus. Five years later, however, the Byzantine armies succeeded in sacking the Paulician stronghold in Western Armenia and thus destroyed for ever the military power of the Paulicians in Asia. But not their doctrines. Notorious heretics, they generally passed in Constantinople for "Manichaeans." Some scholars, including Harnack,[6] have denied such a filiation and have tried, without great success, to absolve the Paulicians of any Manichaean antecedents. We must certainly concede to them that Paulicianism differed in some respects from primitive Manichaeism and that the origin of the Paulician doctrines is more complex than the Byzantine theologians supposed: it is, for example, difficult to deny the influence exerted by Marcionism on the development of the Paulician teachings. But, when these facts are taken into account, the doctrinal and historical connection between Manichaeism and Paulicianism can no longer be doubted today. The principal source of our knowledge of the Paulician doctrines, Peter of Sicily, who was sent in 869 to Armenia as Byzantine ambassador to negotiate a peace between the Emperor and the Paulicians, leaves us in no doubt as to the dualistic character of their teachings. In a treatise, written on the occasion of his visit to the Paulicians,[7] he tells us that they believed in two principles, the one good, the other evil: the evil one is the creator and the ruler of the present world, the good one — the lord of the world that is to come. Holding the material world to be a creation of the evil principle, the Paulicians were naturally led to reject the Christian dogma of the Incarnation and to substitute their own "docetic" Christology, according to which the Body of Christ was of heavenly origin and His Incarnation only "seeming." Moreover, the Paulicians rejected the whole of the Old Testament, interpreted the New Testament in a highly allegorical manner and strongly attacked the whole organization of the Christian Church, including the priestly order. A notable feature of Paulicianism was its extreme veneration for St. Paul (probably the effect of Marcionic influence), but it cannot yet be affirmed for certain that the Paulicians derived their name from that of the apostle of the Gentiles.[8] For the historian of the Balkans the relevance of this treatise of Peter of Sicily, — the *Historia Manichaeorum* — is greatly enhanced by Peter's observation that, while in Armenia, he learnt from the Paulicians themselves that they were planning to send missionaries to Bulgaria to spread their teaching in that country.

A few words must be said about the Massalian sect, the other possible ancestor of Balkan Bogomilism. The Massalians, widespread in Syria and Asia Minor from the fourth century, are attested in Armenia and Asia Minor as late as the ninth. Many of their doctrines were identical with those of the Paulicians; an original and interesting feature of Massalianism was its moral teaching: while its ordinary adepts were pledged to a life of rigid continence and poverty, those who were considered to have attained to perfection were bound by no moral restrictions: this led the Massalians to be accused at once of perverted asceticism and of extreme sexual immorality.[9]

There can be no doubt that the rise of the Bogomil sect in Bulgaria was directly due to the penetration of Paulician heretics into the Balkans: this penetration is attested by historical evidence: not only does the allusion of Peter of Sicily to Paulician proselytism in Bulgaria suggest that at least as early as the middle of the ninth century the

Paulicians regarded the Balkans as a profitable sphere of interest. We also know that on several occasions, in the course of the eighth and ninth centuries, Byzantine Emperors transported large colonies of Syrians and Armenians to Thrace, in order to garrison their northern frontier for their constant wars against Bulgaria. Among these colonists were certainly Paulicians. The Byzantine chronicler Theophanes expressly tells us that these displaced Asiatics were responsible for spreading the Paulician heresy in Thrace.[10] The penetration of the Paulician colonists into Bulgaria was doubtless greatly facilitated by the frequent invasions of Thrace by the Bulgarian armies in the eighth and ninth centuries and especially by the annexation of the great Thracian cities of Sardica and Philippopolis and of parts of Macedonia by the Bulgar khan towards the middle of the ninth century.

During the ninth and first half of the tenth century the notable success of Paulician proselytism in Bulgaria is attested by scattered, though reliable evidence. All the while a gradual process was effecting a fusion on Bulgarian soil between Asiatic dualism and a powerful, and specifically Slavonic, movement directed against the new Bulgarian Orthodox Church. The outcome of this fusion was the rise of Bogomilism in the middle of the tenth century.

The reasons for the successful spread of dualism in Bulgaria before the middle of the tenth century are to be found in the contemporary religious, social, political and economic conditions of the country. Some of the more important of these factors may be briefly enumerated: before the introduction of Christianity into Bulgaria, which began on a large scale after the baptism of the Khan Boris in 864, the teachings of the Paulicians who, for all their dualism, had borrowed many elements from Christianity, must have enjoyed a cultural and moral superiority over Slavonic paganism which, in Bulgaria at least, was never, it seems, a very vital force. We can even suppose that in some cases the Paulicians were the first to bring the knowledge of the Gospels to the pagan Bulgarians, in their own interpretation, of course. After the official introduction of Christianity from Byzantium, the violent struggle between the sees of Rome and Constantinople for the spiritual allegiance of the newly-baptized Bulgarians, which lasted from 866 to 870 and ended in the victory of the Eastern Church, and the embittered polemics between the Latin and Greek clergy in Bulgaria produced a state of religious confusion which, we can safely assume, was exploited by the dualists to discredit the Church in the eyes of the still semi-Christianized Bulgarians. The violently anti-

Byzantine policy pursued at the beginning of the tenth century by the Bulgarian tsar Symeon, despite the outward glory of its military achievements, which still dazzles the imagination of historians, plunged his country at the end into social instability and economic ruin. The internal weakness of Bulgaria on Symeon's death in 927 largely explains the inability of his successor Peter to resist the overwhelming stream of Byzantine influence which seriously crippled the social and economic development of the country. The widespread dissatisfaction caused by the rapid growth of *latifundia* on the Byzantine model and the ruinous taxation provoked during Peter's reign several revolutionary movements which weakened the country and laid it open, after his death in 969, to inner anarchy and to the invasion of the Russian and Byzantine armies, which finally brought about the collapse of the First Bulgarian Empire in 1018. In these circumstances it is not surprising that the Paulicians, hereditary enemies of Byzantium, successfully exploited the anti-Greek feeling in Bulgaria for their own aims. In this respect their social and political role was partly inherited by the Bulgarian Bogomils. Finally, the growth of heresy in Bulgaria towards the middle of the tenth century was also indirectly due to the fact that the Bulgarian Church at that time could no longer command unqualified obedience and respect. Its prelates had become byzantinized and, in the main, had lost that intimate contact with the people, which fifty years earlier had been the strength of men like St. Clement. The minor clergy, monks and parish priests, could not escape the accusation of intellectual and moral decadence levelled against them by one of the outstanding Bulgarian churchmen of the time, the priest Cosmas, whose *Sermon against the heretics* (one of the earliest monuments of Old Bulgarian literature) is directed, significantly, at once against the abuses of contemporary monasticism and against the Bogomil heresy.[11]

A study of these developments in the Near East and in Bulgaria should convince us that the rise of Bogomilism towards the middle of the tenth century was due to the combined effect of two factors: on the one hand, a background of Eastern dualistic doctrines, which penetrated to Bulgaria partly as a result of the colonizing policy of the Byzantine Emperors, and, on the other hand, pre-existing and contemporary conditions in Bulgaria exceptionally favorable to the spread of heresy. The influence of these two factors can be clearly detected in Bogomilism, whose teaching represented essentially a development of Paulician doctrines, and whose moral and social aspects displayed in Bulgaria the features of a specifically Slavonic movement.

The earliest Slavonic source referring to Bogomilism is the *Sermon against the heretics* of the Bulgarian priest Cosmas, probably composed soon after 972.[12] This work was written primarily against the Bogomil sect, and the following words of Cosmas may be regarded as its birth-certificate: "And it came to pass that in the land of Bulgaria, in the days of the orthodox tsar Peter, there appeared a priest by the name of Bogomil. . . He was the first who began to preach in Bulgaria a heresy, of which we shall speak below." Apart from the fact that Bogomil was a contemporary of tsar Peter, who reigned from 927 to 969, and that he was the author of heretical books, we know next to nothing about this greatest heresiarch in the history of the Southern Slavs. It would seem from circumstantial evidence that he taught in the late thirties or the early forties of the tenth century. His name, Bogomil, is generally regarded as the Slavonic translation of the Greek name Theophilos, "beloved of God." The more famous term "Bogomils," a generic name for his followers, seems to have become current in Bulgaria either at the end of the tenth century or at the beginning of the eleventh. Cosmas, who seems to have known them only too well, shows, in a few vivid traits, how to recongize a Bogomil: "The heretics," he writes, "in appearance are lamb-like, gentle, modest and silent, and pale from hypocritical fasting. They do not talk idly, nor laugh loudly, nor give themselves airs. They keep away from the sight of men, and outwardly they do everything so as not to be distinguished from righteous Christians, but inwardly they are ravening wolves. . . The people, on seeing their great humility, think that they are orthodox and able to show them the path of salvation; they approach and ask them how to save their souls. Like a wolf that wants to seize a lamb, they first cast their eyes downwards, sigh and answer with humility. Wherever they meet any simple or uneducated man, they sow the tares of their teaching, blaspheming the traditions and rules of Holy Church." This humble bearing and ascetic appearance of the Bogomils was a source of constant irritation to their Orthodox opponents: a century and a half later, Anna Comnena described the Byzantine Bogomils in strikingly similar terms: "The sect of the Bogomils," she writes in the *Alexiad*, "is very clever in aping virtue. And you will not find any long-haired worldling belonging to the Bogomils, for their wickedness was hidden under the cloak and the cowl. A Bogomil looks gloomy and is covered up to the nose and walks with a stoop and mutters, but within he is an uncontrollable wolf."[13]

The doctrines of the Bogomils are expounded at some length by Cosmas: their central teaching, based on a dualistic cosmology, was that the visible, material world was created by the devil. The devil, in their view, was the son of God and the brother of Christ. He appeared, according to them, several times in the Gospels, concealed in particular under the traits of the unjust steward and the prodigal son. The Bogomil conception of the devil — and hence their cosmological dualism — was, at least outwardly, much nearer to the Christian teaching than the clear-cut and absolute dualism of the Paulicians and the Manichaeans. It must be emphasized that, in contrast to the Paulicians, the Bogomils did not believe in the existence of two parallel principles or Gods, and that their dualism was based on the recognition of the inferiority of the devil and his ultimate dependence on God. Holding matter to be the creation of the devil, the Bogomils were naturally led to deny the Incarnation and to postulate a docetic Christology. In a thirteenth century Bulgarian source (the *Synodicon of the Tsar Boril*) it is stated that Bogomil himself taught that "Christ our Lord was seemingly born of the . . . ever Virgin Mary, was seemingly crucified and . . . ascended in his body which he left in the air." On account of their dualistic cosmology, the Bogomils denied the whole Christian conception of matter as a vehicle of Grace and adopted the anti-sacramental views of the Paulicians and the Massalians. Cosmas tells us that they rejected baptism and the eucharist and spurned the cross, miracles, temples, the order of priesthood and the visible organization of the Christian Church. The moral teaching of the Bogomils was as consistently dualistic as that of the primitive Manichaeans: if the visible world is the creation and realm of the Evil One, it follows that in order to escape his domination and to be united with God all contact with matter and the flesh, which are the devil's best instruments for gaining mastery over the souls of men, should be avoided. Hence the Bogomils condemned those functions of man which bring him into close contact with matter, especially marriage, the eating of meat and the drinking of wine. It is doubtful, however, whether the same degree of continence was equally enforced on all members of the sect. Though we have no precise evidence on this point, it seems probable that the Bogomils, following the example of the Manichaeans, were divided into two groups: the ordinary "believers," who were not bound to rigorous asceticism, and the "perfect," who were expected to live in complete continence. In any case the moral austerity of the Bogomils was, until the decline of the sect in the fourteenth century, invariably recognized by their fiercest opponents: and it is with some justification that they have been called "the greatest puritans of the Middle Ages." But the claim put forward by the Bogomils to lead the pure evangelical life was always rejected by the Orthodox, mainly on account of the dualistic origin of their ethics, partly because of their pharisaic assertion that they alone deserved the name of Christians, and of their angry attacks on the shortcomings of the clergy.

We do not, unfortunately, know very much about the customs and organization of the Bogomil sect in this early period of its history. We should beware of the uncritical assumptions of past historians of Bogomilism, who ascribe to this sect at its beginnings in Bulgaria many features which are attested for the first time by the sources among the Byzantine Bogomils in the late eleventh century. It can scarcely be denied that the ritual and organization of the Bogomil sect underwent considerable evolution in the eleventh and twelfth centuries, mainly it seems, by contact with Byzantine Christianity. But in the tenth century both the ritual and the organization of the sect remained very rudimentary. We know from the evidence of Cosmas that the Bogomils, while rejecting most of the prayers of the Orthodox Church, which they regarded, together with the Liturgy, as "babblings," made wide and apparently exclusive use of the Lord's Prayer, which they recited four times a day and four times a night, with appointed prostrations. Cosmas also accuses them of fasting on Sundays (a practice which existed among the Manichaeans), of confessing their sins to one another and of granting each other absolution; these rites of confession were also performed by women.

The *Sermon against the heretics* gives us a clear and cogent picture of the essential features of tenth century Bogomilism: doctrinally—a mixture of Paulician and Massalian dualism, combined with many Christian elements borrowed particularly from the New Testament and interpreted in a definitely rationalistic and individualistic manner; ethically—a cult of asceticism (though for basically non-Christian motives), with the rejection of the "externals" of religion and a strong emphasis on contemplation and the inner life. Some of the features of early Bogomilism—in particular its refusal to accept any distinction between the priesthood and the laity and the view of Holy Scripture as the unique source of revealed faith, are analogous to traits which we find in later movements of the Reformation.

One last aspect of the tenth century Bogomilism must be mentioned. It is not surprising that at a time when the interests of Church and State were very closely linked, the wholesale rejection of Orthodoxy was tantamount to a rebellion against the secular laws and a challenge to the whole contemporary society. Moreover, a teaching which so unequivocally condemned married life as sinful threatened to undermine the foundations of the family, the community and the state, which were already sufficiently shaken in Bulgaria by the middle of the tenth century. The Bogomils are painted by Cosmas as idlers with no fixed abode, as social parasites, reminiscent, save their heresy, of the *gyrovagi* of Western Europe, "wandering from house to house, devouring the property of the people they deceive" and even "holding that it is unbecoming for a man to labor and to do earthly work." Cosmas puts forward an even graver accusation against the Bogomils—that of preaching civil disobedience. He writes: "They teach their own people not to obey their lords, they revile the wealthy, hate the tsar, ridicule those in authority, condemn the boyars, regard as vile in the sight of God those who serve the tsar and forbid every servant to work for his master." Unfortunately, this much-discussed statement of Cosmas is confirmed by no other contemporary or later source explicitly referring to the Bogomils. It must hence be treated with caution. There seems to be no reason to doubt that the Bogomils, at least on certain occasions, preached a revolutionary doctrine of social equality in opposition to the powerful of this world, which they may have regarded as a reflection on the social plane of the cosmic struggle between good and evil. The fact that the religious and social views of the Bogomils inclined them to espouse the cause of the oppressed against the oppressors, of the serfs against their masters, undoubtedly explains much of the success enjoyed by the sect at certain periods of Bulgarian history, particularly during the Byzantine domination in the eleventh and twelfth centuries. But we must nevertheless beware of attaching too much importance to the social anarchism of the Bogomils, or of seeing in them, as some not always disinterested writers have done, Slavonic communists of the Middle Ages. We must not forget that the Bogomils were always primarily religious preachers, and that their concern with social problems was of a contingent character.

The measures taken by the Bulgarian Church and State to combat the Bogomil heresy are known to us only from later documents. Cosmas contents himself with a dark allusion to "chains and imprisonment" which, on his own admission, only enhanced the prestige of the Bogomils by surrounding them with a halo of martyrdom.

Moreover, their emaciated appearance and ascetic behavior, in an age when monasticism commonly ranked as the highest expression of the Christian life, combined with the essentially popular character of the Bogomil movement, go far to explain the continued success of the sect throughout the four centuries of its history in Bulgaria and in the Byzantine Empire. It can truly be said that after the final defeat of Iconoclasm in the ninth century Bogomilism was the most dangerous enemy of the Orthodox Church in the whole of the Middle Ages.

Of the history of the Bogomil sect in the First Bulgarian Empire we know very little. A variety of reasons — historical and geographical — point to the fact that the original home and subsequent stronghold of Bogomilism was Macedonia. It was moreover in Macedonia that arose a notable proportion of the so-called "Bogomil books," popular literary productions, either adapted from Christian apocryphal writings or specially composed for the propagation of the Bogomil doctrines, and whose study forms one of the most interesting chapters in the medieval history of the Balkans.[14] Finally, certain place names in Macedonia, derived from roots connected with the different epithets by which the Bogomils were known, testify to the prevalence of the sect in that region in the Middle Ages: such are, for example, the topographical names *bogomilsko polje, babuna, kutugertsi.*

In the eleventh and twelfth centuries most of our information on the Bogomils is derived from Byzantine sources. This is primarily due to the fact that after the fall of the First Bulgarian Empire in 1018, as the result of which Bulgaria became for 168 years a province of the Byzantine Empire, Bogomilism, unrestricted by national frontiers, could freely spread from Macedonia over the entire South Eastern part of the Balkan peninsula and even penetrated into Constantinople.

Towards the middle of the eleventh century evidence of Bogomilism in Thrace can be found in the *Dialogus de operatione daemonum* by Michael Psellus,[15] and a letter of the Byzantine monk Euthymius of Acmonia,[16] dated about the same time, shows that the activities of the sect extended over the entire Western part of Asia Minor.

To understand correctly the history of Bogomilism in this period it is essential to realize that, while the Paulician sect directly and permanently influenced the development of Bogomilism, it was not completely merged into the latter sect and for long retained a separate existence alongside the Bogomil movement. It must be admitted that the failure of most scholars to distinguish sufficiently clearly between the different dualistic sects which flourished in the Balkans during the

Middle Ages has led some of them to unjustifiable conclusions regarding the character of Bogomilism.[17]

It is essential, though unfortunately all too uncommon, to distinguish the Bogomils from the Paulicians. Yet the differences between the two sects are clearly apparent and were never obliterated. It can be said that the Bogomil ideal was primarily contemplative, while the life of the Paulicians was largely directed towards action. That is why the Paulicians generally appear in history as restless and troublesome, born soldiers with a marked propensity for fighting, the Bogomils, on the contrary, as meek, humble, ascetic. Moreover, the Balkan Paulicians throughout the Middle Ages remained in self-contained communities, often of foreign origin, living apart from the Orthodox and attempting to convert them from without. The Bogomils, on the contrary, grew from within Bulgarian society and remained in close contact with its people; it is this popular character of Bogomilism that largely explains its appeal and success in the Balkans.

A recognition of these differences should prevent us from confusing, as so many historians have done, the Bogomils with those Balkan Paulicians who, in their traditional hostility to Byzantium, concluded from the eleventh century a series of military and political alliances with the enemies of the Empire — with the Pechenegs and the Normans in the eleventh century and with the French Crusaders in the thirteenth. There is certainly every reason to suppose that the Bogomils were in contact with the Paulicians, particularly in Thrace, round Philippopolis, where, towards the close of the eleventh century, in the words of Anna Comnena, "all the inhabitants were Manichaeans except a few," before the large-scale and celebrated conversion of the Thracian Paulicians by the Emperor Alexius Comnenus about the year 1114. But, again, what we know of the mode of life of the Bogomils precludes the possibility that they ever formed an organized anti-Byzantine party in Bulgaria or that they indulged in warfare.

The growth of Bogomilism in Byzantium in the late eleventh and early twelfth centuries can be studied in some detail in two twelfth century sources, the *Alexiad*[18] of Anna Comnena and the *Panoplia Dogmatica*[19] of the Byzantine theologian Euthymius Zigabenus, the latter composed at the time of the great Bogomil trial at Constantinople around 1110. An interesting — and apparently novel — feature of Bogomilism at that time was the success it gained, on Anna's own admission, among the aristocratic families of Byzantium. We may suppose that it was there, by contact with the theological and philosophical speculations characteristic of the Comnenian Renaissance, that the doctrines of the Bogomils acquired that elaborate and systematic form which they are given in the *Panoplia Dogmatica*. Zigabenus, who agrees with Anna Comnena as to the double derivation of Bogomilism from Paulicianism and Massalianism, expounds in some detail the Bogomil teaching on the devil, which affords an interesting example of this "doctrinal development" among the Byzantine Bogomils. According to them, the devil or Satan, who appears in the Gospel as the "unjust steward," was the first-born son of God the Father and the elder brother of Christ, "the Son and Logos." His original name was Satanael. One day, stricken with pride, he rebelled against his Father, and together with those "ministering powers" whom he had persuaded to follow him, was cast out of heaven. However, he retained his creative power, represented by the last syllable (*el*) of his name, the attribute of his divine origin, and with the assistance of his fallen companions created the visible world, with the firmament, the earth and its products. This, according to the Bogomils, was the creation of the world, described in the Book of Genesis and falsely attributed by the Christians to God Himself. Satanael next created the body of Adam, the first man, but in spite of repeated efforts was unable to animate it. So he begged his Father to send down His Spirit on Adam and promised that man, a mixture of good and evil, would belong to both of them. To this God agreed, and Adam came to life, a compound of a divine soul and a body created by Satanael. The future history of mankind is deduced from this curious mixture of a dualistic cosmology with the Christian teaching on the fall of Satan. The greater part of the Old Testament was the revelation of Satanael and his servant Moses. At last the Father took pity on the human soul imprisoned in the body, and send His second son Christ into the world. Christ assumed a non-material, "seeming" body (the familiar Bogomil docetism), clothed in which He performed His mission on earth, was crucified, died and rose from the dead. During His descent into hell He defeated and imprisoned His enemy Satanael, who was deprived of his divine attributes together with the last syllable of his name, and thus became Satan. Having accomplished His mission, Christ returned to heaven to sit on the throne formerly occupied by Satanael and was resolved into the Father from whom He had proceeded.

The *Panoplia Dogmatica*, apart from its detailed account of other Bogomil doctrines (many of which show a similar development from those attributed to the tenth century Bogomils by Cosmas) throws some light on the ritual of the Byzantine Bogomils: from this it would appear that there existed two distinct ceremonies of initiation into the sect—the first for the catechumens, the second for the "perfect" (the θεοτόκοι, as they were called) — similar to the *abstinentia* and the *consolamentum* practised by the French and Italian Cathari.

The alarming growth of Bogomilism in Byzantium at the beginning of the twelfth century led to a vigorous reaction of the Byzantine ecclesiastical and secular authorities, which culminated about 1110 in the trial and imprisonment of the prominent Bogomils in the capital and the public burning of their chief leader Basil. Anna Comnena has given us a vivid description of this trial, which must have been something of a *cause célèbre*, and in which the Emperor Alexius himself played a prominent role. His drastic measures were at least partly successful: for after 1110 we hear of no widespread outbreak of Bogomilism in Constantinople, though it was still rampant in the provinces, particularly in Asia Minor. But, in the course of the twelfth century, the stronghold of the sect moved back to its original home in Bulgaria, where in the following century, strengthened by its previous growth in Byzantium, Bogomilism reached the summit of its development.

In the middle of the twelfth century, a new outbreak of Bogomilism in Macedonia—the cradle of the sect—is attested in the Slavonic biography of Saint Hilarion, bishop of Moglena,[20] who at the instigation of the Emperor Manuel Comnenus took vigorous and, it seems, momentarily successful action against the heretics. But ecclesiastical penalties proved incapable of stemming the rising flood of Bogomilism. In the second half of the twelfth century, its influence spread from Macedonia to the West, to the neighboring Serbian principality of Rashka. The Serbian Grand Zhupan, Stephen Nemanja, was obliged to summon a general assembly of the land to check this peril. The repressive measures promulgated against the Bogomils by this council and the enlightened ecclesiastical policy carried out at the beginning of the thirteenth century by St. Sava, the first Archbishop of the Serbian Church, prevented the sect from growing any deep roots in Serbia, at least until the fourteenth century, when, in the reign of the Emperor Stephan Dushan, it raised its head for the last time. Not so, however, in Bosnia, where between the eleventh and fifteenth centuries, Bogomilism, considerably modified, and known as the Patarene or Bosnian faith, developed into a large-scale national movement.[21]

In Bulgaria itself Bogomilism reached its heyday at the beginning of the thirteenth century. In 1211 the Bulgarian tsar Boril convened a council at Trnovo, the capital of the Second Bulgarian Empire, to deal with the Bogomil menace. The extant records and acts of this council, known as the *Synodicon of the Tsar Boril*, are extremely important in that they contain the only known formal legislation promulgated by the Bulgarian Church against the Bogomil sect.[22] The Council of Trnovo is contemporaneous with the measures taken by Pope Innocent III to suppress the Albigensian heresy in Southern France. The probable connection between these two events may become almost certain if we remember that the Bulgarian Church at the time was in temporary union with Rome, and note that in 1206 a Român cardinal was sent to Bulgaria on an unknown mission.[23] The whole problem of the relations between the Bogomil and the Albigensian movements still awaits a full investigation. Generally speaking, Western medievalists have not studied the Slavonic Bogomil sources in any great detail, while Slavonic historians have too often taken the filiation of the Albigensian movement from Bogomilism for granted, without studying profoundly enough the dualistic movements of medieval Western Europe. Although their conception of the spread of Bogomilism from the Balkans to Southern France via Northern Italy is often over-simplified, it cannot be doubted that Bogomilism did exert a direct influence on the movement of the Cathars in the twelfth and thirteenth centuries. The name "Bulgarorum haeresis," given to Catharism by its Catholic opponents in France, the proven influence of the Bogomil ritual on that of the Cathars, the Bogomil origin of the *Liber Sancti Johannis*, one of the principal doctrinal books of the Cathars, the view frequently expressed by the dualists of Western Europe that their doctrines originated in Bulgaria, are among the many signs pointing in that direction. There can be little doubt that by the beginning of the thirteenth century the dualistic communities of Southern Europe formed a single international network, stretching from the Black Sea to the Atlantic, though the belief, expressed in some Western medieval sources, that they all owed allegiance to one supreme leader resident in the Balkans — a kind of "Bogomil Pope" — is no doubt fictitious.[24]

Against the background of the spread of dualism over a large part of Europe at the beginning of the thirteenth century the anti-Bogomil council of Trnovo acquires particular significance. Many of the tenets of the sect mentioned in the *Synodicon* are familiar from earlier sources. They are particularly interesting in that they display a marked influence of Byzantine Bogomilism. This applies especially to the organization of the sect. From the evidence of the *Synodicon* and for general reasons, it would seem that the Bulgarian Bogomils in the course of the twelfth century borrowed from their Byzantine co-religionists, and ultimately from the Orthodox Church, a more rigid organization of their communities and a regular hierarchy, in the same manner as the Cathars and Patarenes borrowed many features of their own organization from the Roman Church. The Bogomil sect survived the anathemas of the Council of Trnovo. In 1238 Pope Gregory IX in a letter to the Latin Emperor Baldwin of Constantinople bitterly complained that Bulgaria was "full of heretics" who were apparently enjoying the protection of the Bulgarian tsar John Asen II.[25]

The fourteenth century, which witnessed the fall of the Second Bulgarian Empire under the yoke of the Ottoman Turks, also saw the decline and disappearance of the Bogomil sect in Bulgaria. The increasing decadence of Bogomilism, which forestalled the Turkish invasion, was due to several features inherent in the sect as well as to the general characteristics of the time. In spite of its inner coherence and of the external organization which it had borrowed from Byzantium, Bogomilism always remained a somewhat diffused heresy, eminently changeable and adaptable to circumstances. This peculiarity, which rendered the task of fighting it very difficult for the Church, later became a source of weakness to the sect. Unlike the Paulicians, the Bogomils proved in the end incapable of retaining the purity of their teaching and gradually absorbed from other sects and movements several features which could not fail to have a detrimental effect on their own sect. This applies particularly to some Massalian elements, especially to the practice of sexual promiscuity for pseudo-religious motives. Probably in the course of the twelfth century, a fusion occurred between Bogomilism and Massalianism, which continued throughout the thirteenth and led to their complete identification in the fourteenth. By that time, no doubt under the increased influence of Massalianism, the Bogomils had entirely lost their reputation for moral austerity and had become associated with extreme forms of immorality. This was probably due in part to the general moral decline in fourteenth century Bulgaria, accentuated by the social and economic instability of the reign of John Alexander, which must have weakened the resistance of the Bogomils to the disruptive influence of Massalian practices.

The fight against Bogomilism in the fourteenth century is associated with the name of St. Theodosius of Trnovo, one of the leading Bulgarian Churchmen of his time and a prominent champion of hesychasm. His biography[26] refers significantly to "the Bogomil, that is the Massalian heresy." A council, convened soon after 1350 on the initiative of St. Theodosius, reiterated the previous condemnations of the Bogomils, who were now accused of submitting to the "natural passions" on the grounds that "our nature is a slave to the demons."

The fact that by the fourteenth century Bogomilism had acquired a number of features which would have been disowned by its founder no doubt partly explains the fact that, after the fall of the Second Bulgarian Empire in 1393, the sect apparently disintegrated of itself and the Bogomils disappeared from Bulgarian history. It is probable, by analogy with the behavior of the Bosnian Patarenes a century later, that many Bogomils were sympathetic to the Turks and accepted Islam. In any case, with the establishment of Turkish domination over South Eastern Europe in the fourteenth and fifteenth centuries, the Bogomils vanish for ever from the Balkan countries.

FOOTNOTES ON CHAPTER X

[1] Although the presence in Zoroastrian cosmology of apparently dualist elements is undeniable, the teachings of Zoroastrianism on the nature of man and its moral and social consequences are manifestly opposed to any consistently dualistic view. The dualism between spirit and matter, or the soul and the body, was alien to Zoroastrianism, which taught that man was wholly the product of Ormazd, the Supreme Ruler of the Kingdom of Light, Good and Truth. The Zoroastrian emphasis on man's free will is in marked contrast with the determinism underlying all dualistic systems. In its rejection of asceticism and its emphasis on the holiness of life and the importance of the body Zoroastrianism is also in opposition to every form of true dualism. For the problem of Zoroastrian "dualism," which still awaits a definitive solution, the following works may be consulted: A. V. W. Jackson, *Zoroastrian Studies* (New York, 1928); A. Christensen, *L'Iran sous les Sassanides* (Copenhagen, 1936); H. S. Nyberg, *Die Religionen des alten Iran* (Leipzig, 1938); M. N. Dhalla, *History of Zoroastrianism* (New York, 1938).

[2] The best accounts of the Manichaean doctrines are to be found in the following works: P. Alfaric, *L'Evolution intellectuelle de Saint Augustin* (Paris, 1918); *Les Ecritures Manichéennes* (Paris, 1918); H. H. Schaeder, *Urform und Fortbildungen des manichäischen Systems, Vorträge der Bibliothek Warburg* (1924-1925), pp. 65-157; F. C. Burkitt, *The Religion of the Manichees* (Cambridge, 1925); H. J. Polotsky, article *Manichäismus* in Pauly-Wissowa, *Real-Encyclopädie der classischen Altertumswissenschaft.* Supplementband VI (1953).

[3] See F. W. K. Müller, *Handschriften-Reste in Estrangelo-Schrift aus Turfan...I: Sitzungsber. der K. pr. Akad. der Wissensch.* (1904), pp. 348-352; II: *Abhandl. der K. pr. Akad. der Wissensch.* (1904); C. Salemann, *Ein Bruchstück manichäischen Schrifttums im asiatischen Museum, Zapiski imperatorskoy Akademii nauk (ist.-fil. otd),* Vol. CI (1904); W. Radloff, *Chuastuanit, das Bussgebet der Manichäer* (St. Petersburg, 1909); A. von Le Coq, *A Short Account of the Origin, Journey and Results of the First Royal Prussian Expedition to Turfan in Chinese Turkestan, Journal of the Royal Asiatic Society* (1909), pp. 299-322; E. Chavannes and P. Pelliot, *Un Traité Manichéen retrouvé en Chine, traduit et annoté, Journal Asiatique* (1911), pp. 499-617; 1913, pp. 99-199, 261-394.

[4] See *Ein Mani-Fund in Ägypten. Originalschriften des Mani und seiner Schüler,* von Carl Schmidt und H. J. Polotsky, mit einem Beitrag von H. Ibscher, *Sitzungsber. der pr. Akad. der Wissensch.* (1933), pp. 4-90; *Manichäische Handschriften der Staatlichen Museen Berlin,* herausgegeben in *Aufträge der pr. Akad. der Wissensch.* unter Leitung von Carl Schmidt, Bd. I: *Kephalaia* (Stuttgart, 1935-37); *A Manichaean Psalm-book,* edited by C. R. C. Allberry (Stuttgart, 1938).

[5] See, in particular, E. de Stoop, *Essai sur la diffusion du Manichéisme dans l'Empire Romain, Recueil de travaux publiés par la faculté de philosophie et lettres de l'Université de Gand,* 38ᵉ fasc. (Gand, 1909); F. Cumont, *La propagation du Manichéisme dans l'Empire Romain, Revue d'histoire et de littérature religieuses* (1910).

[6] *Marcion: Das Evangelium vom Fremden Gott,* 2nd edition (Leipzig, 1924), p. 383.

[7] *Historia Manichaeorum qui et Pauliciani dicuntur,* Patr. Graeca, CIV, col. 1239-1304.

[8] C. Astruc and others, "Les sources grecques pour l'histoire des Pauliciens d'Asie Mineure", *Travaux et mémoires du centre de recherches byzantines,* 4 (1970).

[9] For an account of the Massalian doctrines see the article *Euchites* in the *Dictionnaire de Théologie Catholique;* and A. Guillaumont, "Messaliens", *Dictionnaire de spiritualité, ascétique et mystique* X (Paris, 1980).

[10] *Chronographia,* ed. C. De Boor, I, 429.

[11] *Sv. Kozmy Presvitera Slovo na Eretiki,* edited by M. G. Popruzhenko (Odessa, 1907). The text was re-edited by Popruzhenko: *Kozma presviter, bolgarsky pisatel' X veka* (Sofia, 1936). See also now Yu. Begunov, *Kozma Presviter v slavyanskikh literaturakh* (Sofia, 1973).

[12] See A. Vaillant, *Le traité contre les Bogomiles du prêtre Cosmas, Revue des Etudes Slaves,* t. XXI, 1944, fasc. 1-4, pp. 46-89; H.-C. Puech, *Le traité contre les Bogomiles de Cosmas le prêtre* (Paris, 1945).

[13] *Alex., lib.* XV, *cap.* 8.

[14] The "Bogomil books" are the subject of a scholarly study by Prof. I. Ivanov (*Bogomilski knigi i legendi,* Sofia, 1925).

[15] P.G. CXXII, 820 *seq.*

[16] Edited by G. Ficker: *Die Phundagiagiten: Ein Beitrag zur Ketzergeschichte des byzantinischen Mittelalters* (Leipzig, 1908).

[17]This applies even to the work of F. Rački (*Bogomili i Patareni, Rad jugosl. Akad. Znanosti i Umjetnosti*, VII, VIII, X. Zagreb, 1869-1870) which, though a number of its conclusions now stand in need of revision, remains one of the most valuable studies of the Bogomil sect. See now D. Obolensky, *The Bogomils. A Study in Balkan Neo-Manichaeism* (Cambridge, 1948); D. Angelov, *Bogomilstvo v Bŭlgariya* (Sofia, 1969).

[18]*Lib*. XV, *cap*. 8-10.

[19]*Tit*. 27, P.G. CXXX, cols. 1289-1332.

[20]*The Life of Saint Hilarion* by the Bulgarian Patriarch Euthymius was edited by E. Kalužniacki (Vienna, 1901). Reprinted, London 1971.

[21]The still somewhat mysterious problem of the Patarene "Bosnian Church" cannot be treated simply as part of the Bogomil question and hence lies outside the scope of this study.

[22]*Sinodik tsarya Borila*, edited by Popruzhenko (Sofia, 1928).

[23]*Chronica Albrici monachi*, Mon. Germ. Hist., Script, XXIII, p. 886.

[24]See C. Schmidt, *Histoire et doctrine de la secte des Cathares ou Albigeois*, Vol. II (Paris, 1849), pp. 146-147; J. Guiraud, *Histoire de l'Inquisition au Moyen Age*, I (Paris, 1935), pp. 232-234; See now D. Obolensky, "Papas Nicetas: A Byzantine Dualist in the Land of the Cathars", *Harvard Ukrainian Studies*, VII (1983), pp. 489-500.

[25]A. Theiner, *Vetera monumenta historica Hungariam sacram illustrantia* (Rome, 1859-60), I, pp. 160-161.

[26]Edited by O. Bodyansky: *Chteniya v imper. obshchestve istorii i drevnostey rosiiskikh*, Vol. I, Moscow, 1860.

CHAPTER XI

THE CULT OF ST. DEMETRIUS OF THESSALONIKI
IN THE HISTORY OF BYZANTINE-SLAV RELATIONS*

Many historians, I suppose, feel from time to time the urge to fit a particular problem in which they happen to be interested into a wider conceptual framework, by combining the method of analysis with an attempt to paint on a broader canvass. When I was asked to deliver a lecture in your city, under the auspices of the Institute of Balkan Studies, I naturally felt honored by, and grateful for, this invitation.[1] And then, in searching for a subject, I thought that this urge might be satisfied if I chose a theme at once restricted and capable of being viewed within a wider context. The cult of St. Demetrius, which, as you know better than I, occupies a central position in the history of Thessaloniki both in medieval and modern times, can also, it seems to me, be regarded as a particular instance — and one singularly rich in historical content and dramatic overtones — of a process which I have endeavored to study for a number of years: the transmission of Byzantine civilization to the Slav peoples of Eastern Europe.

In the history of the encounter between Byzantium and the Slavs we may distinguish, without perhaps too much oversimplification, three successive stages. The first has been termed the "Dark Age" of Byzantium. It covers, broadly speaking, the period from the late sixth to the early ninth century. In the European sector — the only one with which my paper is concerned — it was marked by the Empire's desperate attempts to defend, first its northern frontier on the Danube, then its lands in the Balkan peninsula, and finally its very life, against the attacks of its enemies from the North—Slavs, Avars and Bulgars. In this struggle for survival, during which most of the North Balkan

---

*Balkan Studies, XV (1974), 3-20.

area, and much of the countryside in central Greece and the Peloponnese, were lost, permanently or temporarily, to these invaders, the
Empire was saved by its ability to retain control of the more important coastal cities, above all, of course, Constantinople and Thessaloniki. The defense of Thessaloniki against the barbarian attacks of the
late sixth and of the seventh century are among the outstanding military achievements of the late Roman and early Byzantine state. In
this achievement the cult of St. Demetrius played a role which it is
impossible to over-estimate. The theme of my paper has thus a particular relevance to the earliest phase of Byzantine-Slav relations.

The second phase begins in the early ninth century and ends in the
late twelfth. It was, for Byzantium, an age of recovery and expansion.
This resurgence, at home and abroad, was crowned by many remarkable achievements. Two of them are of special relevance to my
theme: during the ninth and tenth centuries the Slav tribes, who had
occupied much of continental Greece and of the Peloponnesus during
the preceding "dark age," were subdued, converted to Christianity,
and finally civilized by the Byzantines, thus becoming, in the only
meaningful sense of the word, Greeks. Further north, beyond the
Empire's borders, Byzantine civilization, spreading throughout the
Balkans and thrusting deep into the lands beyond the Danube and the
Black Sea, brought in this period the nascent states of Central and
Eastern Europe into the orbit of Greek Christianity. In the history of
Byzantium's foreign missions there is no more remarkable period than
the sixties and seventies of the ninth century. During these two
decades, through the initiative of rulers and churchmen—especially
the Emperors Michael III and Basil I, and the Patriarch Photius—the
Bulgarians, the Russians and the Serbs were all converted to the
Christian faith, and a mission led by Cyril and Methodius planted
Byzantine Christianity and civilization in the heart of Central Europe.
Of these ninth-century missions that of Cyril and Methodius is particularly germane to the theme of this lecture: for, as I hope to show,
these two Byzantine missionaries were sustained in their arduous task
in this remote land by their conviction that St. Demetrius was there to
assist them in their hour of need.

This age of expansion, associated with the Macedonian and Comnenian dynasties, came to an end, at least on the political plane, in the
last two decades of the twelfth century. It was then that the Bulgarians
and the Serbs revolted against direct Byzantine rule, and the Empire's
hegemony in the northern regions of the Balkan peninsula came to an

end for ever. In this third and last period, which spans the later Middle Ages, Byzantine civilization remained a dominant force in Eastern Europe. Politically, however, the Empire was a dying body. Taking advantage of the new balance of power, several East European nations, although they owed their religion and much of their culture to Byzantium, or perhaps just because of this fact, began to harbor ambitions to supplant their former masters and mentors. Some of their rulers began to claim that the centre of the Christian *oikoumene*, by the supernatural dictate of Divine providence, had moved, or would soon move, from the shores of the Bosphorus to the capital of their own kingdom. These imperialist dreams were but a mirror-image of Byzantine political thought: their roots lay in the idea of the eternal Rome and in the concept of its translation, or migration, which the Byzantines themselves had used to support their belief that Constantinople was the New Rome. On the political plane, this concept was first explicitly extended to an East European country in the mid-fourteenth century: we find it in the claim, made by the court panegyrists of the Bulgarian *tsar* John Alexander, that the centre of the "renovated" Christian Empire had moved from Constantinople to his capital, Trnovo. A century and a half later, after the Byzantine Empire had ceased to exist, these claims were carried a step further in the celebrated theory of "Moscow the Third Rome."

The connection between the idea of the "translatio imperii" and the cult of St. Demetrius may not be immediately apparent. I believe, however, that a link, albeit tenuous and perhaps indirect, can be detected between the two. For if a "copy," or a "mirror-image," of Constantinople, destined to supplant it, could be created in a Slavonic country, there was no inherent reason why the same transposition could not be applied to Thessaloniki. It was, after all, the second most important city in the Empire, and, for so many foreign nations who desired to possess it, appeared, almost as much as Constantinople itself, as a κοσμοπαμπόθητος πόλις.[2] And Thessaloniki, of course, was indissolubly identified with, and personified by, its patron saint Demetrius. So it is not surprising to find, in several Slavonic countries of the Middle Ages, a desire to set up a mirror-image of Thessaloniki. This desire, as I will show in the concluding part of this paper, occasionally even led their rulers or writers to claim that St. Demetrius had forsaken his city and was now extending his posthumous help to the enemies of Byzantium.

Our first period, then, has as its main theme the role of St. Demetrius in defending his city against the attacks of the Avars and Slavs. This theme is vividly illustrated in one of the earliest datable hagiographical works devoted to the saint: the seventh-century document known as the Θαύματα τοῦ ἁγίου Δημητρίου, or *Miracula Sancti Demetrii*.[3] Let me say in passing that I am not so rash as to plunge into the many still unresolved problems involved in the dating and mutual relationship of the numerous medieval writings devoted to St. Demetrius. Halkin's recent edition of the *Bibliotheca Hagiographica Graeca* lists some 40 of these works.[4] They include Μαρτύρια, Θαύματα, Ἐγκώμια, and liturgical hymns stemming from widely different periods. Before they can be safely used by the historian, they must be subjected to a thorough *Quellenkritik*. In the meantime, we can but treat them with caution, and echo the hope, expressed by Professor Paul Lemerle in 1953, [5] that this considerable body of writings will one day be classified, dated and critically edited within what he called a *Corpus Demetrianum*.

The *Miracula Sancti Demetrii* are a shining exception in this fog of textual uncertainty. The first section, or book, was written, between 610 and 620, by John, Archbishop of Thessaloniki. The second book has been reliably dated, on internal evidence, to the ninth decade of the seventh century. We have now fortunately a critical edition (published in 1979-81) by Paul Lemerle. And there is no lack of scholarly works devoted to the *Miracula*: three of them appeared, almost simultaneously and independently: articles by Lemerle[6] and the Bulgarian historian Alexander Burmov,[7] and a book by the Yugoslav scholar Franjo Barišić.[8] More recently, the relevance of this work to our subject has been illustrated by a Greek scholar, Mr. Antonios Papadopoulos.[9]

The first two books of the *Miracula* are so rich in historical content that I can only enumerate some of the types of evidence they provide for the historian: in no other contemporary work will he find so much precise and first-hand information on the military organization and topography of Thessaloniki during one of the most dramatic centuries of its history; on the methods of warfare and the technique of siege-craft used in the Balkan wars of the time; and on the strategy and tactics of the northern barbarians who, thrusting southward in successive waves down river valleys and across mountain passes, sought in the sixth and seventh centuries to gain a foothold on the warm Aegean coastland and to seize its commanding metropolis which always eluded their grasp. And there can be few documents stemming from the Christian world of the Middle Ages in which the belief held by the citizens of a beleaguered city that they stand under the supernatural protection of a heavenly patron is so vividly and poignantly expressed. They were convinced — and to this innumerable passages in the *Miracula* bear witness — that St. Demetrius saved Thessaloniki from epidemics, famine, civil war, and above all from barbarian attacks. Archbishop John describes in detail the first major siege of the city by the Avars and the Slavs:[10] modern scholars date this event variously either to 586 or 597; I personally, for reasons too long to enumerate here, prefer the first of these dates.[11] His account is so precise and vivid that it is hard to resist the impression that he must, at that time, have been a soldier, fighting on the city walls. The barbarian army, he tells us, numbered some 100,000 men and attacked the city with elaborate and fearsome siege-engines. When the assault was delivered, St. Demetrius appeared on the walls in the guise of a warrior (ἐν ὁπλίτου σχήματι)[12] and speared the first assailant who had scaled a ladder. Throughout the week-long siege he continued to instill courage into the hearts of the defenders and fear into the enemy. The defeat of the assailants and the salvation of Thessaloniki were thus his personal victorious achievement (τοῦ ἀθλοφόρου. . .τὸ κατόρθωμα).[13]

The role played by Archbishop John as a historian of his city and panegyrist of its patron saint was taken up, some sixty years later, by the anonymous author of Book II of the *Miracula*. His account of the successive sieges of Thessaloniki by Avars and Slavs in the seventh century, his description of military technology, and the picture he paints of the gradual settlement of Slav tribes in northern Greece, are of considerable value to the historian. The role he ascribes to Demetrius in these military operations is unchanged. Time and again the saint saves Thessaloniki from disaster, encouraging his compatriots by running round the city walls clothed in white (χλαμύδα λευκὴν φορῶν),[14] striking fear into the enemy fleet by walking on the sea, and appearing on horseback to guard the city gates.

The second book of the *Miracula* provides some valuable information about the basilica of St. Demetrius. This building, according to the Μαρτύρια of the saint, was built in the fifth century by Leontius, Prefect of Illyricum. I shall not discuss the controversial problem of the precise time in the fifth century when the church was constructed. Nor do I feel qualified to assess the results of the archaeological work carried out in and beneath the basilica by Greek scholars

such as Professors Xyngopoulos and Pelekanides,[15] and above all by
the late George Soteriou who, in collaboration with his wife, published in 1952 his magisterial book on the basilica of St. Demetrius.[16]
In deliberately side-stepping these complex problems, I can plead in
justification that the history of this building before the seventh century,
and the nature of the site on which it was erected,[17] are of no direct
relevance to the theme of this lecture: my concern here is with the later
role played by the basilica as the focus of the medieval cult of St.
Demetrius. The *Miracula* describe a great fire which burnt down the
church; and the same document tells us that, at the saint's inspiration,
a new and splendid one was, before long, built on the same site.[18] It is
now generally accepted that the fire occurred between 629 and 634.[19]
It is clear, however, that the building was not wholly destroyed, and
some of the mosaics, whose fragments have survived on the church's
west wall, have been reliably dated to the fifth or sixth century.[20] As
for the later cycle of mosaics, executed after the basilica was rebuilt,
and which include the two famous panels on the piers at the entrance
to the sanctuary, representing St. Demetrius between the two restorers
of the church and St. Demetrius with two children, they are dated by
virtually all authorities to the seventh century. It is curious that they
are not mentioned in the *Miracula*; remarkable that they were not
destroyed by the Iconoclasts; and interesting to note that several
authorities believe that the bishop who, in the first of these panels,
stands beside St. Demetrius, is none other than Archbishop John, the
author of the first book of the *Miracula*.[21]

    This remarkable prelate must have done much to shape and prop-
agate the cult of St. Demetrius not only in Thessaloniki, but
throughout the Greek-speaking world. We may surmise that he and
the anonymous author of the second book of the *Miracula* contributed something to the growing tendency to depict Demetrius as a
military saint: the change in his portrayal from a nobleman, clothed in
a chlamys with its senatorial tablion, to a warrior, clad in armour,
bearing a shield and carrying a sword or a spear, is particularly apparent from the tenth century onwards.[22] But the authors of the *Miracula*
must have done much to pave the way for this metamorphosis. The
epithets they lavish on the saint is evidence of this. St. Demetrius for
them is not only the φιλόπατρις,[23] the σωσίπατρις[24] and the κηδεμών[25]
of his city; he is also the ἀθλοφόρος[26] and the ὑπέρμαχος.[27] And the
last epithet calls to mind an even greater power, whose heavenly protection was already then believed to rest on the mother of all Christian

cities, the Πόλις itself. The conviction that Constantinople was placed under the guardianship of the Theotokos is expressed in several contemporary Greek works describing how the Byzantine capital was saved in 626 from the assault of the Avars and Slavs.[28] The origin and date of the Akathistos hymn are no doubt still a subject of debate among scholars. But it is at least possible that the words of its celebrated *kontakion*, τῇ ὑπερμάχῳ στρατηγῷ, were composed at that time as a token of the Byzantines' triumph and gratitude at the salvation of their city.[29] Be that as it may, it is worth noting that in the first half of the seventh century, when the Avaro-Slav invasions threatened to engulf the two foremost cities of the Empire, their citizens were sustained in their struggle by the belief that they enjoyed the supernatural protection of their respective patrons, the Mother of God and St. Demetrius. In this respect the *Miracula Sancti Demetrii* is a work symptomatic of an age when the Byzantines became more convinced than ever before that their empire was divinely protected, and that its victories were those of the Christian religion.

The period of recovery which followed the dark age of Byzantium was marked, as I have mentioned, by a remarkable resurgence of the missionary activity of the Byzantine Church. Freed, after 843, from the burden of the lengthy Iconoclast crisis, the Church was able not only to play an active role in the christianization and the hellenization of the Slavs in Greece; its missionaries abroad, with the support of the imperial government, now gained the allegiance of a substantial part of the vast Slav world. The history of the mission of Cyril and Methodius, the outstanding achievement of the Byzantine Church in the ninth century, is too well known to require any detailed exposition here. I will only remind you that the embassy led by these two brothers to Central Europe in 863, whose original purpose was to preach Christianity in the language of the Moravian Slavs, resulted in the rise of a whole Slavonic culture, rooted in native traditions yet deeply permeated by the civilization of Byzantium. Its success was due initially to the invention by Cyril and Methodius of a Slavonic alphabet which enabled them to create a new literary language, based on the spoken dialect of the Macedonian Slavs, modelled on Greek, and intelligible to the whole Slavonic world. This language, Old Church Slavonic, into which the Scriptures, the liturgy and many works of religious and secular content were translated from the Greek, remained throughout the Middle Ages the third international language of Europe and the sacred idiom of those Slavs — the Bulgarians, the Serbs and the Russians — who received their religion and much of their culture from Byzantium. It proved the most potent of all channels for the transmission of Greek Christianity to Eastern Europe. Among the many hagiographical writings translated into Slavonic during the Middle Ages, the works extolling St. Demetrius occupied a conspicuous place. But the relationship between the Cyrillo-Methodian mission and the cult of St. Demetrius had another, and more personal, aspect. Cyril and Methodius, as you all know, were natives of Thessaloniki. They could not fail to be deeply devoted to the memory of their city's patron saint who, by the ninth century, had become intimately associated with every aspect of its religious and social life. Their ninth-century biographies clearly show that, in the far-away lands of their missionary work — in Moravia where they translated the Greek liturgy and scriptures and trained their disciples, in Venice where they disputed with their Frankish opponents, and in Rome where St. Cyril died in 869 — they never ceased to regard the Byzantine Empire as their fatherland.[30] It is thus not surprising to find that Methodius, acting as Papal legate to the Slavs of Central Europe, beset during the last ten years of his life by countless difficulties due to the hostility of the Franks and the growing indifference of Rome, turned in his loneliness his thoughts to his native city and its patron saint. His biographer tells us that, shortly before his death (which occurred in 885), after completing the translation of most of the Old Testament, he celebrated a liturgy in honor of St. Demetrius on his feast day, the 26th of October.[31] The Slavonic biographers of Cyril and Methodius generally show themselves very conscious of the symbolic significance of the acts performed by their heroes. The eucharistic sacrifice offered by Methodius in memory of St. Demetrius immediately followed the completion of his and his brother's life work: the Christian liturgy and Scriptures had now been made available to the Slavs in their own language. It is perhaps not straining the evidence too much to suggest that the ninth-century author of the *Life* of Methodius wished to imply that their mission had been accomplished under the special patronage of St. Demetrius.

There is another piece of evidence linking Cyril and Methodius with St. Demetrius: and, from the human standpoint, it is more poignant still. The earliest Old Church Slavonic text of the Μηναῖα, preserved in a Russian manuscript dated to the year 1096, contains a canon sung to St. Demetrius on his feast day.[32] The canon, ὁ κανών, is a central part of the office of Matins (the ὄρθρος), and consists of nine (or eight) odes (ᾠδαί), each of which is formed of an εἱρμός and a number of τροπάρια. No Greek original has been discovered for the canon, and its Old Church Slavonic text is ascribed by most present-day scholars, on strong internal evidence, to St. Methodius.[33] Much of it is fairly conventional in content, though local color is provided by repeated references to Thessaloniki and by the description of the saint, in the first ode, as "the glorious patriot of the glorious Thessaloniki." The word I have translated, somewhat inadequately, as "patriot"— *otčestvoljubec* — is obviously a calque of the Greek φιλόπατρις, a term frequently applied to St. Demetrius in the *Miracula*. But in the final ode of the canon, the author seems unable any longer to restrain his personal feelings, and his pent-up emotion bursts through the austere impersonality of the liturgical text. It would surely be hard to find, in the whole corpus of Orthodox hymnography, a more poignant expression of nostalgia for one's native city. Let me quote, in translation, two *troparia* of this ninth ode.

> "Hearken, o glorious one, to us who are poor and belong to you, and pity us, for we are parted and far away from your radiant temple. And our hearts burn within us, and we desire, o holy one, to be in your church and, one day, to worship within it through your prayers."
> "Why, o wise one, are we, your poor servants, deprived of your radiant splendor as, driven by the love of our Creator, we wander through alien lands and cities as warriors fighting, o blessed one, for the humiliation of trilinguals and fierce heretics?"[34]

It has long been apparent to scholars that the mention of "trilinguals" provides a clue linking this canon with the Moravian and Pannonian mission of Cyril and Methodius. For the "trilinguals" were those, mainly Frankish, opponents of the two brothers who attacked the legitimacy of the Slavonic translation of the liturgy by claiming that it was permissible to celebrate the divine office only in three languages—Hebrew, Greek and Latin. Against them Cyril and Methodius and their disciples fought their hardest verbal battles.[35] And, as Roman Jakobson has observed, these troparia, apart from their yearning for Thessaloniki and its basilica, end with what is in effect a battle-cry.[36] Directed against the enemies of the Cyrillo-Methodian mission, it re-echoes with equal force in the ninth-century biographies of the two brothers. And so the last ode of this canon, with its nostalgia and note of defiance, gives us an authentic glimpse into the hearts and minds of the Apostles of the Slavs. Methodius, its probable author, has revealed himself to us at the end, like an artist who has left his signature inconspicuously at the bottom of a picture.

The work of Cyril and Methodius and their disciples did much to spread the cult of St. Demetrius among those Slavonic peoples who, by their conversion to Byzantine Christianity and their adoption of the vernacular tradition which they created, became the beneficiaries of their life-work. These were the Bulgarians, the Serbs and the Russians. The main centers of the propagation of this cult were cities in which St. Demetrius was especially venerated: Ohrid in Macedonia, which became, after the collapse of the Cyrillo-Methodian mission in Central Europe, a leading center of Balkan Slav Christianity; Sirmium in the northern Balkans, where, according to several Μαρτύρια of the saint, a basilica in his honor was built in the fifth century by Leontius, the Prefect of Illyricum,[37] and where a monastery of St. Demetrius, inhabited by Greek, Hungarian and Slav monks, was founded in the eleventh century;[38] later also, as we shall see, the cities of Trnovo in Bulgaria and Vladimir in Rus';[39] and preeminently, of course, Thessaloniki itself. Early in the Middle Ages, its basilica of St. Demetrius became an object of pilgrimage for the whole East Christian world. Some of the Slav pilgrims, whose writings have survived, display in their descriptions of this church almost the same open-eyed wonder and religious awe which they reveal in their accounts of the sanctuaries of the Holy Land and Constantinople.[40] In no small measure was this veneration due to the holy *myron*, which was believed to flow from the saint's relics, and samples of which, endowed with therapeutic and apotropaic powers, were taken back by these pilgrims to their homelands. Within the basilica, they offered their homage and prayers to St. Demetrius in front of the silver hexagonal ciborium, with six columns supporting a dome, standing on the left side of the central nave and which popular piety regarded as the place of the saint's tomb.[41]

The earliest unambigous evidence of the veneration of St. Demetrius in Slavonic lands comes from the late ninth century. In the Macedonian province of Bulgaria, at the close of the century, the leading disciple of Cyril and Methodius, St. Clement of Ohrid, wrote an *encomium* for his feast. It is a somewhat conventional and undistinguished work; yet it is noteworthy as the earliest non-liturgical text composed in the saint's honor in the Old Church Slavonic language. Clement describes him as "the most glorious martyr" and as "the firm foundation of his fatherland."[42]

Of greater interest is the iconographic evidence of the popularity of St. Demetrius in medieval Serbia. Two biographical programmes, each consisting of two scenes, are painted at Dečani and in the Church of St. Demetrius at Peć. The fourteenth-century wall paintings at Dečani represent the saint defending Thessaloniki — anachronistically — against the Cumans, and rebuilding a tower on the city walls. The paintings at Peć, which have been dated to the seventeenth century, depict Eusebius, archbishop of Thessaloniki in the late sixth century, praying before the relics of St. Demetrius, while to the right of this scene, in answer to his prayer, the saint, clad in armor, forces back with a lance a group of enemy soldiers attempting to scale the walls. These paintings were clearly intended to illustrate the story of the Avaro-Slav siege of Thessaloniki in 586 told in the first book of the *Miracula*. They follow the written account with clarity and precision. Mrs. Anka Stojaković, who has studied these paintings, has plausibly suggested that their connection with the text of the *Miracula*, however close, is indirect, and that a pictorial intermediary should be postulated.[43] It is indeed likely that these Serbian paintings reproduced, in summary form, the elements of a biographical cycle from the basilica of St. Demetrius in Thessaloniki. We know from the second book of the *Miracula* that at least one scene of this cycle existed in the seventh century;[44] and several frescoes of this biographical programme were discovered in the church in 1907-8; they perished in the great fire of 1917.[45]

The paintings at Dečani and Peć are interesting for several reasons: they show that works of art which once existed in the centers of the Byzantine world can sometimes be reconstructed with the help of copies or imitations preserved on the periphery of that world; they illustrate the impact of the cult of St. Demetrius on the cultural life of late medieval Serbia; and, depicting as they do the repulse of the Slavs from the walls of a city they so often desired to capture and possess, they testify to the ecumenical spirit which animated the medieval Byzantine Commonwealth, a community in which there was little or no scope for the growth of nationalism in the modern sense of the word.

The Russians did not lag behind the Bulgarians and the Serbs in their veneration of the μεγαλομάρτυς and μυροβλήτης of Thessaloniki. His name — Dimitri, or Dmitri in Russian — has from the eleventh century to the present day been widely popular in all sections of

Russian society. Already in the pre-Mongol period of Russian history it was borne by several members of the ruling dynasty. It was the Christian name of Izyaslav, Prince of Kiev (with two interruptions) from 1054 to 1078. During his reign in the Russian capital Izyaslav founded and richly endowed a monastery dedicated to St. Demetrius which, as the Russian Primary Chronicle tells us, he hoped would eclipse in importance the Kiev Monastery of the Caves, the foremost monastic foundation of Rus'.[46] Several seals of the same prince have been found, on which is represented the standing figure of St. Demetrius, ringed by a Greek inscription.[47] An even more notable bearer of this Christian name was Vsevolod III, Grand Prince of Suzdal' and Vladimir from 1176 to 1212.[48] In 1162, as a young boy, he was exiled by his elder brother to Constantinople.[49] Whether he visited Thessaloniki we do not know; but in those closing years of the twelfth century, when Vsevolod had become the most powerful ruler in Rus', he built in his capital, Vladimir, the magnificent cathedral of St. Dimitri, whose compact majesty and celebrated stone relief carvings belong to the finest achievements of medieval Russian art.[50] On that occasion he had a relic connected with St. Demetrius, which a contemporary Russian chronicler tantalizingly describes as "a tomb slab," transported from Thessaloniki to his capital.[51]

The cult of St. Demetrius in medieval Rus' was also fostered by numerous hagiographical writings. Most of them were translations from the Greek, but several are local and original products. The most popular native saints in the Kievan period were Boris and Gleb, sons of St. Vladimir, the Russian ruler who converted his country to Christianity. In 1015 they were murdered for political motives. Their Christian resignation at the moment of death, and their refusal to defend themselves from their assassins, caused their compatriots to regard them as martyrs, not in the sense that they were killed for the Christian faith, but because, by their act of non-resistance, they chose to die as innocent and voluntary victims in conscious imitation of Christ. Boris and Gleb were canonized by the Russian Church soon after their death; and by a strange paradox, these champions of non-resistance came to be regarded as the heavenly protectors of the Russian people, in war and in peace.[52] One of their Russian biographers, writing in the eleventh or early twelfth century, draws a significant parallel: addressing these murdered princes, he exclaims: "You fight for and help your fatherland, just as the great Demetrius did for his own fatherland."[53] And the town of Vyshgorod near Kiev, where the bodies of Boris and Gleb were laid to rest, is termed by the same author "a second Thessaloniki."[54] It would be hard to find a better example of the spell cast on the minds of the medieval Slavs by the holy places of the Byzantine Empire than this attempt by the Russians, at the dawn of their Christian history, to create in their own country a copy, or a mirror-image, of the shrine of Thessaloniki.

Among the Slavonic texts relating to St. Demetrius for which no Greek model has been found, one, attributed to a late medieval or sixteenth century Russian author, is particularly curious. It tells the story of a pagan chieftan who, while unsuccesfully besieging Thessaloniki, captured two maidens, and took them back home to his country. He then said to them: "I hear that you have a great god called Demetrius, who works many miracles. Embroider me his likeness on an image, so that I might venerate him and defeat my enemies, while I carry his image in front of my army." The maidens, thinking that their captor intended to blaspheme the embroidered image, refused. But threatened with death, they finally consented. The image completed, they tearfully fell asleep. During the night, they were miraculously transported by St. Demetrius to his church in Thessaloniki, where the image remained beside the saint's tomb.[55]

The obviously folkloristic features of this story no doubt explain the fact that it — or perhaps its written source — inspired one of the oral religious poems of Russia. These poems, the *dukhovnye stikhi*, believed to have been composed between the fifteenth and the seventeeth centuries, were recited until recently by groups of itinerant professional singers. One of them tells much the same story, though with several interesting modifications. The image embroidered by the two maidens becomes a magic carpet, on which, with the help of Demetrius and a strong wind, they are carried through the air from the clutches of their tormentor to the safety of Thessaloniki. During the siege St. Demetrius rises from the tomb and defeats the enemy, mounted curiously, but not without pointed symbolism, upon a white donkey. Finally, the poem names the barbarian ruler who besieged Thessaloniki: it is the Tatar Khan Mamai, whose armies were defeated in 1380 by the Russian forces, commanded by Prince Dimitri of Moscow.[56] The anachronistic attempt to graft the story of a miracle performed by St. Demetrius onto the historic victory gained over the Tatars by a Muscovite prince who bore his name may serve to measure the impact which the cult of the Thessalonian saint had upon the poetic imagination of the Russian people.

We have seen how the Russians, by linking the veneration for their national saints Boris and Gleb with the cult of St. Demetrius, created in their country a "copy," or a "mirror-image" of Thessaloniki. But the mirror-image, in certain circumstances, could be used not only to reflect, but also to supersede, its model. As I suggested in my opening remarks, something of the kind was attempted on the political plane in the Middle Ages, when rulers and writers in several Slavonic countries began to lay exclusive claim to the heritage of Byzantium: the concept of the Empire's *renovatio* could thus be used to support the idea of its *translatio*. We must now, in conclusion, consider briefly how far the shift from imitation to substitution can be observed in the attitudes adopted by the Slavs in the Middle Ages towards St. Demetrius and his cult.

The idea that Demetrius has foresaken his city, has changed his allegiance and is actively assisting the enemies of the Empire, may well have originated in the attempt, made by the Bulgarian rebels, to seize Thessaloniki in 1041. The chronicler Scylitzes tells us that during the siege of the city the soldiers of the garrison spent a whole night in prayer by Demetrius' grave, annointed themselves with the *myron* which flowed from his tomb, and on the next day sallied forth to inflict a crushing defeat on the enemy. The Bulgarian prisoners told the Thessalonians that, in the heat of the battle, they had seen a young horseman, leading the Byzantine army and discharging fire which consumed the enemy. This, Scylitzes assures us, was St. Demetrius himself.[57] It was perhaps only natural that the Bulgarians, who in the eleventh and twelfth centuries repeatedly tried to free themselves from Byzantine domination, were tempted to draw a lesson from their defeat, and to enlist on their side the supernatural aid of so formidable a champion. Surprisingly enough, however, the first recorded attempt to make St. Demetrius change sides was made by the Russians. In 907, according to the Russian Primary Chronicle, Oleg, prince of Kiev, besieged Constantinople. The Byzantines, in this hour of peril, attempted to save themselves by sending the Russian ruler poisoned food and wine. Oleg, however, was too cunning to fall for their trick, and declined to partake of the gifts. Whereupon, the chronicler writes, "the Greeks were afraid, and said: 'This is not Oleg, but St. Demetrius, whom God has sent against us.'"[58] This astonishing statement, ascribed to the Byzantines by a Russian monastic chronicler, writing two centuries later and recounting a period when his compatriots were still pagans, has puzzled many a scholar. To my knowledge, the only attempt to explain the appearance of Oleg as an *avatar* of St. Demetrius was made in 1934 by the Danish scholar Stender-Petersen. He has argued, on the whole convincingly, that some of the stories in the Primary Chronicle, particularly those describing military stratagems, go back to a cycle of Viking sagas created by the Scandinavian mercenaries of Byzantium. The story of how Oleg outwitted the Greeks may well be a fragment of one of them. And it is possible, though by no means certain, that the bizarre appearance of St. Demetrius in this tale was the work of the great Viking Harold Hardrada and his retinue, who served in the emperor's Varangian Guard and are believed to have been in Thessaloniki in 1041, the very year of the miraculous defeat of the Bulgarians by the city walls, described by Scylitzes.[59]

The second attempt to appropriate St. Demetrius was made by the Bulgarians. As it is more widely known, I need only refer to it very briefly. In 1185, in northern Bulgaria, the two brothers Peter and Asen raised a revolt against Byzantine rule. The revolt became a war of liberation, and in 1187 the Empire was forced to acknowledge the existence of an independent Bulgaria between the Balkan Mountains and the Lower Danube. Byzantine dominion over this area, which had lasted for 169 years, was at an end. The contemporary Greek chronicler Nicetas Choniates, our main source for these events, states that in the early stages of the revolt Peter and Asen built in Trnovo, the future capital of the "Second Bulgarian Empire," a church dedicated to St. Demetrius, and announced to their followers assembled in it that God had decided to restore their freedom to the Bulgarian people. And, they added, "for this reason Christ's martyr Demetrius had deserted the metropolis of Thessaloniki and the church there in which he had dwelt among the Byzantines, and had come to them (i.e. to Bulgaria) to help and support them in their enterprise."[60] The effect of these claims on the morale of the rebels was, as Nicetas himself admits, considerable; the more so since a few months earlier Thessaloniki had been captured by the Normans.

The Byzantines did all they could to deprive the Bulgarians of this powerful weapon of psychological warfare. This became easier when they recaptured Thessaloniki from the Normans. In 1207 the Bulgarian King Kalojan laid siege to the city, which was then part of the Latin Empire of the Crusaders. Just before he was to deliver the main assault, he died in mysterious circumstances. Once again the Thessalonians ascribed their delivery to the intervention of their patron saint.

John Stauracius, the thirteenth-century Chartophylax of the Metropolis of Thessaloniki, asserts that in the night Kalojan was mortally wounded by St. Demetrius, who appeared before him in the guise of a warrior on a white horse.[61] This story, it is true, was viewed with some scepticism by the contemporary Byzantine historian George Acropolites.[62] But it is symptomatic of the rivalry displayed by the East European peoples of the Middle Ages for the favors and the military assistance of St. Demetrius. The episode of Kalojan's death at his hands could be regarded by the Thessalonians as a kind of revenge for the attempt of his elder brothers Peter and Asen to appropriate the saint for themselves and their country.

We must not, to be sure, exaggerate the importance of this rivalry, nor try to read too much into these factitious efforts of the Slavs to engage in hagiological larceny. It is doubtful whether they were ever intended to be more than temporary expedients or tactical maneuvers. At times when a Slavonic nation was at war with the Empire, to have St. Demetrius fighting on your side was no doubt encouraging for your armies and gratifying to your national pride. But, on a deeper and more permanent level of consciousness, the Slavs knew well, of course, that the supernatural presence of the μεγαλομάρτυς was vouchsafed above all places to his own basilica; and for this reason Thessaloniki always remained in their eyes a holy and prestige-laden city. Of this belief we have seen many instances: Russian pilgrims flocked to its basilica; the saint's victories over the Slavs were depicted on the walls of Serbian and Bulgarian churches; all the Slavs described him by the epithet *Solunski*, derived from the Slavonic name of his city. So great were the healing properties attributed to the *myron* flowing from his basilica in Thessaloniki that it was sometimes used by the Bulgarian church in the fourteenth century instead of the holy chrism in the sacrament of baptism: a practice deprecated by the Byzantine Patriarch Kallistos in a letter to the clergy of Trnovo.[63]

In the last resort, I believe, the attempts sometimes made by the Slavs in the later Middle Ages to appropriate St. Demetrius reflect no more than a certain capacity for "double-think", and a measure of ambiguity in their attitude towards their Byzantine teachers in the Christian faith. This ambiguity is likewise apparent in the realm of political thought: however tempted some of the Slav rulers may have been to lay claim to the universal heritage of Byzantium, few if any of them were seriously or for long disposed to challenge the belief, inherited from their ancestors, that Constantinople was the true center of the Christian Commonwealth, and that he who reigns in that city is its divinely appointed master. Much the same, it seems to me, could be said of the cult of St. Demetrius. To claim his special or exclusive favors may have flattered the national vanity of this or that Slav people. But this embryonic nationalism was, in the Middle Ages, sublimated by the belief that these countries were part of a wider and greater society. For the Slavs, as for all the Orthodox peoples of Eastern Europe, St. Demetrius was not only a local saint whose cult had spread throughout the Greek-speaking world. He was also, in an exact and literal sense, ὁ ἅγιος τῆς οἰκουμένης.

FOOTNOTES ON CHAPTER XI

[1]Except for the notes and a few minor changes, this chapter is identical with the text of a paper read by the author at the Institute for Balkan Studies in Thessaloniki on 18 December, 1973.

[2]For this expression see E. Legrand, "Description des Oeuvres d'Art et de l'Eglise des Saints-Apôtres de Constantinople. Poème en vers iambiques par Constantin le Rhodien," *Revue des Etudes Grecques*, ix (1896), p. 38.

[3]*P.G.*, cxvi, cols. 1203-1384. See now the critical edition by P. Lemerle, *Les plus anciens recueils des Miracles de Saint Démétrius*, 2 vols. (Paris, 1979-81).

[4]F. Halkin, *Bibliotheca Hagiographica Graeca*, 3rd ed. i (Brussels, 1957), pp. 152-165.

[5]P. Lemerle, "La composition et la chronologie des deux premiers livres des Miracula S. Demetrii," *Byzantinische Zeitschrift*, xlvi (1953), p. 349.

[6]Lemerle, *op. cit.*, pp. 349-361.

[7]A. Burmov, "Slavyanskite napadeniya sreshchu Solun v 'Chudesata na sv. Dimitra' i tyakhanata khronologiya," *Godishnik na Sofiyskiya Universitet*, Filosof.-Istor. Fak., xlvii (1952), 2, pp. 167-215. See the critical review of Burmov's article by S. Maslev in *Izvestiya na Instituta za Bŭlgarska Istoriya*, vi (1956), pp. 671-691.

[8]F. Barišić, *Čuda Dimitrija Solunskog kao istoriski izvori* (Belgrade, 1953).

[9]A. Papadopoulos, Ὁ ἅγιος Δημήτριος εἰς τὴν ἑλληνικὴν καὶ βουλγαρικὴν παράδοσιν (Thessaloniki, 1971).

[10]*Miracula* I, 13-15, *P.G.*, cxvi, cols. 1284-1324. Lemerle, *op. cit.*, vol. I, pp. 130-65.

[11]See the arguments in favor of 586 in Barišić, *op. cit.*, pp. 56-64; cf. *ibid.*, p. 10, and, more recently, A. Avenarius, "Die Awaren und die Slaven in den Miracula Sancti Demetrii," *Byzantina*, v (1973), pp. 17-18.

[12]*Mir.* I, 13, 112, col. 1288; Lemerle, I, p. 135.

[13]*Ibid.*, col. 1289. Lemerle, *ibid.*

[14]*Mir.* II, 1, 164, col. 1332. Lemerle. I. p. 178.

[15]S. Pelekanides, Γραπτὴ παράδοση καὶ εἰκαστικὲς τέχνες γιὰ τὴν προσωπικότητα τοῦ ἁγίου Δημητρίου (Thessaloniki, 1970).

[16]G. and M. Soteriou, Ἡ βασιλικὴ τοῦ ἁγίου Δημητρίου Θεσσαλονίκης (Athens, 1952).

[17]For a discussion of these problems see P. Lemerle, "Saint-Démétrius de Thessalonique et les problèmes du Martyrion et du Transept," *Bulletin de Correspondance Hellénique*, lxxvii (1953), pp. 660-694; J. Walter, "St. Demetrius: The Myroblytos of Thessalonika," *Eastern Churches Review*, v, 2 (1973), pp. 159-160; M. Vickers, "Sirmium or Thessaloniki? A Critical Examination of the St. Demetrius Legend," *Byzantinische Zeitschrift*, 67 (1974), pp. 337-50. I would like to express my gratitude to Mr Michael Vickers for letting me see the typescript of his article before publication.

[18]*Mir.* II, 3, 183, col. 1348; A. Tougard, *De l'histoire profane dans les actes grecs des Bollandistes* (Paris, 1874), pp. 144-148; Lemerle, I, pp. 191-3, 195-7.

[19]G. and M. Soteriou, *op. cit.*, p. 25; A. Xyngopoulos, *The Mosaics of the Church of St. Demetrius in Thessaloniki* (Thessaloniki, 1969), p. 6; Cf. R. S. Cormack, "The Mosaic Decoration of St. Demetrius, Thessaloniki," *The Annual of the British School at Athens*, no. 64 (1969), pp. 43-45.

[20]A. Xyngopoulos, *op. cit.*, pp. 12-17.

[21]G. and M. Soteriou, *op. cit.*, pp. 193-194; A. Xyngopoulos, *op. cit.*, pp. 20-21.

[22]See J. Walter, *op. cit.*, pp. 174-177.

[23]*Mir.* II, 1, 164, col. 1332; *Mir.* II, 6, 215, col. 1384. Lemerle, I, p. 177.

[24]A. Tougard, *op. cit.*, p. 142. Lemerle, I, p. 188.

[25]*Mir.* II, 2, 169, col. 1336; *Mir.* II, 4, 185, col. 1349. Lemerle, I, p. 185.

[26]*Mir.* II, 1, 13, 112, col. 1289; *Mir.* II, 1, 167, col. 1333.Lemerle, I, pp. 178, 179, 185.

[27]*Mir.*II, 4, 187, col. 1352. Lemerle, I, pp. 177-8.

[28]For these sources see F. Barišić, "Le siège de Constantinople par les Avares et les Slaves en 626," *Byzantion*, xxiv (1954), pp. 371-395; A. N. Stratos, *Byzantium in the Seventh Century*, i (Amsterdam, 1968), pp. 173-196, 370-375.

[29]See *The Akathistos Hymn*, introduced and transcribed by E. Wellesz (Copenhagen, 1957) [*Monumenta Musicae Byzantinae*, ix], pp. xx-xxxiii; E. Wellesz, *A History of Byzantine Music and Hymnography*, 2nd. ed. (Oxford, 1961), pp. 191-197.

[30]See, in particular, *Vita Constantini*, xviii, 3: *Constantinus et Methodius Thessalonicenses. Fontes*, ed. F. Grivec and F. Tomšič [Zagreb, 1960] (*Radovi Staroslavenskog Instituta, iv*), p. 140; *Vita Methodii*, xvii, 7, *ibid.*, p. 165.

298

[31] *Vita Methodii*, xv, 3, *ibid.*, p. 164.

[32]The text of this canon was published by V. Jagić, *Sluzhebnyya Minei za sentyabr'*, *oktyabr' i noyabr'*, *Pamyatniki Drevnerusskogo Yazyka* (St. Petersburg, 1886), i, pp. 179-190; see also D. Čyževśkyj, "Neue Lesefrüchte," *Zeitschrift für Slavische Philologie*, xxiv (1956), pp. 79-81; and B. S. Angelov, *Iz starata bŭlgarska, ruska i srŭbska literatura* (Sofia, 1958), pp. 19-35.

[33]See R. Jakobson, "Methodius' Canon to Demetrius of Thessalonica and the Old Church Slavonic Hirmoi," *Sborník Prací Filosofické Fakulty Brněnské University*, Ročnik xiv (1965), Řada Uměnovědná, F. 9, pp. 115-121; *id.*, *Selected Writings*, vi, 1, pp. 286-346.

[34]Jagić, *op. cit.*, p. 190; Jakobson, *Selected Writings*, loc. cit., pp. 292-3.

[35]For "the trilingual heresy" see I. Dujčev, "Il problema delle lingue nazionali nel medio evo e gli Slavi," *Ricerche Slavistiche*, viii (1960), pp. 39-60; *Id.*, "L'activité de Constantin Philosophe—Cyrille en Moravie," *Byzantinoslavica*, xxiv (1963), pp. 221-223; F. Dvornik, *Byzantine Missions among the Slavs. SS. Constantine-Cyril and Methodius* (New Brunswick, 1970), pp. 115, 129-130, 144.

[36]R. Jakobson, *Methodius' Canon*, p. 116.

[37]*Passio altera, auctore anonymo, P.G.*, cxvi, col. 1184; *Passio tertia, auctore Simeone Metaphraste, ibid.*, col. 1201.

[38]See K. Jireček, "Das christliche Element in der topographischen Nomenclatur der Balkanländer," *Sitzungsberichte der Kaiserlichen Akademie der Wissenschaften, philosoph.-hist. Classe* (Vienna, cxxxvi, 1897), Abhandlung xi, pp. 93-98; J. Zeiller, *Les origines chrétiennes dans les provinces danubiennes de l'Empire Romain* (Paris, 1918), pp. 81-83; K. Dieterich, "Zur Kulturgeographie und Kulturgeschichte des byzantinischen Balkanhandels," *Byzantinische Zeitschrift*, xxxi (1931), p. 55; V. Popović, "Sirmium, ville impériale," *Akten des VII. Internationalen Kongresses für christliche Archäologie* (Vatican-Berlin, 1969), pp. 665-675.

[39]See D. S. Iliadou, «Ὁ Ἅγιος Δημήτριος καὶ οί Σλάβοι», Πεπραγμένα τοῦ Η΄ Διεθνοῦς Βυζαντινολογικοῦ Συνεδρίου, Θεσσαλονίκη, (1953), iii (Athens, 1958), p. 138.

[40]Ignatius of Smolensk (1405): *Khozhdenie Ignatiya Smolnyanina*, ed. S. V. Arsen'ev, *Pravoslavnyi Palestinskiy Sbornik*, iv, 3 (St. Petersburg, 1887), p. 25; French transl. B. de Khitrowo, *Itinéraires russes en Orient*, I, i (Geneva, 1889), p. 147; Monk Zosimus (c. 1420): *Khozhenie inoka Zosimy*, ed. Kh. M. Loparev, *Pravoslavnyi Palestinskiy Sbornik*, viii, 3 (1889), p. 12; transl. Khitrowo, p. 208; Isaiah of Chilandar (1489), *Skazanie o sv. gore Afonskoy*, ed. Archimandrite Leonid (Moscow, 1882); transl. Khitrowo, pp. 263-264. G. P. Majeska, *Russian Travelers to Constantinople in the fourteenth and fifteenth centuries* (Washington, D.C., 1984).

[41]The role played by the ciborium in the development of the cult of St. Demetrius is discussed by G. and M. Soteriou, *op. cit.*, pp. 18-20, by P. Lemerle, "Saint-Démétrius de Thessalonique et les problèmes du Martyrion et du Transept," *loc. cit.*, pp. 664-673, by N. Theotoka, «Περὶ τῶν κιβωρίων τοῦ ἁγίου Δημητρίου», Μακεδονικά, ii (1953), pp. 395-413, and by J. Walter, *op. cit.*, pp. 160-163.

[42]Kliment Okhridski, *Sŭbrani Sŭchineniya*, i, ed. B. S. Angelov and others (Sofia, 1970), pp. 221-237.

[43]A. Stojaković, "Quelques représentations de Salonique dans la peinture médiévale serbe," Χαριστήριον εἰς Ἀναστάσιον Κ. Ὀρλάνδον, ii (Athens, 1966), pp. 25-48.

[44]*Mir.* II, 1, 167, col. 1333.

[45]A. Xyngopoulos, *Ὁ εἰκονογραφικὸς κύκλος τῆς ζωῆς τοῦ ἁγίου Δημητρίου* (Thessaloniki, 1970), pp. 49-52; J. Walter, *op. cit.*, p. 170.

[46]*Povest' Vremennykh Let* s.a. 1051, ed D. S. Likhachev and V. P. Adrianova-Peretts, i (Moscow-Leningrad, 1950), p. 107; English transl. S. H. Cross and O. P. Sherbowitz-Wetzor (Cambridge, Mass., 1953), p. 141.

[47]V. L. Yanin, *Aktovye pechati drevney Rusi X-XV v.*, i, (Moscow, 1970), pp. 35-36, 167, 249.

[48]*Novgorodskaya 4-aya Letopis'*, s.a. 1154: *Polnoe Sobranie Russkikh Letopisey* iv, 1 (Petrograd, 1915), p. 153.

[49]*Ipat'evskaya Letopis'*, s.a. 1162: *Polnoe Sobranie Russkikh Letopisey*, ii (Moscow, 1962) [reprint of St. Petersburg ed., 1908], col. 521.

[50]See G. H. Hamilton, *The Art and Architecture of Russia* (London, 1954), pp. 37-38, 48-49, 52-53; N. N. Voronin, *Zodchestvo severo-vostochnoy Rusi XII-XV vekov*, i (Moscow, 1961), pp. 396-437.

[51]*Lavrent'evskaya Letopis'*, s.a. 1197: *Polnoe Sobranie Russkikh Letopisey*, i (Moscow, 1962) [reprint of Leningrad ed., 1926], col. 414; cf. *Nikonovskaya Letopis'*, s.a. 1197, *ibid.*, x (Moscow,

1965) [reprint of St. Petersburg ed., 1885], p. 30.

[52]See G. P. Fedotov, *The Russian Religious Mind*, i (Cambridge, Mass., 1966), pp. 94-110.

[53]*Zhitiya svyatykh muchenikov Borisa i Gleba*, ed. D. I. Abramovich (Petrograd, 1916), p. 50; *A Historical Russian Reader*, ed. J. Fennell and D. Obolensky (Oxford, 1969), p. 37.

[54]*Zhitiya*, p. 50; *A Historical Russian Reader*, p. 37.

[55]D. S. Iliadou, Ὁ Ἅγιος Δημήτριος καὶ οἱ Σλάβοι, loc. cit., p. 134.

[56]A. Kirpichnikov, "Osobyi vid tvorchestva v drevne-russkoy literature," *Zhurnal Ministerstva Narodnogo Prosveshcheniya* (1890), April, pp. 306-313.

[57]Georgius Cedrenus, *Historiarum Compedium*, ed. I. Bekker, ii (Bonn, 1839), p. 532; Ioannis Scylitzae *Synopsis Historiarum*, ed. I. Thurn (Berlin, 1973), pp. 412-414.

[58]*Povest' Vremennykh Let*, s.a. 907, i, p. 24; English transl. p. 64.

[59]A. Stender-Petersen, *Die Varägersage als Quelle der altrussischen Chronik*, (Aarhus-Leipzig, 1934), p. 96.

[60]Nicetas Choniates, *Historia*, ed. I. Bekker (Bonn, 1835), p. 485; ed. J. A. van Dieten (Berlin, 1975), p. 371. Cf. V. N. Zlatarski, *Istoriya na Bŭlgarskata Dŭrzhava prez srednite vekove*, ii (Sofia, 1934), pp. 413-414, 431, 440, 472; I. Dujčev, "Vŭstanieto na Asenevtsi i kultŭt na sveti Dimitriya Solunski": *Prouchvaniya vŭrkhu bŭlgarskoto srednovekovie, Sbornik na Bŭlgarskata Akademiya na Naukite i Izkustvata*, XLI, 1, (1945), pp. 44-51.

[61]Ἰωάννου Σταυρακίου λόγος εἰς τὰ Θαύματα τοῦ Ἁγίου Δημητρίου, Μακεδονικά, i, 1940, pp. 371-372; Cf. Zlatarski, *op. cit.*, iii (Sofia, 1972), pp. 252-261.

[62]George Acropolites, *Opera*, ed. Heisenberg, i (Leipzig, 1903), pp. 23-24.

[63]*Acta Patriarchatus Constantinopolitani*, ed. F. Miklosich and I. Müller, i (Vienna, 1860), pp. 436-442.

CHAPTER XII

BYZANTINE FRONTIER ZONES AND
CULTURAL EXCHANGES*

The vastness of the theme which I have been invited to discuss
compels me to concentrate on selected geographical areas and a
limited number of topics. The greater part of my material will be
drawn from the history of Byzantium's borderlands in Eastern Europe
and in the North Pontic region: these comprise the northern part of
the Balkan peninsula, the middle and lower Danube, the Crimea, the
South Russian steppe, and the northern and north-eastern coasts of
the Black Sea abutting on the Caucasus. The Empire's Eastern frontiers, in Asia Minor and Transcaucasia, which will be discussed in other
papers presented to this Congress, will be given only cursory consideration. Furthermore, I propose to confine myself to three principal
themes: I shall first attempt to distinguish between different kinds of
frontier zones which encompassed the territory of the Byzantine
Empire in the early Middle Ages. I shall then consider the role played
by the geographical and physical environment in the process of cultural diffusion across the imperial frontiers. Finally, I shall attempt a
classification of the main types of this diffusion.

1. VARIETIES OF BORDERLANDS

Discussing the diffusion of Mediterranean culture from its mari-
time centers to its continental periphery, Fernand Braudel wrote: "Ce
n'est pas d'une, mais de cent vies diffusées à la fois, ce n'est pas d'une,
mais de cent frontières qu'il doit être question, celles-ci à la mesure de
la politique, celles-là à la mesure de l'économie, celles-là encore à la

---

*Actes du XIVe Congrès International des Études Byzantines, I (Bucharest, 1974), 303-13.

mesure de la civilisation." And, he added, with reference to the central Mediterranean zone: "Il suffit de penser religion, culture, économie pour voir s'élargir ou se rétrécir sa surface."[1]. This judgement is equally applicable to those outer fringes of the Mediterranean world which lay on the periphery of the Byzantine Empire. The "frontiers" of this Empire were not only shifting and impermanent; even in a given historical period they cannot always be precisely delineated. Even the military borders of the Empire, which have a spurious accuracy when drawn on a map, often prove, when examined more closely, to have been more notional than real. The *limes* on the middle and lower Danube, which in some periods came nearest to being a line without breadth, was overrun by the Slavs and Avars in the early seventh century, by the Bulgars in 680, and, though reconquered by the Byzantines in 971, was permanently lost to the Empire in the late twelfth century. Even during the reign of Justinian, when the Danube was still a more or less effective military boundary, the need to defend the Balkans against barbarian invasions caused the Byzantines to build some of their fortifications deep in the interior of the peninsula, as far south as Epirus and the isthmus of Corinth. Moreover, in some cases, particularly when the military frontier did not follow a line traced by physical geography (such as a river or a mountain range), it was skirted by a buffer-zone, and we have not a *limes* but a *limen*. Even the Taurus line, one of the most stable sectors of the Byzantine-Arab frontier between the seventh and the tenth centuries, was open to regular Arab incursions and was flanked by a deserted no-man's land which, according to Theophanes, stretched from Mopsuestia to Armenia IV on the upper Tigris.[2] A similarly imprecise situation seems to have existed on the Byzantine-Bulgarian frontier in Thrace after Krum's wars with the Empire. The imperial fortresses of Serdica, Philippopolis, Adrianople and Develtus, which guarded this frontier, had all been captured by the Bulgarians between 809 and 814. After Krum's death in 814, a section of this devastated frontier, and particularly the cities of Serdica and Philippopolis, were left undefended.[3]

Cultural frontiers are even more varied in character and harder to define than military ones. A distinction can probably be drawn between borderlands which divided societies of comparable cultural level, such as the Byzantine-Arab frontier, where a state of relative cultural equilibrium could be expected to prevail, and those between the Empire and less civilized peoples. Across this type of frontier the encounter between civilization and barbarism (to use Byzantine concepts) took place in conditions of cultural inbalance, and led to more intense diffusion. To use another simile of Fernand Braudel, the greater the difference in voltage, the more powerful the currents.[4] To take a specific example, the relations between Byzantium and its neighbors beyond the Danube frontier and the Black Sea were governed by powerful economic and cultural needs: the Empire was obliged to import raw materials from Eastern Europe and to seek in that area an outlet for its manufactured goods, which were needed by its economically less advanced neighbors. Similarly, the export of Byzantium's civilization to these neighbors was of prime necessity to both sides: the Empire, by taming and civilizing its actual or potential enemies, could hope to render them harmless and to bring them within its cultural and political orbit; and the ruling classes of these more backward countries often borrowed particular cultural traits from Byzantium because of their functional usefulness in solving a social problem or satisfying a material need: thus commercial and ecclesiastical links with the empire satisfied their appetite for objects of luxury, impressive buildings and education; the use of Byzantine technological skill enabled them to carry out difficult engineering projects, such as the building of bridges and fortresses; while the adoption of Byzantine Christianity brought them international prestige and gave to their religious aspirations a new universal dimension.

Cultural and political frontiers seldom if ever coincided. Byzantine civilization had its "internal" and "external" borderlands, the former situated on territory which in a formal and theoretical sense was part of the Empire, the latter sometimes far beyond its political frontier. Thus in the more inaccessible highlands of the Balkan peninsula—the Rhodopes, the Pindus and the Taygetus mountains—Byzantium remained for centuries, and perhaps always, a shadowy power and an ineffectual master, whose provincial governors, tax collectors and Christian missionaries could be largely ignored. As an example of an "external" frontier zone one could cite the forest area of central Russia, where in the eleventh and twelfth centuries the urban and already largely byzantinized culture of the Russian ruling classes was advancing at the expense of the primitive pagan way of life of Slav and Finnic communities. This colonization of Suzdalia and the lands north of the Volga, of which the Russian historian Klyuchevsky painted a vivid picture,[5] resembled in many ways that of the North American frontier. F. J. Turner's celebrated description of the human types that were bred by the American frontier[6] could be made to apply in several respects to the border pioneers of central and northern Rus' in the Middle Ages. These cultural frontiers in Eastern Europe, "internal" or "external", divided from each other lands and peoples which were increasingly marginal to the main centres of Byzantine civilization.

2. ROLE OF GEOGRAPHICAL FACTORS

The lines which marked these cultural frontiers were often drawn by nature. Some of the more impermeable barriers were formed by forests. Procopius tells us that in order to maintain the Empire's control over the Tzani, who lived between Armenia and the Black Sea coast, Justinian carried out a systematic deforestation of the strategic areas of their land: "he cut down all trees by which the routes chanced to be obstructed and, transforming the rough places and making them smooth and passable for horses, he brought it about that they mingled with other peoples."[7] The Russians, at least before the thirteenth century, successfully defended their state, and their Christian civilization derived from Byzantium, by fortifying the fringes of the forest on their southern borders, into which their enemies, the nomadic horsemen from the steppe, ventured only with caution and difficulty. The nomad's distrust of the forest, where ambushes were a constant danger, routes of retreat could easily be cut and his flocks attacked by wild animals, is exemplified more than once in the medieval history of Asia Minor: the wooded highlands of Pontus and Phrygia protected the Nicaean Empire in the thirteenth century from the Seljuqs of Rum, while in north-eastern Anatolia the "Grand Comneni" of Trebizond maintained their independence for two and a half centuries behind the dense screen of the Pontic forests, the "sea of trees" into which the nomadic Turks were for long unable to penetrate.[8]

Next to the forests, the most effective barriers to political expansion and cultural diffusion were mountains. The isolating role of some of the mountain ranges of the Balkan peninsula has already been mentioned. One of the most clearly defined boundaries of the Byzantine Empire before the thirteenth century was the mountain range of the southern Crimea, which separated the narrow coastline, settled from antiquity by Mediterranean colonists, from the semi-arid pasture lands of the central and northern parts of the peninsula, inhabited by nomadic tribes from the Eurasian steppe. The efficacy of this *limes Tauricus* enabled the Byzantine cities on the coast — Bosporus and especially Cherson—to maintain their links with the government in

Constantinople and to remain, in the words of Cicero, "the hem of Greece, sewn on to the fields of the barbarians."[9]

Mountains, of course, were not always in fact obstacles to invaders nor barriers to cultural influence. Xavier de Planhol has observed that the Anatolian mountains proved to be much more of an obstacle to the Arabs, who relied for transport on the fragile and cold-fearing dromedary, than to the Turks, who used the tougher, fur-covered, two-humped Bactrian camel, which could adapt itself to the highlands. As a result, the advance of nomadism at the expense of the farmer's life was much more pronounced on Byzantium's eastern frontier in the Turkish than in the Arab period.[10]

It is possible to be misled by the spurious solidity which natural boundaries seem to acquire when drawn on historical maps. On a physical map of the Balkans, for instance, the Haemus or Balkan Range appears as a continuous line, and one must make an effort to remember that the numerous passes which break its continuity were not only signposts for invaders from the lower Danube thrusting towards the Thracian plain, but also channels for the diffusion of Byzantine civilization into northern Bulgaria and Wallachia. The same may be said of rivers. The Danube in the Byzantine period was at least as much a line of communication as an obstacle to the movement of men, goods and ideas. The author of the *Strategicon* must have had the Danube in mind when he complained that the Slavs were of all peoples the most adept in crossing rivers.[11] Some of the river-valleys of the Balkan peninsula, above all those of the Maritsa and the Vardar, were channels along which commodities and cultural influences from Constantinople and Thessalonica were carried in the Middle Ages to the Empire's neighbors in Eastern Europe.

In discussing the role played by geography in cultural exchanges across frontier zones, the importance of climate must not be forgotten. During the early Middle Ages — approximately from the early seventh century to the late tenth — the boundaries of the Byzantine Empire in Europe roughly coincided with the division between the Mediterranean and the continental climatic zones. The Mediterranean zone formed a fringe of coastal plains round the Balkan peninsula and, at least in the cities, was inhabited by a Greek-speaking population whose economy was sustained by the olive, the vine and fish, and whose way of life was profoundly affected by the proximity of the sea. The continental zone of the North Balkan and Pindus areas, by contrast, has a climate of the central European type; and its mixed population of Slavs, Bulgars, Albanians and Vlakhs was sustained by an agricultural or pastoral economy. In the central areas of the peninsula, in the neighborhood of the forty-second parallel, the natural boundaries between the two zones are the mountains of the Šar Planina and the Skopska Crna Gora, and the hills of Sredna Gora. The continental peoples who crossed this boundary were faced not only with the harsh contrasts of the Mediterranean climate but also with the unfamiliar perils of wine and malaria. These environmental conditions, if they succeeded in surmounting them, hastened their absorption by the local Greek population. The Mediterranean man, on the other hand, who penetrated north of this climatic boundary, encountered no less formidable problems of adaptation: problems epitomized, in Sir John Myres' words, by "the predicament of an oil-bred man transported beyond the frontier of butter-eaters."[12] It is significant that this climatic frontier zone coincided with the line dividing the Slav hinterland from those coastal areas of the Balkans which the Byzantines, between the late seventh and the late ninth centuries, incorporated as themes into the structure of the Empire's provincial administration. It is broadly speaking true that the Slavs who, in the Middle Ages, settled in the Mediterranean region, became Greeks in language and culture, while the Greeks who ventured into the North Balkan continental zone were Slavicized in the course of time.[13] These ecological problems, posed by the crossing of climatic frontier zones, have not been sufficiently studied. They would seem to deserve further consideration.

3. THE TYPOLOGY OF CULTURAL DIFFUSION

Writing of the frontiers of the Chinese empire, Professor O. Lattimore has remarked: "an imperial boundary. . .has in fact a double function: it serves not only to keep the outsiders from getting in but to prevent the insiders from getting out."[14] And, after commenting on this passage, Professor Arnold Toynbee observed with equal justice: "The existence of a *limes* always in practice generates social intercourse — and this in both directions — between the parties whom the barrier is designed to insulate from one another."[15]

What main types of social intercourse can be observed taking place through frontier zones of the Byzantine Empire? The most obvious was in the field of warfare. Facing each other across a fortified though not an impermeable *limes*, the Empire and the "barbarians" could not fail to learn from each other's military technology. In a passage written in 585, John of Ephesus admitted that the Slavs who were then invading the Empire had "learnt to fight better than the Romans."[16] As the context of the passage shows, this grasp of military technique included the mastery of siegecraft; and it is probable that the Slavs acquired this art not only from the Avars, but from the Byzantines as well. A passage in the *Strategicon* of the Pseudo-Maurice suggests that military secrets may have been leaked to the Slavs by East Roman traitors who slipped across the Danube frontier.[17] The Byzantines, for their part, borrowed readily from their trans-Danubian enemies in the military field. In the late sixth and in the seventh centuries, for instance, the Byzantine cavalry took over from the Avars the tactics of the mounted archers of the Eurasian steppe, characterized by the rapid attack, the feigned retreat, reconnaissance, and the harassment of the enemy by methods of guerrilla warfare.[18]

Another field in which frontier zones proved susceptible to cultural osmosis was the economic one. A commodity which, in war as in peace, crossed the imperial borders in abundance was money. Apart from loot, which the barbarians brought home from their campaigns on Byzantine territory, the imperial government periodically paid out large sums to them in tribute. The vast subsidies which it disbursed to the Huns (6000 pounds of gold in 443 alone)[19] flowed across the Danube *limes* into Attila's realm. It is likely that this quantity of gold circulating in Pannonia was one of the reasons which, in the sixth and seventh centuries, attracted Byzantine merchants and artisans to the centers of the Avar Kingdom. And through the merchants who operated on or beyond the frontier, in payment for Byzantine goods purchased by the barbarians, some of this money must have eventually flowed back to its source in Constantinople and other cities of the Empire.

An interesting case of economic "acculturation" across frontier zones occurs when the sedentary and the nomadic ways of life meet and interact on each other. On the Empire's borders in Anatolia there were periods when pastoral nomadism encroached on the peasant's farming economy. For reasons already explained, the Anatolian plateau could never provide a permanent home for the Arabs. During the period of their invasions the advance of nomadism seems to have been largely confined to the lowlands of Asia Minor. By contrast the Turks, particularly in eastern Anatolia, were able to occupy the highlands and to impose more effectively their nomadic way of life on border populations. The cultural pressure which the nomadic Seljuqs exerted on the Empire's eastern frontier was doubtless an important cause of the rapid Turkisization of Anatolia; though, because their summer encampments tended to cluster immediately above the wooded zone, the nomads do not seem to have played a major role in the later deforestation of parts of Asia Minor.[20]

In other frontier zones we observe the reverse process: the retreat of nomadism before farming economy. Often this process was spontaneous, and due to the nomad's desire to exchange the hazards of the arid steppes for the greater security and higher material standards of an agricultural life. In the mid-sixth century the khan of the Utigurs, a Hunnic nomadic people living in the Pontic steppes, bitterly complained to the Emperor Justinian who had recently allowed a number of Kutrigurs, a neighboring and rival tribe, to settle in Thrace. "While we eke out our existence in a deserted and thoroughly unproductive land," the khan wrote to the emperor, "the Kutrigurs are at liberty to traffic in corn and to revel in their wine cellars and to live on the fat of the land."[21] The same desire to exchange a nomadic for an agricultural life may well have prompted the Bulgars to cross the Danube into the Balkans in the 670's. The Magyars, who settled beyond the Empire's northern borders, in Pannonia, in the closing years of the ninth century, seem to have begun to abandon nomadism some fifty years later; and it may well be that this transition to a farming economy was hastened by Christian missionaries who came to Hungary from Byzantium.

The role played by Christian missionaries in the shift from nomadism to a farming economy in border zones is vividly illustrated in the account by a sixth-century Syriac chronicler, the Pseudo-Zachariah of Mitylene, of an Armenian mission to the Huns in the steppes north of the Caucasus. About 542 an Armenian bishop from Arran came to take charge of a Christian community — probably of Sabiri — some of whom had recently been converted by his predecessor. Our chronicler tells us that this missionary, whose name was apparently Maku, "built a brick church and planted plants, and sowed various kinds of seeds and did signs and baptized many."[22] It is clear that he was trying to convert the steppe nomads to a settled, agricultural way of life, and thus to provide a stable frame-work for the religious and cultural growth of their community. The story becomes even more significant if it is recalled that the north Caucasian steppes, where this mission operated, lay in the sixth century immediately beyond the Empire's north-eastern boundary, and that Byzantine diplomats, for strategic reasons, were vitally interested in this sector: indeed we know that the missionary activities of Maku's Armenian predecessor in this area were actively supported by Justinian's government.

Together with military technique, money, material goods, and methods of economic production, Byzantine frontier zones also contributed to the diffusion of political ideas and institutions. This problem is too large to be discussed in general terms in this paper: one instance may be noted, however, which shows that the political thinking of the statesmen in Constantinople could be directly affected by the encounter between Byzantium and its neighbors on the Empire's borders. The Byzantines, like their Roman predecessors, endeavored to attach the neighboring barbarians to the Empire by treaties which imposed upon them the obligation of defending the Empire's frontiers; and they held that imperial territory was ringed by a chain of client states, whose rulers were partly subjects and partly allies of Byzantium. These *foederati*, or *socii populi Romani*, were supposed to guard the imperial borders in exchange for a regular subsidy, the Empire's protection and the right of self-government.[23] This concept of *foederatio*, which defined the status of the Empire's subject-allies, was one which the Byzantine statesmen used to justify both to themselves and to the outside world their claims to universal hegemony, particularly in Eastern Europe and in the Caucasian lands.[24] It is worth noting that this concept, which proved of central importance in the history of Byzantine diplomacy, was born of conditions which prevailed for centuries on the Empire's borderlands.

One last type of contact and diffusion across the Empire's frontiers must be briefly examined. It pertains to the realm of culture in a more specific sense of the word. Its most obvious example was the spread of Byzantine Christianity to the Empire's neighbors. This phenomenon is so familiar that I need do no more that enumerate a few cases, taken from different sectors of the imperial frontier zone. In the Caucasus area, the Lazes, the Tzani, the Abasgians and the Zichians were converted in the sixth century by Byzantine missionaries, and this undoubtedly strengthened their loyalty to the central authorities in Constantinople. The Crimean *limes* also proved highly permeable to the radiation of Greek Christianity: the Crimean Goths, who lived in the mountains between the steppe and the coastal zones of the peninsula and who were thus admirably equipped to serve as intermediaries between the Mediterranean and the Eurasian worlds, were already Orthodox Christians in the early fourth century. In the eighth century

Iconoclast persecution caused an exodus of Iconophile monks to the southern Crimea; and from this frontier outpost they helped propagate Christianity among the people of the Pontic steppe. Cherson, the most important of the Byzantine cities in the Crimea, was captured by the armies of Prince Vladimir of Kiev in 989 or 990; it was probably in that city that the Russian ruler was baptized and the final conversion of his country was planned and initiated. It has been said that the classic example of "acculturation" is the situation described in the celebrated words: "Graecia capta ferum victorem cepit."[25] It is no less true that Cherson took its Russian captor captive. In the Balkans Byzantine Christianity, crossing "internal frontiers", spread in the early Middle Ages to Macedonia, Bulgaria and Serbia. This form of cultural diffusion was not confined to officially-sponsored Orthodoxy. In 757 Constantine V transferred Syrian and Armenian communities from Erzerum and Melitene to Thrace, where they were used to garrison Byzantine fortresses on the Bulgarian frontier. This transfer of unruly populations from the eastern to the northern borders of the Empire had consequences which the Byzantine government could scarcely have foreseen or desired: some of them were Paulician heretics, whose dualist doctrines spread across the frontier into Bulgaria.[26]

The example of the Paulician sectarians in Thrace shows that the diffusion of religious beliefs across the Empire's borders was not only directed outwards, from Byzantium to the neighboring world. At times the influence was the other way. The question has often been raised as to whether Byzantine Iconoclasm, in its early phase, owed anything to the teachings of Islam and other religious movements which proscribed the pictorial representation of the human form. Present-day opinion inclines to the view, strongly upheld by iconophile Byzantine chroniclers, that the Emperor Leo III's decision to attack the veneration of images in 726 was influenced in part by Islamic iconophobia. It is probable, however, that this decision was prompted less by a desire to imitate the policy of the khalifes than by the situation which prevailed on the Empire's eastern borders. As Professor Grabar has shown, Iconoclasm in its early phase found its strongest popular support in central and eastern Asia Minor, where the local population, only superficially hellenized, was subjected to the proselytism of iconophobe sectarians, such as the Paulicians. These sectarians lived in an environment in which Muslim missionary activity was strongly felt.[27] It may well be that the early Iconoclast emperors, Leo III and Constantine V, were conscious of the need to retain the loyalty of their subjects in eastern Anatolia by supporting their aversion to the veneration of images. If this view is accepted, one of the roots of Iconoclasm may be found in the religious beliefs of Byzantine communities on the Empire's eastern borders, beliefs which derived much of their strength from influences coming from beyond the frontier.

In some frontier areas prolonged contact between the Byzantines and their less civilized neighbors created a kind of limbo, or no-man's land, where the cultural boundary that separated Byzantine from "barbarian" was blurred and could easily be crossed in either direction. In the eleventh century this state of affairs prevailed on the lower Danube, where the Byzantine officials of the theme of Paristrion lived alongside a motley collection of nomadic peoples who had filtered across the Danube. According to Michael Attaleiates, every language under the sun could be heard in this ethnic melting-pot.[28] Professor Stănescu has recently drawn our attention to the term *mixobarbaroi* ("semi-barbarians"), used by the Byzantine authors of the time to describe individuals or communities in this area whose origins or behavior showed that they were imperfectly assimilated into civilized society; and it is significant that this term applied equally to Byzantine citizens who were forgetting their civilized habits and becoming contaminated by contact with true "barbarians", and to foreigners who had gone some way towards absorbing Greek civilization.[29] This ambiguous cultural climate, which made it as easy for Byzantines to slide into "barbarism" as it was for "barbarians" to acquire at least the veneer of civilization, had long existed in the Danube borderlands. The author of the *Strategicon* points out that some of the Slavs, especially those who lived near the frontiers of the Empire, can be attracted into imperial service "by promises or gifts."[30] One of these turn-coats was no doubt the famous Chilbudius, who was appointed by Justinian commander of the Byzantine forces in Thrace and who successfully guarded the Danube against his compatriots from 530 to 535.[31] How often Byzantines on the frontier succumbed to the dubious attractions of the "barbarian" life and "went native", we do not know. A vivid portrait of one such renegade is found in Priskos' account of his journey with a Byzantine embassy to Attila's camp in 448.[32] There he met a man, dressed as a well-to-do Hun, who addressed him in Greek. In an ensuing conversation he told Priskos that he was a Greek merchant from Viminacium on the Danube, had been taken prisoner by the Huns and had later purchased his freedom and married a Hun wife. He now enjoyed social privileges in Attila's realm, and much preferred his new existence to his former life as a Byzantine citizen. He justified this view by referring to the constant wars on the Empire's borders, the harshness of imperial taxation, and the helplessness of the poor in their vain attempts to find redress in the Byzantine courts against the lawlessness of the rich. Priskos' attempt in reply to defend the imperial government fails to carry conviction; it was not unfairly described by Gibbon as "a prolix and feeble declamation." One is left with the impression that even moderately prosperous Byzantine citizens, at least in the fifth century, had reasons for preferring the service of a "barbarian" master to the uncertainties of life on the frontier.

It may be suggested in conclusion that several of the problems which I have sketched, all too rapidly, in this paper would require treatment in greater depth by a combined team of sociologists, geographers and historians. Some of its shortcomings, I would venture to plead, could not easily have been avoided: for its theme is an integral part of the historical geography of the Byzantine Empire — a subject which, in her paper presented at the Byzantine Congress in Oxford in 1966, Madame Hélène Ahrweiler rightly described as "une discipline hésitante dans ses méthodes et maîtrisant mal ou peu ses instruments."

FOOTNOTES ON CHAPTER XII

[1]F. Braudel, *La Méditerranée et le monde méditerranéen à l'époque de Philippe II* (Paris, 1949), p. 141.

[2]Theophanes, *Chronographia*, ed. C. de Boor, I (Leipzig, 1883), pp. 363. Cf. E. Honigman, *Die Ostgrenze des byzantinischen Reiches von 363 bis 1071* (Brussels, 1935), pp. 39-42.

[3]S. Runciman, *A History of the First Bulgarian Empire* (London, 1930), p. 74.

[4]Braudel, *op. cit.*, p. 105.

[5]V. O. Klyuchevsky, *Kurs russkoy istorii. Lektsiya 17* (Moscow, 1956), pp. 292-315.

[6]F. J. Turner, *The Frontier in American History* (New York, 1921). Cf. *The Frontier in Perspective*, ed. W. D. Wyman and C. B. Kroeber (Madison, 1957).

[7]*De aedificiis*, 6, ed. J. Haury (Leipzig, 1964), p. 97.

[8]Xavier de Planhol, *Les fondements géographiques de l'histoire de l'Islam* (Paris, 1968), pp. 38, 222-3.

[9]Cicero, *De Re Publica*, II, 4, ed. C. F. W. Mueller (Leipzig, 1898), p. 309.

[10]*Op. cit.*, pp. 39-44, 208-31.

[11]*Fontes Graeci Historiae Bulgaricae*, II, ed. I. Dujčev and others (Sofia, 1958), p. 282.

[12]J. L. Myres, *Geographical History in Greek Lands* (Oxford, 1953), p. 152.

[13]J. Cvijić, *La Péninsule Balkanique* (Paris, 1918), pp. 51-2.

[14]O. Lattimore, *Inner Asian Frontiers of China* (London-New York, 1940), p. 240.

[15]A. J. Toynbee, *A Study of History*, VIII (London, 1954), p. 15.

[16]*The third Part of the Ecclesiastical History of John, Bishop of Ephesus*, transl. R. Payne Smith (Oxford, 1860), pp. 432-3.

[17]*Fontes Graeci Historiae Bulgaricae*, loc. cit., pp. 285-6; *Mauricii Strategicon*, ed. Mihăescu (Bucharest, 1970), p. 284.

[18]E. Darkó, *Influences touraniennes sur l'évolution de l'art militaire des Grecs, des Romains et des Byzantins*, "Byzantion", X (1935), pp. 443-69; XII (1937), pp. 119-47. Idem., *Le rôle des peuples nomades cavaliers dans la transformation de l'Empire romain aux premiers siècles du Moyen Age*, "Byzantion", XVIII (1948), pp. 85-97.

[19]E. A. Thompson, *A History of Attila and the Huns* (Oxford, 1948), p. 192.

[20]C. Cahen, *Le problème ethnique en Anatolie*, "Cahiers d'Histoire Mondiale", II (1954), pp. 347-62; X. de Planhol, *Les nomades, la steppe et la forêt en Anatolie*, "Geographische Zeitschrift", LIII (1965), pp. 101-16.

[21]Procopius, *De bellis*, VIII, 19, ed. J. Haury, II (Leipzig, 1963), pp. 587-9.

[22]*The Syriac Chronicle of Zachariah of Mitylene*. transl. F. J. Hamilton and E. W. Brooks (London, 1899), pp. 329-31. Cf. E. A. Thompson, *Christian Missionaries among the Huns*, "Hermathena", LXVII (1946), pp. 73-9.

[23]T. Mommsen, *Le droit public romain*, VI, 2 (Paris, 1889), p. 269 ff.

[24]See above, Chapter I.

[25]H. van Effenterre, *"Acculturation" et histoire ancienne, XIIe Congrès International des Sciences Historiques. Rapports*, I (Vienna, 1965), p. 37.

[26]Theophanes, *Chronographia*, ed. de Boor, I, p. 429. Cf. D. Obolensky, *The Bogomils* (Cambridge, 1948), pp. 60-1.

[27]A. Grabar, *L'iconoclasme byzantin. Dossier archéologique* (Paris, 1957), pp. 93-7, 103-12.

[28]Attaleiates, *Historia*, ed. I. Bekker (Bonn, 1853), p. 204.

[29]E. Stănescu, *Les "mixobarbares" du Bas-Danube au XIe siècle*, "Nouvelles Etudes d'Histoire publiées à l'occasion du XIIe Congrès des Sciences Historiques", Vienna, 1965 (Bucharest, 1965), pp. 45-53.

[30]*Fontes Graeci Historiae Bulgaricae*, loc. cit., p. 285; *Mauricii Strategicon*, ed. Mihăescu, p. 284.

[31]Procopius, *De bellis*, VII, 14, ed. J. Haury, II, pp. 353-4.

[32]*Excerpta de legationibus*, ed. C. de Boor, I (Berlin, 1903), pp. 135-8.

Index